EXPERIMENTAL CHILD STUDY

The Century Psychology Series
Richard M. Elliott, Editor

EXPERIMENTAL CHILD STUDY

BY

FLORENCE L. GOODENOUGH

PROFESSOR, INSTITUTE OF CHILD WELFARE
UNIVERSITY OF MINNESOTA

AND

JOHN E. ANDERSON

PROFESSOR OF PSYCHOLOGY
AND DIRECTOR OF THE INSTITUTE OF CHILD WELFARE
UNIVERSITY OF MINNESOTA

THE CENTURY CO.
NEW YORK   LONDON

41153

TABLES

PART I
INTRODUCTION

Chapter 1

BRIEF HISTORICAL RÉSUMÉ

SCIENTIFIC interest in children late in developing. In the days of our grandfathers, popular judgment as to the place of the child in society was epitomized by the maxim, "Children should be seen but not heard." Examination of the scientific literature of the time leaves one with the feeling that the admission of children to the visual world was a concession imposed by necessity. As an object of scientific inquiry the child was neither seen nor heard—he did not exist. It is true that early in the seventeenth century such men as Ratke and Comenius on the Continent, and John Locke in England had emphasized the importance of "seeking and following the order of Nature" as a guide to the education of youth. In a sense these men may be said to have laid the foundation, or at least to have pointed the way, for the empirical studies of child development which were to follow. However, almost three quarters of a century elapsed before Locke's ideas were popularized by Rousseau in the *Emile* (1762). Another generation elapsed before Rousseau's theories were put into actual practice by Pestalozzi (1800), and still another before their special application to the education of young children by Froebel (1837). Not until the latter part of the nineteenth century did the scientific study of child development begin to assume systematic form.

From the beginning we can distinguish two very different trends or motivating forces in the study of child development. The first is the practical aim which has for its object the molding of child behavior into some more or less clearly conceived form or pattern. This aim has probably existed in a more or less clearly recognized form in all ages and societies. However, it was not until the eighteenth century that the possibility of utilizing a knowledge of the natural development of the child as a means of facilitating the process of education was clearly recognized. The possibilities of actual experimentation in the education of children were not realized until the beginning of the twentieth century.

The second line of interest, which we may call scientific as opposed to the more purely practical educational interest, may properly be said to date its birth from the publication of Darwin's *Expression of the Emotions in Men and Animals* in 1872. Previous to that time a few scattered studies such as Tiedemann's observations on the development of his infant son had appeared, but the material was not looked upon as having any real scientific importance. In the scientific theory of that time, child psychology had no place. Once its significance had been pointed out, however, interest in the subject developed at an astoundingly rapid rate. Previous to 1872, not more than a dozen major studies devoted to child development had appeared in the literature. Before the end of the century the number had run into hundreds.

Early methods of child study: the child biography. Following the example set by Tiedemann (192),* the early studies of child development are based largely upon more or less incidental observations of single children. In the greater number of instances no consistent plan has been followed with regard to time of recording. The records commonly in-

* The numbers throughout the text refer to the bibliography on page 469.

clude a mixture of remembered instances and facts noted down at the time of observation. Moreover, in many cases there is no clear distinction between the facts observed and the interpretations which are placed upon them. For these reasons, the child biographies have been less useful for their own content than for suggesting problems to be worked out by more adequate methods. Among the best of the diaries which appeared during the last quarter of the nineteenth century are those by Darwin (57), the Scupins (217, 218), the Sterns (234, 235, 236), Major (174), and Shinn (225, 226).

A serious limitation of the diary method soon became evident to most persons who attempted to use it. Since there was no control of the situation in which the child was placed, it became necessary to describe not only the child's behavior but also the varying circumstances under which the responses took place. With advancing age the number and variety of stimuli to which a child would respond multiplied rapidly, and the complexity of behavior-responses increased proportionately. Adequate observation and record of all pertinent facts soon become impossible. It was obviously necessary to limit the field in some way if useful material were to be obtained. Towards the end of the century we accordingly find interest in the general biography, with its attempt to include all facts of importance regarding the child's development, shifting to the more specialized record of the development of behavior of some given type. Among these specialized studies, the records of language development, particularly the development of vocabulary, and the studies of children's drawings occupied a leading place. In these investigations we note also an initial recognition of the need for group study. This tendency is especially evident in the work on children's drawings where many of the studies, even at this early period, were based upon large numbers of cases.

A third type of large-scale investigation, popular at the end of the century, was the study of the concepts formed by young children regarding many items in their environment. Of these, Hall's study on the contents of children's minds on entering school (115) is one of the best known.

The use of children as subjects in controlled investigations of specific problems. During the last quarter of the nineteenth century, at the time when Darwin's influence had aroused intense interest in genetic and comparative psychology, as mentioned in a former paragraph, a second movement of equal or possibly even greater importance was occurring in the field of psychology. This was the development of the experimental method which had its origin in the laboratories of such men as Weber, Fechner, Helmholtz, and Wundt in Germany. The interest of this group centered largely about various problems of the sense organs and sensations. Their work was therefore closely allied to physiology on the one hand and to physics on the other. To them we owe a large part of our present knowledge of the psychology of sensation. Much of the apparatus at present in use in the psychological laboratories was developed by them. Their most important contribution, however, lay in the fact that through their work, psychology, which had previously been regarded as a branch either of physiology or of philosophy, was given a recognized place among the experimental sciences. Investigation took the place of speculation; demonstration replaced theory. However, in the work of the German laboratories of this period, child psychology had no place. Many factors, such as the widespread insistence upon the use of introspective method, the close demand upon attention, and the many long and fatiguing trials necessary to secure reliable data, contributed to make the use of children as laboratory subjects in experiments of this kind hardly practicable. Indirectly, however, the work of these

FOREWORD

The last decade has been marked by a rapidly increasing interest in the field of child development in both its scientific and its practical aspects. Nowhere has this interest been more apparent than in the period of development commonly known as that of "the young child" or "the preschool child."

The need of a book for students of child behavior, teachers, and parents which will describe in simple and understandable form the principles and methods of scientific child study has been sensed by many. In this book, through a series of experiments and exercises, we have tried to outline the methods available for the study of young children both prior to and after their entrance into school, and to give insight into the scientific possibilities inherent in the study of children. In so doing we have drawn extensively upon the modern literature, much of which is relatively inaccessible because of its very recency and because of the fact that the field is one in which the collection of data has outstripped its presentation in textbook form.

The book is the outcome of five years experience in teaching courses in experimental child study. Although there are a number of useful books and laboratory manuals dealing with methods of research in psychology, education, and the social sciences, none are well suited for students in child development since the experiments and methods are, as a rule, devised for adults and older children. On the other hand, neither the monographs and experimental articles on the young child nor the systematic textbooks or outlines of knowledge furnish adequate concrete guidance for the conduct of experiments by the beginning student, because of the degree of technical and statistical knowledge which they presuppose.

In spirit, the book reflects the modern attitude in that it is frankly experimental and observational in tone rather than philosophical. This is an age of scientific inquiry in which theories unsupported by evidence command slight respect. Only through the accurate determination of facts can the principles necessary for the understanding of child nature be formulated.

We have drawn heavily upon the experience and the investigations of the Institute of Child Welfare of the University of Minnesota, which has played its part in the modern movement for experimental child study. Our gratitude to both our present and former colleagues and students can best be expressed by the hope that this volume will prove of value to students of child development, and through them, of service to children.

F. L. G.

J. E. A.

Minneapolis, March 20, 1931.

CONTENTS

vii

Contents

PART III. METHODS OF COLLECTING DATA

Contents

LIST OF FIGURES

work of which was largely modelled along Wundtian lines, his personal interest lay chiefly outside the field of sensation and psychophysics. He was interested in the whole child—how he lived, thought, played and worked, his opinions, attitudes and emotions. In his zeal to throw light on some of these questions, he made such extensive use of the questionnaire method originally devised by Galton that it became associated with his own name. The questionnaire as used by Hall was extremely crude. Both in content and form, the questions violated many of the modern rules for questionnaire construction. Nevertheless, in spite of the inadequacy of his method, Hall was able to secure an enormous amount of valuable data concerning aspects of child behavior which had previously been little studied or understood.

Hall's greatest work is *Adolescence,* published in two large volumes. Among the most important of his studies of younger children may be mentioned his *Aspects of Child Life and Education* (297), his study of children's fears (116), of anger (117), the content of children's minds on entering school (115), and a large number of shorter studies dealing with various aspects of play, attitude toward religion, natural phenomena, social events and relationships, personality, *etc.*

In interpreting his data Hall employed only the simplest methods. His statistical treatment is confined at most to a few percentages. In many instances only generalized statements with no quantitative material are given. In one respect, however, his method is worthy of particular note. Few investigators have examined the literature in the field with more thoroughness in order to relate their findings to those of other workers. In his *Adolescence,* for example, there are almost 4,000 citations from more than 1,200 different authors, and even in his minor studies he always adhered to the principle of relating his findings to those of previous workers.

The development of educational psychology. In a previous section we have pointed out that the earliest development of interest in children was to be seen in the field of education. From the eighteenth century on a steady increase may be observed in the development of educational theory, accompanied by extensive modification in educational practice. Herbart, frequently referred to as the "father of scientific pedagogy," exerted but little influence upon educational theory or practice during his lifetime. A quarter of a century after his death in 1841, his theories became widely known through the work of Ziller and Rein. To him the educational psychology of childhood is indebted chiefly for the wholesome reaction against the extreme naturalistic dogma of the followers of Rousseau and Pestalozzi which set in toward the close of the nineteenth century. Rousseau's doctrine had been that all formal education is harmful, and that natural development alone can be depended upon to fit the child for his place in society. Herbart, in opposition, maintained that all development is profoundly influenced by the external conditions to which the developing organism is subjected, and that it is the task of the educator to provide such conditions as will make for the most healthy growth. Thus, through Herbart's influence, emphasis was shifted from the internal development of the child, over which the educator could have no control, to those external conditions shaping development for which the educator must assume responsibility. Herbart's educational theory was thus both active and dynamic.

Herbart was one of the first proponents of the view that all mental processes are unitary and cannot, except in a very artificial sense, be analyzed into such "faculties" as memory, imagination, judgment, *etc.* He strongly advocated the application of the mathematical techniques used in other sciences to psychological and pedagogical data. However, he was more interested in the mathematical demonstration of abstract principles than in the organization and treatment of concrete data.

In spite of the work of Herbart, for many years educational theory and practice on the one hand, and scientific study and investigation on the other, proceeded in almost complete independence of each other. It was not until the close of the nineteenth century that any sort of effective liaison was established between the two. The union constituted the new science of educational psychology.

Since educational psychology was born out of the convergence of two well-developed lines of interest, its development or appearance is not signalized by any single event nor can its origin be traced to any one source. If we consider both direct and indirect influence, Hall had about as much to do with it as any one, although his interest, as we have seen, centered in the broader personal and social development of the child, rather than training in the formal school subjects. Among the other pioneer workers, we may mention particularly Cattell, who, as Wundt's first assistant at Leipzig, carried out his investigations on individual differences in spite of Wundt's lack of sympathy with the problem. Much of the modern emphasis upon the statistical evaluation of material is to be traced to Cattell's influence. Although he was for a time a student of G. Stanley Hall, their respective contributions to educational psychology have been of a very different nature. Hall's intense interest in children led him to be somewhat careless in techniques of investigation. Cattell had relatively little interest in children as human beings, but was greatly attracted by the possibility of measuring their development, even though his own work was carried out chiefly with adults and college students. His influence upon the study of child development, through the work of his students, has been very great. Among the latter we may mention particularly Thorndike, Woodworth, Dearborn, Hollingworth, Kelley and Gates. In Germany, Meumann, under the influence of Ebbinghaus, carried out an extensive series of learning studies among school children, and tests for measuring educational achievement soon followed. In spite of its late start, interest in educational psychology developed at so rapid a rate that in 1913 Thorndike (339) published a general compendium on the subject in three large volumes aggregating almost 1,200 pages. Of the 348 references cited in his bibliography less than a third were published previous to 1900.

The most outstanding characteristic of educational psychology, as it has developed in America, has been the growth of the testing movement and particularly the work in intelligence testing. Although the first useful intelligence tests were developed in France by Binet and Simon, attempts at constructing such tests had been made in America at a considerably earlier date. In 1893 Gilbert (98) published the results of a series of simple sensory-motor tests carried out with school children. During the same year Münsterberg exhibited a number of tests at the World's Fair in Chicago. These tests were based upon the theories of Galton and Cattell which assumed that the more complex mental processes were simply higher levels or combinations of the more elementary processes; and accordingly that adequate measurement of the higher mental functions might be obtained in terms of such simple performances as speed of tapping, reaction time, *etc.* The assumption, as we now know, proved to be wrong. In France, Alfred Binet, after an extensive series of investigations, covering a period of approximately twenty years, came to a very different conclusion. His findings had led him to believe that the higher mental processes

must be measured directly and that they cannot effectively
be reduced to simpler elements. With the publication of
Binet's work, mental testing in America and elsewhere
started off successfully in a new direction.

Binet and the mental testing movement. Although Binet is
chiefly known for the intelligence tests which bear his name,
his contribution to the study of child development and behavior is far broader in scope. Almost twenty years elapsed
between the publication of his first article on individual
differences and the publication of his first intelligence scale
in 1905. During this time, as stated in an earlier paragraph,
he carried out more than fifty investigations of which the
results have been published. These publications deal with
many different topics, but throughout the list Binet's growing interest in the measurement of individual differences in
mental traits can be observed. He was one of the first to
investigate the question of the relationship between physical
and mental traits, and his conclusions at the end of a number of careful studies were essentially the same as those
held by the best authorities today; namely, that among
individuals of the same age physical size is but slightly, if
at all, related to mental traits (321). He conducted a large
number of investigations on personality traits, the best
known of which made use of his two daughters as subjects
(18). In the search for diagnostic signs of intelligence he
canvassed not only the fields of simple sensory discrimination, reaction time, *etc.*, with which Cattell and his co-work-
ers in America were concerned, but also carried out extensive
investigations on memory, imagination, attention, comprehension, suggestibility, and so on. Even such unlikely fields
as graphology and palmistry were not overlooked.

In evaluating his results, Binet made frequent use of the
comparative method, and particularly the comparison of
extreme cases. For example, he asked teachers to select from

among their students the five brightest and the five most stupid children, and then sought for tests which would differentiate reliably between these groups. He also made intensive studies of persons who had attracted attention through their ability in some highly specialized kind of mental performance. His monograph on the psychology of lightning calculators and great chess players is still a classic in its field.

Binet has laid down for us three criteria of intelligence. It is interesting to evaluate his own work in terms of these three criteria.

1. The power to take and maintain a given mental set. From 1886 to the time of his death in 1911 Binet's investigations were closely centered about a single problem—the measurement of individual differences in mental traits.
2. The power to make adaptations for the purpose of obtaining a given end. We have seen how Binet canvassed almost the entire field of human behavior in his search for diagnostic instruments.
3. The power of self-criticism. Of the many forms of behavior investigated by Binet, only a very small percentage was retained in his intelligence tests as finally published. He never hesitated to throw out any form of reaction which seemed unsuitable for his purpose merely because he had already spent a great deal of time in investigating it.

As a result of the rapid growth of interest in the feeble-minded, public attention was promptly directed to Binet's work. Until the latter part of the nineteenth century, no clear differentiation between the feeble-minded and the insane had been made. With the more intensive studies of mental disorders which grew up during the latter part of the century, it became apparent that there were a certain number of individuals who, from birth onward, exhibited mental defects of a degree which made them incapable of adjusting themselves in the community. The need for early recognition and segregation of these persons became so apparent that, in 1904, the Minister of Public Instruction in Paris appointed a commission to study measures to be taken in the education of children who, by reason of mental defect, were unable to profit by ordinary instruction in the public schools. It was planned to remove these children from the regular classes and to provide instruction for them in a special school, admission to which was to be made on the basis of pedagogical and medical examinations. Binet's first scale was designed specifically to meet this need. During the same year the British goverment appointed the famous Royal Commission, the purpose of which was to ascertain the approximate number of mentally defective persons in England and Wales. Similar surveys of a less extensive nature were carried on in other countries, and social pressure was brought to bear from many sources in an attempt to provide more adequate institutional care for those who needed it. More objective methods of diagnosis were a primary requirement in such a program. In spite of the comparative crudeness of Binet's first scale, it was so far superior to anything previously used that it met with enthusiastic acceptance.

In the beginning, the use of intelligence tests was confined almost entirely to differentiating between the feebleminded and persons of normal intelligence. It was soon found, however, that the method had a much wider range of applicability than had been at first supposed. The tests were useful not only in the differentiation of feeble-minded and backward children, but also as a means of selecting especially bright children who might also profit by special instruction. The "three track system" of education in which the bright, average, and backward children within the schools are segregated for separate instruction thus came into being.

Chapter 2

FUNDAMENTAL PRINCIPLES OF DEVELOPMENT

CONTINUITY rather than discontinuity is character-istic of all development. Although the current use of such convenient terms as "developmental level," "growth stages," "the period of infancy," "of early childhood," "of adolescence," *etc.*, sometimes gives the impression that development proceeds by a series of rapid changes from one well-defined stage to another, it is important for the student to realize from the outset that no such series of marked growth changes exists in nature, and that the expressions which have just been quoted are nothing more than convenient terms for marking off certain parts of a continuous process for purposes of examination and study. The only reason for making such divisions at all is that the entire process is so long and involved that it is impossible to get anything more than a hazy idea of it unless we divide it up in some way and study it a little at a time.

In making such divisions it is customary and convenient to use as the division point the average age or time at which certain prominent events in the field under consideration take place. For example, persons interested in physical growth and development frequently make the following rough divi-sions: the *prenatal* period which is often further subdivided into the periods of the *ovum,* the *embryo,* and the *fetus;* the *postnatal* period which is divided into *infancy,* covering the time from birth to the assumption of the erect posture at about twelve to fifteen months, *early childhood* lasting from about fifteen months to six years, *middle childhood* from six to ten years, *late childhood* or the prepuberal period as it is sometimes called, which lasts from about the age of ten to the time of puberty,* and *adolescence* which extends from the age of puberty until the time when physical growth is terminated, that is, about eighteen in girls and twenty in boys. These divisions are convenient for the anatomist because, in a general way, they mark off periods of slow or rapid physical growth. During infancy and early childhood growth is rapid; during middle childhood it is much slower; during the prepuberal period the growth rate again becomes rapid, and following puberty it slows off gradually and continuously till the final adult standard is reached. The change from one period to another, however, is not abrupt but gradual and continuous. The educator may make a different sort of division, such as the *preschool* period, the *kindergarten* period, the *primary school* or *grade school* period, the *junior high school* period, the *senior high school* period, the *college* period, *etc*. Back in the nineties, when the recapitulation theory was in full swing it was fashionable to make a division of stages in child development along lines which were supposed to parallel the cultural history of the race. There was the "stone age period," the "cave man period," the "big Injun period," *etc*. Persons interested in the playbehavior of children sometimes refer to the *running and chasing* age, the *baseball* age, *etc*. Play interests, however, like other developmental phenomena, come into being and disappear gradually. Although they may be more prominent at certain periods of life than at others, there are no sharply defined stages set off by their presence.

Because of the fact that development is continuous, we are

* Puberty is reached at about thirteen or fourteen years in girls and fourteen or fifteen years in boys.

continually in search of landmarks by which we can describe its progress. The inexperienced person is therefore likely to place great stress upon such developmental events as the coming of the first tooth, the time when the first step is taken unsupported, *etc*. Although such events as these are important in the sense that they furnish objective and clear-cut points of reference from which later progress along the same line can be measured, we must not lose sight of the fact that they are in reality only part of a continuous developmental sequence. Indeed, the most recent studies in mental and physical growth have shown rather conclusively that even birth itself should be regarded as only a conspicuous incident in the developmental progress of the human being.

Increase of factors with age. We can characterize the essential difference between the child and the adult very simply. In contrast to the child who is developing the adult is at a maintenance level. Changes in adult behavior are brought about only as a result of experience.* Since adults seem in general somewhat less plastic, that is, less easily affected by experience, even these changes are of less importance. In the case of the child, on the other hand, we have to deal with the very complex phenomenon of an organism whereof the different parts are growing at different rates, and which is at the same time extremely sensitive to many environmental influences. For these reasons, both the opportunities for scientific investigation of phenomena and the technical difficulties involved in carrying out such investigations are greatly increased in the study of child behavior as compared to adult behavior.

Because of the underlying age factor all developmental processes are interrelated. It is therefore highly important to distinguish between those processes or functions which

* This is true only until the onset of senescence.

have no relationship other than the fact that they are changing with age, and those which are related in other fashions. For example, if we measure the size of vocabulary and the length of index-finger in a group of children who range in age from two to twelve years we shall find that those children who have the longest index-fingers also tend to have the largest vocabularies, but this is only because both the length of index-finger and the size of the vocabulary are increasing with age. If we compare the length of index-finger with the size of vocabulary in children who are all of exactly the same age we shall find little or no relationship between the two. If, however, we compare the length of the right index-finger with that of the left index-finger in a group of children of the same age we shall find that those children who have long right index-fingers tend also to have long left index-fingers. That is to say, there are factors other than age which affect the length of the index-finger, and these factors, whatever they may be, affect the length of both index fingers in approximately the same degree. If, in a similar way, we compare the size of vocabularies with grade placement in school we shall find that even among children of the same age there is some tendency for children with large vocabularies to be in higher grades than those with small vocabularies; that is, the two factors tend to vary together. We cannot say to what extent this may be the result of a tendency to consider the size of vocabulary in determining promotion, to the more complex curriculum of the upper grades acting as a stimulus to learning new words, to the effect of some general underlying factor such as intelligence, or to a combination of all these and other factors which might be mentioned. We can only say that a relationship exists which cannot be entirely accounted for upon the basis of age. We note also that this relationship is considerably less close than that which we found between the length of the index fingers on the two hands. Presumably, therefore, in addition to factors which tend to affect both in the same way, there are other factors operative which may affect one without producing any change in the other.

It is also important to note that developmental relationships change somewhat from age to age. This is because of the fact that different aspects of development may proceed simultaneously for a time but reach their maxima at different periods. For example, walking is a developmental process which reaches complete or practically complete development in early childhood and undergoes little change thereafter. Progress in vocabulary, however, although beginning (in the sense of reaching a level at which we can measure it) at only a slightly later age than walking, continues to increase long after the time when any measurable changes in walking have ceased to occur. During the period when both are developing, some relationship between the two kinds of ability will appear because of the underlying age factor. Thereafter such a relationship ceases to be present.

We may formulate this principle as follows: *In any trait, after the maximum has been reached, developmental relationships to other traits disappear.* Relationships based upon factors other than age will remain even after the developmental period is over.

It is probable that growth proceeds most rapidly during the early years of life. We know that this is true in the case of physical growth where adequate methods of measurement are available. In regard to mental growth we are less certain. It is true that by the age of six years the brain and nervous system have attained ninety per cent of their adult weight, and differentiation of cell structure within the brain seems to be at a corresponding level so far as our present microscopical analysis shows. However, reasoning from structure to function is always hazardous. Mental growth may be dependent in large measure upon facts not revealed by our present microscopes. Common observation, however, lends additional weight to the hypothesis of the early acceleration of mental growth. When we consider that during the first few years of life the child acquires practically all the basic tools of adult behavior, walking, speech, fundamental habits, bodily coördination and manual dexterity, as well as most of the basic mechanisms for social adjustment in an extremely complex environment, it unquestionably appears as though early development proceeds at a rate which is never again equalled. Attempts at measuring the form of the mental growth curve in terms of standardized test scores has, however, yielded inconsistent results. Thorndike (248) as the result of such a scaling technique comes to the conclusion that by the age of three years the child has attained two-thirds of his ultimate mental "altitude." Thurstone (251), however, using a somewhat different method of scaling, finds the curve of mental growth to be approximately a straight line from birth to maturity. We may therefore say that while the weight of evidence seems to be in favor of early acceleration of mental growth, the matter has not yet been irrefutably established.

Development is marked by a serial order. One of the most thoroughly demonstrated principles brought out by studies of child development up to the present time can be stated as follows: *Although children vary greatly in rate of development, the order of development as marked by the successive appearance of various developmental events varies but little from one child to another.* This sequential order is apparent at all ages and in all functions. A few examples may be mentioned. The ability to follow a horizontal movement with the eye develops at an earlier age than the ability to follow a vertical movement, and a vertical movement can be followed before a circular movement. In the eruption of

teeth the incisors precede the molars, and the lower central
incisors practically always appear before the upper ones. A
child can draw a circle before he is able to draw a square,
and the ability to draw a square develops from two to three
years before the ability to draw a diamond. An infant learns
to creep upstairs considerably earlier than he learns to
reverse the process and come down again, either backward
or forward. Later on he will be found to walk upstairs using
only the alternate treads, although he must still come down
one step at a time. He is able to feed himself with a spoon
long before he can spread butter on his bread. He can think
of ways in which two objects are different approximately a
year before he is able to tell you ways in which they are
alike. Almost an endless number of similar examples may be
cited.

Although variations from the usual sequential order do
occur they are relatively infrequent. Generally speaking,
when a child is found to be unable to perform one of the
tasks in such a developmental series we run little risk in
inferring that he will likewise fail on one which ordinarily
develops later, particularly if the two events in the series
are normally separated by a considerable lapse of time.
Children have occasionally been known to succeed on a test
of giving similarities in spite of failure on the test of giving
differences, but this does not often occur. No case has ever
been reported of a child who was able to draw a diamond
but not a square.

Practically, as well as theoretically, the law of the *constancy of developmental order* is of the greatest importance
for the study of child development. Consider, for example,
what would happen to the ordinary mental test if it were
actually necessary to try out individuals on all possible kinds
of performance. A lifetime would hardly be sufficient to complete the task. Recognition of this principle and study of

the order in which various phenomena tend to appear has made it possible for us to select a series of tests so graded in difficulty as to enable us to secure a fairly accurate knowledge of an individual's mental standing within a comparatively short period of time.

Development proceeds from generalized to specific responses. People sometimes think of growth as a building up of larger processes from smaller ones, as a "putting together" rather than a "bringing out." The modern position which is supported by a considerable amount of experimental evidence, is just the opposite. Growth is a process of unfolding, of the development of specific functions from more generalized types of response.

In mental development this progression is noticeable. At first a general response to a total situation is made. Later on the child becomes able to respond to certain specific features in the situation and to give less attention to others. For example, comprehension of speech seems to develop from a stage in which the child is able to make a general response to the total situation—tonal inflection, facial expression and bodily attitude, plus the actual form of the words used. By progressive stages in which more and more of the accompanying situation can be dropped out, a point is reached at which the word alone serves as an adequate stimulus for the response. Nor does the period of differentiation end here. With increasing experience, words which at first had only a highly generalized meaning convey finer and finer subtleties of thought. For the little child, any winged biped is a "birdie" or a "chickie," all food is "dinner," and all timepieces are "tick-tocks." With advancing development these generalized responses become more specific. A countless number of similar examples might be cited.

Integration accompanies differentiation. In the foregoing paragraph it was pointed out that development proceeds from the generalized uncoördinated responses of the infant to the specific and highly differentiated behavior of the adult. There is, however, another aspect of the picture. *Parallel with the process of differentiation which is the result of development, there is going on a process of integration or recombination of responses which is the result of experience.* Although we may distinguish between these two processes theoretically it is impossible to do so in actual practice, since experience without development or development without experience are alike impossible. It is important to realize, however, that the complexity of the integrative or reorganizing process is directly dependent upon the degree of differentiation which has taken place. It is fruitless to attempt to teach either the profound idiot or the child of eighteen months to make the fine distinctions needed to tell the differences between a robin and a wood thrush, or between his right shoe and his left. On the other hand, development alone in the absence of experience or training would never yield such specific items of information. As a result of progressive differentiation, the individual gains the ability to respond to more specific factors in the environment; as a result of experience these responses become organized into the characteristic patterns of response which we call "habits," "personality traits" and so on.

The same situation will induce different responses in different individuals or in the same individual at different times. From the foregoing discussion it should be clear that children in whom the process of developmental differentiation has reached different stages will, upon the whole, show certain characteristic trends in their responses to any given situation from which the level of development may often be inferred. At the earlier stages certain specific types of response will not yet have been differentiated out of the general complex, and will therefore not appear. For the same reason, certain organized reaction patterns will not be present, since the specific reactions needed to make up the general pattern are not as yet completely available. An example is furnished by the definitions of objects given by children of different ages or different stages of mental development. The average child of two or three years has a generalized reaction toward the stimulus word *chair*. When asked, "What is a chair?" he will point it out without hesitation or show his recognition of its purpose by going and sitting on it, but it is unlikely that he will be able to tell you anything more about it. If forced to make a verbal statement he can only say, "A chair is a chair," or "That's a chair." By the age of four or five, however, differentiation has progressed to a point at which the child is able to single out some feature of the general response for particular attention. With most children the "use" factor is one of the first to be differentiated. This gives rise to the well-known "use" definitions of early childhood, such as "a chair is to sit on," "a pencil is to write with," *etc.* As differentiation proceeds, integration goes on in like manner. The partial features which have become differentiated from the total situation are recombined and reorganized in various ways. Objects are now grouped into general classes on the basis of certain features which they possess in common. The early definitions in terms of a single differentiating feature or characteristic may now be replaced by the complete formal definition with classification of the object according to its genus. A chair is a piece of furniture, a horse is an animal.

It is important to realize that whatever the level of development and however generalized or specific the response may be, it is always a response of the whole individual and not of some special "faculty," such as memory, imagination, perception, or what not. Through progressive differentiation and integration, new combinations of partial features in the situation become capable of arousing reactions which are more specifically adapted to these features, and the characteristics of which are more clearly defined. An organism which originally was capable of making only one generalized response to a given total situation gradually becomes sensitive to various partial features and is thereby capable of responding, now to certain aspects and now to others. Although these responses differ in kind according as they are induced through different combinations of partial elements, like the more generalized responses of an earlier period they still involve the organism as a whole. For this reason, a change in a single feature of the situation may modify the entire reaction pattern which is displayed. Within the limits set by differentiation, the particular pattern of response which is displayed by the individual at any given moment will be determined largely or wholly by his previous experience in corresponding situations and by his physical condition at the time.

It is important to bear in mind, therefore, that when modern psychology uses such terms as "memory," "perception," "motor coördination," *etc., the reference is made to the kind of situation to which the individual is called upon to respond and not to the response itself as any sort of mental faculty which operates as a unit.* Nevertheless, there are certain kinds of situations which it is convenient to group together upon the basis of the general characteristics of the response which they tend to elicit from the reacting organism. When we speak of investigations of "memory," for example, we do not mean that we are studying some one part of the individual's mental equipment, but rather that we are concerned with certain aspects of his general behavior rather than others, and that we are setting up certain kinds of situations which are designed to bring these particular aspects of behavior into clearest relief. Every kind of mental process is modified to some extent by previous experience and thus involves memory. The difference between a formal experiment in memorizing and the observations of everyday behavior which involve memory is that in the former case such variable factors as the manner in which the stimulus is presented, the kind of stimulus given, the number of repetitions, the intervals between stimulus and response, *etc.*, are controlled by the experimenter, and thus made uniform for all individuals participating in the experiment. Furthermore, since the experimenter is commonly interested in certain features or aspects of the response rather than others, he centers his attention upon the observation and recording of these partial elements and ignores other features which do not fall within his particular line of interest at the time. In like manner we speak of experiments on sensation, imagination, and so on. Again, the basis for classification lies, not in the subject himself, nor in the particular kind of response elicited, but rather in the *kind of situation which has been set* and in the *selecting of partial elements in the response* for observation and recording. When used in this way, such expressions as "memory," "imagination," "reasoning," and so on are convenient and useful, but the student must not lose sight of the fact that these terms are only *modes of classification* and do not represent independent mental processes of any kind.

Chapter 3

MODERN METHODS OF CHILD STUDY

THE development of methods from problem requirements. Let us suppose that an intelligent and conscientious mother, after reading a book on the health-care of
children, finds that her child is taking less than the recommended amount of sleep. She endeavors to correct the deficiency by putting the child to bed at an earlier hour and
by trying to increase the length of the nap, but without
much success. In the belief that the best way to go about
correcting a difficulty is to ascertain its cause, the mother
finally decides to write out a systematic account of all the
facts in her possession regarding the child's sleeping habits.
With all the evidence before her, it should be, she thinks,
a relatively easy matter to find out where the fault lies.

She begins with the family history. The child's father is
a light sleeper, and one of her own sisters is very nervous
and often complains of insomnia. Is there an hereditary
factor involved? Perhaps, but it seems best to look further.
During the child's first winter there occurred a long visit
from a doting grandmother who, in spite of protests, often
used to rock the baby to sleep. Possibly the child became so
"conditioned" to rocking at that time that it has been difficult for her to go to sleep without it. The books mention
such cases. She is an only child and is therefore put to bed
by herself much earlier than the other members of the family. It may be that in staying awake till a later hour she is
unconsciously trying to imitate the grown-ups whom she

so much admires. Or perhaps she is disturbed by noises from outside. Although she has a room by herself it is not completely isolated from the noise of the household. Last winter she had whooping cough and was frequently wakened during the night by coughing. Were bad sleeping habits set up at that time? Recently she has been having her dinner at night with the family instead of at midday as was her former custom. Can this have anything to do with the matter?

Before the mother has gone very far in setting down possible causes it becomes evident that in any individual child, each form of behavior is closely bound up with all others, and with a multiplicity of different factors in the personal history and home background. It is not surprising, then, that attempts to arrive at the solution of a concrete difficulty by means of *incidental observations,* even when these observations are systematically combined into a descriptive *case history,* are subject to many sources of error. The range of possibilities is so great and the opportunities for verification so few that the findings are likely to be interpreted largely or entirely in terms of personal bias. Since it is impossible to set down everything, there is no guarantee that the facts of greatest significance will not be overlooked.

The mother then begins to wonder how her friends succeed in getting their children to take the recommended quota of sleep. She brings the matter up for discussion at a meeting of the Parent-Teacher Association and finds, to her surprise, that few children are actually sleeping as much as the books recommend. This raises the question of the accuracy of the standards laid down. Perhaps the requirements are too high. It is decided that it would be interesting and worth while to find out how much sleep the average child of each age actually does take, and how much children of the same age vary in their sleeping habits. After some discussion as to the best way in which this information could be secured, the mothers decide to send out a *questionnaire* to the parents of all the children in the school system, asking them to keep records for a period of one week on the amount of time which their children spend in sleep.

The results of the questionnaire show that at least for the children in the city studied, the standards prescribed are considerably higher than the amount of sleep usually taken. But the school nurse immediately points out that this does not necessarily mean that the standards are too high. It may be that most children sleep less than they should. How is this question to be answered?

What are some of the possible results of taking too little sleep? In children, growth and nutrition might be affected. How do the children who take least sleep compare in height and weight, and in the weight-height index with those who take most? *Measurements* of height and weight are accordingly taken and the results compared with the sleep records.

But lack of sleep may affect the child in other ways. He may become more nervous and irritable, or be lacking in physical energy. He may find it harder to give attention to his lessons or to persist at a task for long periods of time. There is no adequate way of measuring such characteristics as these, but it is possible to make judgments regarding them. A series of *rating scales* dealing with a number of traits of the kind just indicated are therefore prepared, and each child is rated on these scales by parents and teachers.

It is then suggested that since recuperation from mental fatigue can best be brought about through sleep, failure to take the needed amount of sleep may actually retard the mental development of a growing child. Each child is therefore given a *mental test* for further comparison with the sleep records.

A mother whose child sleeps less than the average for

his age raises the question of the quality of sleep. Some children are very restless during the night; others sleep more quietly. Is it possible that ten hours of quiet sleep may have as much value for the child as eleven or twelve hours of restless sleep? In order to throw light on this question, a number of mothers volunteer to observe their children throughout one entire night in each week for a period of four weeks, and to record the number of movements made. Nap periods are also to be observed in the same way. The results of these *systematic observations* are to be compared with the length of sleep by way of check on the hypothesis that the more restless sleepers tend to sleep more hours than those whose sleep is quiet. They are also compared with the findings from the measurements of height and weight, the intelligence test scores, and the trait ratings in order to see what relationship, if any, exists between these factors and the degree of restlessness shown during sleep.

After all these matters have been checked up, however, it is found that the differences in the amount of sleep taken by different children of the same age are still not completely accounted for. In discussing the matter, a number of possible hypotheses are suggested. One mother thinks that the amount of time which the child spends in outdoor exercise during the day may affect his sleep. Another places great stress upon the temperature of the sleeping room and the amount of bed-covering. One thinks that a bedtime story has a quieting effect upon the child and causes him to go to sleep more quickly; another is quite certain that stories delay sleep. One believes that the evening meal should come just before bedtime, and cites as evidence the quickness with which young animals and infants drop off to sleep after being fed. Others think that the meal should be scheduled early enough so that at least an hour may elapse between the child's supper and his bedtime.

Some of these hypotheses could readily be made the subjects of *controlled experiments*. For example, one group of mothers might try the earlier supper hour for a time, then change to a later one; while a second group whose children were of similar ages might try first the later, then the earlier plan. The amount of sleep taken by the children in each group under each of the two schedules could be recorded and compared. The bedtime story hypothesis might be tested in a similar way, as could also, within limits, the temperature of the sleeping room and the amount of outdoor play. While it is true that experiment in matters of this kind cannot be carried to a point which is in any way likely to interfere with the child's physical or mental well-being, there are many points where the question of optimum procedure is by no means settled, and upon which carefully conducted experimentation might at least shed some light.

In running through this account of an hypothetical series of investigations, we are immediately impressed with two points. First we note that the method is in each case an outgrowth of the problem to be solved and the devices available for its solution, *The method is fitted to the problem, not the problem to the method*. Secondly, in their attempts to answer the question which they had set themselves to solve, our hypothetical group of mothers have followed much the same line of progress that science in general takes in investigating a new problem. The problem is formulated from incidental observations on a relatively small number of cases. The gross facts are then ascertained by means of a survey of a large number of cases. After these facts have been determined, their relationships to each other and to such other facts as may seem to have a bearing upon their origin are examined. In the course of these investigations, certain hypotheses may be formed. The final step is to set up such crucial experiments as will check the soundness of these hypotheses as completely as possible, Throughout, progress is toward greater specificity in the formulation of the problem, toward organization and definition of procedure and the isolation of single factors for investigation, and toward such control of conditions as will make for clear and unambiguous interpretation of results.

A third point which may be somewhat less evident is worth noting. If a group of parents and teachers sufficiently intelligent and persistent to carry out such a series of investigations were actually to undertake a project of this nature, they might well come out with a greater feeling of ignorance than that which impelled them to start the investigation. It is the way of research to raise more questions than it answers. The beginning student faced with the need of earning so many laboratory credits or of writing a thesis gropes helplessly for a "problem." Let him but undertake the solution of one and a dozen more spring up to confront him. It is a mistaken notion that in order to be worth while, an investigation must provide a final answer to the question with which it deals. Rarely will this be true. What usually happens is that while certain partial aspects of the question under consideration are answered by means of one investigation, at the same time the general interrelationships of all the parts of the problem are brought out and the direction which later research can most profitably take is made more clear. Thus, in the hypothetical case cited, the following facts were presumably established with reasonable certainty:

1. The average amount of sleep taken by children at each age in the locality covered by the survey, and the extent to which these figures conform to the theoretical sleep requirements laid down in certain standard books on child care.
2. The relation of the amount of sleep taken to such factors as physical growth and nutritional status, mental

development, and personality characteristics as judged
by parents and teachers.

3. The relation between amount of sleep and restlessness
during sleep; and between restlessness during sleep
and the factors listed above.

4. The relationship between amount of sleep and certain
factors in the child's daily schedule or in the conditions under which sleep is taken.

Valuable as such information would be, and much as it
would advance our knowledge of the part played by sleep
in child growth and development, many important questions
would still remain unanswered. A large proportion of these
questions might easily be direct outgrowths of the findings
of this study. Suppose, for example, it should be found that
on the average children who are tall for their age sleep more
than those who are short. Does this mean that the added
growth is *caused* by the additional amount of sleep or that
children who grow rapidly require, and therefore take, more
sleep than those whose growth is slower? Or are the longer
hours of sleep and the greater height merely evidences of a
generally superior stock with its usual accompaniment of
better home care? The same question may be raised with
regard to other relationships which may be found. *The
establishment of a relationship does not, in itself, afford
evidence as to the causal basis for the relationship.* We are
not, therefore, provided with an answer to the fundamental
problem involved, but are merely shown whether or not
such a problem exists. In the example cited, if it were
found that sleep and height are unrelated to each other,
further investigation along this line becomes unnecessary
save possibly as a check upon the accuracy of the original
findings.

In the study of child development, as in other sciences, the
advancement of knowledge proceeds through a series of

successive approximations. Problems are formulated, then methods are developed. In the working out of these problems, new questions arise which necessitate other avenues of approach. No one method is adapted to all purposes nor may be applied under all conditions. Some methods, as we shall see, are more likely to yield clean-cut results than others, but each has its own possibilities and advantages, its own limitations and hazards.

A more detailed account of methods is given in Part III of this book.

PART II
EXPERIMENTS

Chapter 4

NOTES TO THE INSTRUCTOR

SECURING subjects. The organization of a course in experimental child study presents certain problems not encountered in the ordinary psychological laboratory where the students themselves commonly act as subjects for the investigations, and the experimental periods may be of protracted length. In carrying out experiments with children, the periods of work with any one child must be of short length, thus greatly reducing the amount of data which can be secured at a single sitting. The difficulty of securing subjects is also a serious problem. It is evident that school-children cannot be withdrawn from their class-rooms for experimental purposes too often, and that there is a limit to the amount of coöperation which can reasonably be expected from teachers in the way of ratings, questionnaires and the like. Even in the nursery-school and kindergarten, where programs are usually more informal and curricular requirements less rigidly defined, too frequent interruption of the activities of the children is unwise. For these reasons it is well to build up as extensive a clientele of subjects as local conditions permit, and to arrange the investigations in such a way as to avoid excessive demands upon any one group. The following are suggested as sources from which subjects can frequently be secured:

1. Individual children in homes known to the student or to his friends.
2. Mother's clubs, parent-teacher associations, and similar organizations.

A brief talk to groups of this kind can usually be arranged. The purpose of the proposed investigation can then be explained and the mothers invited to bring their children to the laboratory or to allow the worker to visit the home. If the invitation is couched in suitable terms, and the requests made are not excessive, the response from such groups is likely to be very gratifying.

3. Birth records and block surveys.

If children of a particular age are desired, these can often be most advantageously located by an examination of the official birth records of corresponding date. Calls can then be made at the homes and coöperation requested. If the situation is handled tactfully, and the request is of a reasonable nature, the number of refusals will usually be small. House to house canvassing may also be used when a somewhat wider range of ages is to be employed.

4. Baby shows, state and county fairs, *etc.*, often afford opportunities for carrying out investigations when only a single sitting of relatively brief duration is needed.

5. Arrangements can often be made with public school authorities to permit children to bring younger brothers and sisters to school for research purposes. When this is done, every precaution should be taken to see that no additional burden is imposed upon principal or teachers. The investigator should arrange for the care of the children during any intervals of waiting or inactivity, as well as during the actual experimental periods.

6. Churches and Sunday Schools with their affiliated organizations afford another means of getting in touch with parents of young children in rather large numbers. It is perhaps unnecessary to add the caution that in order to guard against possible offense, requests for coöperation are better made at the week-day rather than the Sunday services.

7. Public playgrounds and parks attract many children from the "toddler" stage up. When methods and apparatus are simple, it is sometimes possible to find a secluded corner in which experimental work can be car-

ried out on the spot. When controlled observation of "natural" behavior is the method to be used (see Chapter 45), the playground itself becomes an ideal laboratory. If these methods are not feasible, the informal atmosphere of the playground makes it easy to approach mothers or other persons in charge of the smaller children and to arrange for coöperation on another occasion.

8. Social agencies working with young children are usually very willing to coöperate with research agencies or with individual research workers. Among these agencies may be mentioned day nurseries, settlement houses, welfare organizations of all sorts, baby health clinics and milk stations, "behavior clinics" and child placing organizations.

9. Although orphanages and boarding homes for young children will provide many cases, the range of ability is likely to be somewhat restricted.

10. Pediatricians and family physicians can frequently be interested in a research project and persuaded to use their influence to secure coöperation among their patients.

11. Maternity hospitals and nursing homes for dependent or unmarried mothers afford opportunities for research work with young infants.

12. Nursery schools, kindergartens, experimental schools, and "neighborhood play groups," both public and private, are among the most useful as well as the most obvious sources. When the coöperative class method of securing data is used, a stable group of this kind becomes practically an essential. The demonstration or experimental schools connected with most teacher-training organizations afford ideal situations for training in experimental work, since it is possible in such schools to set up a well-organized body of records of the individual children which may be used as a source of much of the supplementary information suggested under the various experiments which follow. These records will also furnish material for many supplementary problems which can be worked out without the necessity of securing further data from teachers or

children. In cases where the coöperation of a nearby orphanage or similar institution can be secured, much the same sort of record-system may be set up.

Methods of organization. There are two general plans by which the laboratory work of a class in experimental child study may be organized; the individual project method and the coöperative or group method. The individual method is likely to be preferable for more advanced students but may also be used with less experienced students when the classes are small enough to permit fairly close supervision by the instructor. When this method is used it is usually desirable to divide the students into pairs. Each member of each pair is assigned a problem or selects one for himself. He then takes the complete responsibility for carrying out the investigation, working up the data, and organizing the results in their final written form. His partner, however, is expected to collaborate with him to the extent of securing whatever independent data are necessary for checking the reliability of the method. These results will be turned over to the main investigator for statistical treatment. In like manner, the first experimenter will secure the reliability data needed by his partner. In working with young children it will often be necessary to make use of hours other than the formal laboratory period. It is therefore wise to arrange partnerships between students who have similar schedules, particularly when the problem chosen is one which requires simultaneous observations.

In case the institution has no connection with an experimental school in which class experiments can be carried out, the individual project method is likely to be the only one feasible. When used, it should ordinarily include at least one regular lecture period per week in which general principles of scientific investigation, statistical methods for the treatment of data, and other problems of general interest to the class may be brought up for discussion. As the individual projects are completed, each one should be reported in full to the other members of the class. When time and the nature of the experiment permit, each student should try to observe one sitting of each experiment carried out by the other members of the group in order to familiarize himself with the methods employed. Each student should also be provided with copies of all the record forms used in other experiments. In this way it is possible to hold each member of the class responsible for a knowledge, not only of his own experiments and those of his partner, but also of those carried out by the remaining members of the group.

When the coöperative method is used the entire class collaborates in the securing of data for each problem. This has the advantage of permitting more detailed explanations of procedures both for the collection and treatment of data and of giving each student first-hand acquaintance with a fairly large number of different techniques. It is therefore preferable for beginning classes who have had relatively little experience with laboratory methods, and whose statistical training is meagre. When circumstances permit it is well to use the group method during the first part of the course and to change to the individual method later on as facility in handling material is gained. When the group method is used, each student is responsible for writing up the results of each experiment in which the class participates.

The experiments. In the following chapters will be found descriptions of a series of experiments and problems suitable for the elementary student. For these experiments no previous training in laboratory methods or statistics is assumed. For the most part the problems suggested require no apparatus or equipment other than that which the students can readily prepare for themselves. As outlined the problems are applicable to children within the range of ages from nursery-school through the primary grades. In some cases they may be used with older children. While the instructions as given follow the plan of the coöperative rather than the individual project, the experiments are equally suitable for the latter method of approach if existing conditions seem to make this preferable.

Since the greater number of the experiments described require several days' time for securing the data, unnecessary delay will result if work on one problem is always completed before another can be taken up. Inasmuch as the data are usually collected outside the class-room, a good plan is to alternate the formal class meetings with free periods. The class meetings may then be devoted to explanations and discussions of methods of organizing and treating the data which have been secured for one problem, while the alternating free periods are spent in securing the data for the next.

It is not to be expected that any one group of students will be able to carry out the entire list of experiments described. Because of the great differences in laboratory facilities and in the number and age of the subjects available in different places, it has seemed wise to make this section sufficiently comprehensive to meet the needs of students working under a wide variety of conditions. Instructors should make such a selection of topics as seems best to fulfill the requirements imposed by the amount of time and the facilities available for their students.

For advanced students who wish to carry out more comprehensive investigations than those outlined in this section, a list of suggested topics will be found in Chapter 40.

Chapter 5

BECOMING ACQUAINTED WITH THE LITERATURE

EVERY scientific worker, no matter what his problem, builds on the work of his predecessors. However new the problem appears, one is almost certain to find in scientific literature accounts of previous attempts to attack either the particular problem or others closely related to it.

The history of science is to be found, not so much in textbooks where scholars, for purposes of exposition, bring together the results of many investigations, as in reports on problems made by research workers themselves. To know first-hand sources is important for grasping the problem and also for formulating methods, techniques and principles of interpretation. The student who begins his investigation by a careful study of the literature on the topic in which he is interested will find, not only that his understanding of the problem and its implications has been greatly broadened, but also that he will secure many useful suggestions as to the technical methods by which it can most profitably be attacked.

But this is not all. A scientific contribution is never set off sharply from other investigations. To be most worth while it must coördinate and integrate the results of previous work. In part, the task of the worker in interpreting his results is to fit them into those obtained in earlier studies. The new findings may then be seen in their true light. Order and meaning may thus be brought out of what was previously chaotic and inconsistent. No one can go far in science unless he develops the habit of reading the work of his contemporaries and predecessors. Nor should he limit the reading of scientific material to his own particular field. Often significant contributions to technique and interpretation come from research outside the field in which a topic would seem logically to belong.

In order to know the literature in a scientific field the student must locate the published work on his problem and others related to it. This involves first of all the building of a working bibliography or list of references. By consulting various indexes, journals of abstracts, textbooks, general reviews and the bibliographies appended to articles and monographs, the student can make a beginning. As he reads he will add other references. It is usually desirable to copy the references on small cards, taking care to write down exactly the author, title and place of publication. Since a title does not always give an accurate picture of what is contained in a scientific article or monograph, the inclusion of more rather than fewer titles is advised.

The preparation of the bibliography is only the beginning. The next step is to work through the list of titles * by going to the articles themselves and determining by first-hand contact, whether or not they contain material of value. Some articles can be dismissed almost immediately with a mere scanning; others will take careful reading; some will be of such importance that they will be referred to many times.

But the quantity of scientific literature is such that no person can keep in mind all that he needs. Notes become necessary. Each article should be abstracted or summarized

* It is a good plan to begin the reading with the articles published most recently and work backward. By this method the student is able to evaluate earlier work in the light of what has since been discovered. He thus avoids falling into many errors of procedure and interpretation which were not discovered at the time the earlier work was published.

at the time it is read. In the preparation of abstracts or summaries a uniform method of note-taking is desirable. Methods vary from scholar to scholar. Some use cards, some bound note-books, some loose leaf note-books and some slips of paper which can be put in envelopes and filed. Whatever the method it should be planned in advance in order that the maximum return may be received. When the student first lays out a plan of note-taking, it may seem rather cumbersome. As he gains experience in its use he will find that it becomes simple and automatic.

It is worth while for the student to devote some time to working out a method of note-taking. If he is to spend a considerable part of his life in scholarly pursuits his notes rank among the most important tools of his profession. If they are effective and accurate they will conserve time and enable him to attack significant problems without unnecessary delay. The student should record every suggestion brought out by his reading as to possible new approaches to scientific problems. If unrecorded these ideas are likely to be forgotten.

After completing his notes on a topic the student will find it desirable to integrate the material into a critical or factual review. Nothing clarifies thinking quite so much as the attempt to organize material in written form. The process of preparing a review gives the student a better understanding of the problems to be attacked, the methods to be used, and the possible results which may be obtained, thus assisting him throughout the entire investigation.

As a guide for the student in reading scientific literature the following outline * for the evaluation of a scientific article has been prepared.

* The beginning student may not be familiar with some of the technical terms used here. They are explained in detail in the chapters dealing with specific experiments, and in the glossary.

Criteria for the Evaluation of Scientific Work

It is obviously impossible to lay down any hard and fast rules which can serve as substitutes for judgment and experience in the evaluation of any piece of scientific work. There are certain general principles which it is well to keep in mind. The student should not lose sight of the fact that technique is not everything; that a brilliant idea, even though poorly carried out, may still constitute a greater scientific contribution than the most thoroughly developed piece of work upon a problem which is not in itself worth while. While bearing these points in mind, it is nevertheless desirable for the student to examine carefully and critically the scientific articles which he reads in order to determine their technical adequacy and the soundness of the conclusions drawn.

I. *The problem itself*

A. Purpose and aim:

Has a definite objective been set for the problem, or does the report consist chiefly of loose records of random experimentation?

It is true that significant findings have sometimes resulted from studies in which no definite objective was laid down, particularly in the investigation of relatively new topics. A certain amount of preliminary exploration of the field is often desirable. An exploratory study is not to be confused with the haphazard collection of poorly organized facts occasionally to be met with in the literature.

B. Orientation in the general scientific field:

1. Is the problem one which may properly be attacked in the present state of our knowledge, or are there basic and essential under-

lying factors which must be investigated, or techniques which must be developed before this problem can profitably be approached?

2. Is the problem given a proper setting with reference to the work of previous investigators? Does the author appear to be familiar with the literature?

II. *Experimental Procedure*

A. Methods:

1. Is the general technique, including tools, units of measurement, *etc.*, carefully thought out and well adapted to the solution of the main problem, or is there careless adoption of the methods used by previous investigators with little regard to their suitability?

2. Have the data been systematically collected according to a definite plan, or do they consist largely of a haphazard array of facts from miscellaneous sources?

3. Has the procedure been kept uniform, or has it been varied to suit the examiner's convenience, prejudices or impulses of the moment?

4. Have uniform methods been followed in handling the subjects, particularly as regards the control of attention and motivation?

B. Subjects:

1. Is the selection of subjects, as regards number, age range, sex, socio-economic status, *etc.*, carefully planned and adequate for the particular problem?

2. Is the amount of data for each subject sufficient to establish reasonable reliability?

3. Has needed supplementary information been secured?

C. Records:

1. Were records taken at the time of observation or at some later period?

2. Was a uniform plan of recording followed throughout?

3. Have negative items and omissions as well as positive items been recorded in all cases?

III. *Treatment of Data*

A. Are the statistical procedures employed:

1. Mathematically sound?

2. Well adapted to the solution of the problem?

B. Has the extent of the experimental error:

1. Been ascertained and reported?

2. Been reduced to a minimum by appropriate weighting or elimination of unsuitable items or by better control of experimental conditions?

Consider here both possible *sources* of error, such as inaccuracy of the measuring instrument, inexpertness of the experimenter, and unfavorable conditions under which the experiment was carried out, and the probable *direction* of error; whether variable or constant.

IV. *Presentation of results*

A. Organization and literary style:

1. Is the article clearly written and well organized as to content?

2. Is there clear differentiation between theoretical material and actual findings?

3. Are table headings, graph titles, *etc.*, clear or ambiguous?

4. Has tabular matter been so arranged as to bring together for convenient comparison those items which it is desired to compare, or is it necessary to shift from table to table or from end to end of the same table in order to interpret the results?

B. Completeness of information:

1. Have all essential facts entering into the set-up of the problem including procedure, subjects, time limits, *etc.,* been described with sufficient detail and clearness so that another investigator could reproduce the experiment exactly?

2. Has all information necessary to the interpretation of results been presented; *i.e.,* if correlations have been used, is the group dispersion stated as well as the P. E. of r? If percentages have been used, is the number of cases stated? *etc.*

V. *Interpretation of results*

A. Extent of generalization:

1. Do the facts presented warrant the conclusions drawn? Has adequate allowance been made for chance variation? Consider here the reliability of the method, the number and selection of subjects, the possible existence of correlated factors for which no allowance has been made, the possibility of correlations between errors as a source of spurious reliability, *etc.*

2. Have all the conclusions which might justifiably have been drawn from the results been pointed out, or have significant facts or trends been overlooked?

B. Integration in the general scientific field:

1. Has the extent of agreement or disagreement with the findings of previous workers on the same problem been pointed out?

2. Has the possible significance of the findings for other related problems been noted?

VI. *Final evaluation in the light of all the above points*

A. Type of problem:

Would you classify this piece of work as primarily

1. A contribution to experimental methodology?

2. A contribution to fundamental knowledge in the field?

3. A contribution to practical diagnosis or procedure?

4. Suggestive of further problems?

5. Of little or no value?

State reason for your classification.

B. To what extent has the problem attacked been solved?

Chapter 6

THE CONDUCT OF AN INVESTIGATION

The Collection of Data

IF the course in experimental child study is to serve its purpose, certain general rules for the securing of accurate data must be grasped and followed. The most important of these may be outlined as follows:

1. *Be sure that all materials are in order.* Since children fatigue and lose interest quickly unless the procedure runs smoothly and automatically, it is essential that instructions be thoroughly memorized in advance. Always try out the procedure with an adult before attempting it with a child in order to make sure that the technique has been thoroughly grasped.

2. *Follow the procedure outlined.* It is impossible even for an experienced investigator, much less a beginning student, to tell without experimentation what changes in response are likely to be introduced by even small changes in procedure. For example, the instruction "Tell me what you see in this picture," will usually call forth a very different type of response from "Tell me what this picture is about." The first question is likely to be answered by simple enumeration of the objects in the picture, while the second is likely to lead to a description of the action portrayed. When a uniform procedure is used the first type of response is characteristic of younger or more backward children, and is therefore regarded as inferior to, or less mature than the second type. A slight change in the wording of the stimulus-question may thus completely invalidate the results obtained from an experiment. Failure to control tonal inflection, direction of glance, and

55

postural changes which may serve as secondary cues by which the subject may guide his responses, are quite as serious errors as changes in the verbal instructions. Young children, to whom language is still a comparatively new acquisition, are far more responsive to non-verbal cues of this sort than most people realize. The experimenter must therefore be continually on his guard to avoid glancing in the direction of the expected response, (or, conversely, in the direction of the wrong response, since the suggestion thus given may cause a timid or overdocile child to make an incorrect response when he would otherwise have made the correct one), and to make sure that his facial expression does not indicate to the child whether or not he is on the right track. A maze problem, for example, might easily be made worthless by carelessness in this respect.

3. *Take records in a systematic fashion from the beginning.* Prepare record forms in advance. Never use loose sheets or odd bits of paper with the expectation of copying afterward. If the recording is at all elaborate, it is best to have the sheets mimeographed, since this insures absolute uniformity of arrangement and facilitates tabulation. If record sheets are prepared by the students themselves, make sure that the same form is used by all. The preparation of a good record sheet demands time and forethought, and should not be left to the inspiration of the moment.

The record sheet should be arranged in such a way that later statistical treatment of the data will be facilitated. In general, items which are to be brought together for comparison should be near one another so as to avoid the necessity of searching about the sheet in order to locate them. Items should be grouped in such a fashion as to make them stand out visually. This can be done by the employment of conspicuous subheads which divide the sheet up into blocks, or by spacing between items and sections. In planning the record forms be sure to allow ample space. Notes are often rendered obscure or even useless by unnecessary crowding. In addition to the formal items, space should always be left on the record sheet foɪ recording any unusual conditions, such as interruptions, poor coöperation on the part of the subject with probable reasons, *etc.* Do not sacrifice time to save paper.

In order to economize time in record-taking, it is advantageous to build up a system of abbreviations or code symbols for terms frequently used, but care should be taken to avoid such indiscriminate use of abbreviations that notes cannot be read after they become "cold." Make a list of all abbreviations used even in rapid note-taking, and place it in the front of your note-book where it will be convenient for reference. Every abbreviation used anywhere in the notes should be found in this list. The following will be found useful.

E—Experimenter
S—Subject
RH—Right hand
LH—Left hand
R—Refusal
Si—Silence
dk—"don't know"
no comp—apparent failure to comprehend instructions

incomp—incomprehensible verbal response
T1, T2, etc.—First trial, second trial
L—Laughter
C—Crying
Int—Interest *
At—Attentiveness *
Ef—Effort *

4. *Label all records clearly and completely.* This rule applies quite as much to the original data as to the final tables. The labelling should show the exact meaning of all data included in the table, and unless the statistical methods employed are completely obvious, notes showing how the figures were obtained should be appended in all cases. It is unsafe to rely upon memory for facts of this kind. The motto, "Label everything," should hang on the walls of every laboratory.

5. *Be sure that figures are written legibly.* Examine your customary manner of writing the digits for the fol-

* These characteristics may be graded roughly as follows: Marked degree + + +, moderate degree + +, slight degree +, somewhat lacking —, decidedly lacking — —, extremely lacking — — —.

lowing or any other bad habits: failing to close the o
so that it looks like a 6, adding an extra curl to the
2 making it look like a 3, carrying the lower part of
the 3 back upon itself so that it may easily be mistaken for a 2, failing to add the upper bar to the 5
so that it is likely to be mistaken for a 3, shortening
the upper part of the 7 until it looks like a 1, or failing
to close the loop of the 9 so that it resembles a 7. All
these are unpardonable sins in any sort of quantitative work. The most painstaking investigation can be
invalidated by faulty computation, and computation
cannot be expected to be correct if the basic data are
copied incorrectly. It makes little difference whether
an investigator's figures are artistic or not. It makes a
great deal of difference whether or not his figures are
so sharply differentiated from one another that they
can be read correctly without a moment's hesitation
or doubt.

The Preparation of Work Sheets

Final tabulations and summaries can frequently be made
directly from the original record forms, particularly if they
have been carefully prepared and the data are not too complex. Occasionally time will be saved by transferring the
original data to work sheets. The work sheet may be a *code
slip* to which data are transferred in order to permit rapid
sorting, reassembling, and resorting; a *master sheet* or large
ruled form to which the data are transferred, or a note-
book. If the data are to be combined in many different ways
the code slip is preferable. This is usually a narrow sheet
of paper or a card on which all the results for each subject
are entered in systematic fashion with corresponding items
always in the same location. A narrow slip is better than a
wide one since it brings each item near a margin and thus
makes it easy to locate. Code slips can be sorted according
to one category, tabulations made, re-sorted according to

another and so on, with a minimum expenditure of time and energy.

If only a small number of items are to be compared with each other, the master sheet may be used. It consists of a large sheet of paper ruled in columns, on which the names of the subjects are entered down the left hand margin, and their scores or responses under appropriate categories in the columns opposite. The master sheet has the advantage of compactness and of suggesting cross comparisons that are not immediately discernible on the code slip.

The tabulation book does not differ in principle from the master sheet. It is useful when the number of subjects or the amount of data for each subject is so great that the master sheet would have to be very unwieldy in order to take care of all the data.

The principles previously enumerated with regard to record forms apply with equal force to work sheets of all types. All entries should be labelled carefully and completely. The data should not be crowded, should be arranged in uniform fashion throughout, and the entries should be legible. Here as elsewhere, care in planning the original forms will more than pay for itself in later saving in time and effort.

Summarizing the Results

In the actual handling of data there are a number of procedures which save time and energy on the part of the investigator. Suppose that the student has collected data with reference to children of both sexes. In his anxiety to find out what his material shows, he may summarize for the whole group of children in the beginning and later be forced to work through the data again in order to treat the material with reference to boys and girls separately. Had he summarized for the sexes separately at the outset, the table for the sexes combined could have been obtained by simple addition and thus much time would have been saved. In general it is best to determine in advance the smallest divisions in which the data are to be handled, summarize for those divisions, and then combine the results in order to obtain the wider generalizations.

Often a much clearer comprehension of relations is gained from charts or graphs than from tables. For this reason it is a good plan for the student to form the habit of plotting as many of his findings as lend themselves to graphic treatment. Here we are not emphasizing the value of graphic methods in the presentation of data so much as their value in bringing the investigator to a clear understanding of the phenomena which he is studying. In many instances the employment of a graphic method brings out relationships which would otherwise be overlooked. Thus a graphic analysis frequently suggests new possibilities of handling the material.

Checking for Accuracy

The handling of data is a complex job in which it is easy to make errors and difficult to locate them once they are made. Every investigator, no matter how experienced, should check his results for accuracy with the greatest care. Every calculation, every transference of material from sheet to sheet, should be carefully checked. If possible this should be done by a different person than the one who made the original calculation or transfer since there is a tendency to make the same errors in going through material a second time. If the original calculations and the checking are done by the same person a different method should be employed. One may start adding at the top of the column rather than the bottom. Subtraction may be checked by addition; multiplication, division or square roots by employing the process opposite to that originally used.

The investigator should also be on the alert for methods of checking his material by comparing the various relationships for consistency with one another. If the investigator is collecting data on boys and girls and finds that within the class intervals of his distribution there is a very large number of girls as compared with boys he should check the original data in order to make sure that the unusual number of girls is correct. The data obtained on boys is used here as a check for the material obtained on girls. If similar studies have been previously done by other investigators he should check his data in some detail against the published material and verify wherever a decided discrepancy occurs. Frequently an investigator works over his material in a number of different ways and so checks one relationship against another. While it is difficult to point out all the possible checks which may be used, nevertheless the importance of being on the alert to utilize every device for checking or cross comparison can hardly be overemphasized. The test of an investigator is not to be found in the amount of data he handles, but rather in the care and precision with which he handles each of its separate phases. Alertness in checking, care in labelling, precision in the manipulation of numbers, are three of the virtues which every person who is undertaking to carry on scientific work should cultivate.

Chapter 7

METHODS OF HANDLING CHILDREN IN EXPERIMENTAL SITUATIONS

THE person who is contemplating scientific investigation with young children as subjects, must not only be familiar with the general principles of research but must also be skilled in the handling of children. No matter how perfect an experiment may be from the technical standpoint, if the child's coöperation is not secured, results can have but little meaning.

Because of the difficulties involved in holding the young child to a rigidly standardized experimental procedure, persons who have had little training in scientific methods are sometimes inclined to vary their procedure from day to day or from child to child according to circumstances. It should be unnecessary to point out the likelihood of serious error entering into results obtained by haphazard methods of this sort. While it is true that experimental procedures must be greatly simplified and must be carried out in an easy informal manner if their application to young children is to be successful, it is nevertheless possible to plan the procedure in such a way that uniformity of method can be insured with no lessening of the child's interest. Methods of controlling motivation will be discussed in more detail in a later section of this chapter. The matter is brought up at this point in order to emphasize the importance of considering the question of interest from the beginning; and of *including in the standardized procedure whatever devices seem necessary*

or desirable for increasing motivation or controlling atten-
tion.

Preliminary adjustment of child to situation. A young
child who is taken for the first time into a strange laboratory
by a person with whom he is unacquainted cannot be depended upon to react immediately in an entirely normal
fashion. Even children who show no particular signs of initial
shyness need to be allowed sufficient time to become acquainted with their surroundings, so that the furnishings of
the laboratory or the noises from without will not serve as
undue sources of distraction. During this time it is better
for the experimenter to avoid thrusting himself too ob-
trusively into the foreground. He should endeavor rather to
function simply as one of the objects or items in the situation which the child may approach or examine at will. Such
advances, when they occur, should be received cordially and
with the suggestion (not too insistent) of further interesting
things to be seen or done presently. By tactful following of
the child's lead it is possible to work up to the actual experimental situation as a natural sequence of events, rather
than as a task which is unreasonably imposed upon the
child by authority which he is very likely to question. Much
of the "artificiality" of the laboratory situation may be done
away with by careful management of the child during the
preliminary stages. The amount of time required for this
preliminary preparation is usually not very great, and will
be more than compensated for by the additional smoothness
and speed with which the later work can be conducted, and
by the greater degree of reliance which can fairly be placed
upon the results. An unwilling, frightened, or excited child
is not likely to react in a typical manner.

A suitable manner on the part of the experimenter will
do much to facilitate the handling of children who are
difficult to manage. Negativistic children in particular, should

never be permitted to detect any signs of uncertainty or annoyance occasioned by their behavior. The experimenter should assume in all cases an attitude of casual, good-natured expectancy, and should make all suggestions in a firm low-pitched tone using words which suggest only one possible alternative. "Now we are going to . . ." accompanied with a smile and general manner suggestive of some altogether delightful event to follow will bring forth a very different response from that likely to result from "don't you want to?" (causing the child to wonder whether or not he really does 'want to', or at least suggesting the possibility of another course of action). A bald "Do this," is to the stubborn child a direct invitation to a clash of wills, which can be avoided by more tactful phrasing of the request or by arousing an interest in some particular part of the task to be accomplished or in some event to follow its successful outcome.

Care must be taken to prevent the voice from becoming high-pitched and to avoid the adoption of a patronizing or artificial tone. The latter is an unfortunately common habit among many persons when speaking to young children. The effect upon the child is always undesirable. It greatly increases shyness and self-consciousness, and among slightly older children frequently leads to "showing off" and similar means of attracting attention. Overactive and distractible children can often be recalled to the task in hand by the simple expedient of momentarily dropping the pitch of the voice.

When children are to be called away from a nursery-school or kindergarten group to take part in a laboratory experiment, every effort should be made to select such occasions as will involve the least possible interruption of their activities. If it is necessary to take a child away from his play, a few moments must be spent in gradually diverting his attention from the activity in which he has been engaged before inviting him to go to the laboratory. This may be done by engaging him in conversation, showing toys, *etc.* If properly managed, children who are being used frequently as laboratory subjects may be trained to look upon these occasions as special treats, while unwise handling may build up a habit of protest which will interfere greatly both with the experimental work and with the nursery-school routine. Children and teachers have rights which must be respected by the research worker. It is hardly necessary to add that when several research projects are being carried on simultaneously, the experimental periods must be arranged in such a way that no child will have excessive demands made upon his time.

Physical condition of child. The extent to which results may be affected by changes in the physical condition of the child due to fatigue, minor illnesses such as colds, recent emotional outbursts, length of time since food was taken, *etc.,* is a subject regarding which we have but little information at present. It has been shown (109) that irritability in young children, as indicated by the frequency of outbursts of anger shows rather marked diurnal variation, but that scores earned on the usual type of intelligence test are but slightly affected by the hour of the day at which the test is given (103). Studies using adult subjects and designed to determine the effect of fatigue upon mental work have usually shown little consistent change in output with moderate degrees of fatigue, but Thorndike (246) has shown that interest and motivation are likely to undergo marked diminution as fatigue increases. Gates (85) found reliable though small diurnal variations in learning efficiency among elementary school children and college students.

It is important to realize that factors such as the above may play a much greater part in the reactions of young children than with older children or adults. Emotional control is not well established at these early ages; hence, if the curve of "satisfyingness" for these children shows a form similar to that found by Thorndike for college students, it is very possible that the curve of "work" may also show a marked decrement, since little children are less able to bring other motivating factors into play to compensate for the loss of interest and satisfaction induced by fatigue. Much additional research is needed before positive statements can be made. In the absence of more valid information, it is the part of wisdom to keep all factors of this kind under as rigid experimental control as possible, by making all experiments at the same hour of the day, and avoiding occasions when the subject is not well or is emotionally disturbed.

Place. There is decided advantage in carrying out experimental work in a place with which the child is at least fairly familiar. When this is impossible, sufficient time for adjustment to the new situation should always be allowed before beginning the actual experiment. The room used should have adequate light, heat, and ventilation, and should be free from interruption. Distracting outside stimuli (noises, *etc.*) are also to be avoided. Furnishings should be simple, attractive, and few in number so that they will not serve as distractions.

Physical set-up of the experimental situation. The arrangement of the situation should always be planned for in advance. As a rule the subject should be placed at the left of the experimenter, since note-taking with the right hand is thereby made more convenient and less conspicuous. The comfort and convenience of both participants should be considered. All material should be kept in uniform arrangement planned to expedite its handling. If the material is at all involved, it is worth while to construct a special container which will prevent items from becoming lost or misplaced. In any case, it is always necessary to check through material to be used before beginning the experiment in order to make certain that everything needed is in its place, and that all pieces of mechanical apparatus are in working order. Make sure that stop watches will not run down in the middle of the experiment.

Fore-exercises. Wherever the nature of the experiment permits, a sufficient amount of preliminary practice to acquaint the subject with the nature of the task to be performed is desirable. First reactions are likely to be unfavorably influenced by a number of factors, such as incomplete or incorrect understanding of instructions, lack of self-confidence, or timidity, incorrect focussing of attention, *etc*. The use of a suitable fore-exercise involving similar but not identical material will ordinarily bring about an appreciable improvement in the reliability of the findings. In the case of certain simple physical tests and measurements in which the practice effect is negligible, the fore-exercise may consist simply of one or more preliminary trials of the actual experiment by way of acquainting the child with the general procedure. Where used, the fore-exercise must be standardized as rigidly as any other part of the experiment, and must be uniform for all subjects.

Verbal instructions. In planning the verbal instructions, clearness, simplicity, and brevity should be the aim. If any changes from the standardized wording are to be permitted, the exact nature of the changes and the conditions under which they are to be used must be defined in precise terms. This frequently involves a considerable amount of preliminary experimentation in order to determine optimum wording of instructions.

Tonal inflection is likewise important. Words or phrases to be emphasized should always be underlined on the outline of procedure; pauses, where not completely obvious, should also be indicated. The rising or falling inflection of the voice at the end of a series of instructions may introduce a considerable element of variation in the results obtained. While absolute standardization of tonal inflection is an ideal exceedingly difficult of attainment the major factors, at least, can be controlled if the experimenter is willing to give sufficient attention to the matter.

As a rule considerable leeway should be permitted in the way of incidental remarks or comments in order to preserve an atmosphere of easy informality. However irrelevant conversation is likely to prove a source of distraction, while remarks about the experiment itself unless very carefully guarded may function as secondary cues which are likely to affect results. An attempt should therefore be made to reduce the number of such comments to the minimum necessary to keep the child happy and at ease. This is usually much less than is realized by the inexperienced worker who frequently attempts to cover his own lack of ease by unnecessary verbiage.

Supplementary instructions. Under this head should be included all illustrations of procedure, gestures, suggestive pauses, changes of facial expression, direction of glance, and expressions of approval or disapproval including smiles, nods, *etc*. Persons lacking experience with young children frequently fail to realize the extent to which the child's responses are conditioned by secondary cues of this kind. Up to the age of two or three years such factors are probably quite as significant elements in the situation as are verbal instructions. Undoubtedly they play an important part at all age levels. It is likely that many inconsistencies in the results of experimental work are attributable to lack of control of factors of this kind. Although, as in the case of tonal inflection, precise regulation of minor variations in these matters is very difficult, the more significant items, at least, can be kept uniform.

Number of trials allowed. Both the number of trials on each item and the number of repetitions of the entire experiment should be uniform for all subjects. If a second trial is to be allowed under any conditions (such as failure to understand instructions, interruption from outside source, fluctuation of attention, or failure due apparently to lack of effort), the circumstances under which such additional trials are to be given, and the number of trials to be permitted must be defined. The same principle holds with regard to the repetition of instructions when, for any reason, the subject fails to respond on the first occasion.

Time limits. Time limits must be defined in all instances. It is also necessary to decide in advance what procedure is to be followed when a child who has not completed the task ceases to make an effort before the expiration of the allotted period. If, under such circumstances, the experimenter sometimes waits until the period is over, sometimes urges, reminds, or offers an incentive for the child to continue, and on other occasions passes on directly to the next phase of the experiment without waiting until the standardized time has elapsed, consistent results can hardly be expected. Because of the marked distractibility of little children and the loss of interest and effort likely to result from a long wait, especially if the task in question is truly beyond their power, it is often desirable to set a minimum as well as a maximum time limit. This will insure general uniformity of procedure, without inducing fatigue or boredom in the less capable subjects.

Time limits should be short because of the limited attention span of young children. Rules for regaining the child's attention during moments of distraction should be formulated in advance. The investigator should make sure that the child is giving attention each time a new stimulus is presented unless attention is itself being studied. The intervals between the presentation of successive stimuli may vary according to circumstances, unless the length of the interval is likely to affect the results.

Incentives and other methods of controlling motivation. Every effort should be made to set up the problem in such a way that it will have intrinsic interest for the children. A natural interest is always more reliable than one aroused through artificial devices not closely related to the total situation. In the latter case there is danger that the interest may be confined to the devices and therefore not carry over to the experimental situation. When special devices are used, they should be introduced in such a way that they seem to the child to be an intrinsic part of the task rather than an unrelated adjunct. The successful completing of a stylus maze may be marked by the ringing of an electric bell which has been wired in circuit; the number of successes in a learning experiment may be marked by pasting an equal number of stars on a prepared chart. On the other hand withholding of rewards for disobedience or naughtiness is a practice which is usually undesirable. Failure to secure the expected reward then takes on the nature of a punishment which is likely to turn the child against the entire situation. If material incentives are used at all they should be simple in nature and should either be assigned upon a basis which is entirely objective from the child's point of view and so arranged as to enable him to observe his own progress from day to day, or else be given uniformly at the end of the experimental period. Studies carried on at the Institute of Child Welfare of the University of Minnesota have tended to show that children place special value upon things made for them in their presence, particularly if there is a connection apparent to the child between the incentive offered and the task performed. In a learning experiment with the Young Slot Maze carried out by McGinnis (173) in which the path is traced by means of a set-in metal shoe which is to be taken to a painted clown at the goal, outline tracings of the "man and shoe" were made and given to the children at the close of each day's sitting. These drawings continued to be prized throughout a fifteen-day series of trials. In another experiment involving the placement of large rings in certain positions on a wooden frame, paper rings of various colors were cut out and given to the children at the close of each day's experiment. In this case, the change in the colors provided an additional source of interest.

No kind of artificial incentive, however, can make up for an unfortunate attitude or manner on the part of the experimenter. Harshness on the one hand or sentimentality on the other, a shrill or rasping voice, nervousness expressed as fussing or nagging—any or all of these may upset the most carefully planned experiment, or outweigh the effect of the strongest incentive which it is feasible to offer. Moreover, the experimenter must not fail to show his own keen interest in the task and in the child's performance. Praise will be more effective and less likely to result in too much self-confidence or "showing off" if directed toward the achievement rather than toward the child. A hearty "That was splendid" will usually be productive of increased effort; a fulsome "My, what a smart boy you are" may produce quite the opposite effect. The importance of making only positive suggestions has been mentioned previously. Punishment, reproof, scolding, or negative criticism are not likely to be effective methods of handling young children.

While the above suggestions on the management of children in an experimental situation will be found generally helpful, it is impossible to lay down a set of formal rules which will make an effective substitute for actual experience.

No one who lacks first-hand experience in the everyday management of young children should attempt to use them as subjects in a controlled experiment until such experience has been gained, or at least until systematic observation of the methods used by skilled nursery-school or kindergarten teachers has been made. What to do when a child is timid, shy, or frightened; how to recognize the beginning signs of fatigue or boredom; how to arouse and maintain interest in a task which has little intrinsic attractiveness; how to handle the negativistic child or the one who is unduly distractible, are likely to become very acute questions indeed with the person who is unskilled in child management. Learning to handle children wisely and effectively is a part of the basic technique of research in child development. Until this technique has been attained little progress can be made.

Chapter 8

THE STUDENT'S REPORT OF AN EXPERIMENT *

A S each experiment is completed, the student is expected to prepare a formal written report to be submitted to the instructor. Reports should be typewritten or written in neat and legible longhand with ink on standard size (8½ by 11 inches) note-book paper. The left-hand margin should be at least two inches in width to provide for criticism by the instructor. Cross-section or ruled paper should be used for all long tables (except where these are typewritten) and for all graphs. The latter may be drawn in colored inks or crayon.

Unless otherwise instructed, the reports should conform to the following plan of organization:

1. *Title of experiment.*
2. *Name of experimenter and of partner if any.*
3. *Date of beginning experiment. Date of submitting completed report.*
4. *List of readings on topic.*†

Give complete bibliographical references as follows. For books give author, title, place of publication, publisher, date

---

* When the entire class is coöperating in the carrying out of an experiment, the instructor will find it convenient to post a tabular form on which results may be entered as soon as possible after they are collected. A definite date by which all records entering into the final summary must be available should be set, in order that the class as a whole may not be handicapped by the tardiness of one or two individuals.

† This may be placed at end of report if instructor prefers.

and number of pages. Indicate which parts of the book were read if it was not read as a whole.

Example:

Baldwin, B. T., and Stecher, Lorle: *The psychology of the preschool child*. New York, D. Appleton and Co., 1925, Pp. vii + 305. (First four chapters were read.)

For articles in periodicals, give author, title, name of journal, year, volume number, and pages.

Example:

Jones, Mary Cover: The development of early behavior patterns in young children. *Ped. Sem.* 1926, 33, 737-785.

Only those references actually read by the student should be included in this list. When the individual project method is used, the student will be expected to make a fairly complete survey of the literature on his topic. When the entire class coöperates in carrying out the experiments, the number of projects in which each student takes part will be considerably greater than when the individual method is used. While, under these circumstances, the reading on each topic will necessarily be less extensive, at least two or three of the most important references should be covered.

5. *Statement of problem and review of previous investigations covered in the literature cited.* Show how the present experiment is related to these investigations and point out any differences in procedure or purpose.

6. *Complete description of experiment including apparatus or material used, method, number and characteristics of subjects, etc.* Cite any difficulties and sources of error which were encountered in carrying out the investigation, and if possible show how they might have been avoided or more adequately handled.

7. *Presentation, analysis and discussion of results.* Organize the findings in tabular form with appropriate table-headings. Supplement the tables by graphs whenever the data can be brought out more clearly in that way. Be sure to label all tables and graphs clearly and completely.

Each computation should be scrutinized carefully, first for its mechanical accuracy since errors in arithmetic may upset the soundest of conclusions, and secondly for the relation of its result to the other parts of the experiment and to the general purpose for which the investigation was designed. Although the numerical findings are the framework of the report, this framework is not complete without a superstructure of interpretation. The superior student is likely to be distinguished from the rank and file, not only by the accuracy of his work, but also by the extent to which he is able to interpret his data, to see its implications, its weaknesses and its possibilities, and to note possible improvements in techniques, or promising trends for future study.

In the discussion of results, take particular pains to interpret all the findings clearly and concisely. Do not attempt to force the figures to come out in any predetermined way. If the results are at variance with expectation, are inconclusive or otherwise disappointing, try to discover the reason without juggling them around to make them fit some theory of your own. Unsatisfactory results may arise from a number of causes. First of all, look to your arithmetic. Are the computations correct, and have the correct formulas been used? Next consider the matter of procedure. When a number of persons collaborate in the collection of data, great care is necessary to insure uniformity of method. Inconsistencies in results may be due to carelessness or misunderstanding of the method on the part of one or two persons. Remember, too, that human behavior is very complex, that no two individuals are exactly alike and that all of us at times react in ways which are not typical of our usual behavior. It is to be expected, therefore, particularly when the number of cases studied is not large, that variations from the normal or typical reactions may produce inconsistent or unusual results. The exceptional event sometimes occurs. But it has a cause and does not occur fortuitously. Results at variance with the usual findings should not be regarded as wrong, but rather considered correct (assuming that technical errors are ruled out) *under the conditions in which the experiment was carried out and for the subjects studied*. It is the student's task to ascertain whether differences in experimental conditions or in the composition of the experimental group account for the unexpected results.

8. *Compare the results obtained with those reported by other investigators in the references cited.* Try to account for any significant differences.

9. *Summarize the findings briefly and concisely at the end of the report.*

Chapter 9

THE MEASUREMENT OF BODILY DIMENSIONS

THE study of child development begins naturally with physical growth, first because bodily dimensions are objective and can be seen and measured directly; and secondly because instruments for measuring these dimensions are already available from the physical sciences. Before mental development or social behavior can be studied effectively, much time must be spent in developing techniques by which the results of observation and experiment can be recorded in terms which will have unmistakable meaning. When we say that a certain child is 49 inches tall, we are making an exact statement which can be understood in only one way. When, however, we wish to describe his mental, social, or emotional level, no such precise terms are at hand, even though much progress toward the establishment of quantitative methods for the study of mental traits has been made during the past few years.

However, we are not interested in the physical dimensions of the child's body simply because they can be easily measured. Growth in size is intimately tied up with many other factors. We naturally think first of health, since failure to make normal growth is suggestive of poor nutritional status or of some other undesirable physical condition. But this is not all. Size undoubtedly plays some part in determining social behavior since the child who is relatively large for his age finds it easier to dominate his companions (all other things being equal) than the one who is small. On the other hand, the child who is exceptionally large physically but is mentally no brighter than the average is sometimes much embarrassed by finding himself the largest child in his class at school. He may thus develop an unwarranted feeling of inferiority which would not have arisen had he been the usual size for his age. Physical growth is thus seen to be closely bound up with the child's general development and social adjustment, and needs to be studied not only for its own sake but as a means of bettering our understanding of the child as a whole. Children do not grow physically on one day, mentally on the next, and socially on the day following. Growth of all kinds takes place simultaneously. It is only by studying the interrelationships of growth factors that an adequate understanding of the whole can be reached.

In order to make accurate measurements of the dimensions of the separate body parts some knowledge of human anatomy is needed. Certain gross measurements can, however, be taken by the untrained student. Among the most valuable of these are standing and sitting height and weight. Methods of measuring height are described in Experiments 1 and 2. Since the taking of weight measurements requires only a good scale and the exercise of care in placing and reading the balance, no formal experiment on weight is included. In recording weight it is important to specify whether it was taken with or without clothing, and if the former, the kind and amount of clothing, (as "light weight indoor clothes," or "heavy woolen suit, heavy shoes and underwear," etc.) should be stated.

Experiment No. 1

Measuring the Standing Height

Using a stadiometer (either standard model or homemade *) measure the standing height of each of the children

* If a regular stadiometer is not available, paper scales can be secured at a small cost from the Child Welfare Research Station of the University

in the experimental group. The subject should stand erect with heels against the wall, arms at side, and chin level. Bring the horizontal bar of the stadiometer down firmly upon the top of the head and take the reading. If the home-made stadiometer described in the footnote is used, a right-angle triangle or a book with stiff binding should first be placed with one side of the angle pressed firmly against the wall, slightly above the level of the subject's head, and from this position be brought down gradually until the base presses against the subject's head as shown in Fig. 1a. Avoid tilting the instrument in such a way that it will distort the reading of the scale. This is very likely to result if a flat object is held in the position shown in Fig. 1b. Make three measurements in immediate succession and take the average of the three as the child's height. Divide the children into age groups and find the *average* or *mean* height for each age and sex by adding together all the measurements for each age and sex group and dividing by the total number of cases in the group. This method of finding the arithmetic mean is known as the *long method*. The formula is:

$$M = \frac{\Sigma \text{ (measures)}}{N} \tag{1}$$

of Iowa, or an ordinary carpenter's wooden rule of at least six feet in length (to provide for the measurement of adults as well as children) may be fastened securely in a vertical position against the wall at a point free from projections such as a baseboard. A third though somewhat less satisfactory substitute can be prepared as follows: Secure a length of heavy brown manila gummed paper about 1-1½ inches wide which is used for sealing parcels. Upon this strip of paper mark off a linear scale in divisions at least as fine as ⅛ of an inch (using a steel ruler or other accurately calibrated measure). An extra space of three or four inches should be left at each end of the scale to allow for pasting to the wall. Select a portion of the wall which is free from any projection and attach the slip of paper at this point, being careful to place it in an exactly vertical position, and moistening it as little as possible so as to avoid stretching. Be sure that the zero point on the scale is exactly even with the floor.

where the Greek letter Sigma (Σ) means "the sum of," M is the arithmetic mean or "average" as it is popularly called, and N is the number of cases in the group.

FIGURE I.

Correct and incorrect methods of measuring standing height with home-made stadiometer.

Are the boys or the girls of a given age in this group taller? Is this in accordance with the usual findings for young children? (See references at end of chapter).

Are the gains in height uniform from age to age? What is the average yearly gain in height for this group of children?

Experiment No. 2

Measuring the Sitting Height

These measurements may be taken on the same occasion as the measurements of standing height, thus obviating the necessity of interrupting the activities of the children a second time. In taking these measurements, the subject should sit on the floor with legs extended straight in front, and the back (including the hips) placed firmly against the wall, hands at side. The measurement is then taken in the same way as in the case of standing height.*

Find the mean sitting height for each age and sex. What proportion of the mean standing height is the mean sitting height for each age and sex group? What general growth trend in the ratio of sitting to standing height is shown by these figures? This is sometimes referred to as the law of *anterior-posterior development*. The head portions of the body are precocious in their development as compared to the extremities. At any given stage of the developmental period, the head and trunk will have completed a greater proportion of their total growth than the limbs. As age advances, the legs gradually catch up to the upper portions of the body with the result that the sitting height of the adult is a smaller proportion of the total height than it is in the young child.

* At least four different procedures have been used for measuring sitting height (a) with the subject's legs extended in the way described above, (b) with the legs hanging unsupported from the knee, (c) with the knees bent and feet planted squarely on the floor as when sitting in the ordinary chair of correct height, (d) and with the knees drawn up against the body. Since each of these measures will yield slightly different results from any of the others it is important to ascertain which method has been followed in comparing experimental results with those reported in the literature. The amount of the difference can readily be ascertained by measuring the same subject several times in each position.

Experiment No. 3

A Comparison of the Experimental Error in Measuring Sitting and Standing Height

Following the procedure just outlined, measure the sitting and standing height of each of two members of the class, designated Subject A and Subject B. If the group contains as many as sixteen students, it may be divided into two sections. The students in the first section should then take the measurements of Subject A and those in the second section the measurements of Subject B. If the class is small, each student should make both measurements for both subjects. Each student should make his measurements independently, without knowledge of the results obtained by other members of the class. The subject should change position between each successive measurement, so that the experiment includes placing the subject in the required position as well as the actual taking of the measurements.

Problems. 1. Find the mean of all the measurements taken for each dimension of each subject. These means may be regarded as the best approximations available for the true measurements.

2. Find the mean *experimental error* of each measurement by subtracting each of the individual measures from the mean (disregarding signs) and then finding the mean of these differences. Express this absolute experimental error as a percentage of the true measurement. Do this for each measurement of each subject. The results obtained are known as the *per cent of experimental error*.

3. Upon the basis of these results, what would you say with regard to the relative accuracy with which the two dimensions under consideration lend themselves to measurement? State possible reasons for this difference.

4. Is there a consistent difference (*i.e.*, taking the same direction for both measurements) in the absolute experimental error obtained for the two subjects? In the percentage of experimental error? What possible explanations can you suggest?

5. Find the ratio of the sitting height to the standing height for the two adult subjects. Compare with the ratios found for the children in the experimental group. How closely do the results check with the ratios reported in the literature?

If time permits it is worth while to find the experimental error of these measurements for one or more kindergarten or nursery-school children. As a rule, both the absolute and the relative experimental error of measurement will be slightly greater for children than for adults because of the greater difficulty in getting a child to take and maintain an entirely uniform posture from one trial to another.

REFERENCES

The student is referred to the following titles in the bibliography at the end of this book (special attention should be given the starred references):

8*, 10*, 144, 272*, 298*, 330*, 342, 343.

Chapter 10

MAKING FREQUENCY DISTRIBUTIONS

FIGURE 2 shows a group of 15 children arranged in order of height. They are standing in a row against a wall, on which lines have been drawn six inches apart. This makes it possible to see at a glance how many children in

FIGURE 2.

Children of different heights arranged by class-intervals.

the group are between 30 and 36 inches in height, how many are between 36 and 42 inches and so on. If we count the number of cases in each of these groups we find it to be as follows:

                30–36 inches......2
                36–42 inches......3
                42–48 inches......5
                48–54 inches......3
                54–60 inches......2

When a set of measurements or other numerical facts is arranged in the manner shown above, with all cases falling between successive limits thrown into single groups, the list or table resulting is called a *frequency distribution,* and the distances within the limits thus defined are known as *class intervals.*

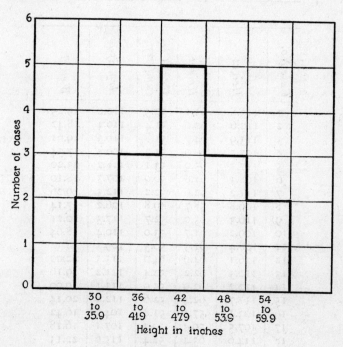

FIGURE 3.
Histogram showing data of Figure 2.

Figure 3 shows the same facts in another way. In this case the boundaries of each class interval are indicated on the base line or *abscissa* of the graph; the smaller values at the left and the larger values at the right. The number of cases falling within each interval is indicated by the height of the class interval or the *ordinate.* Thus the fact that there

TABLE I

PHYSICAL MEASUREMENTS OF CHILDREN BETWEEN THE AGES
OF SIXTY AND SIXTY-THREE MONTHS

BOYS

Case No.	Standing Height	Sitting Height	Head Circumference	Arm Span	Weight
1	113.8	63.1	52.5	110.0	19.25
2	110.6	62.0	51.4	110.4	18.42
3	115.9	64.7	51.8	116.3	19.61
4	107.5	60.0	51.3	106.4	17.34
5	117.2	65.0	53.1	118.2	23.20
6	108.1	61.8	50.0	107.3	18.10
7	111.2	62.6	52.2	112.3	19.26
8	106.8	58.7	49.8	106.2	17.14
9	116.3	65.0	52.7	117.3	20.21
10	109.2	61.7	53.0	110.4	18.64
11	108.4	61.3	50.3	109.1	18.32
12	116.1	64.9	54.0	115.3	22.00
13	110.3	62.2	52.4	111.2	19.16
14	112.2	62.9	52.9	113.1	19.00
15	111.7	62.4	52.6	112.8	20.14
16	103.1	57.1	51.4	104.3	16.42
17	107.5	59.3	50.3	107.1	16.18
18	114.6	63.4	52.4	115.6	22.13
19	115.3	64.0	54.1	117.2	23.11
20	112.8	63.0	50.2	113.4	20.50
21	112.2	62.8	53.3	112.2	20.42
22	110.1	61.4	51.8	111.3	19.51
23	111.4	62.5	52.6	109.4	18.62
24	115.1	64.1	53.1	114.2	21.13
25	109.3	61.3	53.7	108.1	20.14

TABLE I *(Continued)*

PHYSICAL MEASUREMENTS OF CHILDREN BETWEEN THE AGES
OF SIXTY AND SIXTY-THREE MONTHS

Case No.	Standing Height	Sitting Height	Head Circumference	Arm Span	Weight
1	109.6	62.0	50.6	108.2	18.39
2	110.5	62.3	50.9	107.4	17.24
3	114.6	64.0	52.1	112.6	19.36
4	112.3	62.5	51.0	110.4	20.42
5	107.1	60.1	49.8	105.1	16.38
6	105.2	59.4	48.2	102.2	15.21
7	103.1	56.0	47.1	101.3	13.19
8	110.6	59.6	49.2	107.5	18.14
9	109.7	61.7	50.2	108.2	17.16
10	111.1	62.8	50.3	111.3	19.24
11	110.8	62.1	51.4	110.1	21.16
12	111.3	63.0	51.5	109.4	23.21
13	112.4	63.2	52.3	110.2	19.14
14	113.6	63.8	50.6	111.1	20.13
15	110.4	62.4	50.0	108.4	18.41
16	108.2	61.2	49.2	107.3	16.28
17	107.1	60.1	49.8	106.5	17.14
18	109.6	61.0	50.4	108.1	18.39
19	112.3	62.6	51.1	111.3	19.21
20	111.5	63.1	50.6	110.1	19.30
21	110.2	62.1	51.3	109.5	18.41
22	109.1	61.8	52.2	109.2	17.22
23	112.1	63.2	50.6	111.0	17.39
24	110.5	63.0	50.5	108.1	18.24
25	110.6	63.3	51.0	107.4	18.05

are two cases in the interval 30-36 is indicated by making that column two units high, and so on.

It will be noted that in this case the greatest number of cases is found in the middle interval, while the number either of very tall or of very short children is decidedly less than the number who are of medium height. This form of distribution in which the cases tend to cluster about the mid-point is much more frequent than any other in biological measurements of all kinds. In its most typical form it is known as the *normal frequency distribution* or the *normal probability curve*. Much of the data with which we have to deal is distributed in a fashion similar to this, though the curves will not often be so symmetrical.

Examples: Table I lists the results of a series of physical measurements taken upon a group of kindergarten children all of whom were between the ages of sixty and sixty-three months. All the children were of North European stock. All measurements were taken without clothing. A stadiometer was used for measuring sitting and standing heights. The sitting height was taken with the legs extended straight out before the child; head circumference was taken by means of a tape placed horizontally around the head just above the top of the ears; arm span was taken from finger tip to finger tip with the child standing and the arms extended horizontally at the level of the shoulders against a calibrated measuring beam. The group was composed of twenty-five boys and twenty-five girls. All measurements are expressed in metric units to facilitate computation. The linear measurements are given in centimeters, weight in kilograms and are listed in the order in which the children happened to be measured without attempt at arrangement.

If we wish to organize the results of any single series of measurements so as to give a clear picture of the group as a whole, our first task is evidently that of grouping those measurements which are of nearly the same value into single classes. In other words, we need to organize the material into *class intervals* as was done in the example at the beginning of this chapter. The simplest way of doing this is first to find the *total range* of the measurements included (that is, the difference between the largest and smallest measurements), and then to decide upon a class interval of a size which will make the kind of distinctions necessary for the particular problem under consideration. For reasons which will be apparent later on, it may be said that if the problem is to make a graphic analysis of the form of the distribution, from 5 to 9 class intervals will usually be sufficient. For purposes of statistical treatment a somewhat finer division, say from 11 to 21 class intervals is preferable. If the number of class intervals is large, only a small proportion of the cases will fall within any one interval and the curve will therefore be comparatively flat. If the number of intervals is smaller, those measurements which are most nearly alike will tend to fall within the same interval so that the general form of the distribution will be more clearly seen. This is particularly true when the number of measures is small. We may illustrate this by arranging the data of Column 1 (standing height for boys) in two ways, first using a class interval of 1 cm. and secondly, one of 2.5 cm. The *total range* of the measures is first found by subtracting 103.1 cm. (the height of the shortest child in the group) from 117.2 cm. (the height of the tallest child). The difference is 14.1 cm. Since it is more convenient to fix the boundaries of our class intervals in round numbers, we may set our lowest division point at 103.0 and proceed by 1.0 centimeter intervals thereafter. In preparing a frequency table it is customary to place the lowest value at the bottom as shown in Table 2.

The lowest class interval will then include all cases

TABLE 2

FREQUENCY DISTRIBUTION OF MEASUREMENTS OF STANDING
HEIGHT OF BOYS: GROUPED BY CLASS-INTERVALS
OF ONE CENTIMETER

(Data taken from Table 1)

Class interval	Cases	f
117.0–117.9	I	1
116.0–116.9	II	2
115.0–115.9	III	3
114.0–114.9	I	1
113.0–113.9	I	1
112.0–112.9	III	3
111.0–111.9	III	3
110.0–110.9	III	3
109.0–109.9	II	2
108.0–108.9	II	2
107.0–107.9	II	2
106.0–106.9	I	1
105.0–105.9		0
104.0–104.9		0
103.0–103.9	I	1

measuring from 103.0 to 103.9 centimeters, the next, those measuring 104.0 to 104.9 centimeters, and so on. The frequency table itself may now be prepared as follows: The first child in the list measured 113.8 centimeters. This should be indicated by making a tally mark opposite the class interval 113.0 to 113.9. The next child measured 110.6 centimeters. This is indicated by a similar tally mark opposite the class interval labeled 110.0 to 110.9. Each of the other cases should be indicated in a corresponding fashion until the entire list of 25 has been included. After the checking has been completed, the list should be gone over a second time and a dot placed above each tally mark as the cases are checked off in order to insure accuracy. The number of cases in each class interval should then be counted and entered in the column labelled *f*.

These results may now be shown graphically in the form of a *frequency surface* or *histogram* such as Fig. 4. The preparation of such graphs will be greatly facilitated by the use of cross-section paper. Select paper which is ruled ac-

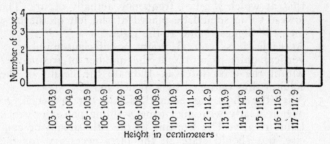

FIGURE 4.

Histogram showing distribution of standing-height of twenty-five five-year-old boys.

Measurements grouped by class-intervals of one centimeter.

cording to a decimal system, *i.e.*, either in centimeters and millimeters or in inches and tenths of an inch. The successive steps in preparing a frequency surface may be outlined briefly as follows:

1. Mark off a base line the length of which is an even multiple of the number of class intervals to be included.

2. Note the greatest number of frequencies in any single class interval. With this in mind, select a unit of height which will give a pleasing proportion to the curve. For example, in Fig. 4 each class interval is represented by a horizontal base of five millimeters and each frequency within an interval is represented by a corresponding vertical space of five millimeters. It is not, however, necessary to have the unit representing the frequency equal to that of the class inter-

val, and unless the total number of cases is small the latter will ordinarily be much smaller than the former.

3. Directly below the base line, write neatly the range of values included within each class interval. Note that the extremes should be represented as of an equal length with the others, even though this involves the extension of the range to a point somewhat beyond that at which the last frequency actually occurs. The lowest value should be placed at the left of the base line, the highest value at the right.

4. At each class interval, count a sufficient number of vertical units to represent the number of frequencies within the class interval. Indicate the height of the column thus obtained by a pencil mark.

5. After the chart has been thus laid out in pencil, go over it neatly with ink, using a ruling pen if possible. Label clearly. The wording of the title should be concise, but should state all the facts necessary for the interpretation of the chart.

It will be seen that when as many as 15 class intervals are used for a distribution containing only 25 cases, the form of the curve appears to be rather flat, without any very clear tendency for the cases to center about one point rather than another. Table 3 and Fig. 5 show what happens when the data are grouped by intervals of 2.5 cm.

TABLE 3

FREQUENCY DISTRIBUTION OF MEASUREMENTS OF STANDING HEIGHT OF BOYS: GROUPED BY INTERVALS OF 2.5 CENTIMETERS

(Data taken from Table 1)

Class interval	f
115.5–117.9	4
113.0–115.4	4
110.5–112.9	7
108.0–110.4	6
105.5–107.9	3
103.0–105.4	1

While the data are not so symmetrical as those shown in Figure 3, the tendency toward a piling up of cases in the center of the group with a smaller proportion at the extremes is apparent. When, as in this case, there are more cases at one extreme than at the other we say that the distribution is *skewed* toward the end at which the smaller

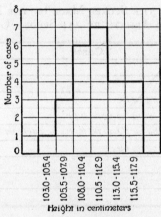

FIGURE 5.

Histogram showing distribution of standing-heights of twenty-five five-year-old boys.

Measurements grouped by class-intervals of 2.5 centimeters.

proportion of cases appear, or toward the opposite end from that at which the extreme cases are massed.

In preparing a frequency table, the checks or tally-marks should be grouped by fives, with the fifth check crossing the others at an opposite angle. The groups of five should be separated from each other by a space which is at least equal to two or three check marks, and the successive groups in each class interval should be placed exactly below each other. When this is done, the tally marks themselves will show the form of the distribution almost as clearly as a formal graphic analysis. This is well illustrated in Table 4, which shows the distribution of scores made on the Mc-Carty test of drawing ability (171) by 244 second grade boys between the ages of seven and seven-and-a-half years.

TABLE 4.

DISTRIBUTION OF THE SCORES MADE ON THE McCARTY TEST OF DRAWING ABILITY BY 244 SECOND GRADE BOYS

Score	Cases	f
19-20	//	2
17-18	𝗧𝗛𝗟	5
15-16	𝗧𝗛𝗟 𝗧𝗛𝗟 𝗧𝗛𝗟 𝗧𝗛𝗟 𝗧𝗛𝗟 𝗧𝗛𝗟 𝗧𝗛𝗟	35
13-14	𝗧𝗛𝗟 𝗧𝗛𝗟 𝗧𝗛𝗟 𝗧𝗛𝗟 𝗧𝗛𝗟 𝗧𝗛𝗟 𝗧𝗛𝗟 𝗧𝗛𝗟 𝗧𝗛𝗟 𝗧𝗛𝗟 /	51
11-12	𝗧𝗛𝗟 𝗧𝗛𝗟 𝗧𝗛𝗟 𝗧𝗛𝗟 𝗧𝗛𝗟 𝗧𝗛𝗟 𝗧𝗛𝗟 𝗧𝗛𝗟 𝗧𝗛𝗟 𝗧𝗛𝗟 𝗧𝗛𝗟 𝗧𝗛𝗟 𝗧𝗛𝗟 𝗧𝗛𝗟 𝗧𝗛𝗟 𝗧𝗛𝗟 𝗧𝗛𝗟 𝗧𝗛𝗟 ////	94
9-10	𝗧𝗛𝗟 𝗧𝗛𝗟 𝗧𝗛𝗟 𝗧𝗛𝗟 𝗧𝗛𝗟 𝗧𝗛𝗟 𝗧𝗛𝗟 ////	39
7-8	𝗧𝗛𝗟 𝗧𝗛𝗟 ///	13
5-6	𝗧𝗛𝗟	5
	Total	244

By inspection of the tally marks alone, it is seen that the curve approaches the normal frequency distribution rather closely, since by far the greater number of cases are clustered near the midpoint with only a small proportion at either extreme. There is a very slight positive skewness, shown by the greater scattering of cases at the upper end of the scale and by the massing of cases somewhat nearer the lower than the upper end.

Exercise. Arrange the data of each column in Table 1 in the form of frequency tables, using a system of classification in which the data are grouped into from 11 to 21 class intervals of equal length; then reorganize the material into frequency tables in which a uniform class interval of one centimeter is used for the linear measurements and one kilogram for the weight measurements without regard to the range of measures in the group. Draw histograms to show the data according to both plans of organization. Keep the frequency tables for use in the statistical exercises of the following chapter.

REFERENCES

The student is referred to the following titles in the bibliography at the end of this book:

384,* 397.*

Chapter 11

A SHORT METHOD FOR FINDING THE MEAN

THE method of finding the average or *arithmetic mean* by summing the individual measures and dividing by the number of cases, which was described in Chapter 9 is suitable for use only when the number of cases is small. In dealing with larger groups, particularly when the measurements themselves are expressed in terms of several digits, the adding becomes very laborious and a more convenient method is needed. The procedure commonly used is known as the *short method* of finding the mean by the use of an *arbitrary origin* or, as we sometimes say, by working from a "guessed mean." In using this method, the data are first arranged in the form of a frequency distribution as described in the last chapter. If the original measurements are fine enough to permit it, the distribution should be planned to include from 11 to 21 class intervals in order to prevent undue loss in accuracy from grouping. As an illustration we may take the distribution of the measurements of standing height in which a class interval of 1 cm. was used. We wish to find the mean of these measures by the short method.

By inspection of the frequency distribution it is possible to guess with more or less accuracy at about what point the mean will fall. This will be somewhere near the midpoint of the distribution if the data are distributed evenly, but if there are a greater number of cases near one end than the other, the mean also will be moved towards that end of the curve. In this case, since there are rather more cases

96

near the upper end of the distribution than at the lower
end, we may guess that the mean will fall somewhere between 111.0 and 111.9. An inaccurate guess does not affect
the accuracy of the computation; it means only that the
work of computation will be slightly increased since we
shall have to deal with somewhat larger numbers. It is a
good plan to set off the class interval chosen as the guessed
mean by heavy lines as shown in Table 5.

TABLE 5

COMPUTATION OF MEAN STANDING HEIGHT BY THE SHORT
METHOD

Intervals	Cases	f	x	fx	
117.0–117.9	/	1	+6	6	
116.0–116.9	//	2	+5	10	
115.0–115.9	///	3	+4	12	$\Sigma (+fx) = 36$
114.0–114.9	/	1	+3	3	$\Sigma (-fx) = 34$
113.0–113.9	/	1	+2	2	Difference =
112.0–112.9	///	3	+1	3	2 cm.
111.0–111.9	///	3	0		Correction (c)
110.0–110.9	///	3	−1	3	$= D/N = \dfrac{2}{25}$ or
109.0–109.9	//	2	−2	4	.08 of a class
108.0–108.9	//	2	−3	6	interval.
107.0–107.9	//	2	−4	8	
106.0–106.9	/	1	−5	5	
105.0–105.9			−6		
104.0–104.9			−7		
103.0–103.9	/	1	−8	8	

We shall now assign a numerical value to each class interval in terms of its distance above or below the guessed
mean. Starting from the mean as a zero point, we number
the successive steps above and below this point as shown in
the column labeled x (Table 5). From now on these x

values will be used for all computations exactly as if they were the true measurements of those cases. In the column headed *fx* we record the product obtained by multiplying the number of cases (*f*) in each class interval by the new or *x* value which we have given to that class interval. Thus in our top class there is one case whose measurement has an *x* value of 6. The *fx* value for this interval is therefore $1 \times 6 = 6$, and this is entered in the *fx* column. The values of the remaining class intervals are listed in like manner. Values above the guessed mean are counted as plus, those below the guessed mean as minus.

FIGURE 6.

Graphic representation of the data in Table 5 to illustrate the location of the mean.

Turn now to Fig. 6 which represents graphically the facts shown in Table 5. Here we have a series of weights set irregularly at intervals along a rod which is to be balanced upon a support. The problem is to find the point at which the fulcrum should be placed so that the weights with their present arrangement will exactly balance each other. This point corresponds to the true mean. It is the point which divides the measurements in such a way that the sum of the measurements on one side exactly equals the sum of the measurements on the other side of the point of division. If we now check the accuracy of our guessed mean according to this criterion, we find that the sum of the $+ fx$ values is 36 while the sum of the $- fx$ values is 34. The difference is 2. Since the number of cases is 25 it follows that the average amount which must be added to the minus values or subtracted from the plus values in order to achieve a balance is 2/25 of a class interval. 2/25 of 1.0 centimeter is .08 centimeters. The fulcrum must therefore be shifted .08 centimeters toward the top of the scale. Had the excess been below instead of above the guessed mean, the correction would have been subtracted.

We have now determined how large a correction needs to be applied to the guessed mean in order to make it correspond to the true mean. Before we can do this, it will be necessary to turn back to the original data as given in Table I and consider a little more precisely just what these figures signify. It is important to realize from the beginning that any measurement of a *continuous quantity,* that is, a quantity such as length, time, weight, *etc.,* which has no natural division points or breaks, always refers to a class interval and not to a fixed point. When the interval is very small, however, its boundaries are often implied rather than expressed. Thus, when we say that John is 57⅞ inches tall, we mean that in height he belongs somewhere in the interval between 57 13/16 and 57 15/16 inches (if we are measuring to the nearest eighth of an inch). In the case with which we are dealing the measurements are expressed in terms of .1 of a centimeter, but finer measurements than this might have been made if it had seemed profitable to do so. Actually, then, what has been called 113.8 centimeters in the first measurement on the list really denotes a measurement which falls somewhere between 113.75 and 113.85 centimeters. All measurements falling within this range have been grouped together in the original measures and given the common value of 113.8 centimeters. When we arrange our data in class intervals we merely impose a coarser system of grouping upon data which have already been grouped into finer units. In both cases the value ascribed to all cases falling within the group or class interval is the midpoint of the group. We find this midpoint by adding ½ the size of the interval to the lowest value which would be included within that interval. Our guessed mean then would fall at the midpoint of the interval 111.0 to 111.9, and we have ascertained that it is necessary to shift this value 0.08 centimeters higher up. The lower boundary of the class interval will be the lower boundary of the lowest score included within that class interval. The lowest score included within the class interval containing the guessed mean is 111.0. The lower boundary of the measurement recorded as 111.0 is 110.95. One-half the size of the class interval is ½ (1.00 cm.) = .50 centimeters. The midpoint of the interval is therefore 110.95 + .50 or 111.45 centimeters. The true mean, therefore, when the error in guessing is corrected is 111.45 + 0.08 centimeters (the amount of the correction) or 111.53 centimeters.

We may sum up the steps involved in calculating the mean by the short method as follows:

1. Find the total range of the distribution by subtracting the lowest from the highest measurement in the series.
2. If this range is sufficiently great to make it desirable to group these measures into coarser units, select a class interval of such a size that the total number of steps or intervals will be somewhere in the neighborhood of 11 to 21.
3. Using these class intervals, prepare a frequency table with the measures increasing in size from the bottom of the table to the top.
4. Enter the separate measures in the frequency table by placing a tally mark opposite the appropriate value for each case. Recheck this distribution to make sure that no errors have been made in placing the scores.
5. Count the number of tally marks in each class interval and enter the sums in a column to the right labeled *f*.
6. By inspection of the distribution, guess the approxi-

mate point at which the mean will fall, and set off this class interval by heavy lines.

7. Taking the guessed mean as the zero point, assign values to each successive class interval in terms of distance above or below the mean. Enter these values in a second column to the right of the f column. This column is called x.

8. Multiply the scores in the f column by those in the x column, and enter the products in a third column labelled fx.

9. Find the difference between the sum of the $+ fx$ scores, (that is, those above the interval containing the guessed mean), and the $- fx$ scores (those below this interval). If the sum of the $+ fx$ scores is greater than the sum of the $- fx$ scores, the guessed mean is too low, and the amount of the correction must be added to the midpoint of the class interval containing the guessed mean. If the sum of the $- fx$ scores is greater than that of the $+ fx$ scores, the guessed mean is too high, and the amount of the correction must be subtracted from the midpoint of the class interval.

10. Find the mean amount of the correction by dividing the difference between the $+ fx$ and the $- fx$ scores by the number of cases in the group. Multiply this result by the size of the class interval.

11. Find the midpoint of the class interval in which the mean was guessed by adding one half the size of the class interval to the lower boundary of the lowest score included within that class interval.

12. Add or subtract, according to its sign, the amount of the correction to the midpoint of the class interval within which the mean was guessed. The result will by the true mean.

The formula for finding the mean by the short method is written as follows:

$$M = \text{Arbitrary origin} + \frac{(\text{Class interval}) \, \Sigma \, fx}{N} \quad (2)$$

where $\Sigma fx =$ the *algebraic* sum of the fx values, that is the difference between $\Sigma(+ fx)$ and $\Sigma(- fx)$.

The advantages of the short method over the long method of finding the mean will become apparent as soon as the student has become moderately proficient in its use. Since the long method requires the handling of large numbers and often of decimals, the procedure becomes very laborious. The substitution of scale values expressed in terms of integers of small denomination greatly reduces the labor of calculation, and thereby increases its accuracy. Moreover, as will be seen later on, the arrangement of the data in frequency distributions facilitates the carrying out of other statistical processes which we shall wish to use.

Practice Exercises. 1. Using the short method, find the mean of each of the other columns in Table 1. Compare the sexes with regard to each of the separate measures.

2. Compute the mean of the last column by both the long and the short method, and record the time required for each process. What is the difference between the means obtained by the two methods? This difference may be regarded as the loss in accuracy due to grouping of the data. Express this grouping error as a percentage of the mean for the group. What is the time required for finding the mean by each method (including checking)? *

REFERENCES

The student is referred to the following titles in the bibliography at the end of this book:

384*, 396*, 397*.

* It is a good plan to have different members of the class select different columns for the comparisons of time and accuracy. If this is done, the results for the class may be combined so as to show (a) the mean difference in the time required for computation of the mean by the two methods, and (b) the mean per cent of grouping error.

Chapter 12

SLEEP

THAT the growing child needs more sleep than the adult whose growth is completed is well known. During the first few weeks of life, the tiny infant sleeps most of the time; his waking time is confined almost wholly to the hours when he is being fed and bathed. As age advances the proportion of time spent in sleep gradually decreases; but most children continue to spend more than half of the twenty-four hours in sleep until they are well past the third birthday (5).

Because of the importance of an adequate amount of sleep for the child's physical and mental well-being, a

TABLE 6

TOTAL AMOUNT OF SLEEP (NIGHT SLEEP PLUS NAPS) TAKEN BY MINNESOTA CHILDREN AT DIFFERENT SEASONS (5)

Age	Fall hrs. min.		Winter hrs. min.		Spring hrs. min.		Summer hrs. min.		All Seasons hrs. min.	
1 mo.–6 mo.	(Too few cases)				14	55	15	29	15	3
6 mo.–1 yr.	14	1	14	31	14	15	13	37	14	9
1 yr. –1½yr.	13	22	13	38	13	10	13	24	13	23
1½yr. –2 yr.	13	20	13	20	13	0	12	39	13	6
2 yr. –3 yr.	12	38	12	47	12	47	12	37	12	42
3 yr. –4 yr.	12	8	12	13	12	5	12	0	12	7
4 yr. –5 yr.	11	44	11	53	11	40	11	34	11	43
5 yr. –6 yr.	11	18	11	25	11	20	11	11	11	19
6 yr. –7 yr.	11	1	11	11	11	2	11	2	11	4
7 yr. –8 yr.	10	55	11	3	10	59	10	55	10	58

comparison of the amount of sleep taken by any child with the averages found by studying a large number of children of his age is well worth making. Fortunately, such standards are now available. Table 6 shows the average amount of sleep taken by Minnesota children during each of the four seasons of the year. These figures are based upon a week's record which was kept for approximately a thousand children at each season. It should be noted that these averages represent "time asleep" and not "time in bed," *i.e.*, the time required to go to sleep has not been included.

Experiment No. 4

The Amount of Sleep Taken by Young Children

Request * the parents of the children in the experimental group (nursery-school, kindergarten or primary grades) to keep a record of the amount of sleep taken by the children during a period of one week. Prepared record forms should be provided for the purpose. The arrangement shown on the opposite page has been found satisfactory.

Written instructions for keeping the records should accompany the blanks, even when the interview method is used for securing coöperation. These instructions should point out (a) that time is to be recorded as exactly as possible (b) that in case the child lies down for a nap but fails to sleep, the time of lying down and of getting up should be recorded and a zero (o) placed in the space labeled "was asleep at," and (c) that no attempt should be made to

* Care must be taken to arouse the interest of the parents in the project in order to insure their coöperation. Requests may be made by telephone, by letter, or by personal interview. The last method is likely to be most satisfactory if time permits. If the interview is used, it is well to secure the data on food preferences (see following chapter) on the same occasion. The results of the latter study can then be worked up in class during the week that the sleep records are being kept.

Child's name.......... *Sex*.... *Age: Years*.... *Mo*.....

	Sun.	Mon.	Tues.	Wed.	Thurs.	Fri.	Sat.
Health: well, fair, ill							
Day nap: was in bed at							
Did he go willingly?							
Was asleep at (hr.)							
Awake at (hr.) ...							
Night Sleep: was in bed at							
Did he go willingly?							
Was asleep at (hr.)							
Up at (hr.)							

Record for week beginning with nap (if taken) on_____
Date
Recorded by ....

modify the child's usual schedule while the records are being taken. Although having the records made in terms of clock time rather than in hours and minutes involves some additional labor for the investigator, such records are likely to be much more accurate than would be the case if the parents were asked to make the subtractions themselves. In treating the results, it is evidently necessary first to transmute the clock time records into time units for each day, and then to find the weekly averages for each child. Since this involves a separate retabulation of the data before the final organization can be made, it is well to prepare separate code slips for each child upon which the subtractions can be entered. These slips can then be sorted into age and sex groups. The following form is suggested:

Code Slip for Recording Children's Sleep

Name ....

Age: Yr..... *Mo*..... *Sex*.... *Grade*....

Night

	WFI	BT	w	TBS	LOS	TS
S						
M						
Tu						
W						
Th						
F						
S						
M						
MV						

Nap

	WFI	BT	w	TBS	LOS
S					
M					
Tu					
W					
Th					
F					
S					
M					
MV					

On this slip the state of health (well, fair, or ill) is to be recorded in the first column for each day, using the initial letter of the word only. "BT" in the second column stands for "bedtime" which is to be copied directly from the original record; "w" stands for "willingness" and is to be recorded as + or —; "TBS" for "time before sleep" is to be obtained by subtracting the hour at which the child was put to bed from that at which he was judged to be asleep. "LOS" stands for "length of sleep," obtained by subtracting the hour at which the child is said to have fallen asleep from that at which he awakened. The last column in the section on night sleep is headed "TS" for total sleep in 24 hours. It is found by adding the length of the day nap to the length of the night sleep for that day.

The weekly averages for each child are to be entered at the bottom of each column in the space marked "M" (Mean). Since there are only seven days' records in each average the long method will be preferable to the short method for finding these means. The spaces marked "MV" are for the recording of the mean variations, a term which will be explained shortly.

I. **Comparisons of the amount of sleep taken by individual children with Minnesota standards for different ages and seasons.** When the data for each child have been summarized in this fashion, it will be found interesting to compare the results with the standards obtained for unselected children in Minnesota (5) (see Table 6) in order to ascertain which children are sleeping more and which less than the average for their age at the season of the year at which the records were obtained. Table 6 gives the standards for total sleep only. Other comparisons such as length of nap, average number of naps per week, usual bedtime, usual waking time, *etc.*, are worth making. For those the student is referred to the monograph cited.

II. Regularity of sleep habits of the individual children.
It is important to know, not only how much sleep an individual child takes on the average, but also to know something about how much his sleeping habits vary from day to day. While a single week's record is not long enough to yield an entirely typical picture in all cases, it is sufficient to be at least suggestive. There are many different ways of computing and expressing the variance from an average, but one of the easiest to compute and understand is the *average deviation* from the mean (*A.D.*) or, as it is often called, the *mean variation* (*M.V.*). This is computed in exactly the same manner as the *experimental error* taken up in Chapter 9, *i.e.*, each individual day's measurement is subtracted from the mean for the week (disregarding signs), and the mean of these differences computed in the usual fashion. When this difference has reference to the variation among individual measures within a group, we speak of the result as the *mean variation* or the *average deviation* from the mean. When the method has reference to the variation in measurements which are supposed to be the same, since they are taken on a single individual or object on a single occasion we refer to it as the *experimental error*. The mean variation, then, may refer either to the average amount of divergence from his own most typical performance or habit which is shown by the same individual on different occasions (as in the instance under consideration), or to the average amount of departure from the mean of a group which is shown by its individual members. It refers, therefore, to differences which are presumed to be actually existent, while the *experimental error* has reference only to differences arising from imperfect measurement of a fact which is presumed to remain constant during the period of measurement. The method of computation is identical for both.

Find the mean variation of each child during the week

of observation in each of the following: bedtime, time required to go to sleep at night, length of night sleep, time of lying down for nap, time required to go to sleep, length of nap, and length of total sleep.

Divide the cases into age groups. Then subdivide each age group into the 50 per cent taking most sleep in 24 hours and the 50 per cent taking least sleep by arranging the cases in order and dividing the group in half. For each group separately, find the mean of the individual mean variations in each of the factors listed in the foregoing paragraphs. From these results what would you conclude with regard to the importance of a regular schedule in increasing the weekly quota of sleep during early childhood?

III. **Additional exercises:** (a) Arrange the individual averages for the children of each age group into frequency tables and find the group mean and the mean variation from the group mean for each of the measures listed.

(b) Do the children whose health was recorded as "fair" or "ill" show any consistent tendency to sleep more or less than the averages for their ages?

(c) Is there any difference either in the length of sleep or in the time required to go to sleep between the children who are said to have gone to bed willingly and those who went unwillingly.

IV. **The preparation of seriatim curves.** A *seriatim curve* is a graphical representation of the changes which occur in a function during a continuous time period, either as a result of growth and development or as a result of other factors such as practice in the case of a learning experiment. Strictly speaking, a seriatim curve refers to changes in the same individuals, but the method may also be used for data in which the successive stages are based upon the measurement of different individuals, who, it is assumed, are similar except for the age factor. When either very large groups or smaller groups of carefully selected individuals are used, the assumption that the differences found correspond on the average to the changes which would take place in any single group during the age period covered is

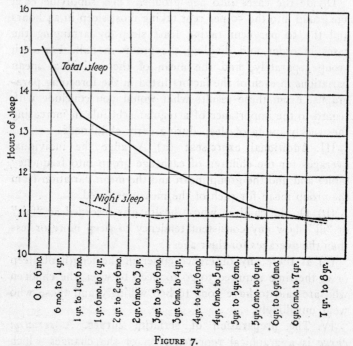

FIGURE 7.

Seriatim curve showing relation of length of sleep to age.

likely to be fairly safe. With smaller unselected groups the differences in the sampling of subjects at the various ages is likely to cause more or less irregularity in the curves, although general trends may still be suggested.

The method of drawing a seriatim curve is shown in Fig. 7 which depicts the age changes in the mean amount of sleep taken in 24 hours by Minnesota children between the ages of 6 mo. and 7 years 11 mo. This curve is based upon the averages for the four seasons.

The time variable (in this case, age) is entered along the abscissa, the changes in amount or level of the function in question along the ordinate. The use of cross-section paper will facilitate the drawing of the curves. Note that the points indicating the means for the successive age groups are placed at the midpoints of the divisions separating these age groups. The student should be able to state the reason for this.

If enough cases are available prepare seriatim curves showing the age changes in the mean amount of sleep taken in 24 hours by the experimental group. If the group includes ages in which there are usually daytime naps place a second curve on the same chart showing the age changes in the amount of night sleep. Compare with the findings in the Minnesota study previously cited.

Draw similar curves showing age changes in bed time; in time of waking, in mean length of nap when nap is taken, in mean number of naps taken per week.

V. **The calculation of the median and of the per cent of overlapping between two groups.** We frequently speak of a measure which is regarded as the most typical single expression of a group value as a *measure of the central tendency* of that group. The *arithmetic mean* or *average* is such a measure. There are other ways, however, of expressing the central tendency which for some purposes or under certain conditions may be preferable to the mean. Next to the mean, the *median* is the most commonly used of these measures. The median is defined as the point above and below which exactly 50 per cent of the cases will fall. Thus, if all the cases are arranged in rank order from the lowest to the highest the score made by the middle person if the number of cases is odd, or the point half-way between the two middle persons if the number of cases is even, may be taken as the median. When the number of cases is small, this method of arranging them in order of size and then counting through to find the midpoint is commonly employed. It is known as the "counting method." When the number of cases is large and the data are arranged in the form of a frequency distribution a second method which will be explained later is commonly employed. If the cases are distributed in a symmetrical fashion, the median will be identical in value with the mean, but if the cases tend to cluster around one or the other extreme the two values will not coincide. The median is not affected by the occasional inclusion of one or two sporadic cases, *i.e.,* cases which differ very greatly from the rest of the group, and for this reason is often to be preferred to the mean as a measure of central tendency. However it is affected to a greater extent than is the mean by chance shifting about of cases near the center of the group. For the latter reason it is, in most cases, a less stable measure than the mean, that is, the medians of two supposedly similar groups are likely to differ more from each other than the means of those groups. However, the median is less affected by inequalities in scaling (*e.g.,* as in many kinds of mental test scores) than is the mean. Whether the mean or the median is to be regarded as the more adequate measure will therefore depend upon the kind of measurement used and the distribution of cases in the sampling. For a more complete discussion of this point the student is referred to any of the standard textbooks on statistical methods.

A special use of the median in the comparison of groups is known as the *per cent of overlapping,* that is, the percentage of the cases in one group which equals or exceeds the median score of the other group. This method of comparison has been much used because it is so easily calculated and so readily understood. The method of computation is indicated by the name of the process. First, find the median score of the group which is to be used as the standard. Then count the number of cases in the second group whose scores are equal to or greater than this amount, and express this number as a percentage of the total number included in the second group. Thus if the median number of naps per week taken by a group of two-year-old children is 7, and if 11 out of 33 four-year-old children, or 33 per cent, take 7 or more naps per week, then we may say that 33 per cent of the four-year-olds equal or exceed the two-year-olds in median number of naps taken per week.

Tables 7 and 8 show (a) the mean time of going to bed, (b) the mean time of falling asleep and (c) the mean time of waking both for day and night sleep for two groups of young children, one group between the ages of two and two-and-a-half years, the other between the ages of five and five-and-a-half years. The data are taken from records secured in the Minnesota study on the sleep of young children (5). Each item represents the mean obtained by averaging the records for seven consecutive days as recorded by the mothers on the blanks sent them.

Exercises. 1. What percentage of the five-year-old children equal or exceed the median of the two-year-olds in amount of night sleep? Compute the same value for amount of total sleep, for number of naps taken per week, for mean length of nap when nap is taken. Which of these measures shows the greatest percentage of overlapping, *i.e.*, the greatest amount of difference between the two age groups? Note that the percentage of overlapping provides a method of comparing directly the amount of the difference between two groups even though the units of measurement are unequal.

TABLE 7

ANALYSIS OF SLEEP RECORDS OF 25 TWO-YEAR-OLD CHILDREN

Case no.	NIGHT SLEEP			DAY SLEEP			No. of maps during week
	Mean bedtime	Asleep at	Awake at	Bedtime	Asleep at	Awake at	
1	8:32	8:40	8:24	11:50	11:57	1:51	7
2	8:16	8:37	7:15	12:25	12:37	2:25	7
3	7:05	7:22	7:02	12:50	12:10	1:42	7
4	7:15	7:31	7:05	1:05	1:17	3:04	7
5	7:24	8:08	7:16	1:36	1:52	2:58	6
6	7:00	7:22	7:36	1:20	1:37	3:08	7
7	7:38	7:54	7:15	12:10	12:21	2:28	7
8	6:56	7:07	7:22	1:28	1:41	2:56	7
9	7:01	7:09	6:54	12:34	12:51	2:18	7
10	7:41	8:05	7:48	1:15	1:30	2:25	7
11	8:07	8:28	7:38	1:10	1:25	3:02	5
12	8:28	8:46	6:54	1:08	1:25	2:10	6
13	7:35	7:47	7:28	12:15	12:42	2:18	7
14	9:17	9:37	7:10	1:45	1:56	3:25	6
15	6:30	6:42	7:18	1:00	1:21	3:10	7
16	7:21	7:26	7:14	2:20	2:28	3:15	7
17	7:09	7:22	8:15	1:15	1:32	2:58	7
18	6:54	7:06	6:50	1:42	2:00	3:15	6
19	8:19	8:34	7:15	1:50	2:02	3:35	7
20	8:01	8:17	7:40	12:15	12:38	1:54	6
21	7:13	7:21	7:45	1:00	1:10	2:56	7
22	7:15	7:29	7:30	2:08	2:15	3:48	6
23	8:00	8:34	7:10	1:50	2:08	3:57	6
24	7:58	8:18	7:50	1:15	1:38	3:10	7
25	8:54	9:36	7:20	1:41	2:12	3:56	6

TABLE 8

ANALYSIS OF SLEEP RECORDS OF 25 FIVE-YEAR-OLD CHILDREN

Case no.	NIGHT SLEEP			DAY SLEEP			No. of naps during week
	Mean bedtime	Asleep at	Awake at	Bedtime	Asleep at	Awake at	
1	7:51	8:00	7:10	...	...	...	0
2	8:09	8:24	7:16	...	...	...	0
3	7:11	7:56	7:50	...	...	...	0
4	8:14	8:33	7:02	...	...	...	0
5	7:55	8:15	7:32	1:15	1:38	2:56	2
6	9:28	10:05	8:05	1:25	1:48	2:55	6
7	8:09	8:16	7:45	1:10	1:32	2:54	3
8	7:44	7:55	7:15	...	...	...	0
9	7:24	8:05	7:30	...	...	...	0
10	7:19	7:42	7:10	12:50	1:17	2:15	4
11	8:13	8:26	7:00	...	...	...	0
12	7:41	7:52	7:48	12:39	12:52	2:15	7
13	7:30	7:41	7:25	...	...	...	0
14	8:09	8:15	7:30	...	...	...	0
15	7:09	7:29	6:55	...	...	...	0
16	8:12	8:32	7:00	12:50	1:15	2:05	1
17	7:19	7:37	7:02	1:35	1:56	3:02	3
18	7:34	8:22	7:10	...	...	...	0
19	9:15	9:35	7:00	...	...	...	0
20	7:41	8:00	7:30	1:00	1:15	2:25	4
21	7:32	7:55	7:00	...	...	...	0
22	7:31	8:22	8:15	...	...	...	0
23	7:45	8:10	8:00	1:15	1:30	2:15	2
24	8:10	8:17	7:15	...	...	...	0
25	7:05	7:25	7:00	1:20	1:35	2:45	3

2. Compare the mean time of going to bed for the two age groups.

3. Compare the groups with regard to the mean length of nap when a nap is taken; the mean number of naps taken per week.

4. Of the various single factors considered, which one would you say is chiefly responsible for the difference in the total amount of sleep taken by the two age groups?

Additional exercises for statistical practice. The data of Tables 7 and 8 may also be used for practice in finding the mean by the short method and in computing the mean variation from the mean. In case it is not feasible to carry out the investigation on the sleep of children in the local group, the data of Tables 7 and 8 may be used for the statistical exercises described in the preceding sections.

REFERENCES

The student is referred to the following titles in the bibliography at the end of this book:

5*, 25*, 72, 77, 242*, 244.

Chapter 13

FOOD PREFERENCES

FOOD faddism among children is one of the very common problems reported by the parent who is endeavoring to rear her child according to modern dietary standards set by the best authorities on child care and training. Feeding difficulties of one kind or another head the list of problems among the one hundred normal children studied by Foster and Anderson (76). Among these children, the percentage of children with feeding problems rises sharply to a peak at the age of three years and falls off more slowly thereafter, but eating habits continue to be problems for more than a fourth of the children in this group up to the age of six years.

Studies of the food preferences of children usually show that their likes and dislikes are not purely individual matters, but that certain foods are quite generally unpopular while others are almost universally liked. That these dislikes can be overcome by proper management (including special methods of preparing and serving the less popular foods) is shown by several studies carried out in nursery-schools, in which the number of objections to or refusals of food is usually much smaller than will be found for children in the home. Among the methods which have been found successful in handling cases of refusal to eat certain foods are, first to make sure that the unpopular food is prepared and served in as attractive a fashion as possible, and that it is given early in the meal (usually at the beginning)

117

while hunger is still keen; secondly to serve rather small portions, particularly during the beginning of the period of training and to insist that these portions be eaten before other food is given; and finally and most important, to treat the child's meal period as a casual event, about which no one is going to become disturbed whether he eats or not. Many feeding problems arise because the child learns that by refusing food he can easily become the center of attention— a position which to many children as well as to many grown-ups is sufficiently desirable to warrant some sacrifice.

Experiment No. 5
Food Likes and Dislikes

Prepare a list of the most common foods regarded as important in the dietary requirements of children. Include vegetables both starchy and leafy, cereals, protein foods, fats such as butter, common desserts, and fruit.

Arrange a record form such as is shown on the opposite page. This form may be mimeographed or copies may be prepared by the individual members of the class. Each member of the class should secure one or more interviews with mothers of children in the experimental group (nursery-school or kindergarten).* On the basis of the mother's report, each item of food listed is to be classified according to the child's habitual attitude toward it under one of the following categories:

Likes it (*L*), is indifferent toward it (*I*), dislikes but eats it (*E*), refuses to eat it (*R*), is never offered it (*O*). In case of cooked foods, ascertain also the method in which the food is usually prepared. Records for at least twenty-five children

* If the coöperation of the parents for the sleep study is obtained by means of an interview, it is well to secure this information on the same occasion. The results can then be worked up during the week for which the sleep records are kept.

Attitude Toward Food

Child's name............ *Age: years*.... *mo*..... *Sex*....
Data collected by....... *Information furnished by*.......

List of foods	Child's attitude				
	L	I	E	R	O

should be secured, and the findings will be more reliable if a greater number of cases can be included.

Problems: Combine the results so as to show:

1. Which foods are most generally liked? *
2. Which are most often disliked?
3. Is there any difference in the usual method of preparing any specific food between the groups by whom it is liked and those by whom it is disliked?
4. Which foods are rarely offered to this group?
5. According to accepted standards, which children have specific dietary deficiencies?

* In computing the percentages of liking, disliking, *etc.*, the number of cases to whom the food is never offered must be subtracted from the total number of cases in the group before computing percentages.

Graphic exercise. The making of bar diagrams. The purpose of the bar diagram is to afford a graphic comparison of the differences between two or more groups in regard to some specified measure. The manner of constructing these diagrams is very similar to that used in preparing the fre-

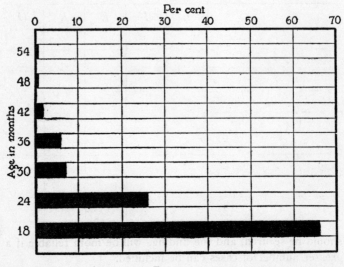

FIGURE 8.

Example of a bar diagram showing percentage of incomprehensible language-responses given by children of different ages. Adapted from McCarthy (170).

quency surface described in the previous chapter, except that it is customary to show the frequencies along a horizontal instead of a vertical axis. Compute the percentages to be compared and decide upon a convenient unit of measurement. Draw horizontal bars of lengths corresponding to these percentages, separated from each other by a distance approximately equal to the width of the bars. Label each bar clearly. (See Fig. 8.)

Arrange the foods listed in order of (a) liking, (b) disliking, (c) refusing. Construct three series of bar diagrams as described above, showing the proportion of children who react toward each of the foods in the manner indicated.

REFERENCES

The student is referred to the following titles in the bibliography at the end of this book:

25, 58*, 92, 130*, 191, 249, 331*.

Chapter 14

RATE OF TAPPING

THE "tapping test" is one of the oldest methods employed for the study of individual differences in a behavior function. It has been used experimentally for many purposes—for the study of fatigue, the effect of drugs, the determination of handedness, as a part of several industrial or "trade tests," *etc.* Upon the assumption that speed of motor action is related to intelligence, a tapping test was included in the early series of mental tests developed by Gilbert (98), but further investigation has shown that when children of the same age and sex are considered, tapping speed is at best but slightly related to intellectual differences as usually measured. However, since the rate of tapping increases fairly rapidly with age, a positive relationship between standing on intelligence tests and tapping speed will ordinarily be found when children of different ages are studied. The student should be able to state the reason for this. In a comparison of the tapping rates of kindergarten children and college students, Goodenough and Tinker (112) found that the average maturity of performance of the children, when measured in terms of the per cent of the average adult speed attained by them, varied according to the muscle groups employed in the different methods of tapping which were used. For example, when the hand was strapped to a palm rest in such a way that only the fingers could be moved, the children averaged only 14 per cent as many taps with the little finger of the left hand as the adults were able to make in the same length of time (253). When whole arm and elbow movements were used as in the pencil tapping method about to be described, the children attained more than 50 per cent of the adult speed. Other methods involving chiefly wrist and hand movements yielded intermediate results. These findings illustrate the well-known principle that the larger muscle-groups are functionally in advance of the smaller muscle-groups during childhood, and that little children should not, therefore, be expected to carry out tasks requiring fine coördination of the smaller muscles.

A number of different methods for measuring speed of tapping have been employed. One of the most convenient makes use of a metal plate on which the subject taps with a stylus. The plate is wired so that the taps are registered on an electric counter. See Fig. 9. If this apparatus is available it may be used instead of the paper and pencil method described in Experiment No. 6. However the latter method has been shown to be about equally reliable although the process of counting the dots is somewhat tedious. An ordinary key-drive adding machine is useful for measuring finger tapping and this may be used either with or without a palm rest and strap for restraining accompanying movements of the hand and arm. A telegraph key is sometimes used in the same way. Other methods complicate the simple tapping by requiring the subject to exercise care in placing his taps, as one tap in each of a series of squares, or by using some sort of a rhythmic sequence instead of a hit-or-miss method. Each of these variations has its advantages for certain kinds of problems. Experiment No. 6 describes one of the simplest of the standardized methods. This method has the further advantage of requiring no apparatus except pencil and paper.

Experiment No. 6

Rate of Tapping in Children and Adults

Material: A number of sheets of cross-section paper and some soft blunt pencils. A stop-watch or ordinary watch with second-hand if the stop-watch is not available.

Subjects: * This experiment may be carried out either with kindergarten children or with children from one or more of the primary grades. If time permits, two groups of children may be used, *e.g.,* a group of kindergarten children and one of children from the third or fourth grades. The members of the class will serve as the adult subjects.

Procedure: The method to be employed is the pencil tapping method described by Goodenough and Tinker (112). The subject is seated comfortably at a table with elbows resting upon its top. He is given a soft blunt pencil and a sheet of cross-section paper † is placed before him. The following instructions are then given.

"When I say 'Go,' I want you to show me how fast you can tap on this piece of paper with the pencil. Hold the pencil straight up in your hand like this (illustrating vertical position), rest the elbow on the desk, and tap just as fast as you can. Keep on tapping until I say 'Stop.' Do you understand?"

The experimenter should demonstrate the procedure, and allow the subject a five second practice period in order to make sure that he understands the directions. A ten second trial is then given with each hand separately, using a sepa-

* Experiment No. 7 described in the following chapter may be carried out on the same occasion as Experiment No. 6, since only a few minutes time is required for each. This does away with the necessity of interrupting the children more than once.

† The use of cross-section paper rather than plain paper will greatly facilitate the counting of the dots.

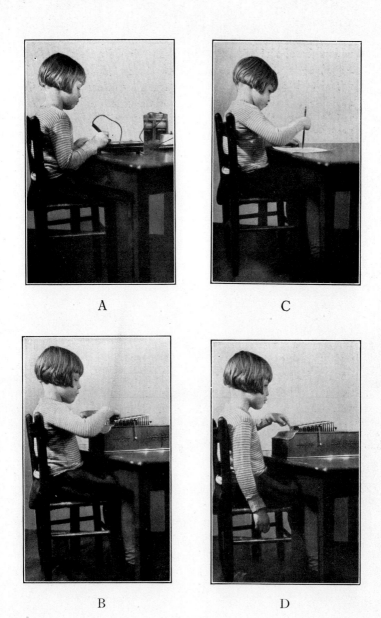

A   C

B   D

FIGURE 9

Different methods of measuring rate of tapping

rate sheet of paper for each, and labeling so there will be no confusion. Two fresh sheets of paper are then supplied, together with an extra pencil. The experimenter then says, "Now we'll see which hand can tap the faster. Hold a pencil in each hand and when I say 'Go,' begin tapping with both hands at once as fast as you can. Keep on until I say 'Stop.' Ready, go." The time limit is ten seconds. Count the number of taps made with each hand as shown by the number of dots on the paper, and record the scores separately for right and left hand and for both unimanual and bimanual tapping. It is well to have blank forms for this purpose prepared in advance, as shown below:

Name of subject................ *Age*...... *Grade*......
Trial......... *Date*........... *Examiner*..............

Score in Unimanual Tapping   Score in Bimanual Tapping
Right........ *Left*........   *Right*........ *Left*........

Each subject should be tested twice on consecutive days by different persons working without knowledge of each others' results. The method and time limit is the same for both trials and for all subjects.

I. Comparison of mean scores and of practice effect in children and adults. 1. Using the short method, find the mean tapping score for each group of subjects with each hand, for each method and for each trial. Keep the distributions for use in a later problem.

2. What percentage of the average adult speed has been attained by the children? Compute these percentages separately for each hand, each method, and for both trials.

3. Is any effect of practice apparent when the mean score of the first and the second trials are compared with each other? Is this effect greater for the children or for the adults? For each group separately, find the per cent of practice effect

by dividing the mean gain by the mean score on the first test. Do children or adults show upon the whole the greater percentage of practice effect?

II. **Variability in the tapping rates of children and adults. Finding the standard deviation.** In a previous chapter it was pointed out that it is quite as important to know how much individuals vary in regard to any type of performance as to know the central tendency or average of their performances. We have already learned how to compute one measure of such variability, the *mean deviation* or as it is sometimes called the *average deviation* from the mean. Another, and for many reasons a somewhat better measure of variability is known as the *standard deviation* which is usually written as *S.D.* or σ (Greek sigma). The *standard deviation* is defined as the square root of the mean of the squares of the deviations of the separate measures from the mean of the group. There are two important reasons why the standard deviation is in general to be preferred to the average deviation as a measure of variability. In the first place, it is usually a more stable measure, that is, less affected by chance fluctuations of sampling. Secondly, it is used in the computation of many other statistical facts as will be shown later on. We shall illustrate its computation by the use of data from Table 1.

Arrange the measurements in Column 1 of Table 1 in the form of a frequency distribution as shown in Table 5 and prepare columns f, x, and fx, as was done before. Our definition calls for the sum of the squares of the separate deviations from the mean and then the average (or mean) of these squares, but since this procedure would involve the use of very large numbers and frequently of decimals we shall find a shorter method of arriving at the facts. This method makes use of the same two devices which were found to be convenient in computing the mean. That is, we shall make our computations from a guessed mean rather than from the true mean, and use the number of steps away from the mean as substitutes for the true value of each class interval. When both the mean and the standard deviation are to be computed for the same set of facts, the same guessed mean and the same class interval should be used for both series of computations.

We now add a fourth column to our table which we shall call fx^2. The values for this column are obtained by multiplying the numbers in the fx column by those in the x column. Since the product of two numbers which have the same sign is always plus, all the values in the fx^2 column will be positive. The sum of these numbers divided by the number of cases in the group will be the mean of the squares of the deviations from the guessed mean expressed in terms of class-intervals. To this we must make a correction according to the amount of error which was made in guessing the mean. We previously found (page 97) that in this case the correction amounts to 2/25 or .08 of a class interval. This correction must first be squared in order to reduce it to units similar to those in the fx^2 column and its value subtracted from the uncorrected mean fx^2.

Note that the squared correction is always to be subtracted, since it can easily be shown that whenever the deviations are computed from any point other than the true mean their value will be increased above that which would be found if they had been calculated from the mean itself. The square of .08 is .0064. We therefore subtract .0064 from 12.00 and find the square root of the result. This is 3.46. We now have the standard deviation expressed in terms of class intervals. Since in this case each class interval is equal to 1.0 centimeter of actual measurement the true value of the standard deviation is 3.46 × 1 cm. or 3.46 cm. (See Table 9.)

TABLE 9

FINDING THE STANDARD DEVIATION

(Data from Column 1, Table 2)

Intervals	f	x	fx	fx²	
117.0–117.9	1	6	6	36	$N = 25$
116.0–116.9	2	5	10	50	$\Sigma fx = +2$
115.0–115.9	3	4	12	48	$c = +.08$
114.0–114.9	1	3	3	9	$c^2 = +.0064$
113.0–113.9	1	2	2	4	Σfx^2
112.0–112.9	3	1	3	3	$\dfrac{\Sigma fx^2}{N} = \dfrac{300}{25} = 12.00$
111.0–111.9	3	0			
110.0–110.9	3	1	3	3	
109.0–109.9	2	2	4	8	$\sqrt{\dfrac{\Sigma fx^2}{N} - c^2} = \sqrt{11.9936}$
108.0–108.9	2	3	6	18	$= 3.46$
107.0–107.9	2	4	8	32	
106.0–106.9	1	5	5	25	
105.0–105.9	0	6			$\sigma = 3.46 \times$ the value of
104.0–104.9	0	7			the class interval or 3.46
103.0–103.9	1	8	8	64	cm. since the class inter-
Totals	25		+2	300	val in this case is 1 cm.

The steps involved in computing the standard deviation may then be summarized as follows:

1. Arrange the data in the form of a frequency distribution and proceed with steps 1 to 10 inclusive as outlined on pages 100 ff. under the computation of the mean by the short method, except that the correction is to be left in terms of class-intervals.
2. Add a fourth column called fx^2. Multiply the values in the x column by the corresponding values in the fx column and enter the products in the fx^2 column. Divide the sum of the values in the fx^2 column by the number of cases in the group.
3. Square the correction previously found and subtract from the result just obtained. Extract the square root

and multiply by the size of the class interval used. The result is the standard deviation.

The formula for finding the standard deviation by the long method is

$$S.D. \text{ (or } \sigma\text{)} = \sqrt{\frac{\Sigma x^2}{N}} \qquad (3)$$

or by the short method which is commonly used

$$S.D. \text{ (or } \sigma\text{)} = \text{Interval}\sqrt{\frac{\Sigma fx^2}{N} - c^2} \qquad (4)$$

where $\Sigma fx^2 =$ the sum of the squares of the deviations of the separate measures from an arbitrary origin instead of the true mean and $c =$ the amount of the correction, or the difference between the arbitrary origin and the true mean.

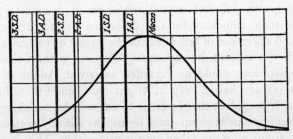

FIGURE 10.

Showing the relative values of the average deviation ($A.D.$) and the standard deviation ($S.D.$ or σ).

Figure 10 shows the relative values of the standard deviation and the average deviation in a normal distribution. Remember that both these values are measured on the base line of the curve starting from the mean; and that the area which is set off by a given distance on the base line represents the proportion of the total number of cases in the group measured which fall within the limits thus defined. In a normal distribution, 68.26 per cent of the cases will fall within the area lying between $+$ 1.00 *S.D.* and $-$ 1.00 *S.D.*, and 54.46 per cent between $+$ 1.00 and $-$ 1.00 *A.D.*

Problems. 1. Using the distributions previously worked out in finding the means, compute the standard deviations of tapping rate for each group of subjects on each trial, keeping hands and methods separate. Do the children or the adults show greater individual differences in tapping rate?

2. Compare the standard deviations of the first trial with those on the second trial for both groups of subjects. Upon the whole do individual differences in tapping rate appear to increase or decrease with practice?

III. **Relative as opposed to absolute variability. The coefficient of variability.** In comparing the variabilities of two groups with different central tendencies it is necessary to make some allowance for this difference in interpreting results. A difference of one ounce in the weight of two mice is a significant amount, but an equal difference in the weight of two elephants would be regarded as trivial. Adults of the same sex and height vary in weight much more than do infants. It is evident that in order to express the variability of different groups in comparable terms, the size of the mean of each group must be taken into consideration. This is done by means of the *coefficient of variability*. The coefficient of variability may be regarded as analogous to the per cent of experimental error in that it is obtained by dividing the absolute variability or *S.D.* by the mean of the group.*

Problems: Express each of the standard deviations which

---

* Some writers have recommended that the coefficient of variability as computed by the method just described be multiplied by 100. This has no effect except to change the decimal point, and is commonly not done except in those cases where the variability is so small in proportion to the mean that the decimal point is followed by two or more zeros. In such a case multiplying the result by 100 will remove the zeros and leave the significant figures for comparison.

were computed in the last section as coefficients of variability. Make the same comparisons as were outlined in Problems 1 and 2 of Section II. Do the results show a similar trend?

IV. **The tapping test as a rough measure of handedness.** A comparison of the scores made by the two hands will show that the tapping test may be used as a rough indication of handedness. Prepare a series of handedness scores for each subject by subtracting the score made by the left hand from that made by the right hand. When the right hand exceeds the left the score is positive; when the left exceeds the right the score is negative. Four scores are then available for each subject, *viz.*, those derived from the unimanual and the bimanual tapping separately on each of the two occasions. Which subjects would be classified as right-handed by all four tests? Which as left-handed by all four tests? Which show inconsistencies from test to test?

If possible secure from the home a statement as to the handedness history of each child. Ask parents to state whether the child has always shown a right-hand preference so far as they have observed, has always shown a left-hand preference, or has never shown any marked preference for either hand. Inquire also which children showed an early left-hand preference but were trained to use the right hand. What percentage of each of these cases falls within each of the three handedness groups as determined by the tapping test?

V. **The reliability of the tapping test.** By the reliability of a measuring device is meant the extent to which the device tends to show consistent results upon consecutive remeasurements of the same subjects under similar conditions. The reliability with which the behavior of living organisms can be measured is affected by three general factors: the amount of the experimental error, the extent to which the behavior of the individual varies from time to time under similar circumstances, and the size of the sample of behavior which is measured. Thus if we attempt to measure the comparative activity of each of a number of persons, the consistency or reliability of our findings will depend upon the accuracy of the method used, and also upon the extent to which individuals vary in activity from time to time during the period of measurement. Some individuals are on the average more active than others, but the same individuals are sometimes more active than they are at other times. Evidently if we secure only a very small amount of data for each subject, we may, by chance, select occasions for measuring certain subjects when their activity is not at all representative of their usual behavior. If we take one measurement on Monday and another on Tuesday the behavior on the two occasions may be quite different. In general it may be said that the larger the sample of behavior included in the measurements, the more adequate will be the result, and the closer will be the correspondence between measurements taken on different occasions. Moreover, if we are careful to take all our measurements under conditions which are strictly comparable for all subjects, we may expect the results to be more consistent than when such factors as hour of the day, fatigue, *etc.*, are permitted to vary from subject to subject or from time to time for the same subjects. Since the amount of time available for any particular experiment is always more or less limited, a very practical problem arises in determining how much confidence we are warranted in placing in the results of any obtained measure from the standpoint of the amount of consistency to be expected upon remeasurement. To what extent is generalization warranted? May we assume that children who show a low tapping rate on the first test are really inferior in this respect to those who tapped more rapidly on this occasion, or did they "just happen" to do poorly the first time? A comparison of the scores made on the two occasions gives us some idea as to the answer, but we need a method of reducing these comparisons to a single numerical expression or statement. Such an expression is furnished by the *coefficient of correlation* between the two series of scores. Before describing the method of computing this coefficient we may consider some of its properties.

In measurements of human beings and particularly in psychological measurements, we are usually less concerned with the absolute value of the measurements taken than we are with the extent of the differences between individuals revealed by them, or the amount of change introduced by known modifications of experimental conditions. In the matter of reliability we are not so much concerned with the gross amount of change which takes place from measurement to measurement as we are in the extent to which such changes as do occur affect the rank order of the individuals making up the group. If the dispersion of the group is large, that is, if the individuals differ from each other in regard to the trait in question by rather large amounts, small differences between successive measures will not greatly affect their standing with reference to each other. If, however, the differences between individuals are small, then even small changes in measurement upon retest may disturb their relative standing very greatly. Since in our measures of reliability we are chiefly concerned with the question of changes in the rank orders of the subjects, we may use the frequency and extent of such changes as a criterion of the consistency of the measurements we are making. This method of determining the relationship between two series of measures is known as the *Spearman rank-order method,* and its written symbol is the Greek letter rho (ρ). We shall use this method to determine the reliability of the tapping tests just described. For purposes of illustration the hypothetical values in Table 10 will be used. This table shows the tapping scores made on two consecutive occasions by fifteen kindergarten children.

TABLE 10

METHOD OF COMPUTING THE RANK-ORDER CORRELATION BE-
TWEEN THE TAPPING SCORES MADE ON TWO CON-
SECUTIVE DAYS BY FIFTEEN KINDERGARTEN
CHILDREN

Sub-ject	Score 1	Score 2	Rank 1	Rank 2	d	d^2	
A	22	26	15	15	0	0	
B	15	17	6.5	8	1.5	2.25	
C	11	12	2	2	0	0	$96.5 \times 6 = 579.0$
D	19	17	12.5	8	4.5	20.25	
E	10	13	1	3	2	4	$15 \times 15 = 225$
F	15	17	6.5	8	1.5	2.25	$225 - 1 = 224$
G	19	24	12.5	14	1.5	2.25	$224 \times 15 = 3360$
H	18	21	11	12	1	1	
I	16	15	8.5	5	3.5	12.25	$\dfrac{579}{3360} = .172$
J	13	14	4	4	0	0	
K	20	23	14	13	1	1	
L	17	16	10	6	4	16	$1 - .172 = .828$
M	16	20	8.5	11	2.5	6.25	
N	12	10	3	1	2	4	$\rho = .828$
O	14	19	5	10	5	25	
						$\Sigma = 96.5$	

Columns 1 and 2 show the scores made on each occasion by each of the fifteen subjects. The first task is to rank each series of scores in order of their respective size. Ranking may be done either from high to low, or low to high, but the same procedure must be followed with each series of scores. In this case we shall make our rankings from low to high. On the first test the lowest score was made by Subject E who is therefore given a rank of 1. (Column 3). The next lowest score was made by Subject C who is given a rank of 2, and so on for Subjects N, J, and O, who are given ranks of 3, 4, and 5, respectively. Since Subjects B and F made scores of equal value, they are each assigned the average of ranks 6 and 7, that is 6.5. Likewise Subjects I and M receive the average of ranks 8 and 9 or 8.5 and Subjects D and G are given the average of ranks 12 and 13 or 12.5. Note that the total number of ranks must always be the same as the total number of subjects in the group. The rank order of the scores on the second test are found in the same way and entered in Column 4. In one case here we have three subjects making identical scores. These are subjects B, D and F, each of whom makes a score of 17 and therefore receives a rank of 8 which is the average of the three ranks 7, 8, and 9.

We now proceed to ascertain the number and extent of the changes in the rank order of the different subjects on the two tests. This is found by subtracting the two ranks for each subject, disregarding signs. The results are entered in the column headed d (standing for the difference in rank). Each of these differences must be squared * and the squared value entered in the column headed d^2. The sum of the d^2 column is then multiplied by 6 and the product divided by $N (N^2 - 1)$ (where N is the number of cases in the group). The difference between this quotient

---

* A convenient device for squaring numbers ending in 5 may be noted here. Multiply the number preceding the 5 by the next higher number in the original series. Write 25 after the product. This will be the square desired. For example, the square of 6.5 is 6 × 7 (the number preceding the 5 multiplied by the next higher number) or 42, +.25 which is 42.25. Likewise, the square of 4.5 is 20.25 (4 × 5 with 25 in the next two digit places). The 25 will of course always be a decimal if the final 5 is a decimal.

and 1 is the rank order correlation coefficient. The complete formula then is

$$\rho = 1 - \frac{6\Sigma d^2}{N(N^2 - 1)} \qquad (5)$$

Let us consider the meaning of this coefficient a little further. If there is perfect correspondence between the rank orders of each of the cases on the two tests the correlation will be + 1.00. Under these circumstances we should say that the test has perfect reliability, since no changes have occurred which were of sufficient magnitude to disturb the relative positions of the subjects from one occasion to another. If there is no correspondence between the ranks on the two occasions, that is if a subject testing very high on one occasion is no more likely to do so on the second occasion than another who at first ranked very low, the correlation will be zero. If the positions of the subjects were exactly reversed from one trial to another so that the highest ranking subject on the first test became the lowest on the second and so on the correlation would be − 1.00. As a rule, correlation coefficients of values intermediate between these extremes will be found. It is important for the student to realize from the beginning that the size of a correlation coefficient obtained in this way is simply an indication of *the degree of correspondence between the rank orders on two successive measurements of the subjects who differ from each other to the extent indicated by their respective scores in the experiment under consideration.* If a different group of subjects were selected who resembled each other in the trait measured more closely than did the members of this group, differences between the successive scores of the same gross amount as those in the example given would disturb the rank orders to a much greater extent, and the correlation would therefore be lowered. If, on the other hand, an even more heterogeneous group were used, differences of the amount shown would be less likely to affect the rank orders and therefore a higher correlation would be expected. *It is impossible to compare correlation coefficients directly, without reference to the dispersions of the groups from which they have been derived.* In speaking of correlations, therefore, the nature of the sampling of subjects from which the coefficients were derived must always be stated clearly. Thus, we may say that a given test or measurement has a reliability of .83 for kindergarten children between the ages of 5 and 6; of .91 for children in grades 1, 2, 3, *etc.* Simply to state the reliability coefficient of a test without reference to the amount of difference existing between the subjects who are to be classified by its use is meaningless.

At first thought, it may seem to the inexperienced person that this dependence of the reliability coefficient upon the dispersion of the group measured makes the coefficient itself very difficult to interpret. A little consideration, however, will show that this very property gives it a more precise and more general meaning than would otherwise be possible. In the case of the scores listed in Table 10, for example, we are not made much the wiser by being told that the subjects varied in their performance from one test to the other by amounts ranging from − 2 to + 5 points. These differences might be quite insignificant or they might be great enough to upset completely any conclusions as to individual differences which might be drawn from the measurements. It was pointed out in an earlier section that differences of as much as an ounce in the weight of two individuals, or in two consecutive measurements of the same individual may be highly significant in the case of mice and quite trivial in the case of elephants. The reliability coefficient tells us how adequately a given measuring device distinguishes between individuals who differ from each other by amounts which are known or can be described. It is to be expected that coarse distinctions can be made more readily than fine ones. If we find, therefore, that one measuring device has a reliability of .80 when used with unselected children between the ages of five and six, while another device has a reliability of .80 for children who range in age from five to fifteen years, we can say at once that if the characteristic measured is one which changes with age, the first device is considerably more accurate than the second, since it makes the fine distinctions necessary to arrange five-year-old children in their correct rank-order as accurately as the second makes the coarse distinctions which are all that are necessary in the second case. *The description of the group tells us in a general way how fine are the distinctions which the measurement or test in question has been called upon to make; the magnitude of the reliability coefficient tells us how effectively it makes these distinctions.*

The student must also be careful to avoid confusing the numerical significance of the correlation coefficient with any sort of percentage value. This point will be taken up more fully in connection with the Pearson product-moment formula which will be described in a later chapter. For the present, it is sufficient to note that in the example given, a correlation of $+ .83$ is obtained between the two series of scores although only three of the cases maintain exactly the same rank order on both occasions, and in one case the change in rank is as great as five places, which is $1/5$ of the entire range. Nevertheless, it is true that *on the average* the subjects ranking low on the first test continue to rank low on the second, and vice versa. For many kinds of relationships, we may say that the percentage of identical factors determining standing on the two occasions is indicated by the square of the correlation coefficient. Thus, in the case under consideration where the correlation is $+.83$ it may be said that 69 per cent ($.83^2 = +.6889$) of the factors determining individual differences in performance were the same on the two occasions. However there is no substitute for experience. Continued practice in computing correlation coefficients, noting the amount of difference found between ranks with correlations of different magnitude, will give a more concrete understanding of the meaning of these coefficients than can possibly be obtained in any other way.

Problems: 1. Find the reliability of the tapping-scores for each hand by each method, and for both groups of subjects. Is there any consistent difference shown (a) in the comparative reliability of the tapping performance of adults and children? (b) in the reliability of the unimanual as compared to the bimanual tapping? (c) in the comparative reliability of the test for the two hands?

2. Find for each group the reliability of the total tapping scores when the sum of the four scores (right and left hand for both unimanual and bimanual tapping) on each trial are combined to give a single score. This reliability coefficient will ordinarily be higher than those for the single scores since chance errors in the individual scores will tend to cancel each other in the total.

3. Find the reliability of the handedness scores for unimanual and bimanual tapping separately, also for the total. The handedness scores are obtained by subtracting the number of taps made by the left hand from the number made by the right on each trial. Positive scores indicate right-handedness; negative scores left-handedness.

4. Do the tapping scores themselves or the handedness scores derived from them show the higher reliability? Can you suggest any reason for the difference?

5. Compare the results obtained in this experiment with those reported by Goodenough and Tinker (112).

REFERENCES

The student is referred to the following titles in the bibliography at the end of this book:

24, 66*, 67*, 89, 98, 112*, 125, 135, 144, 209*, 253*, 378*, 382, 384, 387.

Chapter 15

GENERAL BODILY COÖRDINATION AND ACTIVITY

IN the last chapter, the differences among children and adults in the speed of arm and hand movements were studied. Marked individual differences are also to be found in the control of the larger muscles of the legs and trunk. Some children move clumsily and balance badly; others are much more agile. Similar differences may be noted among adults.

A number of devices for measuring bodily coördination in young children have been worked out. Among these may be mentioned particularly the "walking board" (10) which consists of a narrow board raised three or four inches above the floor. The test consists in having the child walk the length of the board without stepping off. A modification of the walking board test is described in Experiment No. 7.

Experiment No. 7

General Bodily Coördination in Walking a Twenty-five-foot Line

Material: On a 27 ft. strip of white shelf paper, paste a 25 ft. length of gummed manilla paper 1 inch wide, which is used for sealing parcels. The gummed strip should extend down the center of the shelf paper, and a short length of the gummed paper should be pasted at right angles across each end to mark the starting point clearly. A stop-watch or an ordinary watch with a second hand is also needed.

Subjects: Nursery-school, kindergarten, or primary grade children may be used. If time permits it is well to have two groups of subjects of different ages as in the preceding experiment. If the subjects used in the tapping experiment are also used here, both the walking experiment and the tapping test can be given on a single occasion, thus doing away with the necessity of interrupting the children more than once.

Procedure. The experiment is carried out as follows: Spread the length of paper down a hall or other convenient place. With the child standing on the cross-strip at one end, give the following instructions: "Have you ever seen acrobats walk a tight rope in a circus? You know how they have a rope fastened to two posts away up in the air, and the acrobat walks along the rope without falling off? Let's make believe that this brown paper is a tight rope, and see if you can walk all the way from one end to the other without stepping off at all. You have to put one foot ahead of the other like this (demonstrate by taking a few steps), and you must be very careful not to step off the rope. When I say, 'Go,' start from your end and walk all the way down to this end as quickly as you can. Be sure not to step off the rope. All ready, go." With very young children a practice series may be needed to make sure that the child understands.

Start the stop-watch when the child starts to take his first step. An ordinary watch with a second hand may be used if no stop-watch is available. Record the time to the nearest number of seconds. The number of errors, that is the number of steps in which more than half the foot is off the paper strip should also be recorded. Allow three trials in immediate succession, and record time and errors separately for each trial. The test should be repeated on the following day by a different investigator, working without knowledge of previous results.

Problems: 1. Find the reliability of the time scores by correlating the total time required for the three trials on the first occasion with the corresponding total on the second occasion. Totals should be found by adding the number of seconds required for each of the three trials.

2. Find the reliability of the error scores in the same way. Does the length of time or the number of errors constitute a better method of differentiating between children of this age on the task in question?

3. Using the rank order method, find the correlation between time and errors on each of the two occasions. What does this suggest as to the relationship between these functions?

4. If the same subjects were used for the walking test and the tapping test, find the correlation between total tapping scores (hands, methods, and trials combined) and the sum of the time scores on the two occasions. Do the same for the error scores. What relationship, if any, between gross bodily coördination and manual speed is suggested by these results?

Experiment No. 8

Physical Activity as Measured by Distance Traversed Spontaneously in Free Play during a Constant Period of Time

Prepare a chart of the playroom or playground used by a group of nursery-school, kindergarten, or primary grade children. This chart must be carefully drawn to scale and the position of a sufficient number of permanent features indicated to serve as landmarks. The chart should be mimeographed, and should have space provided for recording the name of the child observed, the day and hour of observation, the name of the observer, and other facts which may be of interest. A space for general notes should always be included. Students should work in pairs. Each pair is to observe the activities of a single child simultaneously during a five minute interval, and record his progress from one part of the playroom or playground to another by means of a line traced on the chart. Pauses of fifteen seconds or longer should be indicated by numbered circles as shown

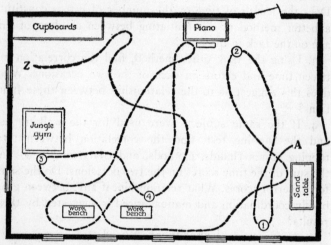

FIGURE 11.

Showing a five minute record of the activity of one child

Adapted from Thomas (245)

Circles indicate pauses (15 sec. or more).
A indicates beginning of record.
Z indicates end of record.

Pauses

1. Looking out of the window ....—20″
2. Talking to teacher ....—18″
3. Climbing on jungle gym ....—95″
4. Watching other children at work bench ..—35″

Scale = 5 ft. = 1 inch.

Distance traversed = 26 × 5 = 130 ft.

in Fig. 11. The length of the pauses and the activities occurring at these times should be recorded at the bottom of the chart. At the end of a five minute observation of one child, both students should observe another for five minutes, and so on to the end of the period. The experiment should be repeated on succeeding days until a total of not fewer than ten five minute observations have been secured for each subject. The greater the number of records, the greater should be the reliability of the total. If there are as many as ten students in the class, each student should aim to secure one five minute record for each child. If there are fewer than ten students, two records from each will probably be needed to make the data sufficiently reliable.

Find the total distance traversed by each child during each five minute period by measuring the length of the lines with a chartometer.* If no chartometer is available, a fine thread may be laid along the line and subsequently measured, but this method is more laborious and less accurate. Convert the measurements into the original units in terms of the scale used in preparing the chart. Note that this scale should not be too small, since a slight error in drawing on a small scale will produce a large error when the measures are converted to the original units.

It is evident that a method such as this does not give a complete picture of the actual energy expenditure, since the time spent on a "jungle gym" alone may readily involve more activity (though here recorded as a pause) than is required by the total amount of running about the room which is recorded. On the average, however, it is probably true that the most active children will move from one part of the room to another more frequently than do the quiet children. Marston (176) used a method somewhat similar to this in connection with his study of introversion-

* Can be obtained from C. H. Stoelting and Co., Chicago, Ill.

extroversion in young children and Thomas (245) used it as one method of studying social behavior.

Problems: 1. Find the reliability of a single five minute observation of activity by correlating for each pair of students separately the distance traversed by each child according to one student's record against the corresponding record obtained by his partner. The result tells nothing as to the variability of the behavior of the same children from day to day, but it does indicate the extent to which their rank orders are likely to be disturbed through errors of observation, recording, and measuring. In other words, it indicates to what extent the *experimental error* alone affects the accuracy of discrimination.

2. Have each student find his own mean experimental error by computing the mean difference between his own scores and those of his partner. What is the average experimental error for the group as a whole? What percentage is the mean experimental error of the total range of scores, *i.e.,* of the difference between the mean scores earned by the most active and the least active children in the group? The experimental error differs from the correlation between simultaneous observations in that the results are expressed in terms of the absolute or actual amounts of error in measurement. The correlation coefficient shows the extent to which the method makes it possible to arrange the results of the various observations in order of the true magnitude of the distances traversed. As has been pointed out before, the significance of an experimental error must always be interpreted in terms of the degree of precision in measurement which is needed for the problem at hand. For example, if we are interested in knowing how the amounts of physical activity as measured in this way vary at different hours of the day, under different room temperatures, before and after naps, or in accordance with any other

known or measureable change in conditions, we shall require an instrument which is sufficiently precise to arrange the measurements in rank order with a relatively small number of displacements. If the differences between the separate measurements are large, so that only rather coarse discriminations are required, a comparatively accurate arrangement may often be secured in spite of somewhat large experimental errors; but if the differences are small, so that fine discriminations are necessary for accurate arrangement, even small experimental errors may invalidate the results.

We are often interested, however, not so much in the activity displayed by any given child at a given moment, as in securing a measurement which will tell us at least roughly how he compares with other children of his group with regard to his habitual or characteristic degree of activity. We may secure such a measure for each child by summing the scores obtained by all the observers on all the occasions that he was observed and taking the mean or average of these scores as affording an indication of his characteristic activity. If this is done for all the children in the experimental group, it will be found that the scores thus obtained differ considerably from child to child. We need to know how much confidence we are warranted in placing in these scores. In other words, what is the probability that if we were to secure the same amount of data for each of these children a second time under similar conditions the individual subjects would hold the same or approximately the same positions with reference to each other? Would the children who were found to be most active in the first series of observations also be the most active in the second series and vice versa? Problem No. 3 describes a method for answering this question.

3. Find the reliability (or consistency) of the children's

behavior from day to day by summing the scores obtained by half the observers for each child and correlating against those obtained by the other half. In dividing the observers for this purpose, the scores obtained by both members of an original pair should be placed in the same variable and the average of their observations used as the child's score for that occasion, in order to avoid the spurious result which would arise from correlating behavior with itself.

The size of this correlation coefficient is a measure of the amount of dependence which can be placed in the combined observations of one-half the total number of observers. The student should note the size of the correlation coefficient obtained and compare with the number and magnitude of the changes in the rank order of the individual cases. The actual magnitude of these changes in rank order should, of course, be thought of in reference to the number of cases in the group, that is, the maximum change possible. The significance of the differences in rank order may be made more concrete to the inexperienced person if they are expressed in terms of the number of cases which would be transferred from the most active to the least active twenty-five per cent, from the upper half to the lower half, *etc.*

Since the correlation between independent halves of the observational series tells us only the reliability of one half the amount of data actually obtained, it is desirable to get an estimate as to the reliability of the total. If all the scores for each subject were combined, and the results correlated with a second series, what would be the most probable value of this correlation? The formula used here is known as the *Spearman-Brown prophecy formula.* It is written

$$r_{nn} = \frac{n\,r_{11}}{1 + (n-1)\,r_{11}} \tag{6}$$

Strictly speaking, this formula applies only to correlations derived by the product-moment method which is to be taken up in a later chapter. The symbol for the product-moment correlation is r. However, since results by the two methods usually agree quite closely, we shall not be doing much violence to our data if we substitute ρ for r in the prophecy formula which will then read.

$$\rho_{nn} = \frac{n\rho_{11}}{1 + (n-1)\rho_{11}} \qquad (7)$$

Here ρ_{nn} is the most probable value of the reliability coefficient which would be found if the number of observations for each child were to be increased n times; n is the number of times the length of the present sample has been (theoretically) multiplied; ρ_{11} is the obtained correlation between independent halves. In the present example, $n = 2$, since we are assuming that a second series of observations, equal in length to the first has been obtained for correlation with the first series. If the correlation between halves has been found to be .60, it is to be expected that the reliability of the total series as found by correlating with a hypothetical second series would be

$$\frac{2\,(.60)}{1 + .60} = \frac{1.20}{1.60} = .75$$

4. By applying the Spearman-Brown formula as described, correct the reliability coefficient obtained for independent halves of the activity scores to the value which presumably would be found for the total series.

5. Prepare a frequency surface showing the distribution of activity scores for the entire group. The mean of all the observational records for each child should be used as the score for that child.

6. Using the same scale of measurement, prepare a second frequency surface showing the distribution of experimental errors for all the cases and all the observations. The experimental errors, it will be recalled, are computed by sub-

tracting the scores made by the two simultaneous observers for each subject on each occasion. How does the range of experimental errors compare with the range of individual differences in the scores made by the different subjects?

REFERENCES

The student is referred to the following titles in the bibliography at the end of this book:

10*, 38*, 54, 93*, 95, 126, 144, 225, 245*, 261, 269, 272, 308, 310, 319, 331*, 378.

Chapter 16

COLOR DISCRIMINATION

TESTS of color matching or of color naming have been much used in psychological laboratories as a means of gauging the speed of perceptive reaction. With little children, however, such tests serve a somewhat different purpose, since at these ages children have not yet learned to recognize colors with complete accuracy. The average child does not learn to associate colors with their correct names before the age of four or five years. Recent experiments appear to show that red, yellow, and blue are learned at an earlier age than green. In standardizing the Merrill-Palmer tests in which a test very similar to the one described here was used, Stutsman (376) found that at the age of 24 months, among the children who received partial credit red was always correct, blue was failed but once, yellow was correct only once, and green was failed by all. The total number of cases and the number making complete failures is not stated. Somewhat similar results were obtained by Staples *
in a study of the responses to color of children between the ages of six months and two years. Staples' method was to show the infant a large card on which were pasted two discs of colored paper, of equal brightness but differing in color, and to record for which disc the child reached or to which he pointed. She found a marked preference for red, yellow was next in popularity, while blue and green were chosen much less often. The finding of such marked differences in

* Unpublished thesis, The University of Minnesota.

reaction to different colors at these early ages suggests strongly that color perception is not fully developed at birth, and that even as late as nursery-school age, children do not react to all colors with equal readiness. However, these investigations, like most which have been carried out with young children up to the present time, need further verification with other groups. It is therefore well worth while to carry out additional investigations in this field to see whether similar results will be obtained. Experiment No. 9 describes one method by which the reactions of young children to different colors may be studied.

Experiment No. 9

Color Matching

Material: Sixty one-inch discs cut from heavy colored paper, a tray for sorting, and a set of six small boxes with sliding covers into which the discs are to be sorted. Ten discs in each of the following colors should be prepared: red, yellow, blue, green, black, white. Boxes should be labeled by pasting an additional disc on the cover, using a different color for each box.

Subjects: This problem may be carried out with children between the ages of two and five years. It is too easy for children beyond the age of five and therefore has relatively little value for them.

Procedure: Seat the child at a low table and place before him the tray containing ten discs in each of the six colors including black and white, (60 discs in all) which have been thoroughly shuffled. The six small boxes are to be placed directly above the tray within easy reach, with the boxes drawn half-way out of the sliding covers to permit placing the discs. The following instructions are then given:

"Do you see this pretty ball?" selecting one of the discs

at random. "It belongs in one of these boxes up here (*pointing*). In which box do you think it belongs?"

If the child does not understand or points to the wrong box the experimenter should correct him by saying, "No, each ball belongs in the box which has a ball just like it on the top. Where is the one just like this? If child does not then point out the correct box, examiner shows him, saying, "See, here is the one. This ball is just like the one on the cover of the box." Examiner then selects another disc of a different color and repeats as before until one disc of each color has been placed in its appropriate box. As much help as necessary is given throughout this demonstration series. Examiner then says, "Now I am going to see how quickly you can put all the balls back into their own boxes. Find the boxes and put in the balls as quickly as you can, but be sure not to make any mistakes. Every ball must go in the right box. Do you understand? All right, go ahead."

If the child stops to play or chatter before completing the task, urge him to continue by saying, "That's fine, you're doing splendidly. Hurry up and get them all back in their boxes." Record the total time required for placing all the colors and the number of errors for each color separately, *i.e.*, the number of discs of each color which are placed in the wrong box.* The demonstration series is not counted. Do not correct errors after the demonstration series has been completed. When all the colors have been placed, ask the child to tell you the name of the color on the top of each box. Record responses verbatim.

I. **Age differences in color matching.** *Problems:* 1. Classify the children according to age, and prepare frequency distributions for each age group separately, showing the

---

* If two-year-old children are used it is better to have only five discs of each color placed at a single sitting in order to avoid fatigue and loss of interest.

total number of errors made in matching and the total time required for matching. What percentages of the children in each age group equal or exceed the median time score of the age group next older? What percentage equal or exceed the median error score? Thus, if the age range used has included children of three, four and five years, find the percentage of three-year-olds who equal or exceed the median score of the four-year-olds, and also of the five-year-olds. Also find what percentage of the four-year-olds equal or exceed the median score of the five-year-olds.

Upon the basis of these results would you say that the time scores or the error scores show a clearer developmental trend?

2. Arrange the colors in order of matching difficulty as judged by the total number of errors made in matching by the entire group, also by each age group separately. Is the order of difficulty approximately the same at all ages?

3. Find for each age group separately the rank order correlation between the time required for matching and the total number of errors made in matching. Upon the whole, do the most accurate children of any age take more or less time than those who make a greater number of errors?

4. Considering each color separately, divide the children into two groups; those who named the color correctly and those who did not. Age should be disregarded. Compare these groups as to the mean number of errors made in placing each color.

II. **The standard error of the mean and the reliability of differences between the means of different groups.** If we were to divide the members of this class into groups of five each, selecting each group purely at random, and then were to measure the height of each person and find the mean height of each group, it is unlikely that all the means would be exactly alike. If, on the other hand, we should take all the college students in America, and after shuffling them thoroughly so that a random selection could be made from all parts of the country, were to divide this large and miscellaneous group into five subgroups, we should probably find that the mean height of each of the five groups would correspond very closely. The reason for the large differences between the means of the small groups as contrasted with the small differences between the means of the large groups is that when the measurements of many cases are combined, the number of very tall persons will usually be about equal to the number of very short persons. These differences will then tend to balance each other. When the number of cases is small the balance is likely to be less perfect, since the chance inclusion of one or two very tall or very short persons in such a group may greatly change the value of the mean. Errors of this kind are known as *errors of sampling*. It is evident from the example just given that they are more likely to be found in small than in large groups. It should be noted, however, that even in very large groups, sampling errors of importance may still be found if a selective factor of any kind is present, that is, if the entire group has not been thoroughly shuffled previous to dividing it into subgroups. Thus, in the example given if all the students from such a state as Minnesota, (where, because of the large admixture of Scandinavian stock, the inhabitants tend to be distinctly taller than the average for the population as a whole) happened to be placed in one group, and all the Italians and Oriental students were placed in another group, significant differences would still appear between these groups in spite of the large number of cases included in each.

When we wish to ascertain how much confidence we may place in a difference which is found to exist between two groups of subjects, we must take into consideration, first, the size of the group; secondly, the amount of variation which is ordinarily found between the members of such groups. We must also be able to state with reasonable assurance that the groups are closely similar or have been thoroughly shuffled as regards all factors except the single one which has formed the basis for the division.

Many years ago it was shown that the relative *frequency* of the occurrence of certain events can be foretold with considerable accuracy, even though the individual events are determined purely by chance and therefore cannot be predicted at all. No one can tell in advance what will be the sex of any individual unborn baby, but if we know the birth-rate of a country we can predict with accuracy how many male and how many female babies will be born in a year. Again, provided the toss is made fairly, we cannot say whether a falling coin will show heads or tails, but when a large number of such tosses are made, we can state not only that the total will show a fifty-fifty ratio of heads and tails, but also approximately how many times one, two, three, or four heads will be thrown in succession. We can thus predict for the group as a whole what can not be predicted with accuracy for the individual members of the group. Because of this principle, life insurance companies are able to function, gambling houses maintain a successful balance in spite of occasional "runs of luck" for individual patrons, traffic policemen can be stationed at the most crowded crossings before the day's traffic really commences, and the restaurant keeper can apportion his days' marketing on the basis of the usual food habits of his clientele, although he does not know what any individual customer may order. Whether we are aware of it or not, statistical method and particularly the theory of probability is used by every one of us in his daily living. Formal statistical devices merely furnish more precise ways of organizing the results of our own experience and that of others in such a way as to yield more accurate prediction.

Let us return to the question of the amount of confidence to be placed in a difference actually found between two groups divided in some known fashion. Suppose we were to find that on a test of speed in tapping the mean number of taps in a ten second period made by 25 four-year-old boys was 18 and the standard deviation 10.0. For 25 girls of the same age, tested in the same manner, the mean score was 16 and the standard deviation 8. We wish to know the probability that if other groups of similar age were tested in the same way, the boys would continue to make higher average scores than the girls.

We first need to know how great differences we may reasonably expect to find between the means actually obtained for these two groups and the means of other samples taken from the same general population. We express the probable dispersion of the means derived from a series of successive samples of this kind in terms of the standard *error of the mean*,* which may be defined as the standard deviation of the *theoretical* distribution of the means of an infinite number of groups similar to the one actually measured. It is obtained by dividing the standard deviation of the scores earned by the tested group by the square root of the number of cases in that group. The formula is therefore:

$$\sigma_M = \frac{S.D.}{\sqrt{N}} \qquad (8)$$

In the case under consideration the standard deviation of the boys' scores is 10 and the number of cases 25. 10 divided by the square root of 25 is 2. Following the same procedure

---

* The term *standard error* refers to the standard deviation of a theoretical distribution while the term *standard deviation* is used for the dispersion of concrete groups actually measured.

for the girls we find that the standard error of their mean is 8 divided by the square root of 25 or 1.6. We now have

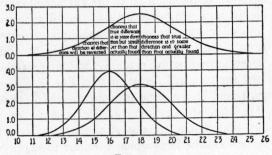

FIGURE 12.

Showing the reliability of a difference between independent measures.

the situation shown in Fig. 12 above, with the distribution of probable changes in the value of the two means for other similar groups expressed by the forms of the two lower

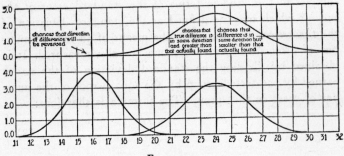

FIGURE 13.

Showing the effect upon the reliability of the difference of increasing the difference between the means.

curves. Note that although the number of cases in each group is the same, the probability that large differences will be found between the means of different samplings of boys is

Color Discrimination 159

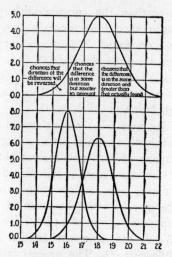

FIGURE 14.

Showing the effect upon the reliability of a difference of increasing the number of cases in the sampling.

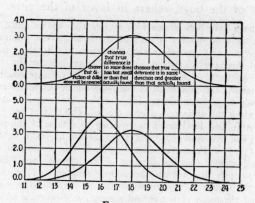

FIGURE 15.

Showing the effect upon the reliability of a difference of correlation between measures.

somewhat greater than the corresponding probability for girls. This is as it should be, since in the group actually tested the boys were found to show greater *individual differences* (S.D. = 10) than the girls (S.D. = 8). The larger standard error is shown by the relatively flat curve of distribution of probable means for the boys as compared to that for the girls.*

Let us consider now what results would be obtained if we were to compare the mean of each successive sampling of boys with the mean of each possible sampling of girls. All samples are of the same size, in this case 25 for each sex. We begin by taking one random sample of 25 girls and finding the difference between the mean of this group and that of a corresponding group of 25 boys. This difference we may call D_1. We do the same with another pair of samples and call the difference D_2. The process is continued until the difference between the means of each possible pair of samples has been ascertained. These differences would be of varying magnitude and it is probable that some would be in favor of the boys, others in favor of the girls. If they

* All curves have been drawn with area of 1600 square units. The area represents the total number of chances; the height of the ordinate erected at any given point represents the proportion of the total number of theoretical means which would have the value indicated by the scores entered along the abscissa; the area cut off by an ordinate erected at any point represents the proportion of the total number of theoretical means which would have values greater (or less) than the score indicated by the point at which the ordinate has been erected. The student can easily plot curves of this kind for himself by referring to a table of the probability integral [The Kelley-Wood table given as an appendix in *Statistical Method* (390) or Pearson's tables (395)]. If this is done on millimeter paper the likelihood that the direction of the difference would be reversed in other samples drawn from the same population can be checked by counting the number of square millimeters in the difference curve which fall beyond the mean of the second group. The proportion which this is of the total area of the difference curve will correspond to the probability (percentage of an infinite number of samplings) that the direction of the difference will be reversed in succeeding trials.

were arranged in the form of a frequency table, however, it is likely that the distribution would follow the form of the *normal frequency curve.* The standard deviation of a curve obtained in this way is known as the standard error of a difference. However, since we have postulated that the distribution curves comprising the means of all the samplings for each sex are each made up of an infinite number of such samplings, a lifetime would be insufficient actually to prepare such a table. Fortunately a statistical short cut is available by which we can determine the standard error of the theoretical distribution of differences which is most likely to correspond to that between a single pair of samples actually obtained. We need to know the standard errors of the means of these samples, and the amount of correlation between the members of the two groups in the trait measured.* If there is no correlation, the formula for the standard error of the difference is:

$$\sigma_D = \sqrt{\sigma_1{}^2 + \sigma_2{}^2} \tag{9}$$

where σ_1 is the standard error of the mean of the first group and σ_2 is the standard error of the mean of the second group.

Fig. 12 shows graphically how the standard error of a difference is interpreted in terms of probability. The lower curve on the left represents the standard error of the girls' mean in the example given on page 157. The right-hand lower curve represents the corresponding facts for the boys. The upper curve shows the theoretical distribution of the *differences* between the means of successive samplings of boys and girls; each sample being made up of exactly 25 cases. Since there is as much likelihood that either one of the obtained means from the samples actually tested is too high

* For the derivation of the formulas given here, the student is referred to the discussion by Kelley (390) or Yule (403).

as that it is too low, the midpoint of the difference curve is placed at the mean of one of the samples. It does not matter which one is chosen for this purpose, since all the curves are symmetrical. By applying the difference formula given above to the data given on p. 157 we find that the standard error of the difference in this case is

$$\sigma_D = \sqrt{1.6^2 + 2.0^2} = 2.56$$

The difference curve has therefore been drawn with a standard error of 2.56 but with the same area and on the same base as the curves showing the standard errors of the means for the sexes. The means of the two lower curves thus divide the difference curve into three parts. Fifty per cent lies to the right of the boys' mean. This represents the probability that in other samplings drawn from the same population the difference between the means of the sexes would be in the same direction and greater in amount than that actually found. The remaining fifty per cent of the chances is divided into two parts. The portion lying between the two means represents the probability that the difference lies in the same direction, (in this case that the boys would continue to be found superior to the girls), but is smaller than the amount actually found in the samples tested. The proportion falling below the girls' mean represents the probability that in other samples the direction of the difference would be reversed, that is, that the girls would be found superior to the boys. The proportion which this area is of the entire area of the difference curve may be found from a table of the probability curve as follows: First divide the actual difference between the means of the two groups tested by the standard error of the difference curve. This locates the point of division of the "questionable" half of the curve in terms of its own dispersion, and the areas thus determined will be uniform proportions of the total, regardless of whether the curve is flat (*i.e.*, has a wide dispersion) or peaked (indicating a narrow dispersion). Find this value in the $\dfrac{D}{\sigma_D}$ column of Table 11 which is an abridged form of the *probability table* showing the areas falling beyond any given point on the abscissa. Then read across the table to the corresponding value in the column marked "chances in 1000" which shows the proportion of the total area of the difference curve which is included in the portion falling below the mean of the second group. If the total area is assumed to be 1000, then this figure may be said to represent the number of chances in a thousand that in other samplings drawn from the same population the direction of the difference would be the reverse of that actually found in the two groups which were tested.

TABLE 11

SHOWING THE PROBABILITY THAT A DIFFERENCE WHICH IS A
GIVEN MULTIPLE OF ITS STANDARD ERROR WILL
OCCUR BY CHANCE

$\dfrac{D}{\sigma_D}$	Chances in 1000	$\dfrac{D}{\sigma_D}$	Chances in 1000	$\dfrac{D}{\sigma_D}$	Chances in 1000
.00	500	.70	242	1.90	29
.05	480	.80	212	2.00	23
.10	460	.90	184	2.10	18
.15	440	1.00	158	2.20	14
.20	421	1.10	136	2.30	11
.25	401	1.20	115	2.40	8
.30	382	1.30	97	2.50	6
.35	363	1.40	81	2.60	5
.40	344	1.50	67	2.70	4
.45	326	1.60	55	2.80	3
.50	308	1.70	45	2.90	2
.60	274	1.80	36	3.00	1

Suppose, now, that the difference between the two means were increased as indicated in Figure 13, where the mean for the girls remains at 16 but the boys' mean has been moved forward to 24. Since the number of cases and the standard deviations remain the same, the form of the curves representing the theoretical distribution of the means from successive samples (the standard error curves) is unchanged; the only difference is in their position with respect to each other. Likewise the form of the difference curve is identical with that of Figure 12, but because of the increased distance between the two means the portion of the difference curve which extends beyond the mean of the second group and represents the likelihood that the direction of the difference would be reversed in other samples is very small, only 1/1000 of the total area.

Now look at Figure 14. Here the difference between the two means is the same as in Figure 12, but the number of cases in the samplings has been increased to 100. The greater the number of cases, the more dependable is any statistical measure derived from them and the less likely is it to vary from sample to sample. This increased stability of the mean is shown in the relatively small spread of the two lower curves representing the standard errors of the two means, and it is likewise reflected in the smaller spread of the difference curve. Thus although the difference between the two means is the same as that shown in Figure 12, we are warranted in placing more confidence in an assumption that a "true" sex difference exists because of the greater stability of measures based upon larger numbers of cases. In the first case there are 218 chances in 1000 that the direction of the difference would be reversed in other samples; in this case the chances of reversal have been reduced to 59 in 1000.

In the three instances which have been given we have assumed that there is no correlation between the scores made by individual members of the two groups. Suppose, however, that the successive samplings had been made up entirely of brothers and sisters, and that the trait measured was one in which a familial relationship exists. In such a case, the differences between the samples would be lessened in proportion to the amount of family-resemblance, and the standard error of the distribution of differences will likewise be smaller than is the case when the variables are uncorrelated. The formula for the standard error of a difference between correlated measures is:

$$\sigma_D = \sqrt{\sigma_1{}^2 + \sigma_2{}^2 - 2r\sigma_1\sigma_2} \qquad (10)$$

If $r = 0$ the last term of this formula drops out and the formula for independent measures remains.

Figure 15 shows the effect of a correlation of $+ .75$ between the paired measures in the two samples when all other conditions are identical with those shown in Figure 12. The lower curves showing the standard errors of the two means are unchanged in form and position, but the standard error of the difference curve has been reduced from 2.56 to 2.04 as a result of the correlation. This gives it a higher central peak and a shorter spread, and the area overlapping the second mean is thereby reduced from 218/1000 of the total to 164/1000.

The difference formulas which have just been given apply not only to the difference between means but to the difference between any two statistical measures whose standard errors are known. In using these formulas, computation may often be facilitated by combining the difference formula with that used for finding the standard errors of the measures to be compared. For example, when the standard error of the difference between the means of two independent groups is the only value desired, we may substitute the formula for the standard error of the mean for σ in the difference formula as shown below:

$$\sigma_D = \sqrt{\left(\frac{S.D^2}{N}\right)_1 + \left(\frac{S.D^2}{N}\right)_2} \qquad (11)$$

The question of the reliability of obtained differences between groups is one of the most important concepts in the entire field of measurement and experimentation, and the student should make sure that he has thoroughly grasped the underlying theory. Note that the assumption is always made that the two groups have been drawn from the same population and that this population has been thoroughly shuffled, so that the factor constituting the basis for the division is the only selective agent present. It is of the highest importance therefore that before applying these formulas, the nature of the sampling be examined carefully to make sure that the data are free from systematic errors of sampling. An additional point to be kept in mind is that the exceptional event sometimes really occurs, and that even though it be found that a given difference would occur by chance only once in ten thousand times, the present occasion *may* be the ten-thousandth chance. One occasionally finds statements in elementary treatises on statistical method to the effect that if a given difference is so many times its standard error it may be regarded as "significant"; the limits set for "significance" varying somewhat from textbook to textbook. Such statements are likely to cause erroneous concepts of the situation. There is no single point which divides the significant from the non-significant or the probable from the improbable, and it is well to recognize this fact from the outset. As the ratio of an actually found difference to its standard error increases, the likelihood that the direction of the difference would be reversed by further investigation decreases very rapidly. There is no point at which such a reversal becomes theoretically impossible, though the chances may be so few that we may with reasonable safety ignore them. It is better, therefore. instead of speaking about significant or non-significant differences, to speak of differences which by chance would occur with a specified degree of frequency as not over once in a hundred or once in a thousand times.

Problems: 1. Find the reliability of the differences between the mean number of matching-errors made on all the colors combined by the children of each age. What is the probability that these differences are the result of chance?

2. Find the reliability of the differences in the time required for matching all the colors by children of different ages. Do the time scores or the error scores show the more reliable age trend?

3. Find the reliability of the differences between the number of errors made in matching the different colors. Are the age differences or the color differences more reliably established?

4. Find, for each color separately, the reliability of the differences between the number of errors made in matching the color by those children who named the color correctly and those who did not. (See Problem 4, p. 154).

REFERENCES

The student is referred to the following titles in the bibliography at the end of this book:

10, 30, 226, 228, 254*, 276, 376*, 384, 390*, 403*.

Chapter 17

PERCEPTION AS A SELECTIVE PROCESS

COMMON observation teaches us that two persons looking at the same thing at the same time do not always
"see" it in the same way. The artist may look at a machine
and note chiefly its general form and symmetry, while the
engineer, looking at the same machine observes the functional relationships of the separate parts to each other and
pays little attention to their artistic proportions. The proof-
reader notes errors in word-form which completely escape
the observation of the ordinary reader who is interested in
the subject-matter. If a dozen people inspect the contents of
a crowded show window they will usually carry away widely
different impressions of the objects displayed. Not only do
individuals differ from each other with regard to their most
characteristic modes of perception, but the same individual
will perceive the same object differently from time to time
according to his most recent experiences, his immediate
physiological condition and so on. At the end of a long walk
on a winter's day, one may enter a wayside lunch room and
eat heartily without "seeing" the dirty table-cloth or "smell-
ing" the stale odors of which at another time he would have
been most unpleasantly conscious. Perception is thus a selective process in which certain features of a situation are
singled out for attention and others neglected. What these
factors shall be, however, varies considerably from individual to individual, and in the same individual at different
times. Among the factors which determine the nature of the

selective responses to partial elements in a situation, age undoubtedly plays an important part. It is therefore both interesting and valuable to compare the responses of individuals of different ages to a situation in which the variations of response are reduced to a single choice between two alternatives.

Experiment No. 10

The Relative Potency of Color and Form Perception at Different Ages

The purpose of this experiment is to determine whether the perception of color or the perception of form plays a major part in the total apprehension of an object by individuals of a given age, and whether this relative potency tends to change with age. Since the responses obtained will show considerable variation from time to time, clear-cut results can be expected only if the number of subjects at each age is fairly large, say 20 or more as a minimum. Unless this number can be obtained, the experiment had better be omitted.

Material: Four of the surface forms used by Brian and Goodenough (30) should be used. These forms are as follows: a two inch circle, a two inch square, an equilateral triangle two inches on each side, and a diamond two inches on each side. These forms should be cut from heavy colored cardboard, or if the colored cardboard is not available the forms may be cut from plain cardboard and covered with colored paper. The colors to be used are red, yellow, green, and blue. One copy of each form in each of the four colors should be prepared, making sixteen pieces in the entire set.

Subjects: If possible four groups of subjects should be used as follows: Nursery-school children between the ages of two and three years, kindergarten children between the ages of four-and-a-half and five-and-a-half years, school children between the ages of seven and eight years and a group of adults or high school children.

Procedure: The subject should be seated at a table facing the experimenter who says, "Now watch and see what I have to show you." A screen is then interposed while the experimenter arranges two of the figures differing both in form and in color behind the screen, placing them about

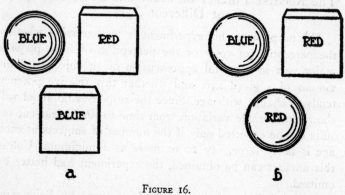

FIGURE 16.
Illustrating placement of forms before child.

eight inches apart and equidistant from the child. Constancy of distance and position can be easily insured by using as a base a sheet of neutral gray cardboard with crosses to indicate the points at which the forms are to be placed. When the forms have been placed in position the screen is removed and a third form, chosen so as to match one of the first two forms in respect to form and the other in respect to color, is placed in a position intermediate between the first two figures and six inches nearer to the child. (See Fig. 16a). The experimenter then says, "Do you see these two things? And see this other one. Now which of the two things up here is just like this one?" (*pointing to the single form.*) The question may be repeated if the child does not seem to understand.

As soon as the choice is made the experimenter should record it and then replace the screen. The third form is then removed, but the first two are left in their original positions. In place of the third form a fourth is substituted so chosen that the color and form combination is reversed from that used originally. (See Fig. 16b). A child who first chose the form on the left would then have to choose the one on the right or else reverse the apparent basis for his choice. After the choice has been made and recorded, the screen is replaced and an entirely new series of different form and color is presented, and both alternatives tried successively as before. This is continued until four different combinations of figures involving eight choices have been presented. The positions of the two upper figures should be changed systematically in such a way that a child who matches consistently on the basis of either form or color will be obliged to make his choices in the following order: left-right, right-left, left-right, right-left, *etc.*

The experimenter must exercise great care not to suggest by glance or gesture which of the two figures is to be chosen. All comments on the child's performance must be deferred until the sitting is completed, since praise for the first reactions may cause the child to attempt to make his later choices on the basis of what he conceives to have brought forth the praise, and thus modify his performance. A cheerful encouraging attitude should, however, be maintained throughout.

The experiment should be conducted in a brisk, lively fashion so as to discourage undue deliberation on the part of the subject, since it is desired to have the reaction represent the subject's first impression rather than a reasoned choice.

Problems: 1. What percentage of the total number of choices at each age are made on the basis of form? What percentage on the basis of color?

2. Draw curves showing the age changes in the comparative percentages of form and color choices.

3. What percentage of the total number of subjects at each age made all eight of their choices on the basis of form? of color? Draw curves showing age changes in the percentage of entirely consistent choices.

4. Compare these results with those obtained by Brian and Goodenough (30).

Experiment No. 11

Individual Differences in Tactual Acuity among Kindergarten Children

Prepare four samples of sandpaper ranging from very coarse to very fine. Each sample should be two inches square and should be glued to a separate base of heavy cardboard. The subject should be seated at a low table and blindfolded by the use of a pair of goggles with lenses covered with heavy paper. A paper napkin should be interposed between the child's eyes and the goggles in order to guard against possible infection. The napkin also makes it impossible to see the sandpaper from underneath the goggles.

Place two of the samples of sandpaper on the table before the child, and bring the fingers of his right hand lightly into contact with one of them. Say to him, "Here you have two pieces of sandpaper. One of them is rougher than the other. Feel them both carefully and tell me which is rougher." Move the child's fingers from one sample to the other as instructions are given. Record the choice, remove one of the samples and substitute a third. Say, "Now try these two and tell me which is rougher. Use the other hand

this time." Alternate the position of the two samples so that
the coarser one is sometimes at the right and sometimes at
the left. Do not follow an exact order in rotation, however,
since the brighter children are likely to "catch on" to such
a system and be guided by it in making their choices. Continue the experiment with each subject until each of the four
samples has been matched with each of the others twice,
once for each hand. Record the judgments for the two hands
separately. Since there are four samples there will be six
possible combinations or twelve judgments in all, six with
the left hand, six with the right.

Problems: 1. What is the correlation between the number
of correct judgments made with the right hand and the
corresponding number for the left hand? What does this
correlation suggest?

2. When the scores for the entire group are combined,
which hand shows the higher percentage of correct judgments? How reliable is the difference in the tactual acuity
of the two hands? Do the individual differences in the scores
for the two hands seem to show any relationship to handedness? If the same subjects were used, compare the results
obtained with those of Experiment 6, Chapter 14, on tapping. Otherwise a report from teacher or parent as to the
child's usual hand preference may be secured.

3. What is the relationship of tactual acuity to chronological age within the kindergarten range? If mental test
scores are available, find the relationship to mental age.
Would you conclude from these results that a test of tactual
discrimination such as this would be a useful element in an
intelligence test for kindergarten children?

4. Find the mean combined score on the two hands for
the sexes separately. How reliable is the difference obtained?

5. Draw bar diagrams showing the percentage of correct
judgments for each pair of samples.

REFERENCES

The student is referred to the following titles in the bibliography at the end of this book:

10, 30*, 225, 228, 335*.

Chapter 18

ATTENTION

THE word *attention* as used by most psychologists has two aspects, the first referring to the limitation or narrowing of the *range* of stimuli to which the subject is responding, the second having to do with the *intensity* of the response to the limited stimuli. We judge attention in others chiefly in terms of muscle tension. When the subject's eyes are fixated upon some object with only slight exploratory movements as he examines one part of it after another, we say that he is giving attention to that object. As a rule, not only the eyes but the entire body is oriented in the direction of the stimulus object, and the more complete the orientation and the greater the apparent muscular tension, the more intense we judge the attention to be.

An essential feature of the state of attention seems to be that the organism is not merely responding to a rather sharply defined stimulus object, but is, as it were, mobilized for further response. In large measure, then, attention is a *preparatory reaction,* an adjustment of the organism toward an expected event.

There is a question whether the ability to give sustained attention is generalized, in the sense that persons who attend well to situations of one kind are more likely than others to attend well to stimuli of a different kind. The question is not easy to answer, since a given stimulus may not have the same interest value or "strength" for all persons who are subjected to it. The housewife listens with eagerness to a radio talk on how to remodel last year's dresses into this year's styles, while her husband is equally absorbed in the sports page of the newspaper. If the situation were reversed, so that the woman was obliged to turn her attention to knockouts and batting averages while the husband was initiated into the intricacies of basques and boleros, each would find it far harder to keep the attention from wandering. Popular opinion, however, usually assumes that some people, either by nature or habit are "flighty," "distractible" or "absent-minded" while others have great power of "concentration." It is interesting, therefore, to see whether the individual differences shown by young children in maintaining an "attentive" attitude in a situation likely to have strong interest value for all, appear to be related to their usual habits of attention as judged by their teachers.

Experiment No. 12

Sustained Attention in Waiting for a Delayed Stimulus

Material: A series of three jack-in-the boxes, each of a different kind. The ordinary commercial boxes which can be purchased at a small cost may be used, or a home-made variety consisting of an amusing toy fastened to a coiled spring the other end of which is attached to the bottom of a wooden box with a strong hinged cover will serve the purpose. The box should be of a depth such that the spring will be depressed when the cover is fastened down, thus causing the "jack" to spring up when the cover is released. A stop-watch or ordinary watch with second hand is also needed.

Subjects: Nursery-school or kindergarten children. If possible two groups of different ages should be used in order to see what changes take place with age.

Procedure: Seat the child at a low table with the first box directly before him. Tell him to watch it carefully, without looking away for a single moment, and he will see something funny. Start the stop-watch and observe the child's eyes carefully. As soon as the attention wanders, spring the catch of the box and record the time. Follow the same procedure with the second and the third boxes, and record time for each separately. Keep a record of child's comments and note whether there is a general bodily adjustment (leaning forward in chair, shifting of position to bring body in more direct line with the box, planting of feet more firmly on floor, etc).

Problems: 1. For each group of subjects separately find the rank order correlation between the attention time on the first and second boxes, the second and the third, the first and the third. Which of these correlations is highest? Is the order of the three coefficients the same for both groups of subjects?

2. Compare the two age groups with reference to mean attention-time on each of the three boxes. Is the direction of the age-difference the same for all three boxes? Find the reliability of these differences by dividing the actual difference by its standard error as described in Chapter 16. Do the same for the total time on the three boxes.

3. For each age group separately, compare the sexes with regard to the total attention time on the three boxes. Is the difference in the same direction for both ages? Find the reliability of these differences by the method described in Chapter 16.

4. If possible have the children ranked * for attentiveness as shown in school by one or more of their teachers. Find the rank order correlation between these rankings and the total time on the three boxes. How do the correlations com-

* See Chapter 44.

pare with the usual findings for teacher's rankings in such traits as general intelligence? (243.)

REFERENCES

The student is referred to the following titles in the bibliography at the end of this book:

31, 32, 56*, 75, 138, 140*, 141*, 176, 287, 288, 290, 297.

Chapter 19

MEMORY

IN everyday speech the term *memory* is used as a kind of blanket expression covering a number of mental processes which investigation has shown to be rather loosely related to each other. For example *recall* in which the subject is required to reproduce or to describe a stimulus after it has been withdrawn is a much more difficult task than *recognition* in which he has only to select from a number of objects the one which was previously a stimulus. Either recall or recognition may be asked for immediately upon withdrawal of the stimulus (immediate reaction) or after an interval of time (delayed reaction). Somewhat different results will be obtained according to whether the particular sensory field which is stimulated is visual, auditory, tactual or what not. The difficulty of recall or recognition is also largely dependent upon whether the material to be memorized is meaningful or nonsense. For most children a sentence of 12-15 words of simple meaning can be repeated after a single hearing about as easily as a series of five unrelated digits or nonsense syllables. Many other factors might be cited but the foregoing are probably sufficient to show that the popular idea of memory as a single characteristic or method of classifying individuals is not sufficiently exact to be very useful. Instead of speaking vaguely about studies of "memory," both the kind of task set and the conditions under which it is to be carried out should be stated in all cases.

Experiment No. 13

Delayed Recall of Logical Prose Material *

Material: Select a story of approximately 400 words in length, of a kind which will be interesting and not too difficult for children of the ages to be used. Make sure that the story is one which is not already familiar to the children. Have this story mimeographed with double spacing so as to permit writing between the lines. At a number of critical points in the story an essential word or phrase which can not be filled in on the basis of context alone should be enclosed in parentheses. A separate copy of the story should be used for each child on each occasion.

Subjects: This experiment is best suited to children within the age range of three to seven years. At least three age groups should be used if possible, in order to compare developmental changes.

Procedure: Students should work in pairs, one acting as reader and the other as recorder. In order to avoid confusing the children, it is better for each student to act as reader or as recorder throughout the series of sittings with each individual child, but to alternate between the rôles of reader and recorder for different children.

The reader should sit on the floor or in a low chair beside the child with her back to the recorder. The situation is introduced by saying to the child, "You like stories, don't you? I am going to read you a story about ————" (whatever the title of the story may be). On the first day of presentation a story is read through at an ordinary rate of speed with no pauses. On each successive day thereafter, the reader should pause at the points indicated by the parentheses, look expectantly at the child, and wait from

* Procedure adapted from Foster, (74).

two to three seconds before reading the part in the parentheses. If the child fills in the pause either by supplying the correct word or by some other word or phrase, the recorder, who is supplied with one of the mimeographed sheets, should record the fact directly above the corresponding word or phrase. A plus mark may be used if a verbatim completion is given; but any changes from the stereotyped phrase should be recorded verbatim. If, on the second rereading of the story, the child does not begin to supply words spontaneously, the reader may prompt him by saying after the usual pause, "What?" The child's attempts at completion should at first be rewarded by a *"good"* from the reader, thereafter they should always be acknowledged by a smile and nod. If incorrect completions are given the reader should repeat the correct word firmly enough to show the child that his completion was not exactly right, but with no touch of a reproof which might discourage further efforts. The child should be allowed to continue telling the story as far as he is able to go on each completion until an error is made, when the reader should interrupt and read on to the next pause. The recorder meanwhile should keep an exact record of everything said by the child.

If time permits, as many as ten readings on the story may be given, but five readings (the original reading and four rereadings), each on a separate day, will be sufficient to show the general trend. After trying out several different methods of scoring these results, Foster found that the total number of *correct* words supplied by the child in any single sitting yielded the most consistent results. A word is classed as correct only when it is the verbatim expression used in telling the story.

Problems. 1. On the basis of the total number of correct words supplied at a single hearing, draw learning curves for each child separately as described in Chapter 12. If children of different ages have been used, find the average score on each repetition for each age group separately, and compare the learning curves for these ages.

2. Using the entire group of subjects, find the rank order correlation between the scores earned by each child on the first repetition as compared to the second repetition, the third repetition, and so on. Then find the correlation between the second and third repetition, the second and fourth and so on, until the correlations for all possible pairs have been worked out. As learning progresses, what general tendency is apparent in the size of the correlation coefficients between successive repetitions? Compare also the correlations between successive repetitions and those which are more widely separated.

3. All other factors being equal, one would expect that differences in attentiveness might be associated with differences in the ability to learn the story. If the same children were used in both this and the preceding experiment it will be interesting to correlate the total time for the three boxes with the total number of words supplied in all repetitions of the story. Name all the factors you think of which might account for a low relationship between these two measures. Is it known that the child who is more than usually attentive in one kind of situation will also be more than usually attentive in another situation of a different kind? What factors other than attentiveness itself might operate to affect the apparent relationship, either negatively or positively?

4. Compare the results with those given by Foster (74).

Experiment No. 14

Immediate Recall of Visually Presented Stimuli

Material: Two sets of ten familiar objects; a practice set of five other objects. There should be no duplicates. A suggested list is as follows: Practice set: a ball, a pencil, a cup, a bottle, and a book.

Set No. 1: A small doll, a spoon, a pair of scissors, a watch, an apple, a ruler, a toy horse, a pitcher, a knife, an eraser.

Set No. 2: A fork, a box, a key, a handkerchief, a toy engine, a teddy bear, a tumbler, a child's shoe, a fountain pen, an orange. Other similar objects may be substituted if more convenient. A screen with three sides large enough to conceal the objects completely is needed, also a stop-watch or ordinary watch with second hand.

Subjects: Children from three to ten years may be used.

Procedure: Arrange the objects of the practice series in a predetermined position on a low table, behind the screen. Seat child at table and say, "Behind this screen I have a lot of things for you to see. When I take the screen away you must look carefully and see what is there. Afterward I'm going to see whether you can tell me everything that is on the table, so look carefully."

At the words, "look carefully" the screen should be removed and the stop-watch started. At the end of ten seconds the screen is replaced and the experimenter says, "Now tell me what you saw." If there are any omissions, experimenter should prompt by saying "Was there anything else?" and if this does not elicit the correct reply, "Did you see the ———? And the ———?" naming omitted objects. Exact replies should be recorded.

The two regular series are then shown in the same way, the objects being arranged behind the screen as before, with care that the child does not see them before the screen is removed. If kept in a covered box, this can usually be managed without difficulty. Be sure that the arrangement of each series is kept constant for all subjects. At the end of each series, after the child has named all the objects he can remember, and has been questioned as to his memory for

the omitted objects ask, "Did you see the ———? And the
———?" *etc.*, naming five objects not actually used in any
of the experiments. These fictitious objects should be the
same for all subjects.

Records can be made most expeditiously if a mimeographed sheet is prepared on which the objects used for each
experiment are listed in order, followed by the names of the
fictitious objects. In making the records, the following symbols can then be used to indicate the child's response for
each object: S to indicate that it was named spontaneously,
previous to urging; N to indicate that it was named in response to the question "Was there anything else?"; + to
indicate an affirmative reply to the question, "Did you see
the ———?"; and — to indicate a negative reply to the
same question. Space should be left at the bottom of the
sheet to record any objects spontaneously named by the
child which were not actually shown.

Problems: 1. Find the mean number of objects spontaneously named by the children in each age group on
Series I and II combined. Draw a series of frequency surfaces on the same base line, showing the overlapping of the
scores from age to age. Do the same for the total number
named correctly with or without urging, that is, when the
S and the N responses are combined. Which method shows
the clearer distinction between age groups?

2. Find the reliability of the scores earned by each of the
two scoring methods, by correlating the number of objects
named on Series I with the number named on Series II,
and correcting by the Spearman-Brown formula. Which
scoring method yields the more consistent results?

3. Compare the age changes in the positive replies to the
"suggestibility" questions when the results of the two series
are combined. Is there evidence of a sex difference in suggestibility as shown by (a) the consistency of the direction

of the differences between the sexes from age to age, or (b) the reliability of the difference between the means for the sexes when the ages are combined?

4. For each age group separately, compare the mean number of positive replies to the "suggestibility" questions made by the children whose memory scores were above the median for their age group with those whose scores were below the median.

5. Is there any evidence of transference from one experimental situation to another, *i.e.*, are there instances when an object actually shown in an earlier experiment is named in a later experiment? Is there any relationship between such transference and the number of objects correctly named? the number of positive replies to the "suggestibility" questions?

6. Arrange the objects used in order of size, using the mean judgment of the class to settle doubtful cases. Find the correlation between the size of the object and the total number of times it was correctly named.

7. If the same children were used in this and in the preceding experiment on verbal memory, find the correlation between their combined scores on the two series (using the scoring method which was found to have the higher reliability) and the total number of words correctly supplied in all sittings combined. What do the results suggest as to the relationship between memory performances of different kinds? (Age groups should be kept separate).

REFERENCES

The student is referred to the following titles in the bibliography at the end of this book:

10, 14, 42, 74*, 101, 115, 155*, 177, 179, 234, 299, 309, 311, 335*, 378.

Chapter 20

THE DEVELOPMENT OF LOGICAL THINKING OR PROBLEM SOLVING

EVERYDAY observation of children when confronted with problems affords striking evidence of the extent to which their immaturity and their lack of experience combine to affect their thought processes. To the little child "time's arrow" is not fixed or unchangeable. An event may precede as well as succeed its cause, the relationships of "yesterday" and "tomorrow" are not clearly distinguished or an intent may be "discovered" by the child only after he has completed an act. It is worth while, therefore to endeavor to develop methods whereby the sequence of development in logical thinking may be traced.

One approach to the study of thought processes is to present a series of problems for solution and observe and classify the methods by which children of different levels of development attempt to solve them. In so doing, we may depend either upon the child's verbal reactions or upon his overt behavior in situations offering a considerable possibility of variation in response.

In Experiment No. 15 the first method is used; in Experiment No. 16 the second.

Experiment No. 15

Problem Solving in Children of Different Ages *

Material: Thirty squares of cardboard prepared as follows: Six of the squares are to have on one side a plain con-

* Adapted from Heidbreder. (122).

186

ventional figure drawn in outline in black ink, using the following designs, a circle, a diamond, a triangle, a clover, a star, and a cross. On the reverse side of each of these squares is to be pasted a large red or gold star or some other interesting device. A duplicate set of six cards is to be prepared without the star. Six other squares are to bear the same figures with a small flower drawn in red ink added in the center. These also have a star on the reverse side. A third set should contain the same series of figures as the first set, and in addition a series of red dots around the edge of each card. Again, one set of six should have a star on the reverse side which is omitted from the duplicate set.

Subjects: If possible, three groups of subjects should be used, one of three-year-old children, one of five-year-old kindergarten children, and one of children from the fifth or sixth grade. Each student should try the experiment with one or more children in each age group.

Procedure: * 1. The squares with plain conventional figures are used for the first problem. The child is seated at a table facing the experimenter who first shows him some of the materials and says, "Do you see these cards? They have pictures on the front and some of them have something on the back, too. Look and see what is on the back." After the child has examined several of the cards, both with and without stars, the experimenter says, "Now we are going to play a guessing game. I shall show you two of the cards and see if you can tell me which one has the star." A screen is then interposed, behind which two of the squares are arranged corner to corner. The square on the right-hand side nearer the child has a star; the other has not.

* The method followed by Heidbreder (122) has been somewhat shortened in order to make it possible to secure all the data at a single sitting without unduly fatiguing the subjects. As a result a smaller number of solutions may be expected than were found by Heidbreder.

The screen is then removed, and the experimenter says, "Which one do you think has the star?" As soon as the child indicates his choice he is told to see whether he was right. The experimenter then asks, "What made you think it was that one?" or "How did you know which one to take?" Each successive choice is recorded as + or — and the reason for the choice is recorded verbatim. The situation is repeated five times using different cards, with the arrangement the same, that is, the square with the star always in the nearer right-hand corner. After each choice the child should be asked to state his reason for making it. However he should not be urged too strongly if he says he does not know. After five presentations the arrangement is changed. The left-hand square is now placed nearer the child, and the right-hand square farther away. Again, the right-hand square is to be chosen. This should be continued until five successive arrangements have been shown.

These two arrangements are then presented in random order until ten successive reactions have been made. The problem is considered solved if the last five or more reactions are all correct, that is, if the right-hand square is taken regardless of whether it is the nearer or the farther, or if the correct verbal solution is given on the last three or more trials.

2. Two kinds of squares are used for this problem, those with plain figures without the star, and those with red flowers in the center of the figure and with the star on the back. The solution consists in choosing the square with the flowered design, regardless of its position. In the first five situations the flowered square is placed on the right of the plain one, then the flowered square is placed to the left for five trials, after which the two arrangements are given in random order for ten trials as before. Procedure and rules for determining solutions are the same as in Situation A.

3. Again two kinds of squares are used, those with the plain figures and those which have red dots around the border. In the first five presentations two squares with plain figures are used, one immediately behind the other, the star always on the further square. In the next five presentations the squares with dots are used with the same arrangement, except that the star is always on the nearer square. The two kinds of situation are then presented in random order for ten trials. The solution consists in always taking the farther square if the plain figures are used, and the nearer square if the dotted figures are used.

Problems. 1. Compare the age groups with reference to the proportion of children in each who solve each of the three problems. Is the order of difficulty as indicated by the percentage of children making correct solutions the same for both age groups?

2. Compare the age groups with reference to the percentage of the total number of reactions on each problem for which reasons of any kind were given. In what percentage of the cases was the correct reason clearly stated at the end of the series?

3. What percentage of the reasons given by the children of each age group fall within each of the following classes:

a. Reasons based on observations after the action, such as "Because it had the star on it."

b. Non-specific reasons, such as "Because I drew it," or "I just guessed it."

c. Reasons based on preferences or aesthetic values, such as, "Because I liked that one best," or "Because it is pretty."

d. Reasons based on particular features without indication of preference such as "The one with the cross," or "Because it has a flower on it."

e. Reasons based on spatial features or relationships, in

which a word or a gesture shows that the spatial factor is the basis for the reaction. Examples: "The one on this side" (pointing), or "The one on the right."

f. Reasons based on past success or failure, as "Because it was right before," or "Because last time I took the other one and it was wrong."

g. Social reasons, such as "Because I thought you'd try to fool me and make it different this time."

Which class of reasons is most commonly given by the younger children? By the older children? Compare with results secured by Heidbreder.

Experiment No. 16
The Solving of Problem Situations by Nursery-School Children

Apparatus and arrangement: From the ceiling of the laboratory, suspend an animal cracker at such a height that it will be about eight to twelve inches beyond the reach of the child to be tested. At a distance of about six feet from the cracker place a low chair on which is laid a ruler, and about half way between the chair and the cracker place side by side two boxes, the combined height of which when piled one on another will enable the child to reach the cracker although either one alone is too low.

Subjects: Nursery-school children, preferably under four-and-a-half years.

Procedure: Bring the children into the room one at a time. Say, "Do you like animal crackers? There is one which you may have if you can get it." Start the stop-watch and record child's reactions, including verbal responses as they occur, together with time of occurrence. Give no suggestions, but encourage child from time to time by saying "I think you can get it if you try." Allow a total time of five minutes for each child. If he succeeds in getting the cracker before the end of the five minutes send him back to the class-room and bring in another child. On the following day, repeat the experiment with the same children and compare responses.

Problems: 1. What percentage of the children at each age succeed in getting the cracker on the first day? On the second day? Did any who succeeded on the first day fail on the second? What percentage of the children who succeeded made use of the chair? Of the boxes? Of the ruler?

2. Among the children who succeeded what was the mean time required for success?

3. In what proportion of the successful cases was an unsuccessful method tried first?

4. List all the unsuccessful methods, and see if you can work out a scheme for classifying them as was done for the reasons in the preceding experiment.

5. Compare the reactions of the children with those of the apes studied by Köhler (157) and with those of the children used in Alpert's experiment (1).

REFERENCES

The student is referred to the following titles in the bibliography at the end of this book:

1*, 28, 122*, 123*, 157*, 175, 189, 203, 204*, 205, 319, 330, 335.

Chapter 21

LEARNING AND HABIT FORMATION

WITH increasing practice, children become more expert in the performance of various acts. The infant when given a spoon for the first time uses it awkwardly and makes many unnecessary movements. After an interval in which he has handled the spoon many times much improvement in the facility and ease with which he manipulates it can be observed. We say that he has *learned* to use a spoon, and speak of the process by which this ability has been gained as the *acquisition of skill*. Since the greater part of his active life will be spent in the acquisition of skills, the study of the manner in which they are developed has great practical significance as well as much scientific interest.

The transition from the slow, awkward performance of the beginner to the smooth running, almost automatic movements which characterize the later stages in the learning process may be analyzed in several ways. One of the most useful and readily understood methods of analysis is found in the graphic representation of the course of learning by means of *learning curves*.

Learning curves. If a beginner who is learning to typewrite keeps an exact account of the number of letters written correctly in a standard period of time on each day of practice, and then plots the results on cross-section paper with the abscissa of the curve representing the successive days of practice and the ordinate showing the number of words written each day, he is likely to secure results similar to those shown in Fig. 17. The curve rises somewhat more rapidly during the first few days of practice than it does later on. If practice is continued long enough, eventually a point is reached at which little or no further gain is made. We speak of this point as the *physiological limit*, since its position seems to be determined chiefly by physiological factors such as speed of reaction, muscular control, *etc.*

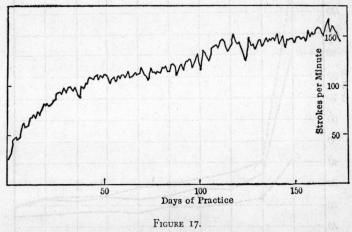

FIGURE 17.

Learning curve for one subject practising typewriting (after Book).

In such complex tasks as typewriting, the physiological limit is commonly reached only after a rather long period of training. If a somewhat simpler task is set, such as tracing a maze, the physiological limit is reached much sooner and the rapid improvement during the earlier stages, with slowing off in rate of gain during later trials, shows up more clearly. (See Fig. 18). In the learning of complex motor skills which involve the simultaneous coördination and coöperation of many muscles (such as ball tossing, golf, throwing at a moving target, *etc.*) the limit of improvement is reached, if at all, only after very prolonged practice, and the learning curve is likely to be marked by many irregularities. These irregularities include: (a) "plateaus" when no appreciable advance seems to be made for prolonged periods, (b) regressive periods, when the temporary setting

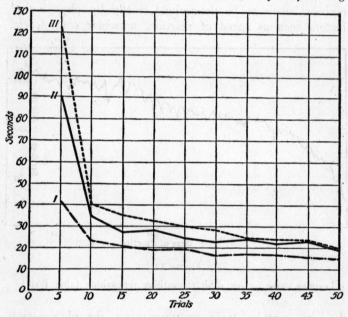

FIGURE 18.

Learning curves for children on Young Slot Maze. From McGinnis (173).
I = 3 year olds, II = 4 year olds, III = 5 year olds

up of a bad habit results in the performance becoming steadily worse, and (c) periods of rapid gain when the correction of a single factor which has been retarding progress suddenly makes apparent the improvement which has been taking place all along in other parts of the total performance. (Fig. 19.)

In many of the experimental situations used for the study of learning, the reliability of the score earned on a single trial is not high. As a result, the curves plotted from the original data show many fluctuations which may partially obscure the general trend. It is customary, therefore, to subject these curves to a process known as *smoothing,* the purpose of which is to average the day-to-day fluctuations and

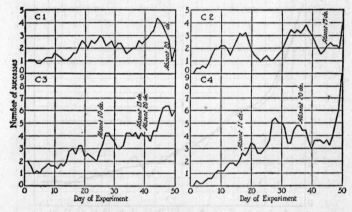

FIGURE 19.

Learning curves for individual children in ring-tossing. From Goodenough and Brian (110).

thus bring out the general form of the curve more clearly. A number of methods of smoothing or "curve-fitting" are in use, but for our purposes a relatively simple procedure known as smoothing by the *method of a moving average* will be sufficient. We may illustrate it as follows: Suppose that the number of seconds required by John Doe to trace a finger-maze such as is described in the next experiment were as follows: 278, 210, 156, 138, 140, 129, 110, 80, 92, 74, 69, 40, 71, 52, 47, 36, 40, 29, 35, 31.

If the data are plotted as they stand, the resulting curve

would be that shown by the light line in Fig. 20. While this curve shows clearly that much improvement has taken place in the course of the twenty trials, there are a number of irregularities which are probably the result of chance factors. If this assumption is correct, the more regular curve in Figure 20 which was obtained by averaging the scores in

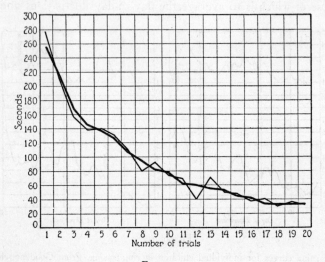

FIGURE 20.

Illustrating the effect of smoothing by means of a moving average.

adjacent trials depicts the rate of progress in a more truthful manner.

The optimum number of scores entering into each successive average depends upon the amount of day-to-day fluctuation. If the data are very irregular, as many as seven adjacent scores may be averaged. However, this is somewhat hazardous since true changes in the form of the curve, resulting from factors which are not chance and the nature of which might be revealed by a more careful analysis may thereby be obscured. For this reason, the number of scores to be averaged should not as a rule exceed five, and in most cases three is sufficient. In the example given the smoothing has been done by threes as follows: For the first smoothed score the original first score is multiplied by 2 (since there is no preceding score to be used in averaging) and to this is added the second score. The sum is then divided by 3 and the result recorded as the first score in the column of smoothed values. The second point in the curve is obtained by taking the mean of the first, second, and third raw scores; the third point is the mean of the second, third, and fourth raw scores, *etc.* If a five point instead of a three point smoothing had been used, the method would have been very similar. The first point would have been obtained by multiplying the first raw score by 3, adding the second and the third score and dividing by 5. The second point would be $1/5$ the sum of twice the first score + twice the second score + the third score. The third point would be the mean of the first five raw scores, *etc.* Note that by this method each point on the smoothed curve is based upon an average of an equal number of the scores preceding and following it. Hence an odd rather than an even number of scores should be used in computing the successive averages. As the end of the curve is approached, a weighting system corresponding to that used at the beginning should be employed.

Exercises: Plot each of the following learning curves in three ways: (a) from the original unsmoothed data, (b) by a three point moving average, (c) by a five point moving average. Which method seems to you to give the most truthful picture in each case? Why?

1. Time in seconds required for each trial in learning to trace a maze. 456, 328, 320, 156, 236, 204, 140, 118, 97, 82, 80, 61, 75, 73, 51, 29, 46, 32, 49, 22.

2. Time in seconds required for 20 successive sortings of a pack of 100 cards according to pattern. 37, 38, 31, 34, 28, 32, 27, 24, 28, 30, 21, 19, 22, 23, 18, 15, 17, 20, 14, 12.

3. Number of successes made in trying to toss a ring over a wooden post, allowing 20 trials per day for 20 days. 1, 0, 3, 0, 0, 2, 1, 4, 4, 5, 3, 1, 0, 0, 0, 1, 5, 7, 6, 10.

Are the learning curves for the three tasks described similar in form? Compare with those shown in the references at the end of this chapter.

Experiment No. 17

A Comparison of Maze Learning in Children and Adults

Material: A multiple T maze of the high relief type. A screen or goggles and paper napkins for blindfolding. Stopwatch.

The maze can easily be constructed by the students themselves according to the directions given by Miles (182). From a lumber dealer secure a panel of three-ply cedar wood from 16 to 18 inches square. Secure a length of German silver wire, No. 14 in size (one-sixteenth of an inch in diameter) and cut into lengths, each of which is about three-fourths of an inch longer than the separate units to be used in the maze pattern. Using a pair of pliers, bend the ends into long square cornered staples. These ends may then be driven into the wood in such a way as to form the pattern (182). After the pattern has been completed drop a bit of solder at each joint and rub with emery paper so as to form a smooth path. Rubber feet which may be obtained at any furniture store should be placed on the back of the panel at each of the four corners to prevent slipping when the board is placed on a table. The starting point is marked by a single small staple driven astride the main wire; the goal by two staples fastened in the same way.* Each cul-de-sac is numbered.

Subjects: Each student should arrange to have the maze learned by one child of five or six years and by one adult who has never seen the pattern.

Procedure: The subject is first blindfolded unless the learning is to be done under a screen. In either case it is essential that he does not see the maze at any time until the learning has been completed. The subject is seated at a table of comfortable height, with the maze before him. His forefinger is put on the starting point of a small practice maze in the corner. The experimenter then says:

"I am going to see how quickly you can follow this wire with your finger to a place where there are two wires on top of the main wire. Move your finger along the wire without taking it off until you find this place and I will keep track of the time it takes you. If you come to a place where your finger slips off the end, that means you have taken the wrong turning and you will have to go back until you get on the right track again. When I say 'Go' start and go as fast as you can till you find the place which has two wires on top of the other wire.† Do you understand? All right, go!"

When the sample maze has been traced twice, the experimenter places the subject's finger on the starting point of the main maze and says, "Now we are going to do a bigger one. You will have to go quite a long way to find the two wires in this one but keep on trying and pretty soon you will get there. Remember that when your finger slips

* Or a small iron toy may be set at the goal by means of a thumb-tack soldered to its base. This adds interest to the task for young children, particularly if several different toys are used and the child does not know in advance which one he is going to find.

† If a toy is used to mark the goal, instructions should of course be changed accordingly.

off the end, you are on the wrong track and must go back until you find the right way. All ready, go!"

Start the stop-watch as soon as the subject's finger begins to move. Record all errors as they occur, using the numbers marked on the board. Take time to the nearest whole second for each trial. Allow five trials a day for a total of five days, or better, if time permits, until five successive errorless trials have been made. Exactly the same procedure should be followed for children and adults.

Problems: 1. Using the time scores, draw learning curves (both smoothed and unsmoothed) for each of the individual subjects separately, also for the combined scores for each group of subjects. Are the individual curves or the group curves more even and regular? Why?

2. Place the smoothed curves for the children (combined scores) and the adults on the same base so as to facilitate comparison. Compare the two groups as to (a) mean initial speed, (b) rapidity of learning as shown by steepness of slope, and (c) final level reached.

3. Do the same for the error scores. What is the mean total number of errors made by each group in the course of 25 trials?

4. What is the mean number of errors made on each cul-de-sac by each group? Find the rank order correlation between the relative difficulty of the cul-de-sacs for children and adults. Does this correlation suggest that certain cul-de-sacs are intrinsically more difficult than others? What features seem to be characteristic of the difficult cul-de-sacs? Of the easy ones? Consider particularly whether a cul-de-sac leads toward or away from the goal, whether it occurs near the beginning, middle, or end of the maze pattern, whether it leads inward (toward the median line of the body) or outward, *etc.* Find the reliability of any differences which seem well marked.

REFERENCES

The student is referred to the following titles in the bibliography at the end of this book:

10, 88, 89, 97, 137, 144, 173*, 182*, 269, 280*, 292*, 330, 339.

Chapter 22

THE ACQUISITION OF COMPLEX SKILLS

IN learning complex skills such as ball tossing, tennis, or golf the task not only involves a linking up of responses formerly learned into a new sequence but also learning to integrate actions previously used independently or in other and different combinations into a new form of organization. In golf or bowling not only must a number of actions be carried out simultaneously but these organized groups of reactions must follow each other in a rhythmic sequence in which the time relations are quite as important as the order. In such an organization involving the coördinated action of many different muscle-groups an error in any part of the action disrupts the total. Because of the number of coördinations involved and the inflexibility of the time relations, learning curves for the acquisition of complex motor skills rise slowly. Occasional periods when there is no measurable advance or even an apparent loss in efficiency may occur.

Because of the length of time required to secure meaningful results, studies in the acquisition of complex skills are not well adapted to general class demonstration. If time and opportunity permit it will be worth while for those members of the class who have continued access to one or two children to carry out an experiment such as the one about to be described, in order to analyze the factors influencing the child's progress in the manner indicated here.

Goodenough and Brian (110) had twenty four-year-old

children practice throwing rings over a post set at a distance of about five feet. Ten of the children were given practice without instruction or criticism; six were given verbal instruction and criticism but were not required to adhere to a constant method of holding and throwing the rings; while four were taught a definite procedure in throwing and were not permitted to experiment with any other method. Each child was given twenty trials per day for a period of fifty days. The children in the third group who were required to adhere to a constant procedure throughout the experimental period showed distinctly greater improvement than either of the other two groups. The most interesting results, however, were obtained not from the comparison of the group curves but from an analysis of the individual records in the light of certain general factors which were found to hold good for the group as a whole. These analyses were made possible by very careful records of the daily performances of the children.

In order to facilitate record-taking, the floor of the room in which the experiment was carried out was first divided into quadrants by means of lines drawn with chalk which intersected at the post over which the rings were to be thrown, while distance from the post was indicated roughly by means of concentric circles drawn with the post as a center. Mimeographed duplicates of the floor plan were prepared and used as the daily records sheets for each child. Records were taken by writing the serial number of each throw in the space on the record sheet corresponding to the point on the floor on which the ring fell when thrown. Thus if the child's first throw struck in the farther left quadrant between the first and second of the concentric circles, the number 1 was written in the corresponding space on the record blank; if the second struck in the near right quadrant within the smallest circle, the number 2 was written in that space on the blank, and so on until all twenty throws had been recorded. In addition, careful observation and record was made of the child's manner of holding and throwing the rings, his apparent interest and effort, and any other pertinent factors, together with verbatim records of all remarks and comments on the situation or on his own performance.

In this experiment the rings used were made of ¾″ manilla rope joined with adhesive tape. They were 7 inches in diameter. The post was 6 inches in height and was fastened to a heavy oak platform 12″ x 14″ x 1″. In carrying out the individual experiments suggested, if smaller rings are used the distance should be shortened somewhat to allow for the added difficulty. The optimum distance will depend both upon the size of the rings and the age of the subjects.

A statistical analysis of the results obtained for the group as a whole seemed to warrant the following conclusions:

There was practically no relationship between gain in skill and initial score, or between total score earned during the fifty days performance and intelligence test standing.

Boys made significantly higher scores than girls.

Improvement in skill occurred in the course of the daily practice periods as shown by the fact that the last five of the twenty trials included 13.6 per cent more successes than the first five.

The results suggest that the effect of interruption of practice through absence is differential, varying according to whether the habits which are being formed at the time of the absence are favorable or unfavorable to success. If an absence occurs at a time when the child's performance is showing rapid improvement through the establishment of good methods of throwing, considerable loss in skill may result; but if the absence occurs when the setting up of bad habits is retarding progress, the effect may be quite favorable, since the interruption of practice permits the bad habits to become weakened through disuse.

The effect of the pleasurable emotion aroused by success was shown in a much greater tendency to throw beyond the mark in the case of those errors following a successful throw. Apparently the delight ensuing upon success caused the children to throw the rings with greater vigor than was displayed after unsuccessful attempts.

The way in which these and other recorded factors seemed to affect individual performance is illustrated in the following descriptive accounts of the performances of three children in the group who were given no instruction or criticism. Table 12 shows the daily records of these children expressed in terms of the number of successful throws per day. These records should be subjected to a five point smoothing as described in Chapter 21. The learning curves should then be plotted and compared with the descriptive accounts.[*]

"Subject 1A made seven correct throws on his first day of practice, which is a greater number than was made at the start by any other child in the group. Although his mother was quite certain that P—— had never played with it, a small ring toss game had been packed away with some discarded toys in the family attic, hence it is possible that there had been some previous practice in this case. He was extremely proud of his superior performance and boasted about it repeatedly. 'I get more ringers than anybody else, don't I?' 'Gee! what a lot of stickers I have on my card!' were frequent comments during the first few days. For the first three days his errors were nearly equally divided between overthrows and underthrows. On the fourth day a pronounced tendency toward overthrowing became apparent, with 9 out of 13 errors overthrown. This tendency increased steadily until during the period from the thirteenth to the

[*] Quoted from Goodenough and Brian (110).

TABLE 12

DAILY RECORDS OF THREE FOUR-YEAR-OLD CHILDREN IN LEARNING A RING-TOSS GAME

	SUBJECTS				SUBJECTS		
Day	1A	6A	9A	Day	1A	6A	9A
1	7	1	3	26	2	2	4
2	2	0	1	27	2	2	4
3	3	0	1	28	3	1	8
4	7	1	0	29	5	3	4
5	4	1	2	30	1	0	2
6	3	0	1	31	6	1	2
7	5	0	1	32	1	3	7
8	2	1	1	33	5	3	6
9	3	2	1	34	2	3	6
10	1	0	2	35	3	1	6
11	2	1	0	36	0	2	6
12	2	1	2	37	5	4	7
13	1	0	0	38	1	1	5
14	2	0	3	39	1	0	2
15	4	1	3	40	1	3	8
16	0	2	5	41	4	6	1
17	1	1	0	42	3	3	4
18	2	1	4	43	3	1	3
19	2	0	4	44	4	3	4
20	3	0	4	45	0	0	3
21	2	0	5	46	2	3	6
22	1	1	3	47	2	1	1
23	0	0	4	48	3	7	5
24	4	1	4	49	2	2	6
25	7	3	8	50	1	0	6

seventeenth days inclusive, 73 out of 92 errors were overthrown. About this time new charts were given out, P——'s array of stickers no longer presented so imposing an appearance, and his self-confidence began to wane. 'I hope I'll get a lot to-day,' or 'Maybe I can get better to-morrow,' are characteristic remarks of this period. Overthrowing became much less frequent, dropping to 47 per cent of the total number of errors made between the 20th and 24th days. On the 18th day he had discovered for himself that the rings balanced better if held at the point of junction. From that time on he continued to be very punctilious about this point, frequently remarking "I must always take them here, mustn't I?" This discovery, together with correction of the tendency to overthrow the mark, apparently accounts for the rise in the curve at this point. The second falling off in performance which began about the 35th day, and, with the exception of a brief period of improvement around the 40th day, continued to the end of the practice period appeared to be the result of a curious association of meaning with the word *careful* which to him seemed to be synonymous with *gentle*. 'I must be careful today, mustn't I?' he would say repeatedly. Taking the ring gingerly between finger and thumb he would toss it with the utmost gentleness, with the result that it often fell a considerable distance short of the mark. He appeared to see no connection between his *carefulness* and the resultant error; and on several occasions remarked after a failure of this sort, 'I'll be carefuller this time,' and repeated the performance exactly. During the last eight days of the practice period, 75 per cent of the errors were underthrown. It is not known how this peculiar verbal association arose, as the expression had not been used by the experimenter at any time."

"This case furnishes an interesting example of retrogressive learning through the setting up of incorrect modes of response in spite of excellent effort on the part of the subject. Interest was apparently very keen throughout the experimental period; he was always eager to come to the laboratory to "play the ringer game," was delighted at each successful throw and disappointed at each failure. Indeed, this very interest appears to have reacted unfavorably for success in his case; first through creating over-self-confidence, and later on through the development of undue anxiety and caution."

"Subject 6A at first threw the rings with a decided twist of the wrist, producing a whirling movement by which the rings often fell almost at her feet. From this she changed to raising the rings high above her head, then throwing them downward with much force but little attention to the angle at which they were held, so that they frequently struck upon the edge. For the first twenty-three days she alternated from one to the other of these methods, during which time her curve shows but little progress. An eleven day vacation then intervened, and on the first day after her return she spontaneously adopted an overhand pitch which was quite different from either of her former methods. She adhered to this method until the end of the practice period and made steady improvement throughout. Special inquiry was made at the home to ascertain whether or not any instruction or practice had been given during the vacation period. There had been none. It seems, therefore, that the chief importance of the eleven day interval lay in the fact that it permitted the former undesirable habits to become weakened through disuse, so that a new method was more readily adopted."

"Subject 9A, after a brief period of experimentation, developed a constant method of holding and throwing the rings to which she adhered throughout the experimental period. She was careful to grasp the rings at the point of juncture, raised them shoulder high, and threw downward. Steady improvement was shown, except for a single brief drop which coincided with certain unusual activities elsewhere and may have been an expression of slight fatigue. With this exception, improvement continued steadily until after the Christmas vacation, when there is a marked drop in efficiency which is only just beginning to be made up at the end of the experimental period. This record, taken in conjunction with those of Subjs. 6A and 7A, suggests that interruption of practice in the acquisition of a motor habit may function either to the advantage or disadvantage of the learning individual, according as the particular habits which are in process of formation are desirable or undesirable. If the subject is improving his efficiency, a temporary discontinuance of practice may result in a loss of skill previously attained. If, on the other hand, continued practice is operating merely to fix undesirable habits more firmly, a period without practice, which permits the undesirable habits to become weakened through disuse, may be the best possible preparation for the establishment of more desirable habits."

REFERENCES

The student is referred to the following titles in the bibliography at the end of this book:

10, 87, 110*, 127, 128*, 155, 173, 308, 310, 330, 339.

Chapter 23

LANGUAGE DEVELOPMENT

LEARNING to talk may fairly be called the most important single developmental process which takes place in the human infant. Man shares most of his abilities with the lower animals; but in the possession of an organized system of language he is unique. In man, the use of language is so intimately tied up with thought processes that some psychologists have put forth the view that the two are identical—that thinking is merely subvocal speech. Whether or not this is literally correct, it is clearly true that words act as convenient symbols without which the formation of clear ideas would be greatly hampered. Language is thus a *symbolic process* by which simple vocalizations or groups of written characters function in place of the cumbersome material objects or the time consuming acts for which they are substituted. We use language symbols so easily and glibly that it does not often occur to us how inconvenient it would be if we were forced to employ the complete actions or real objects signified by these linguistic symbols. Through the use of language, moreover, we are able to deal with abstractions, generalizations, qualities and attributes as easily as with the concrete material objects in our environment.

In this connection it is most enlightening to read Helen Keller's account of her mental life before the acquisition of language, and of the rapid expansion of her ideas and thought processes as new words were learned. After reading her reminiscences of this period it is hard to escape the conclusion that whether or not thought processes are identical with language processes, the use of language symbols greatly facilitates and clarifies the formation of ideas, while in the absence of language, thought is greatly hampered.

Thus far, we have considered language only in its relation to the individual. But man is a social being, and there can be little doubt that social interaction has played a dominant rôle in the development of civilization. Whether we are interested in the individual or the group, in mental organization or social relationships, the study of language behavior offers one of the most promising means of investigation. It is doubtful whether any other source of data lends itself to so many different uses, or affords an equally adequate means of obtaining insight into complex aspects of human behavior. For this reason, it is worth while to examine the techniques available for the study of language with much care.

In the study of any form of behavior, the first problem with which we are confronted is that of reducing our descriptive accounts of observed events to quantitative terms. In the earlier studies of language development, complete vocabulary records covering the first few years of life were kept for a number of cases. Although this method is valuable if time and opportunity permit, it is evidently not suited to the study of large groups of unselected children for the purpose of establishing developmental standards. Moreover, vocabulary studies alone do not throw light on the functional or social aspects of language from which important inferences with reference to personality, interests, *etc.*, may often be drawn. For this purpose, larger language units such as sentences and continuous conversation are needed.

A method which has shown itself to be serviceable both for the purpose of furnishing quantitative data on language development *per se,* and as a means of classifying language behavior on a functional or social basis has been developed by McCarthy (170). It is described in the following experiment.

Experiment No. 18

Language Behavior of Children in a Controlled Situation

Material: A number of interesting toys and picture books. The following were used by McCarthy: a little red automobile, a cat that squeaked, a telephone with a bell, a little tin mouse, a music box and a small ball. Two picture books were also used. The first which was preferred by the younger children contained pictures of animals, usually with one central object in each picture. The other contained group pictures illustrating various Mother Goose rhymes. It is probable that minor changes from this list will not materially affect results.

Subjects: If comparison is to be made with McCarthy's standards, children should be selected at a time within two weeks of the yearly or half-yearly birthday. However, if this is not convenient, interpolation can be made with fair accuracy. Children between the ages of 18 and 54 months should be used. Each student should secure data on three children: a two-year-old, a three-year-old, and a four-year-old.

Procedure: Each child should be tested individually in a familiar environment (home or nursery-school). After enough preliminary conversation to insure freedom of response the experimenter says: "I have some things to show you. Which would you like to see first—toys or picture?" In most cases a preference will be indicated, but if not, the experimenter presents the toy which seems best suited to the age, sex, and apparent interest of the child. If this fails to bring forth verbal response within a minute or two another toy is produced. No constant order is followed in presenting the material.

After showing the first toy, every verbal response or expressive vocalization should be recorded verbatim. This is continued until 50 consecutive responses have been secured. If a response is incomprehensible (as will be true with some of the younger children) it should be recorded phonetically as nearly as possible. This should also be done in the case of incomprehensible elements in semi-comprehensible responses. A single response is defined as (1) each complete sentence in continuous conversation, or (2) any response, whether or not it is a complete sentence, which is set off by distinct pauses, or (3) incomplete sentences in practically continuous conversation which are clearly set off as distinct language units by reason of their content.

Since the aim is to secure *spontaneous* responses, the child is addressed as little as possible during the observation. In the case of very quiet or unresponsive children it may be necessary to stimulate conversation by remarks or questions. If this is done, all such remarks should also be recorded and the responses classified as *elicited* rather than spontaneous.

The time required to secure the 50 responses should be recorded to the nearest minute in all cases.

Analysis of individual records: 1. Quantitative analysis. Classify the responses as incomprehensible, semi-comprehensible (in which some words, but not all, could be understood) and *entirely comprehensible*. Prepare frequency distributions for the comprehensible responses, showing for each child the number of one word responses, two word responses, three word responses, *etc*. Find for each subject (a) the mean length of response, (b) the total number of words used including repetitions, (c) the total number of different words used, (d) length of longest sentence used,

(e) the most typical sentence length (the crude mode).* These figures should be based on the comprehensible responses only. Find also the per cent of the total number of responses falling within each of the three main classes: comprehensible, semi-comprehensible, and incomprehensible.

2. Functional analysis: Classify each comprehensible response according to McCarthy's (170) modification of the Piaget analysis (203). A brief outline of the method used by McCarthy is given below.

A. Egocentric speech.
   (1) Repetition or echolalia
   (2) Monologue
   (3) Dual or collective monologue
B. Socialized speech
   (1) Adapted information
      (a) Naming
      (b) Remarks about the immediate situation
      (c) Remarks associated with the situation
      (d) Irrelevant remarks
   (2) Criticism
   (3) Emotionally-toned responses
   (4) Questions
   (5) Answers
   (6) Social phrases
   (7) Dramatic imitation

"By *egocentric speech* Piaget means that in which the audience is disregarded. The child talks either for himself or for the pleasure of associating any one who happens to be there with the activity of the moment. He speaks only about himself and makes no attempt to place himself at the point of view of his hearer."

* The crude mode is the class interval in a frequency distribution which includes the greatest number of frequencies.

"*Repetition* or echolalia means repetition of words and syllables for the pleasure of talking, with no thought of talking to any one, nor even, at times, of saying words that will make sense. *Monologue* occurs when the child talks to himself as though he were thinking aloud, without addressing any one. In *dual or collective monologue* an outsider is always associated with the thought or action of the moment, but is expected neither to hear nor to understand. The point of view of the hearer is never taken into account. The child talks about himself without collaboration with his audience or without evoking dialog."

"*Socialized speech* occurs when the child addresses his hearer or considers his point of view, tries to influence him or actually exchanges ideas with his hearer. The first category of socialized speech, according to Piaget, is *adapted information* in which the child really exchanges his thought with others, either by telling him something that will interest him, influence his action, or by actual interchange of ideas." The four sub-categories are adequately defined by their titles. *Criticism* applies either to objects or persons. *Emotionally toned responses* includes commands, requests, threats, "wish-words" and also single word sentences uttered with a decided emotional inflection. *Questions* include all sentences having an interrogative function, whether or not they are expressed in interrogative form, but do not include declarative sentences with an interrogation added as a matter of form or simply for approval or affirmation, as "I made it go, didn't I?" *Answers* includes all elicited responses except those made in response to remarks which were not questions. The latter are usually classified under *adapted information. Social phrases* includes expressions which occur only in social situations which the child has been taught to say parrot fashion, as "thank you," "by-bye," *etc. Dramatic imitation* includes all talk in imitation of the conversation of adults such as imaginative conversation, also imitation of the sounds made by animals, trains, *etc.*" *

The student should prepare a table showing the number of sentences for each child falling within each functional category.

3. Construction analysis: Classify each response under one of the following heads: (a) incomplete sentences, in which essential structural elements are missing in a way not sanctioned by adult usage as "doggie bark" (for "the doggie is barking," or "will bark," *etc.*); (b) sentences which are functionally complete but structurally incomplete when the construction is also employed by adults, as "All finished, now?" or "Bad weather to-day," (c) sentences which are complete both structurally and functionally though they may contain grammatical errors. The last group should be further subdivided into (1) simple sentences without a phrase, (2) simple sentences with one phrase, (3) sentences with two or more coördinate clauses without modifying phrases, (4) complex sentences with one dependent clause and no phrases, (5) elaborated sentences containing at least three clauses or phrases (including the major clause). Prepare a table showing the number of sentences for each child falling within each structural category.

4. Word analysis: Classify each word used according to the part of speech (noun, pronoun, *etc.*). Prepare a table showing the number and percentage of each part of speech used by each child, basing the frequencies both on the total number of words used including repetitions of the same word and on the total number of different words excluding repetitions.

Class problems: After the individual tables have been prepared, results for the entire class may be combined, keeping ages and sexes separate. Using these results compute:

* Quoted from McCarthy (170), pp. 39-42.

1. The mean length of sentence used by children at each age. McCarthy's results are given below for comparison.

2. The mean total number of different words used at each age. Compare with McCarthy.

3. Sex differences in mean length of sentence; in mean number of different words used.

4. Percentile graphs for each age based upon the combined frequency distributions for length of response.

TABLE 13

MEAN NUMBER OF WORDS PER RESPONSE BY CHRONOLOGICAL AGE AND SEX

From McCarthy

	18 mo.	24 mo.	30 mo.	36 mo.	42 mo.	48 mo.	54 mo.
Boys	0.96	1.38	3.18	3.09	4.18	4.34	4.55
Girls	1.33	2.14	3.09	3.81	4.41	4.41	4.74
Sexes combined	1.16	1.82	3.13	3.41	4.27	4.38	4.63

It is often useful to know what percentage of children at any age equal or exceed a given level of performance. A common way of expressing this is by means of *percentiles* which show the level below which a given percentage of cases fall. For example, the 30th percentile is the level below which 30 per cent and above which 70 per cent of the cases lie.*

There are a number of ways of computing percentile or decile values but the graphic method is usually the easiest. From the combined frequency tables for each age and sex find what percentage of the total number of comprehensible sentences used by the two-year-olds are one word in length, what percentage are two words in length, three words in

---

* Unless the number of cases in the group is very large, only the successive ten per cent intervals are commonly indicated. These divisions are known as *deciles*.

length and so on. Enter these percentages in a column to the right of the frequency column. In a second column enter the *cumulative* values of these percentages by adding each successive percentage to the total lying below it. These figures show what percentage of the sentences consisted of one word, what percentage of not over two words, what percentage of not over three words and so on. Using a sheet of decimal-ruled paper, lay off along the ordinate the successive lengths of sentence, as one word, two words, three words, *etc.,* spacing equally. On the chart at each of these points place a dot representing the cumulative frequencies in terms of percentages. Draw lines connecting these dots as shown in Figure 21. The values of the successive deciles can then be read directly from the chart by first locating the 10 per cent line on the abscissa and reading across to the point at which it intersects the curve, then doing the same for the 20 per cent level, *etc.* Do the same for the children of three and four years and tabulate the results.

Draw percentile graphs for the class data, placing the boys and girls of each age on the same graph and the totals for both sexes at the three age levels on a fourth sheet to facilitate age and sex comparison.

The distances set off by the 25th, 50th and 75th percentiles are known as the *quartiles,* since they are the points which divide the entire distribution into four parts, each including a quarter of the total number of cases. One-half the distance from the 25th to the 75th percentile is known as the *semi-interquartile range.* In a normal distribution this will be identical in value with the *probable error* or *P.E.,* and for this reason the terms have been used interchangeably by some writers. This is a regrettable practice, since few distributions based upon concrete data are precisely normal in distribution. Chance fluctuations of sampling will usually introduce small departures from normality unless

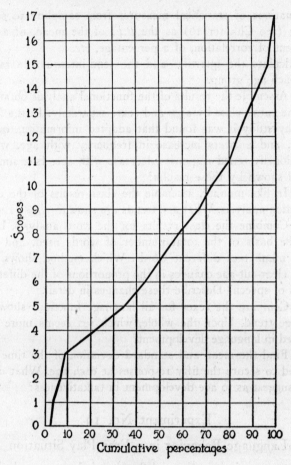

FIGURE 21.

Method of drawing percentile curves.

the number of cases is exceptionally large. For this reason
it is better to reserve the use of the term *probable error*
for the theoretical distributions representing the probable

fluctuations of statistical measures from sampling to sampling (see Chapter 16) as the *P.E.* of the mean, of a coefficient of correlation, of a percentage, *etc*.

Calculate the quartiles and the semi-interquartile range for each age group.

5. Assemble the results of the functional analysis obtained by the entire class by ages and sexes separately. In the McCarthy study it was found that adapted information, questions, and answers increase in frequency with age, while emotionally toned responses decrease with age. Is a similar trend shown by these results?

6. In like manner, assemble the class results of the construction analysis. What age trends are shown?

7. Combine the class results for the word analysis, both on the basis of the total number of words used, and the total number of different words. Which method shows the most clear-cut age changes in the proportions of the different parts of speech? Describe these changes in detail.

8. Compare the sexes for all language functions showing an age trend. Upon the whole, which sex seems more advanced in language development?

9. Find the mean and standard deviation of the time required to secure the fifty responses at each age. What does this suggest as to age development in talkativeness?

Experiment No. 19

Language Behavior in a Free Play Situation

If opportunity permits and the class is large enough, it is interesting to carry out a check study, using the same subjects but recording the language responses during the free play hour when the child is in a group of other children near his own age. It is hardly worth while to have both studies done by the entire class, but if the number of students is sufficient they may be divided into two groups, one of which carries out Experiment 18, the other Experiment 19. Results may then be assembled for comparison of the language behavior in the two situations. In this case the observer takes up a position near enough the child to hear all that is said but without addressing him or entering into the play-situation in any way. Each language response is recorded as it occurs, until fifty responses have been observed. The time required to secure the data should also be recorded.

Results should be analyzed in the same manner as in the preceding experiment. Compare the findings. In what respects does language behavior seem most directly dependent upon the situation in which it takes place?

REFERENCES

The student is referred to the following titles in the bibliography at the end of this book:

17, 26, 29, 78, 115, 169*, 170*, 195, 196, 198*, 203*, 213*, 225, 233, 235, 238, 263, 281, 307, 313, 319, 330, 335, 342, 394*.

Chapter 24

VOCABULARY

SINCE language is a symbolic process, it is not surprising that a rather close relationship exists between facility in the use of language and intelligence as measured by standard tests. The latter are constructed upon the assumption that "intelligence" is the power to think in abstract terms, to see relations, to make use of what has been formerly learned in adapting to new situations, *etc.* The relationship of intelligence test standing to language has been shown most clearly with reference to vocabulary. As Terman (241) has pointed out, a good vocabulary test is one of the best short intelligence tests available, provided that the children tested come from English speaking homes where they have had normal opportunity to learn the language. The relationship between size of vocabulary and intelligence test scores appears to be about equally well marked at all ages.

Apart from its indirect significance as an index to general mental level, the possession of a good vocabulary is important in its own right. Imperfect knowledge of words is a great handicap to any child who must gain much of his information through the printed page. Vocabulary studies in the early grades are of much importance since the handicap arising from a deficient vocabulary becomes more serious as the child advances further in school and gains more and more of his information through reading.

Experiment No. 20

A Standard Vocabulary Test for Primary Grade Children

Give the vocabulary test in the Stanford achievement scale (362) to second, third, and fourth grade children. This is a group test, requiring only ten to fifteen minutes for its administration to an entire class. Instructions for giving the test are to be found in the manual which accompanies the test blanks. Divide the children on the basis of age, grade, and sex.

1. Find the differences between the means of successive age groups and the reliability of these differences.

2. Find the differences between the means of successive grade groups and the reliability of these differences. On the whole, are the age differences or the grade differences absolutely greater? In which case is the difference more reliably established?

3. Compute a "vocabulary quotient" for each child by dividing his "vocabulary age" according to the standards given in the manual of instructions by his chronological age. Compare the "vocabulary quotients" of children who are accelerated in school with those of retarded children.

Experiment No. 21

Word-Knowledge and Class Standing

From one of the school textbooks (a geography or history is preferable) select a list of 50 difficult words which occur at least three times and for which no definition is given. Prepare a vocabulary test of the "multiple choice" type in which the child is required to select from among four words the one which most nearly corresponds to the test word in meaning. Examples are given below:

Underline the right word in each line.

1. *Altitude* means: attitude, height, garret, a vegetable.
2. *Ancient* means: history, salty, expensive, old.

Give the test to children in the grade in which the textbook is used (fourth to sixth grade children preferably). Compare the number of errors made by each child with their class marks in the subject from which the words were selected. Discuss the results.

REFERENCES

The student is referred to the following titles in the bibliography at the end of this book:

29, 61, 62, 63, 83, 93, 136, 195, 213, 233*, 235, 238, 241*, 247, 258, 275, 301, 313, 319, 335.

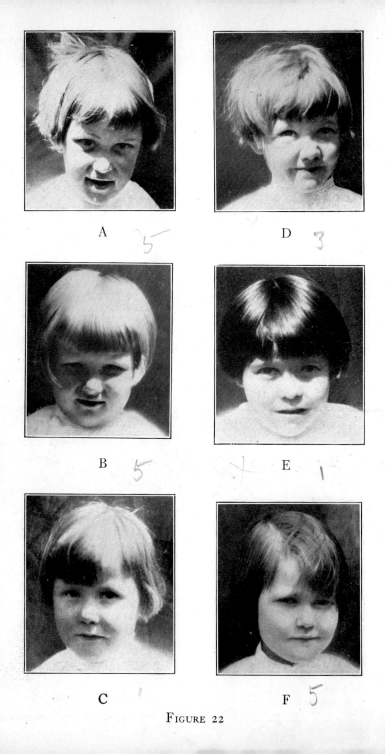

FIGURE 22

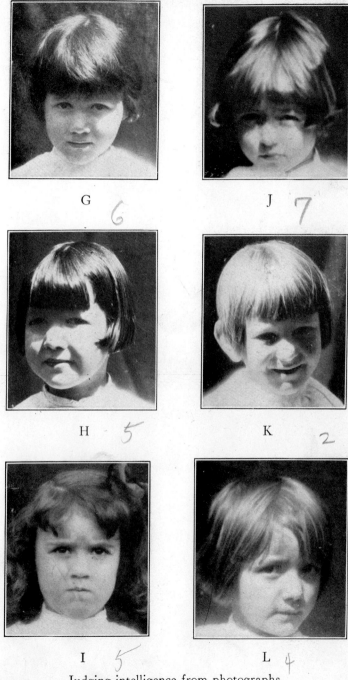

G   6   J   7

H   5   K   2

I   5   L   4

Judging intelligence from photographs

Chapter 25

GENERAL INTELLECTUAL DEVELOPMENT

THE popular use of such terms as "measuring intelligence," "mental tests," and the like may lead the layman to assume that "intelligence" is an organized and independent "faculty" or "ability" which exists in man, much as a canary exists in its cage, or a goldfish in its bowl. Of course this is not true, nor is it true that we are able to *measure intelligence* at all, in the sense that the word "measurement" is used in the physical sciences. We can, however, *classify individuals* with respect to their ability to perform certain tasks which experience has shown to be more or less diagnostic of ability to succeed in school or college or in the more "intellectual" occupations of adult life. While our devices for making these classifications are not completely accurate either in the sense that two persons applying the same test to the same individual on succeeding days will secure exactly the same result, or in the sense that the measurements taken yield a perfect prediction of accomplishment along "intellectual" lines; nevertheless they have shown themselves to be more useful than any other methods developed for this purpose.

Owing to the fact that the term *measurement* is used in different senses in the physical and mental sciences, some people have regretted that the expression *mental measurement* ever came into popular use. However, no real misconception need arise if the student remembers that in the latter case we are dealing with a *principle of classification* only. Words vary in meaning according to the context in which they are used. The dentist "extracts" a tooth, the mathematician "extracts" a square root, and the lawyer "extracts" information from an unwilling witness. The fact that the same name is given to very different processes does not trouble us. Neither should the difference between mental and physical "measurements," provided we bear in mind that in the case of physical measurements we are employing units which are universally applicable to all objects which occupy space. Mental measurements, on the other hand, have a very limited range of applicability. They have no meaning apart from the performance of other persons who have been measured in the same way. Thus we say that a certain child has a "mental age" of seven years, meaning that on the test used he did as well as the average child of seven. Or we may say that he ranks in the 90th percentile for his age; meaning that out of a hundred children of his age who had been given this test, only ten did better than he. In the same way we say that a child is as tall as the average seven-year-old; or that he is among the tallest 10 per cent of his class. But in addition to this, we may say that he is 50 inches or 128 centimeters in height. No such general measurement which is independent of the performance of other persons on the test used is available as yet in the field of mental measurement. Our tests, then, *classify* the individual with respect to his position in the group, but do not *measure* him in any way which is independent of the group to which he belongs.

The administration of the more exact individual mental tests, such as the Binet test, requires a considerable amount of special training on the part of the examiner. There are, however, a number of simple tests, the administration of which requires little or no special training and which can be scored by very simple and objective methods. The student should realize that tests of this kind are not sufficiently exact to yield anything more than a rather crude estimate of individual differences in mental development. They should never be used for diagnosis if any matter of real importance for the child's future is involved. Nevertheless such tests if carefully given according to instructions fill a very useful purpose as a basis for tentative classification or as a means of making a preliminary sifting of children to be tested in more detail before admitting them to special classes or granting extra promotion. Among the tests of this kind which are suitable for use with kindergarten children may be mentioned the Detroit Kindergarten Test (347), the Rhode Island Test (350), and the Pintner-Cunningham Test (370). For children in the first and second grades, the Haggerty Delta I (356), the Pressey Primary Classification Scale (373), the Pintner-Cunningham Test (370) or the Detroit First Grade Test (349), are suitable. For children with special language handicaps such as those coming from foreign homes, the Pintner Non-language Test (369) or the Goodenough Test based on spontaneous drawing (354) will be found useful.

In using any of these tests the inexperienced examiner must bear in mind that even minor departures from the standardized procedures may cause differences in the results which will invalidate any comparison with standardized norms. The examiner should familiarize himself thoroughly with the procedure before attempting to give the test and should follow the instructions verbatim. This rule applies alike to the manner of giving and of scoring the tests.

In using these tests, two new expressions will be used which may need to be explained here.

Mental age is the level of performance expressed in terms of crude score or "points passed" which is most typical of children of any given chronological age. In the manuals of instruction accompanying the tests suggested in this chapter there will be found tables of "mental age norms" which show the scores earned by the average child of each chronological age. To find the mental age of any child, it is necessary only to locate in the table the score which he earned on the test. The entry opposite will give the *mental age equivalent* of that score. Thus a child of 4 years 0 months, who makes a score of 15 on the Detroit Kindergarten Test is said to have a mental age of 5 years 0 months, which means that on this test he did as well as the average child of five.

But for a child of four to be advanced a full year in mental age means much more than it does for a child of ten to be equally advanced, since the ten-year-old has had ten years' time in which to gain his advanced standing while the four-year-old has had but four years. We need some method of relating the amount of advancement or retardation to the age of the child. A simple and useful method is that of the *intelligence quotient* or IQ which is obtained by dividing the mental age by the chronological age. It is customary to carry this division to two decimal places and to express the result as a whole number (omitting the decimal). Thus in the example just given, the four-year-old with a mental age of 5 would have an IQ of 5/4 or 125. A five-year-old with a mental age of 4 would have an IQ of 4/5 or 80. The child who is exactly "average for his age" will have an IQ of 100.

In order to interpret the IQ correctly, a knowledge of the approximate frequency in the general population of IQ's of various degrees above or below 100 is needed. Since certain tests have a greater "spread" or variability than others, account should be taken of the "spread" in interpreting the results. However, the following interpretations may be used tentatively for tests such as have been mentioned in this chapter.

5

IQ	*Interpretation*
130 or above	Very superior
120—130	Superior
110—120	Slightly superior
90—110	Average
80—90	Slightly retarded
70—80	Retarded, may or may not be serious
Below 70	Decidedly retarded, should have special examination

Experiment No. 22

A Mental Test for Kindergarten Children

Each student should give one of the tests mentioned at the beginning of this chapter to from three to five kindergarten children. At this age it is better to give the tests individually, even if the instructions state that it is permissible to give them to small groups. Score the results and compute the mental age (MA) and IQ for each child. Compare with results of other tests if any have been given, and with teacher's estimates of children's ability.

Experiment No. 23

A Group Intelligence Test for Primary Grade Children

If opportunity permits, it is worth while for each member of the class to give one of the standard primary group tests to an entire class of children within the range of first to third grade.* Higher grades may be included if desired. All tests should be scored *independently* by two members of the class who will exchange their papers for this purpose. The

* A list of tests is given in Section III of the bibliography.

tests must be given and scored in the exact manner described in the manual.

Problems: 1. Prepare frequency surfaces showing the distribution of mental ages within each grade. Do the same for the distribution of IQ's.

2. Find the median score for each grade. What percentage of children in each grade equal or exceed the median score of the next higher grade? What percentage in each grade fall below the median of the grade next lower?

3. In each grade, what is the correlation between chrono logical age and score on the test?

4. If possible, have the teacher in each grade arrange the children in rank order for general class standing, and correlate the results with the rank orders on the test.

REFERENCES

The student is referred to the following titles in the bibliography at the end of this book:

7, 10, 13, 39, 53, 55, 61, 64, 93, 103*, 119, 144, 207, 215*, 237, 243*, 244, 248, 286, 293, 323*, 330, 334, 340. *See also Section III. Titles* 347-380.

Chapter 26

JUDGING INTELLIGENCE FROM PERSONAL APPEARANCE

MANY people believe that in some way the mental capacity of an individual can be judged from his appearance. In making these judgments some people state that they rely chiefly upon the shape of the head, others upon general facial expression, others upon special features such as the eyes, the nose, the height of the forehead and so on. This reliance upon personal appearance as a means of estimating other characteristics is so general that many business firms, professional organizations such as Boards of Education, and so on, require that all applicants for positions must submit a photograph as a part of their application. In estimating the ability of their pupils, teachers frequently admit that they are guided in part by the fact that the child "looks bright" or "looks stupid." It is interesting, therefore, to see how closely such estimates of intelligence agree with the results of standardized tests.

Experiment No. 24

Judging Intelligence from Photographs

Material: In Figure 22 there will be found a series of photographs of children, all of whom were between the ages of four and five years. A uniform garment is used in order to eliminate the possibility of the judgment being influenced by the clothing.

231

Subjects: The members of the class will act as judges.

Procedure: The photographs in Figure 22, page 226 should be cut apart, together with their identifying letters, and mounted on separate sheets of cardboard. The student should then select two photographs at random, and after comparing them with each other, decide which of the two children appears to him to be more intelligent. This photograph should be placed to the right of the others on the desk before him. A third photograph should then be selected and compared with each of the others in turn. If the third child is thought to be more intelligent than the first but less intelligent than the second, it is placed between them in the row, if more intelligent than either it is placed at the right, and if less intelligent than either at the left of the other two. A fourth photograph is then taken and compared with each of the other three in turn and thus placed in its appropriate position in the series. When all the photographs have been arranged in this way, the student should check the arrangement by looking through them first from left to right, then backwards from right to left. Any changes in position which seem desirable should be made until he is satisfied with his arrangement. The identifying letters of the photographs should then be recorded in order as they are ranked. After the arrangements have been made and recorded the students should turn to page 517 of this book where the intelligence quotients of these children will be found. These figures are based upon an individual mental test given by a competent psychologist. Students should not consult the test results until after the photographs have been arranged and should not confer with each other when making the arrangements.

Problems: 1. Each student should correlate the rank orders of the children according to his judgment of their ability with the rank orders for test-intelligence as indicated by the scores given on page 517.

2. Find the mean rank orders given to each subject by all the members of the class. Rerank these means and correlate the rank orders thus obtained with the rank orders according to the test results. How does the judgment of the group compare with the individual judgment of the members of the group with regard to accuracy in judging intelligence?

3. Each student should subtract his own rankings from the sum of those given by all the members of the group, and find the correlation between his rankings and those of the remaining members of the class. On the average, do the individual rankings show a closer agreement with the compound judgment of a number of other people or with the test results? What explanation can you offer?

4. Compare the results obtained by this group with those reported in the literature. Upon the basis of these combined findings, what conclusions would you draw with regard to the usefulness of photographs as a means of estimating intelligence?

REFERENCES

The student is referred to the following titles in the bibliography at the end of this book:

84, 206*, 300*.

Chapter 27

SOCIO-ECONOMIC STATUS

BEFORE drawing conclusions with regard to results obtained from any limited group, it is frequently necessary and always desirable to know something of the selective factors which have determined the composition of the group. Since individuals may be classified in many different ways, there are many different standpoints from which the composition of a group may be judged. Although the precise factors which need most to be taken into consideration in any individual problem will depend upon the nature of the facts which are being investigated, there are certain factors which have been found to affect the results of so many different kinds of investigations that it is rarely safe to ignore them. A general standard of reference is needed, in order that we may know to what extent the group with which we are dealing departs from that standard. In the field of intelligence tests for example, we have set the standards in such a way that an "average" group will be found to have a mean IQ of 100 with a standard deviation of about 16 to 18 points of IQ (271). In the case of physical measurements, standards have been developed from the measurements of large numbers of individuals of different ages by means of which we can state with reasonable assurance that a given group averages shorter or taller, lighter or heavier, and so on, than the average for the population as a whole. Other tables have been prepared showing the average amount of sleep taken by children of different ages, their average caloric intake and so on.

Among the more general factors, *socio-economic status* appears to be related to an unusually wide variety of traits and functions. Upon the average, children who come from the better socio-economic classes stand higher on intelligence tests (103), are more advanced in language (170), sleep more (77), have more toys (230), are less likely to fail in school (46), and so on through a long list of related characteristics which cannot be completely enumerated here. While it must be remembered that these are only general tendencies which show many individual exceptions, nevertheless the relationships just enumerated will commonly be found to hold on the average for large groups.

Whether the advantages offered by the homes of superior social status tend to increase the intelligence of children, or whether the superior ability of the parents which enables them to attain positions of higher social status is transmitted to their offspring is uncertain. From correlation alone it is impossible to say which of two related variables is cause and which is effect, or whether both are effects of a common underlying cause. The fact that two variables are positively related to each other means nothing more than that variations from the average in one variable are likely to be accompanied by corresponding variations in the other variable. The reason for such an association must be determined from other information.

When we find that socio-economic status is related to an unusually wide variety of other factors we do not imply that it is the *cause* of these differences. We can say, however, that socio-economic status is one of the factors which needs to be examined very carefully in all studies where comparison is to be made between groups. Suppose, for example, that we wish to study the effects of a daily story period upon the development of vocabulary. Two groups of children are used. To one group stories are told for half an hour daily, while the other has no story period. At the end of a definite period of time, both groups are tested for extent of vocabulary. If it should chance that one group was made up of children from the upper social classes while the other was recruited from children of the laboring class, extremely erroneous conclusions might be drawn from the results of the experiment, since a greater gain on the part of the first group might be a function of the social status, and in no way connected with the story telling. Even though the groups were matched for size of vocabulary at the beginning of the experimental period, the effect of the systematic error of sampling might still appear, since the absolute difference between social classes in language development has been shown to increase with age. If experimental results are not to be vitiated by errors of sampling, a knowledge of the social composition of the groups studied is highly important.

Increasing recognition of the importance of factors such as these has led to a number of devices for measuring social status, each of which attacks the problem from a somewhat different angle. While the results obtained by the different methods show some agreement with each other, nevertheless there is sufficient disagreement to show that they do not measure exactly the same phenomena. The selection of a method must be determined by the purpose for which it is to be used.

We shall consider three devices which differ both in content and in the manner of obtaining the data.

In any study in which the results are expected to serve as standards with which the scores made by other individuals are to be compared, one of two procedures is necessary. Either all the individuals to whom the obtained standards are expected to apply must be studied, or a representative sample used. Since the former is rarely possible, some way of testing the sample for systematic errors is needed. The matter is not as simple as it seems, since we cannot tell how closely a sample resembles the remainder of the population from which it has been drawn unless we are in possession of knowledge regarding the entire population. This means that we must use as our criterion for the adequacy of the sample some measure for which information regarding the entire population is available. The most accurate information available for all the population is found in the reports of the United States Census Bureau, in which there are complete tabulations of the occupations of all employed persons. Separate tables are given for the country as a whole, for the states, and for the larger cities.

In Appendix A will be found a list of the occupations of adult males for the United States as a whole as given in the report of the 1920 census and the number of cases in each class. These occupations have been divided into seven main groups which may be roughly characterized as follows:

	Percentage of employed males in United States population (1920)
Group I.—Professional	2.54
Group II.—Semi-professional and managerial	4.70
Group III.—Clerical, skilled trades, and retail business	14.42
Group IV.—Farmers	18.74
Group V.—Semi-skilled occupations, minor clerical positions and minor business	27.40
Group VI.—Slightly skilled trades and other occupations requiring little training or ability	13.25
Group VII.—Day laborers of all classes	18.96

The percentages in each of these general categories for the entire male population of the United States are shown in the column at the right.

While occupation is only a crude measure of social status, the fact that complete and reasonably accurate comparative data for the entire country and for its principal divisions are available makes an occupational classification particularly useful as a means of examining the composition of selected groups.

Experiment No. 25

Testing the Social Composition of an Experimental Group in Terms of Paternal Occupation

Using the scheme of classification given in Appendix A, find the percentages in each class for the local community (state or city). The occupation of the fathers of the children in the experimental group or school may then be compared either with the local population or with the population for the country as a whole in order to determine by how much and in what direction the standards derived from this group may be expected to diverge from a more representative sampling of the community. Find the percentages of each occupational class within the group and express each of these percentages as a multiple of the normal quota found in the general community.

Two other methods of classifying occupations have been developed. The first is the Taussig Industrial Classification based upon "non-competing" groups (336); the second is the Barr Scale (11) for occupational intelligence in which a group of judges ranked a list of 100 selected occupations according to their judgment of the relative degree of intelligence necessary to attain an average degree of success in each. Scale values for each occupation were worked out on the basis of these ratings. Reference to these studies will be found in the bibliography. The classificatory scheme given here is in part based upon the Barr and the Taussig Scales.

Experiment No. 26

The Chapin Scale for Measuring Living Room Equipment

This is a method of studying socio-economic status based upon the material equipment of the family living room. Use of this scale requires a visit to the home. Since no standards for the general community are available, the scale is more suitable for use in problems requiring differentiation among the members of a specified group than for testing the representativeness of any sample. For purposes of individual study, however, it is probably more accurate than a rating based upon the occupation of the father alone. A copy of this scale will be found in Appendix B.*

Problems. 1. Have the homes of all the children in the experimental group rated on the Chapin Scale. The students should work in pairs, visiting each home together but making their records independently. The reliability of the scoring may then be found by correlating the scores of the first member of each pair against those of the second member.

A difficulty hitherto unencountered is found here; that of determining which student is to be regarded as the first and which as the second member of a pair when the results from a number of different pairs of investigators are to be included in the same correlation. If in arranging the table there is a constant tendency to place the higher of the two paired scores in variable x and the lower in variable y, a serious error will be introduced which will raise the correlation coefficient above its true value. A situation similar to this is found in the measurement of like-sex twins and in other cases in which there is no objective way of determining

---

* Blank forms for making these records can be obtained at a small cost from the Institute of Child Welfare, University of Minnesota.

which of the two scores should be considered as the *x* variant and which as the *y* variant. In all such cases it is customary to use what is known as the *double entry method*. Each score is entered twice, first in the *x* column and then in the *y* column. Although the rank order method of determining the correlation may be used, the fact that each number is entered in each series of scores to be ranked means that unless the number of cases is very small, doubling the number of cases in each column makes the process of ranking very laborious. A better and quicker method is to be found in a modification of the Pearson product moment method of determining correlation. The general method will be taken up in a later chapter, but since the procedure is simpler and more readily understood when the variables are interchangeable we shall begin with this method.

If we are dealing with two measurements of the same thing expressed in the same terms, and these two measurements agree perfectly with each other, a deviation from the mean in one variable will be exactly paralleled by a deviation from the mean of the paired score in the second variable. If the two measures are perfectly correlated with each other but are expressed in different units, it is necessary to reduce these units to similar terms before the measurements can be compared, just as it is necessary to reduce two fractions to the same denominator before adding or subtracting. One way of doing this is to reduce both to rank orders as we have previously seen. Another method of reducing the variables to similar units is to express each in terms of the number of standard deviations above or below the mean of its group. In this case a perfect correlation between two measures is indicated, not by exact numerical agreement of the paired variables (since in this case the gross measurements are expressed in different terms and therefore the numerical values do not have the same significance) but by agreement in the extent to which each individual member of the pair departs from the mean of its own group when this departure is expressed in terms of standard deviations of the distribution. When *in every instance* a variation of an *x* measure from the mean of the *x* variable (expressed in terms of standard deviations of *x*) is exactly equal to the variation of its paired measure in the *y* variable (expressed in terms of the number of standard deviations of *y*) the agreement is just as complete as if the measures had been expressed in similar units in the first place. The correlation is therefore 1.00. Moreover, in this case the sum of the products of the deviations of the individual members of the pairs from their respective means will be exactly equal to the product of the standard deviations of the two distributions multiplied by the number of cases. If, however, the agreement between the two variables is less than perfect, a high measurement in one is not certainly but only probably associated with a high measurement in the other. This is the condition commonly found. In such cases the sum of the products of the deviations of the pairs will be less than the products of the standard deviations multiplied by the number of cases. This principle is expressed in the basic formula for correlation by the product moment method which is as follows:

$$r = \frac{\Sigma xy}{N \sigma_x \sigma_y} \qquad (12)$$

In the case under consideration where each member of each pair is entered twice, first as an *x* variate and then as a *y* variate, the two distributions become identical and therefore have the same mean and standard deviation. In place of $\sigma_x \sigma_y$ we shall then write σ^2 in the denominator. And since the mean is the same in both variables, the deviations from the mean (*x* and *y*) are both taken from this mean as origin. We therefore enter all the scores obtained by all the members of the group in a single frequency table and find the mean and standard deviations of this series of scores. This table, it will be noted, contains two scores for each home rated.

Returning to the original paired scores, we find by how many class intervals each member of each pair deviates from the mean of the entire group. If, for example, in the first pair of measures considered, student No. 1 gave to the first living room visited a score which is 5 class intervals above the mean of the group, while her partner gave a score which is 4 class intervals above the mean, the xy value of this pair is $5 \times 4 = 20$. We enter this in a separate column, headed xy. The same procedure is followed for each pair of scores until all the xy products have been found. Remember that if one student should happen to give to a room a value above the mean (that is, a $+x$ value) while her partner gave a value below the mean (a $-y$ value), the xy product would have a minus sign. The algebraic sum of the xy column is then taken as Σxy required in the formula. If, as is customary, the mean and standard deviation have been computed from an arbitrary origin (a guessed average) instead of the true mean, both the x and the y values will differ from the true mean by the amount of the correction, and the xy product will differ from its true value by the product of the corrections. Since in this case the x and the y distributions are the same, the corrections will be equal and the product of the two corrections will be equal to c^2. And since each of the individual pairs is in error by this amount, the squared correction must be multiplied by the number of pairs (in this case the number of homes) and the result subtracted from the sum of the xy product found by computing from the arbitrary origin. The result obtained will be the true Σxy. A corresponding correction must of course be made in the denominator (See Chap. 14).

The product moment formula for computing the correlation between interchangeable variables is therefore:

$$r = \frac{\Sigma xy - Nc^2}{N\sigma^2} \qquad (13)$$

The steps in its computation are outlined as follows:

1. Arrange all the scores for both members of the paired variables in a single frequency distribution. Find the mean and the standard deviation of this distribution.

2. Find the products of the deviations (x scores) of the individual members of each pair from the guessed mean. Enter these products in a new column headed xy, giving regard to signs. (If there are many xy scores it is better to make two columns, one for the $+xy$ and the other for the $-xy$ values in order to avoid confusion). The difference between the sum of the $+xy$ and the $-xy$ values will be the sum of the xy products (Σxy) taken from the guessed average.

3. Make a correction for the error in guessing at the true mean by multiplying the square of the correction by the number of paired scores in the series. Subtract this from the sum of the xy values. The result will be the true Σxy. Write this value as the numerator of the fraction representing the correlation coefficient.

4. Find the denominator of this fraction by multiplying the square of the standard deviation of the single distribution (corrected for the error in guessing) by the number of paired values in the group.

5. Divide (3) by (4). The result is the correlation coefficient desired.

Experiment No. 27

The Chapman-Sims Scale for Socio-Economic Status

A third method for measuring socio-economic status has been devised by Chapman and Sims (45, 229). The information for this scale may be obtained from the parents at the time the home visit is made. With older children or adults, data may be obtained by the use of a prepared questionnaire filled out by the subjects without necessitating a visit to the home itself.*

Problems: 1. Find the correlation between the Chapman-Sims scores and the mean scores obtained by the two observers on the Chapin Living Room Scale.

2. Divide the children in the experimental group into classes according to paternal occupation as described in Section 1. For each of these groups find the mean score on the Chapman-Sims Scale and also on the Chapin Scale for living room equipment. Draw curves showing the mean scores on each of these scales for the successive occupational classes. Which of these two curves shows more regular and even progression from one occupational category to another?

3. If intelligence test scores are available for the children, find the correlation between the IQ's and each of the three measures of socio-economic status. Which of the three shows the closest relationship to intelligence-test score?

REFERENCES

The student is referred to the following titles in the bibliography at the end of this book:

5, 9, 11, 43*, 44*, 45*, 46, 96, 100, 106*, 146, 170, 229*, 330, 336, 385*.

* Forms may be obtained from the Public School Publishing Co., Bloomington, Ill.

Chapter 28

SOCIAL BEHAVIOR

IF we observe the behavior of those around us, our attention is at once directed to the marked differences in their manner of reacting to other persons. Although social reactions vary according to the particular company in which the individual happens to be placed, and are likewise affected by such incidental circumstances as bodily health, recent experiences, fatigue, or anxiety, it is nevertheless true that in the course of time every one builds up a system of social habits or pattern reactions which he is likely to display with fair consistency under a wide variety of circumstances. These habits become so well established or pronounced that after some acquaintance with an individual it is possible to predict with more or less certainty how he will behave when confronted with a given social situation. When we say of another person that he is bashful, forward, friendly, sympathetic, irritable, or jealous, we mean nothing more than that he has built up certain *habits* which make him more likely than others to behave in the manner indicated by these terms. The irritable man does not always behave in an irritable fashion but does so more frequently, on the average, than do those to whom we do not apply the term. The bashful person is not bashful with every one, but shows this form of behavior so frequently as to merit the description.

By the *social traits* of an individual we refer to those forms of reaction which have become so habitual that he displays them more frequently and under a wider variety of conditions than does the average person. A social trait is nothing more than a habitual way of reacting to social situations.

If we regard the social traits of an individual as largely, if not entirely, the result of *habits* which have been set up through experience, the importance of developing methods for studying the formation of such habits becomes evident. It is difficult, however, to reproduce the social conditions of everyday life in the laboratory without making them highly artificial. Attempts to do so have thus far not been very successful. For the present it is probably better to develop methods whereby observations of behavior in everyday life can be recorded and organized in a systematic fashion. Techniques of this kind suitable for use with young children are particularly needed if we are to study the early stages of social behavior.

Experiment No. 28

An Observational Method of Studying Social Behavior in Children

A number of observational devices for studying social behavior have been developed. We shall consider here the modification of the Olson (199) technique which was developed by Parten (201) at the University of Minnesota for use with nursery school children. The method can also be used with children beyond nursery school age. It makes use of a series of short time samples, during which children are observed on occasions when they are free to do as they wish with reference to the particular phenomenon studied. The method may be described briefly as follows: A series of graded categories descriptive of social behavior is worked out upon the basis of preliminary observation. These categories are described in as detailed and objective a manner as possible. The categories refer directly to the kind of situations in which the children are to be observed. Only one child is observed at a time. The observer who is provided with a convenient record blank chooses an inconspicuous position from which he can see and hear the subject easily. Each observation is continued for a set period of time which is checked with a stop-watch. At the end of this period the behavior is classified and recorded according to the system previously devised. The observer then moves on to the next child in the group and classifies his behavior in the same way. This is repeated until one record has been secured for each child. On the following day, another record is secured for each child and so on until a sufficiently large number of samples have been obtained for each subject to yield a reliability coefficient high enough to serve the purposes of the investigation. The greater the number of samples secured for each child the higher will be the reliability. It has been shown that the Spearman-Brown prophecy formula (see page 148) may be used to ascertain the approximate number of additional samples needed at any stage of the investigation in order to secure a reliability coefficient of a given magnitude. Thus, if 20 samples are found to have a reliability coefficient of +.70, 40 samples may be expected to show a reliability not far from +.82; 100 samples, which is five times the original number, would be expected to yield a reliability coefficient of approximately +.92, *etc.* In computing the reliability coefficients the records taken on the odd numbered days are compared with those taken on the even numbered days.

Before beginning the actual observations each student should spend one or two preliminary periods in familiarizing himself with the method. Observations should be carried out in a definite order to make sure that the children will not be selected for observation at a particular time because of some unusual or striking aspect of their social behavior.

Parten was able to distinguish six different types of social behavior among nursery school children, defined as follows:

1. *Unoccupied behavior.* The child does not appear to be playing but occupies himself with casual or momentary observation of the activities of others, or plays with his own body and clothes, gets on and off chairs, or merely stands around, follows the teacher, or sits in one spot glancing around the room. His general attitude and behavior do not suggest any kind of purposeful activity.

2. *Solitary play.* The child plays alone and independently with toys which are different from those used by the children within speaking distance of himself. He makes no effort to get close to other children, or to join in what they are doing. He pursues his own activity without reference to others.

3. *Onlooker behavior.* The child spends most of his time watching the other children playing. He often talks to the children whom he is observing, asks questions or gives suggestions but does not enter into the play himself. His behavior differs from that of the unoccupied child in that he is definitely observing particular groups of children rather than allowing his gaze to flit at random from one group to another. The onlooker stands or sits within speaking distance of the group whom he is observing so that he can see and hear everything which is taking place.

4. *Parallel activity.* The child plays independently, but the activity which he chooses is one which naturally brings him among other children. He plays with toys which are like those which the children around him are using, but he plays with the toys as he sees fit, and does not try to influence or modify the activity of the children near him. He plays *beside* the other children rather than *with* them. There is no attempt to control the coming or going of other children in

the group. The difference between parallel activity and solitary play is thus seen to be at least in part accidental, since it is determined by the character of the play and the chance presence of other children. The play of young children at the sand table is likely to be of this character.

5. *Autonomous group play.* The child plays with other children who recognize a common interest in their toys or games. This recognition is shown by a borrowing and loaning of play material, conversation about their common activity, and mild attempts to control the group membership. However, there is little or no group organization; the children do not subordinate their individual interest to that of the group. There is more or less mutual exchange of suggestions and material, but each child's part in the play is individually determined. Concentration of leadership in the hands of one or two individuals does not exist.

6. *Organized group play.* The child plays in a centralized group which is organized for the purpose of making some material product, striving to attain some competitive goal, dramatizing situations of adult and group life, or playing formal games according to simple rules. All the children show a marked sense of belonging or not belonging to the group. The control of the group situation is usually in the hands of one or two of the group members who direct the activity of the others in the group. Both the goal and the method of attaining it necessitate a division of labor. The various group members play different parts, and the organization of the activity is such that the efforts of one child are supplemented by those of another. Thus in playing house, one child takes the part of the father, another that of the mother, while others play the parts of the children, of visitors, and so on. Or a group of children may unite in building a railroad track, each child contributing his own efforts to those of the group. The difference between this type of activity and autonomous group play is thus seen to lie primarily in the

subordination of individual interests or activity toward a common goal, and secondarily in the fact that this subordination of interest usually involves a greater or less degree of specialization in the rôle played by each individual child.*

In carrying out this investigation, it is desirable for the members of the class to work in pairs, each pair observing the same child simultaneously but classifying and recording the behavior independently. Although Parten used a one minute time sample, it has been found feasible and somewhat more reliable to divide the minute into two periods of thirty seconds each and classify the behavior for each thirty second period separately, since the form of social reaction in young children not infrequently changes even within a period as short as one minute. Each child is then to be observed for one full minute at a time and two records of his social behavior set down, one for the first half minute, the other for the second half minute. At the end of the minute the observers should move on to the next child and repeat the procedure and so on until all the children in the group have been observed. If possible, at least 40 one minute samples of behavior should be secured for each child. All samples should be taken at about the same time of day and only one pair of observers should observe the child during the same minute.

Problems: 1. Find the mean error of observation by computing the percentage of the total number of observations in which there is disagreement as to classification of behavior between the two simultaneous observers. Is this error approximately the same for all children, or are there certain children whose behavior is consistently more difficult to classify than others?

2. In what percentage of the total number of observations

* Adapted from Parten's descriptions (201).

was the behavior classified by one or both of the observers under each of the six categories listed? Find for each category separately the percentage of time in which the observers agreed as to their classification as compared to the percentage of times they disagreed. Which of these six categories would you say is the most difficult to classify? Can you suggest any improvement in the definition or description given which would help to clear up this difficulty?

3. In arranging the observations partners should, if possible, rotate them in such a way that each student carries out approximately the same number of observations with every other student. If this is done, each student should compute his own observational error by determining the percentage of his observations in which his classification disagrees with that of his partner. If such a system of rotation is not possible, the relative accuracy of the various pairs of observers can be computed in a similar fashion. Under these circumstances, however, there will be no way of determining which of the two members of a pair is the more accurate.

4. Prepare bar diagrams for each child showing the total number of times his behavior was classified under each of the various social categories. Examine these figures and state what form of social behavior seems to be most typical of each child.

5. Combine the data for the individual children to show the age changes which take place in each form of social behavior. Express the results graphically in the form of overlapping frequency polygons.

6. By comparing the individual results with the group curves, divide the children roughly into three groups: those whose social behavior seems to be in advance of that usual for their age; those whose behavior corresponds fairly closely to that of others of their age; and those who seem somewhat retarded in social development, that is, whose behavior re-

sembles that most typical of younger children. What is the mean IQ of the children in each of these groups?

7. Find the reliability of the observations in each category separately, using the method described in the study of physical activity outlined in Chapter 15. The magnitude of these reliability coefficients will depend upon several factors, of which the following may be particularly mentioned: the size of the observational error (problems 1 and 2), the consistency of the children's behavior from day to day, and the relative frequency with which the form of behavior under consideration took place. The last point may require some further explanation. If the form of behavior is one which occurs only rarely, the number of samples on which the determination of reliability is based will be small, and consequently the chance occurrence of one or two instances of non-typical behavior will affect the reliability of the total to a much greater extent than if the number of samples had been large. All other things being equal, the categories containing the greatest number of frequencies will be more reliable than those which were more rarely observed.

8. Arrange the six reliability coefficients for the different categories in order of magnitude. Compare this rank order with (a) the rank order of the same category with reference to the total number of times the form of behavior was recorded, (b) according to the comparative size of the observational errors for each as found in Problem 2. Which of these two factors appears to have been more important in lowering the reliability coefficient for the particular category considered?

9. Why is it desirable to have the observations taken on different occasions rather than in immediate succession? What are some of the spurious factors which might affect the validity of observations, all of which were made during a brief time span (e.g., within the same hour)? How would

these factors be likely to affect the obtained reliability coefficients?

10. Compare the results obtained with those reported by
Parten (201).

REFERENCES

The student is referred to the following titles in the
bibliography at the end of this book:

47, 48, 70, 91, 104, 108*, 121, 201*, 245*, 268, 330, 333*,
335.

Chapter 29

THE SOCIAL REACTIONS OF INFANTS

VERY early in life, the infant learns to distinguish between human beings and other objects in his environment. That the kind and amount of social experience which he undergoes at this time exerts an effect upon his later social development can hardly be doubted, even though we are not yet able to say how the effect is manifested. A careful follow-up of the social development of a group of infants from birth to maturity, together with systematic records of the amount and kind of social stimulation which they have received would do much to clarify our understanding as to the manner in which patterns of social behavior are laid down.

Experiment No. 29

Dominant Behavior in Infants

This experiment can best be carried out in a baby health clinic, milk station, or similar place where fairly large numbers of infants are brought together. Infants between the ages of six and eighteen months or, with slight modifications in method, older children may be used as subjects. If no organization of the kind just described is accessible, it is often possible for the members of the class to locate a few babies among their friends.

Procedure: Two babies differing but slightly from each other in age should be used for each experiment. The children are placed on the floor or in a crib facing each other,

254

FIGURE 23

Social Behavior in Infants
(From Shirley)

with pillows to support the back if they are unable to sit without support. An attractive toy is first dangled before them for a moment and then dropped on the floor midway between their feet. The stop-watch is started as soon as the toy is dropped, and the behavior is observed for a period of two minutes. Records should be made on a prepared form so arranged as to provide space for recording the behavior of both children. A convenient method is to use a single sheet with parallel columns for checking the various forms of behavior as they occur. A sample form of this kind is shown on page 256.

The form should be mimeographed, or, if this is not possible, each student should prepare a sufficient number of copies for his own use. The headings should be filled in before beginning the experiment. *Place* refers to the place of making the experiment (note whether or not it is familiar to either or both children). *Ex.* should be followed by experimenter's name or initials. *Hour* refers to the time of day. Under *Special Conditions* should be noted any special features of the *experimental conditions,* such as an unduly hot or cold room, interruptions, noises from outside, *etc.* Since relative size as well as age may affect social interaction, the weight of each child should be recorded, also the height if this is known. The ages of other children in the family may also be taken in order to see whether children who are accustomed to the play of other children differ in their reactions from those who have had less social experience. Under *Notes* should be recorded any pertinent facts relating to the child's physical condition, recent emotional upsets, *etc.*

The record form is divided into twelve time intervals of ten seconds each. A list of abbreviations for the more common forms of behavior is given at the bottom of the page. Items not listed may be written in the spaces provided. The

Place.... Hour.... Ex.....	Sp. Cond..................	

Child..... Age.... Sex....	Child..... Age.... Sex....
Weight..... Age of sibs....	Weight..... Age of sibs....
Notes....................	Notes....................

Time	Behavior	Behavior
0—00		
0—10		
0—20		
0—30		
0—40		
0—50		
1—00		
1—10		
1—20		
1—30		
1—40		
1—50		

Abbreviations

RT—Reaches for toy
RC—Reaches for other child
ST—Secures toy
OT—Offers toy to other child
PT—Tries to pull toy away
RE—Resists
Y —Yields without perceptible resistance
PV —Protesting vocalization

C —Crying
V —Vocalization (undescribed)
WC—Watches other child
WT—Watches toy
L —Looks about aimlessly
WO—Watches other persons in room

behavior of each child *during each ten second period* should be recorded in as much detail as possible. Each student should carry out from five to ten experiments either with different infants (if clinical or social service agencies are used) or with the same pair of infants on different occasions if this is more convenient.

Problems: 1. Write out a descriptive account of the social interaction taking place in each experiment. If the same infants have been used on each occasion compare their reactions on successive trials. If different infants have been used, contrast their behavior.

2. If a sufficient number of different infants have been used, combine the results obtained by the entire class in such a way as to show what characteristic changes take place with age.

3. Compare the behavior of only children with those who come from homes where there are other children.

4. In what proportion of the total experimental time did the heavier child have the toy in his possession? The older child? Are any sex differences apparent?

REFERENCES

The student is referred to the following titles in the bibliography at the end of this book:

34*, 35*, 71, 95, 153, 163, 164, 225, 228, 265*.

Chapter 30

PLAY EQUIPMENT AND PLAY BEHAVIOR

A^N investigation by Skalet (230) shows the number and kind of toys and other play equipment in the homes of a group of 120 children between the ages of two and four years, selected to include a representative sampling of the population of Minneapolis according to the distribution of paternal occupation described in Appendix A. The toys were classified under several general heads, the proportion in each classification was computed as was also the number of homes in which at least one toy of each type was found. The data were obtained by actual visits to the homes.

The following table shows the way in which the toys were classified and the proportion of the total number of toys falling within each general class.

TABLE 14

PERCENTAGES OF DIFFERENT CLASSES OF TOYS FOUND IN A
REPRESENTATIVE SAMPLING OF THE HOMES OF CHILDREN
BETWEEN THE AGES OF 2 AND 4 YEARS IN THE
CITY OF MINNEAPOLIS

Kind of toy	Number	Per cent of total
Animal toys	379	7.20
Balls	378	7.18
Blocks, including boards and boxes (12 blocks counted as one toy)	462	8.78
Climbing apparatus (chiefly of an informal character but including all apparatus on which the child is permitted to climb)	142	2.70

258

Kind of toy	Number	Per cent of total
Dolls, doll dishes, and doll furniture	849	16.13
Garden tools (including sand toys)	295	5.60
Hand work materials such as scissors, crayons, beads for stringing, etc.	262	4.98
Household equipment including both the child's toy equipment and household possessions which the child is permitted to use..	232	4.41
Jumping ropes and horse reins...	16	0.30
Live pets such as goldfish, canaries, dogs, etc.	30	0.57
Manual training equipment including child's own toy hammers, etc., and those belonging to the household which he is allowed to use	118	2.24
Mechanical toys	164	3.12
Musical toys—drums, horns, etc..	182	3.46
Picture books	722	13.72
Puzzles and table games used by child	15	0.28
Representative toys (toy soldiers, etc.)	26	0.49
Riding and coasting toys such as kiddie-cars, bicycles, sleds and wagons	339	6.44
Sand	105	1.99
Swings and slides	41	0.78
Transportation toys (trains, trucks, etc., not large enough for child to ride in himself)	218	4.14
Unconventional manipulative materials used as toys (includes boxes, clothespins, toilet articles, soap, old shoes, etc.)	289	5.49

At least one of each of the following toys was found in 90 per cent or more of the homes: animal toys, balls, blocks, dolls, garden tools, handwork materials, picture books.

The following types were represented in from 50 to 89 per cent of the homes: climbing apparatus (informal), household equipment, riding and coasting toys, manual training equipment, mechanical toys, musical toys, sand, transportation toys, unconventional manipulative materials.

Toys of the following type were found in fewer than half the homes: jumping ropes, pets, puzzles and games, representative toys, swings and slides.

Experiment No. 30

An Inventory of Play Equipment

Using the system of classification just described, make a list of all the play equipment in the experimental nursery school or kindergarten. Compare the proportions falling within each of the main categories with the corresponding percentages for the home as reported by Skalet. What are the most outstanding differences between the amount and type of play equipment provided by the school and that found in the homes of Minneapolis children? If time permits, a similar inventory of the play equipment in the homes of the children in these schools may be made, and the results compared with the school equipment and also with Skalet's findings.

Experiment No. 31

A Comparative Study of the Uses Made of Different Pieces of Play Equipment

Each member of the class should select one piece of typical play equipment for observation during the free play hour in the experimental kindergarten or nursery-school or on the school playground. Public playgrounds may also be used for this purpose. The length of the observational period should be uniform for all observations. It should not be less than one hour. From two to four hours' observation should be secured if possible for each piece of apparatus. Two or more students may observe the same piece of apparatus or type of play equipment at different times, thus adding to the amount of data obtained for each. Prepared record forms arranged in such a way as to facilitate recording should be used. The planning of this record form is left as an exercise for the student. The form should be worked out by the class in advance and all students should make their records in a uniform manner. Compare the different types of play material with regard to each of the following:

1. The number of different children who make use of the equipment during the observational period.
2. The mean length of time spent by each child in consecutive play with the equipment (disregard minor interruptions and distractions).
3. The number of children who leave the apparatus or equipment and later return to it, with average length of time spent at each visit.
4. Mean number of children using the material at any one time. Compute by dividing the total length of time spent by all children with the apparatus by the total length of time the apparatus was observed.
5. Keep a record of the number of times each child speaks during the observational period. The records for the different children may be thrown together to facilitate recording, since the purpose is not to secure evidence regarding the talkativeness of the separate children, but rather to determine the extent to which conversation is likely to be associated with the use of each piece of equipment. Although verbatim records are unnecessary, each remark should be classified as a remark about the play or the play equipment, a part

of the play itself (as in playing house or playing store), or as irrelevant to the occupation at hand.

6. Make a list of the number of different ways each piece of apparatus is used.

7. Which pieces of equipment are clearly preferred by the boys? Which by the girls? Which are about equally well liked by both sexes? Are there any sex differences in the way in which any given piece of apparatus is used?

8. Which pieces of apparatus are preferred by the older children in the group? By the younger children? Which are popular at all ages? Which are liked by a relatively small number of children?

9. Which pieces of apparatus seem most conducive to social play? To solitary play? Which show greatest variety in manner of usage?

10. From the above findings what kinds of play equipment would you recommend for a child of four years who is in good health but appears to be (a) unduly lethargic, (b) inclined to day dream, (c) solitary, (d) overactive?

REFERENCES

The student is referred to the following titles in the bibliography at the end of this book:

10, 31*, 32*, 138, 139, 162*, 230*, 232, 245.

Chapter 31

THE PEARSON PRODUCT MOMENT METHOD OF CORRELATION

IN Chapter 27 the general principles underlying the product moment method of computing correlation were discussed and a simplified formula for use when the paired variables are interchangeable was given. In this chapter we shall take up the more usual condition in which the variables are not interchangeable and a single entry instead of a double entry is used. Unless a calculating machine is available the work will be facilitated by arranging the data in the form of a *scatter-diagram* or *scattergram,* as it is sometimes called. In using this method the values for one variable are arranged along the ordinate of a chart and those for the other variable along the abscissa. We shall illustrate the procedure by using the data for standing height and weight of five-year-old boys in Table 15.

By inspection of the data we find that the range in height is 9.9 inches and that the range in weight is 20.0 pounds. If we group the height measurements by class intervals of 0.5 in. and the weight measurements by class intervals of 1.0 lb. we shall have 21 class intervals in each variable. There is no fixed requirement as to the number of class intervals, nor is it necessary to have exactly the same number of class intervals in each of the two variables. It is better, however, not to use too coarse grouping.

Using cross-section paper with ruling not finer than four lines to the inch, rule off a section including twenty-one

TABLE 15

MEASUREMENTS OF THE HEIGHT AND WEIGHT OF 50 FIVE-
YEAR-OLD BOYS

Case No.	Height* (inches)	Weight* (pounds)	Case No.	Height* (inches)	Weight* (pounds)
1	44.6	42.50	26	39.0	41.00
2	36.9	34.75	27	40.2	40.75
3	46.2	45.00	28	41.5	46.50
4	43.1	40.25	29	42.4	45.00
5	46.1	52.75	30	43.1	44.00
6	41.6	40.50	31	40.7	45.25
7	43.3	42.75	32	39.4	38.25
8	44.0	44.25	33	40.4	43.50
9	39.5	37.50	34	44.2	50.75
10	43.0	41.50	35	44.8	47.00
11	40.7	38.75	36	44.3	53.00
12	42.4	41.50	37	43.2	47.50
13	46.2	49.25	38	42.5	45.50
14	38.5	33.75	39	41.6	43.75
15	45.1	44.25	40	40.7	43.25
16	46.8	48.50	41	42.7	48.25
17	42.3	49.00	42	46.7	53.75
18	44.2	45.25	43	45.3	46.75
19	38.8	36.00	44	42.6	46.25
20	45.2	47.25	45	41.7	43.50
21	43.0	40.50	46	41.0	44.50
22	40.2	39.75	47	39.6	40.75
23	41.0	42.25	48	43.7	49.25
24	41.6	43.50	49	43.5	47.50
25	44.1	48.75	50	42.6	45.00

* Age is taken at the nearest birthday; height at the nearest tenth of
an inch, weight at the nearest quarter of a pound.

squares in each direction, or prepare a standard correlation chart such as is shown in Figure 24.* When the prepared correlation form is used the labor of computing the correlation will be much simplified.

After having decided upon the size of the class intervals, enter the value of each interval in the y variable (in this case, height) along the ordinate of the chart, and the x values along the abscissa as shown in Figure 24. Turn now to the paired measurements of the fifty children as given in Table 15. The first child measured 44.6 inches in height and 42.50 pounds in weight. Find the class interval which includes his height, which in this case is the sixth interval above the arbitrary origin. Follow the horizontal row of cells to the one which intercepts the column which includes his weight. This chances to be the first column to the left of the arbitrary origin chosen for the weight measurements. Place a tally mark in the cell which marks the point of intersection of the height and weight measurements. In like manner find the cell which marks the point of intersection of the height and weight measurements of the second child. Place a tally mark in this cell. Continue until all the paired measures have been entered.

Now observe the chart. Note that although the tally marks scatter considerably, they tend to cluster about the diagonal line extending from the lower left to the upper right corner. The measures which are lower than the average both in height and weight fall in the lower left quadrant, while those above the average in both measures fall in the upper right quadrant. Since these two quadrants include the majority of the cases, it is evident that in this group the tall

* The chart shown in Fig. 24 is the Anderson correlation chart which can be obtained from the Educational Test Bureau, Minneapolis. A number of similar charts differing slightly in arrangement from this one are available. (See references in bibliography.)

y \ x	33.0	34.0	35.0	36.0	37.0	38.0	39.0	40.0	41.0	42.0	43.0	44.0	45.0	46.0	47.0	48.0	49.0	50.0	51.0	52.0	53.0	f	y	fy	fy²	Σxy +	Σxy −
46.5																/					/	2	+10	20	200	150	
46.0													/				/			/		3	+9	27	243	153	
45.5																						0	+8				
45.0												/		/	/							3	+7	21	147	56	
44.5										/					/							2	+6	12	72	24	6
44.0												/	/			/		/			/	5	+5	25	125	125	
43.5															/		/					2	+4	8	32	40	
43.0								//	/	/		/			/							6	+3	18	54	15	27
42.5													//	/		/						4	+2	8	16	24	
42.0									/				/				/					3	+1	3	3	8	2
41.5								/			///			/								5	0				
41.0										/		/										2	-1	2	2	1	1
40.5						/					/		/									3	-2	6	12	10	4
40.0							/	/			/											3	-3	9	27	21	
39.5					/			/														2	-4	8	32	36	
39.0						/			/													2	-5	10	50	35	
38.5	/			/																		2	-6	12	72	102	
38.0																						0	-7				
37.5																						0	-8				
37.0																						0	-9				
36.5		/																				1	-10	10	100	90	
f	1	1	0	1	1	2	1	5	3	3	5	4	6	3	4	3	3	1	0	1	2	50 n		+85	1187	890	40
x	-10	-9	-8	-7	-6	-5	-4	-3	-2	-1	0	+1	+2	+3	+4	+5	+6	+7	+8	+9	+10		$cx = \frac{\Sigma fx}{n} = 0.80$	$cy = \frac{\Sigma fy}{n} = 1.7$			
fx	10	9		7	6	10	4	15	6	3		4	12	9	16	15	18	7		9	20	40	$\sigma x = \sqrt{\frac{\Sigma fx^2}{n} - cx^2} = 4.454$				
fx²	100	81		49	36	50	16	45	12	3		4	24	27	64	75	108	49		81	200	1024	$\sigma y = \sqrt{\frac{\Sigma fy^2}{n} - cy^2} = 4.566$				

Date Nov-24-1930
Cal. by FLG

Correlation between
x. Weight.
y. Height.
Boys Age 5.

x Data
$cx = +0.8$
$cx^2 = 0.64$
$\sigma x = 4.454$
Mx =

y Data
$cy = +1.7$
$cy^2 = 2.89$
$\sigma y = 4.566$
My =

$$r = \frac{\frac{\Sigma xy}{n} - cx . cy}{\sigma x . \sigma y} = \frac{17.00 - 1.7 \times 0.8}{4.454 \times 4.566}$$

$$r = \frac{15.64}{20.337}$$

$r = +0.769$

P.E. = ±0.039

FIGURE 24.

Correlation between height and weight of five-year-old boys.

children tend to be heavier than the short children. A positive correlation between the two variables therefore exists. If the relationship were perfect, that is, if a child who is one standard unit above the average in height is also one standard unit above the average in weight and so on through all the cases, all the measurements would fall exactly on the diagonal line extending from the lower left to the upper right corner.* The fact that not all the measurements fall on this diagonal, but merely scatter around it, shows that we are dealing with a correlation which, while positive, is not perfect. The student should notice carefully the extent to which the measures scatter away from the diagonal in this and other correlation charts, and compare the amount of scatter with the value of the correlation obtained.

When perfect correlation exists, a deviation from the mean in one of the measurements is always accompanied by an equal deviation of its paired measure from the mean of the second variable.† The sum of the products of these deviations will be exactly equal to the product of the two standard deviations multiplied by the number of cases. This is the principle upon which the product moment formula is based.

The small numbers in the upper left corner of each cell in Figure 24 show the xy value of that cell, that is, the product of the distances of the cell (in terms of class intervals) from each of the two arbitrary origins. Note that those cells which lie exactly on the diagonal line have a value which is the square of the distance of the cell from the lines of arbitrary origin. Since the standard deviation is defined as the square root of the mean of the squares of the individual deviations from their means, it is evident that only those

* Provided that the data are similarly grouped so that a class interval represents the same proportion of a standard deviation in each variable.
† Both deviations must be expressed in standard units.

paired measures which fall directly on the diagonal line will contribute to the xy value in the same measure as they contribute to the two standard deviations. Whenever an individual entry departs from this diagonal line, the xy value will be less than the contribution which the measures make to the standard deviations of the two variables. The farther away from the diagonal, the greater is the discrepancy between the xy values of the paired measures and the part which they play in increasing the standard deviation, and the lower, consequently, will be the correlation.

It will be noted further that the heavy lines marking the boundaries of the intervals containing the arbitrary origins divide the chart into four quadrants. The entries in the lower left and the upper right quadrants have positive values, since in these quadrants the sign of both variables is the same. Those in the upper left and the lower right quadrants have negative values, since the scores are above the arbitrary origin in one measurement and in the other below it.

In computing the coefficient of correlation, which, as we have seen, is the ratio of the mean of the xy products to the product of the standard deviations of the two variables, we begin by finding the two standard deviations in the usual manner. If we are concerned only with the value of the correlation and not with the size of the means or standard deviations we may work in terms of class intervals throughout, without transmuting into original values. The product of the two standard deviations is entered in the denominator of the fraction. The xy value of each cell which contains a frequency is then found by multiplying the number of steps above or below the arbitrary origin in the x variable by the corresponding number of steps in the y variable. A cell which is located 5 steps above the mean of the x variable and 7 steps above the mean of the y variable would have an xy value of 5×7 or 35. The Σxy product for that cell will then be the value of the cell multiplied by the number of cases within it.

In the manner just described find the Σxy products for all the positive frequencies in each horizontal row and enter these values in the column headed $\Sigma + xy$. Do the same for the negative values, if there are any, and enter the sum in the column headed $\Sigma - xy$. The difference between the $\Sigma + xy$ and the $\Sigma - xy$ values is the algebraic sum of the xy products computed from an arbitrary origin. We need the mean of this value. This is found by dividing the algebraic Σxy by the number of cases in the group (here 50). Since these products have been computed from an arbitrary origin in each variable rather than from the true mean a correction is necessary. This correction is found by multiplying the x correction by the y correction (taking account of signs). The product of the two corrections is then subtracted from the mean xy value, $\left(\dfrac{\Sigma xy}{N} \right)$ and the result entered as the numerator of the fraction. The quotient obtained when the corrected mean of the xy products is divided by the product of the two standard deviations is the coefficient of correlation, which in this case is $+.769$.

The steps in computing the product moment correlation may then be summed up as follows:

1. Construct a *scatter-diagram* or *scattergram* using coarse ruled cross-section paper or, preferably, one of the standard correlation charts. Decide upon the size of the class intervals to be used in each variable and enter the values of the class intervals of the x variable along the abscissa, and the values for the y variable along the ordinate of the chart.

2. From a table showing the paired scores of the individual subjects on the two variables (or measurements) enter a tally mark for each individual on the correlation chart at the intersection of the row and

the column corresponding to his scores on the two measurements. Continue until all the paired measurements have been entered. *These entries should always be rechecked for accuracy.*

3. Find the sum of the number of frequencies in each horizontal row of cells and enter the total in a column at the right marked *fy*. In like manner sum the frequencies in each column and enter the results at the bottom of the columns in a horizontal row marked *fx*.

4. The *fx* row and the *fy* column are simple frequency tables for the *x* variable and the *y* variable respectively. Since the inexperienced student often finds it difficult to place the tally mark in the appropriate row and column, it is a good plan to prepare an ordinary frequency distribution for each of these variables on a separate sheet of paper, using the same class intervals that were used on the correlation chart, and making each frequency table independently of the scores in the other variable. These distributions may then be compared with those obtained by summing the tally marks on the correlation chart. If no error has been made in checking, the two frequency tables for each variable should correspond exactly. After sufficient practice has been gained in entering the tally marks on the correlation chart, a simple rechecking of the entries will usually be adequate. This checking should never be omitted, even with experienced workers, since misplacement of the tally marks is one of the most common errors in computing correlations.

5. After the tallying has been checked, find the standard deviation of each of the two frequency tables and record these values in the appropriate place on the correlation chart, or in some consistent position on the sheet if ordinary cross-section paper has been used.

6. If a standard correlation chart * is not used, find the *xy* value of each cell which contains a frequency by multiplying its distance from the *x* origin (the class interval in which the *x* mean was guessed) by its

---

* In the standard charts, the xy value of each cell is usually indicated on the chart itself, hence need not be computed separately.

distance from the y origin. Multiply the cell value thus obtained by the number of cases or frequencies within the cell and enter these results in the $+ xy$ column if both measures have the same sign and in the $- xy$ column if they are of opposite sign.

7. Find the algebraic sum of the xy values and divide by the number of cases in the group. In order to correct for errors in guessing the mean, subtract from this result the product of the corrections to the means of each of the two variables. Note that this is an algebraic subtraction, hence the signs of the two corrections must be considered.

8. Divide the mean xy product as thus obtained by the product of the two standard deviations ($\sigma_x \sigma_y$). The result is the product moment coefficient of correlation or r.

The formula is:

$$ r = \frac{\frac{\Sigma xy}{N} - c_x c_y}{\sigma_x \sigma_y} \text{ or } \frac{\Sigma xy - N c_x c_y}{N \sigma_x \sigma_y} \tag{14} $$

The regression lines. In a previous paragraph it was pointed out that in the case of perfect correlation, all the frequencies will fall within the cells lying on the diagonal line extending from the lower left to the upper right corner, provided that the plotting has been done in such a way that the class intervals in the x variable represent the same proportion of a standard deviation of x as those in the y variable do of a standard deviation of y. In case the correlation is less than 1.00 some of the frequencies will scatter on either side of the diagonal lines. (See Figures 25, 26, 27.) If we find the means of each of the successive rows in the y variable, that is, the mean x value corresponding to each class-interval of y, and indicate the position of each successive mean by a dot on the scattergram, and then rotate a stretched thread which passes through the point of origin (the point determined by the true means of the x and y

variables) until it appears by inspection to make the best
fit to the means of the rows, we shall find that in the case
of a positive correlation which is less than 1.00, this line
will form an angle of less than 45° with the vertical line
which passes through the *x* mean (the *x* axis). In other
words, the line of best fit to the means of the *y* arrays, as it
is customary to call the horizontal rows of cells in which the
y scores are entered, will have *regressed* from the 45° angle
which it occupies in the case of perfect correlation toward
the *x* axis and will occupy some position intermediate between the diagonal and the vertical line. If we now do the
same for the columns (the *x* arrays) we shall likewise find
that the line of best fit to the means of the *x* arrays will, in
the case of a correlation which is less than perfect, have
regressed toward the *y* axis. The greater the amount of regression, that is, the nearer the *regression lines* approach the
two axes of origin the lower is the correlation. In case the
regression is complete, so that the lines of regression coincide with the lines of origin (the means) the correlation is
zero. If the regression lines pass beyond the lines of origin
(the *x* and *y* axes) so that the frequencies scatter about
the diagonal line running from the lower right to the upper
left corner of the correlation chart, the correlation is negative, that is, a high score in one variable is likely to be accompanied by a low score in the other variable and *vice
versa*. Note that a negative correlation has exactly the
same significance as a positive one, and can always be expressed in positive terms by reversing the terminology. For
example, with increasing age, the time required to perform
many kinds of intellectual tasks decreases. It is therefore
correct to say that a negative correlation exists between age
and *time required* to perform a task of this kind. But it is
equally correct and less confusing to say that a positive
correlation exists between age and *speed* on such a task. As

a general rule it is preferable to plot data to be correlated in such a way that a correlation between desirable, or more advanced, or superior traits will be expressed in the positive

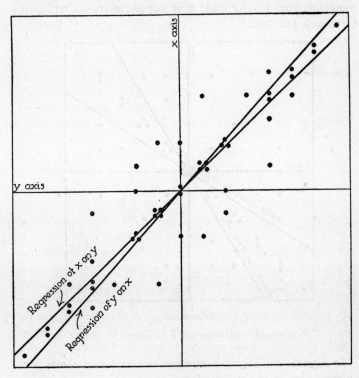

FIGURE 25.

Scattergram and regression lines when r = + .93.

form. If the customary arrangement is followed, the values which are *interpreted* as lowest (although numerically they may be the highest) will then be placed at the bottom in the *y* variable, and at the left in the *x* variable. Although this arrangement is purely arbitrary the practice is so general that it is well to adhere to it. It is hardly necessary to say that if, after a correlation has been worked out, it is thought desirable to express it in the opposite form, only the terminology need be changed; it is not necessary to replot or to rework the data.

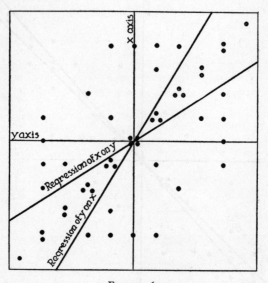

FIGURE 26.

Scattergram and regression lines when r = + .62.

In Figures 25, 26, 27 a number of correlation charts are shown in which the standard deviations in the two variables are plotted in equal units, so that the conditions making for equality of slope of the two regression lines with reference to their respective axes are fulfilled. Only when this is done, is the statement that perfect correlation is indicated by coincidence of the two regression lines with each other at an angle of 45° with the axes or lines of origin literally true. But in order to equalize the standard deviations be-

fore plotting, a considerable amount of unnecessary computation is required. Since the product moment formula as
given on page 271 is so arranged that inequalities in the
standard deviations will enter equally into both the numerator and the denominator of the fraction and will therefore
not affect its value, such equalization is rarely performed

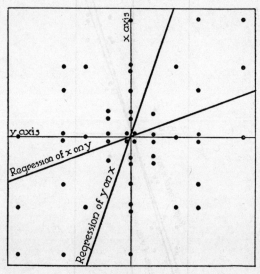

FIGURE 27.

Scattergram and regression lines when r = + .36.

except for purposes of demonstration. When the standard
deviations are not equalized, the line of perfect correlation
at which the two regression lines coincide will depart somewhat from the 45° angle, but the accuracy of the correlation computed from such a scattergram is not necessarily
affected.

Figure 28 shows the data used for the correlation shown
in Figure 25 when plotted without equalizing the standard

deviations. In this figure one variable has intentionally been grouped into a much smaller number of class intervals than the other, to illustrate the change in the slope of the regres-

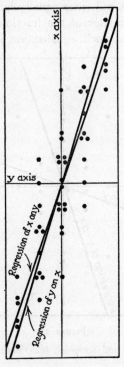

Scattergram and regression lines for data of Figure 25 when one variable is compressed into a small number of class-intervals.

sion lines which occurs when such an arrangement is necessitated by the fact that the original data are given only in a small number of coarse units. The student should note the change in the appearance of the charts resulting from these differences in grouping.

The regression lines, when properly fitted, have a highly important meaning. Since they pass through the points which give the best approximation to the position of the means of each successive array, they enable us to predict the most probable score in one variable which will be made by a subject whose score in the other variable is known. If, for example, we know the mean x score made by all the subjects whose y score was a given amount, we can say that this mean is the most probable x score corresponding to the y score in question. It is not necessary to compute all the means separately in order to make the necessary translation of the scores from one variable to another. This is done more simply by means of the *regression equations* which are:

$$\overline{y} = r . \frac{\sigma_y}{\sigma_x} . x \text{ or } \overline{x} = r . \frac{\sigma_x}{\sigma_y} . y \qquad (15)$$

where y and x indicate the most probable or mean value of a given y or x score expressed in terms of the other variable.* For example, suppose we wish to know what would be the most probable standing on a certain reading test of a child who has earned a score of 32 on a group intelligence test which correlates with the reading test to the extent of .75. The group for which this correlation was found had a mean score of 24 on the intelligence test with a standard deviation of 6.0. On the reading test the mean was 52 and the standard deviation 12.0. This child, then, stands 8 points above the mean on the intelligence test. If we consider the intelligence test scores as the y variable and the reading scores as the x variable and substitute the numerical values just given in the regression equation we have:

$$\overline{x} = .75 \frac{12}{6} 8 = 12.$$

* Note that there are two regression equations which cannot be used interchangeably.

A child who rates 8 points above the mean on the intelligence test would then be most likely to rate 12 points above the mean in the reading test. Since the latter mean is 52 points, the most probable score of this child would be 52 + 12 = 64. Note that although the difference in terms of score points is greater in the case of the reading test than in the intelligence test, its significance, when expressed in terms of standard deviations is less, as the regression line would indicate. On the intelligence test the child is 1.33σ above the mean; on the reading test only 1.00σ.

Although the regression line affords a basis for estimating the *most probable* standing of an individual in one measure when his standing in another correlated measure is known, we have seen in the scatter-diagrams that only when the correlation is perfect do all the actual measures fall exactly at the means of the arrays. Whenever the correlation is less than perfect, the measures in any array scatter about its mean, and the greater the scatter the lower the correlation. We therefore need some measure of the reliability of the predicted scores;—a measure which will tell us how far away from the mean of an array the individual scores are likely to scatter. This measure is furnished by the *standard error of estimate* of a $\overline{y}$ or an $\overline{x}$ score. The formula is:

$$\sigma_{\overline{y}} = \sigma_y \sqrt{1 - r^2} \qquad (16)$$

or conversely

$$\sigma_{\overline{x}} = \sigma_x \sqrt{1 - r^2} \qquad (17)$$

where $\sigma_{\overline{y}}$ and $\sigma_{\overline{x}}$ are the standard errors of the estimated scores and σ_y and σ_x are as usual the standard deviations of the distributions in the y and x variables respectively. These standard errors are interpreted in the same manner as the standard errors of any of the statistical constants which have been dealt with previously; that is, they indicate the standard deviations of the theoretical distributions of scores about the mean of the array. The formula is a highly important one for the understanding of correlation, and we shall return to it again in connection with the interpretation of the correlation coefficient.

In the product moment formula it is assumed that the lines of best fit to the means of the arrays (the regression lines) are rectilinear. While this is the most common condition in the kind of data with which we are dealing, it is not always true. Sometimes a curved line gives a better fit. If this is the case, neither the rank order method nor the product moment method is suitable for finding the correlation. A third method, known as the *correlation-ratio*, should be used. For this method the student is referred to any of the standard textbooks on statistical method.

The standard error of the correlation coefficient. Like other statistical measures, correlation coefficients computed from different samplings of a supposedly "well-shuffled" population may nevertheless be expected to vary somewhat from each other. The amount of such variation will depend upon the number of cases used in computing the correlation and the size of the coefficient itself. The formula for predicting the probable amount of variation is:

$$\sigma_r = \frac{1 - r^2}{\sqrt{N}} \tag{18}$$

When the rank order method of computing the correlation is used, the standard error is slightly larger. The formula becomes:

$$\sigma_p = 1.0471 \frac{1 - \rho^2}{\sqrt{N}} \tag{19}$$

The difference formulas (pp. 161 and 165) used for finding the reliability of a difference between two statistical measures apply to the difference between two correlation coefficients as well as to the other measures for which they have been suggested.

The interpretation of the correlation coefficient. If we are told that Johnny Jones read ten pages of a book and made only four errors, we are not much the wiser as to Johnny's reading ability unless we know something about the difficulty of the book from which the ten pages were read. If Tom Brown reads ten pages from a different book and makes the same number of errors as did Johnny, it would be quite unsafe to say that the reading ability of the two boys is equal. If Johnny chanced to be reading from an easy primer and Tom from one of Emerson's Essays, it would obviously be absurd to say that because the two boys made the same number of errors, one is as good a reader as the other.

In their interpretation of correlation coefficients, inexperienced students (and sometimes workers of more experience) often make an error which is much the same as the one just described, namely, of assuming that when two correlation coefficients derived from different samplings of the population chance to have the same magnitude their meaning is necessarily the same. In reporting reliability coefficients, for example, it is very difficult for some people to avoid the conclusion that if Mr. A. gives a certain test to a group of children in his town and finds a reliability coefficient of +.80, while Mr. B. gives another test which purports to measure the same function to a group of children in his town and also finds a reliability coefficient of +.80 that the two tests must be equally reliable. This does not necessarily follow, any more than it follows that Tom and John are equally good readers because they made the same number of errors in reading from different books. Such an assumption is safe only if it can be shown that the individual differences in the two groups of children were of approximately equal extent. Coarse distinctions can always be made more easily than fine ones. Unless the *difficulty of the task which the test is called upon to perform* in the two instances, namely, that of distinguishing between the reading ability of the different subjects, is approximately equal, it is impossible to compare the reliability coefficients directly. It is possible to secure a reliability coefficient of only .4 for a test within a very limited range where the task of discriminating between individuals is difficult, and a reliability coefficient of .9 for the same test with a group having wide individual differences. Only when equally fine distinctions are called for, are we warranted in making direct comparisons between coefficients of correlation derived from different groups. The child who makes ten errors in reading a page of Shakespeare may nevertheless be a better reader than the child who makes only two errors in reading an equal amount from a primer.

Experiment No. 32

The Effect of Heterogeneity in the Data upon the Reliability Coefficient

Prepare ten cards of Bristol board, three by ten inches in size. Upon each of these cards draw a heavy line in black ink. These lines should vary in length from five to six inches by intervals of one-tenth of an inch. No two lines should be exactly the same length. On the back of the cards write the correct length of the lines, also letters to serve as an identification mark. The letters should be assigned in random order so that they will furnish no clue to the actual lengths of the line. Provide the members of the class with paper and pencils and say to them, "I am going to show you some cards on which lines of different lengths have been drawn. You are to look at the cards and guess the length of each line as nearly as you can. Express your guesses in terms of inches and tenths of an inch. You will have ten seconds for each card. Write your estimates in order as the cards are shown and do not omit any. Remember that no two lines are alike, so none of your estimates should be the same."

As soon as all the cards have been shown say, "I will now read a series of letters which you will use for identifying the cards later on. These letters are arranged in random order, and do not correspond with the length of the lines in any way. They are to be used purely for identification purposes." The instructor should then read the identification letters in the order in which the cards were shown and the students should write them down in a column opposite their estimates. The cards should then be thoroughly shuffled, after which they are again shown to the class, who are to write down their estimates as before. The identification letters should then be read again in the new order in order that the students may match their first estimate for each line against the second estimate. The reliability of all the estimates should then be computed by correlating the estimates on the first trial with the corresponding estimates on the second trial.

A second series of ten cards should then be shown. In these the lines vary by one-fifth inch intervals from four and a half to six and a half inches. Two trials should be given as before. The reliability of these estimates should then be determined. Which series shows the higher reliability? Explain.

Kelley (390) has devised a method for estimating the reliability in one range when its reliability in another range is known and the standard deviations of both ranges are given. The formula is as follows:

$$\frac{\sigma}{\Sigma} = \frac{\sqrt{1 - R}}{\sqrt{1 - r}} \qquad (20)$$

In this formula σ and Σ are the standard deviations of the scores in the two groups: r and R are the reliability coefficients.

We may apply this formula to our data in the following manner. Call the reliability coefficient for the first series r. Find the standard deviation of the true lengths of the lines in this series and call this σ. Do the same for the second series and call the results R and Σ. Substitute the numerical results thus obtained in Formula 18 and see how accurately the prediction is fulfilled.*

The significance of this principle for the interpretation of coefficients of correlation should be clear. If we substitute tests or other instruments of measurement for the judges, and compare the relative accuracy with which individuals can be differentiated by these tests, we shall find that the accuracy of placement (test reliability) varies with the difficulty of the task which the test is called upon to perform. Just as the number of errors which a child makes in reading varies with the difficulty of the reading material, or the ability of an observer to differentiate between lines of different length varies with the amount of difference (in proportion to the total length) between the lines whose length is judged,

---

* Formula (20) assumes that the measure used is equally reliable over the entire range considered. This is not completely true in the examples given, since Weber's Law applies to the judgment of the length of the lines within this range, consequently the lines should differ by a constant proportion of each successive length, rather than by a uniform increment. The task of estimating the length would therefore be somewhat more difficult with the longer than with the shorter lines in each series and the reliability at the upper limits would accordingly be somewhat less than at the lower limits. However, the error in this case is not great, and since the matter is likely to be somewhat confusing to the beginner, it has been disregarded in setting up this experiment.

so also will the reliability of a measuring instrument or the correlation between the measurements of two related traits in a group of individuals vary with the heterogeneity of the group.

Differences in heterogeneity may be brought about in many ways, but in the case of young children one of the most important factors is age. Since most of the physical and mental traits of children are changing with age, a positive relationship between such traits will usually be found when the measurements of a number of children who differ in age are thrown into a single correlation table. Such a correlation may mean only that the older children rank higher in both traits, even though no intrinsic relationship between the traits exists. The age factor has introduced an element of heterogeneity into the group which is similar for both variables. The obtained correlation is due to the fact that both measurements differentiate the children on the basis of *age*. The greater the age variance the better will be the age differentiation and the higher the correlation. There are many other factors which may bring about systematic heterogeneity within a group and thereby produce an apparent correlation between traits which are fundamentally unrelated, or which may raise a reliability coefficient far above the point which it would occupy if the extraneous factor or factors were controlled. Among these may be mentioned differences in motivation, emotional factors operating in a similar way throughout a series of measurements, misunderstanding of directions or the lack of an adequate fore-exercise.

From the examples which have been given, two principles of fundamental importance may be formulated.

1. A reliability coefficient, or a coefficient of correlation between two different variables must be interpreted

in terms of the heterogeneity of the group measured; that is, in terms of the fineness of the distinctions which the instrument is called upon to make. A high reliability coefficient means nothing more than that the measuring instrument has been set a task which it is able to perform with accuracy. If a more difficult task, requiring finer distinctions between individuals is set for it, its reliability in that situation will be lower. For this reason the *variability of the group for which the correlation was obtained must always be stated* if coefficients of correlation are to have meaning.

2. Since extraneous factors related to both variables may bring about systematic heterogeneity resulting in an apparent correlation between traits which have no intrinsic relationship to each other, correlational data should be examined with much care in order to make sure that confusing elements of this kind have been adequately controlled.

The dependence of the correlation coefficient upon the heterogeneity of the group has been emphasized at the outset because of the difficulty experienced by many people in seeing the connection between a measure of relationship and a measure of dispersion. Paradoxical as it may seem, correlation is a function of dissimilarity rather than similarity. Its fundamental requirement is that the individuals measured shall differ among themselves. If correlation exists the individual differences found in one measurement will be related to those found by another measurement (either of the same or of a different characteristic) in such a way that standing in one can be predicted from standing on the other with better than chance accuracy. Correlation means nothing more than concomitant variation.

The significance of a correlation coefficient then reduces itself essentially to a question of the accuracy of the prediction which can be made from it. This question has two aspects. First, how accurately has the true magnitude of the correlation been determined? The answer to this question is given by the standard error of the correlation coefficient (Formulas 18, 19). Reference to Table 11 will show the probability in terms of the number of chances in a thousand that in other samplings drawn from the same population, fluctuations above or below the obtained value of the correlation may be expected to occur. Thus, if in the sample studied the correlation between two measures was found to be +.34 with a standard error of .17, Table 10 shows that there are approximately 158 chances in a thousand that in another sampling the correlation obtained would be as much as one standard error higher (+.51 or more) and an equal number that it would be as much as one standard error lower (+.17 or less). There are about 23 chances in each direction that it would differ by as much as two standard errors, that is, that it would become as high as +.68 or as low as .00. Evidently, when the standard error of a correlation is high, one cannot place much dependence upon the relationship. If the coefficient is not more than two or three times its standard error we cannot be sure that it is not the result of chance.

Suppose, however, that the correlation in question has been obtained from such a large number of cases that its standard error is negligible for most purposes, say not greater than .001, so that we may fairly accept the coefficient at its face value. Under these circumstances, what does a given degree of correlation mean in terms of prediction?

If we know nothing about the correlations of the measure which we wish to predict, but do know its mean and standard deviation for the group under consideration, our best "guess" as to the measurement of any individual case would of course be the mean of the group, since by definition the mean is the point about which the deviations of the separate measures are at a minimum. The standard error of such a guess would then be equal to the standard deviation of the group. Now if in order to make this guess somewhat more accurate we wish to make use of a knowledge of the score attained by the subject on some other measurement which is correlated to a known extent with the measurement to be predicted, we shall make use of the regression equation which enables us to change our estimate of the subject's standing from the mean of the entire group to the mean of the particular *array* which corresponds to his measurement in the other variable.

But we have seen before (p. 278) that while it is true that the mean of this array is the best approximation which we can make to the probable standing of the individual on the trait in question, whenever the correlation between the two measurements is less than perfect, not all the measures will actually fall at the mean but will be scattered around it. The error of estimate involved when the mean of the array is taken as the best expression for each of the individual measurements within the array is the standard error of the array or $\sigma\sqrt{1 - r^2}$. (Formulas 16, 17.) But when no account is taken of the measurement in the correlated variable, and prediction is made solely on the basis of the mean of the group, the error of estimate is equal to the standard deviation of the group or σ.

The comparative size of the two errors of estimate is then given by the ratio

$$\frac{\sigma\sqrt{1 - r^2}}{\sigma}$$

The use of the correlated measure as a means of predicting or estimating the most probable standing of the individual subjects on the trait with which we are concerned will reduce our *errors of estimate,* on the average, to a magnitude which is only $\sqrt{1-r^2}$ as great as they would otherwise have been. Expressed conversely, the mean percentage of *gain in accuracy of prediction* secured in this way is $1-\sqrt{1-r^2}$.

We can make this more concrete by considering a few examples. If $r = .50$, $\sqrt{1-r^2} = .866$ and the average gain in accuracy brought about by predicting scores in the second variable on the basis of those made in the first is 13.4 per cent. If $r = .707$, $\sqrt{1-r^2} = .707$, and the error of estimate has been reduced 29.3 per cent. If $r = .866$, $\sqrt{1-r^2} = .50$, and the error of estimate is only half as great as it would otherwise have been. If $r = .98$, $\sqrt{1-r^2} = .199$, and the error of estimate has been reduced to a fifth of its original amount.

The value $\sqrt{1-r^2}$ is known as the *coefficient of alienation*. It measures the lack of relationship between two variables just as r measures the presence of relationship. Because of its frequent use in statistics it is often denoted by the letter k.

To some persons, the discovery that the actual predictive value of a correlation is so much smaller than its numerical value had led them to expect is very disappointing. A little consideration, however, will show that this feeling is unwarranted. Whether or not a given correlation is to be regarded as significant or useful depends upon a number of factors, and cannot be determined from its absolute magnitude alone. From the scientific standpoint, the existence of any relationship, no matter how small, is, if true (that is, if the standard error is small enough to be negligible), a fact to be explained. A correlation so small that no one would think of using it for predictive purposes in the guidance of individual behavior may nevertheless have important implications for the understanding of behavior in general. Moreover, even from the practical standpoint, a measurement which on the average reduces the error of estimate by as little as 5 or 10 per cent is by no means to be despised, provided the method is not too costly in time and effort, and the end served is an important one. A gain of five per cent may be of enormous total value if applied to a very large number of cases. In the financial world, an investment which yields such a return is respected. The field of human behavior is surely quite as complex as the stock market. Need we be surprised if the methods available for the study of child behavior usually fail to yield one hundred per cent prediction?

From earliest times, the layman has been inclined to look upon the experiments of the scientist with a curious mixture of credulity and distrust. This leads to a rather widespread conviction that in some way an error in advice or treatment which is consequent upon an error in an attempted measurement exerts a far more pernicious effect upon the subject than a similar or even a greater error resulting from individual prejudice, ignorance, or neglect. There is no reason why this should be true unless the alleged measurement is falsely endowed with a reputation for infallibility which it does not in fact possess, thus making it difficult to correct the errors resulting from its use. Provided its limitations as well as its possibilities are clearly recognized, an instrument which materially lessens the probability of error, even though it does not preclude it, may be well worth using. If, moreover, the results obtained by its use are carefully recorded and evaluated from time to time in the light of later events, the way to improvement in the method will often be made clear. The danger in the use of fallible instruments lies not so much in their fallibility as in the failure of the uncritical user to recognize their limitations.

REFERENCES

The student is referred to the following titles in the bibliography at the end of this book:

380, 382, 384*, 389*, 390*, 391, 393, 397, 401, 403

Chapter 32

INTROVERSION AND EXTROVERSION

FOR years some psychologists and psychiatrists have been interested in the .possibility of classifying individuals into definite personality "types" distinguished by fairly well-marked patterns of reaction. Jung, a pupil of Freud who rejected many of Freud's original ideas, first used the terms *extroversion* and *introversion* as ways of describing two opposed kinds of emotional reaction. According to Jung, *extroversion* is characterized by an outward movement of interest toward the object, while *introversion* is characterized by a movement of interest away from the object toward the subject. We may express this more simply by saying that in the extroverted form of behavior the subject's interests and emotions are expressed freely and promptly with little attempt at concealment, while in the introverted form of behavior there is much less active expression of interest in external objects or events, and the subject's attention seems to be turned inward upon himself. Although emotional states are expressed less freely, feelings or moods often persist for considerable periods of time. This is in marked contrast with the behavior of the extrovert with whom emotional expression is commonly more violent but relatively transient.

The following descriptions which are taken from Marston's (176) account of the behavior of young children while visiting a museum of natural history illustrate these points.

"B.G. ran about the room, commanding the experimenter to follow and plying him with questions about the exhibits which greatly interested him. He was easily distracted, however, and for a time eagerly followed the janitor about the hall. His behavior was determined by an objectively directed but rapidly shifting interest. He was ready to leave the museum after eleven and a half minutes." (Extroverted behavior.)

"J.K. walked around and around the center section of the museum. He moved slowly and quietly, observing the exhibits with casual interest, seldom stopping to examine them closely. He retraced his course several times and did little exploring. The environment failed to attract him, and, although he was undoubtedly bored, he would not ask to return to the school but continued his monotonous walking. According to both ratings and experiments, J.K. is a pronounced introvert."

It is thought by some that introverts and extroverts constitute two distinct types of personality, in the sense that practically all individuals can be classified under one head or the other with comparatively few intermediate or undetermined types. The rating scale which will presently be described was constructed according to this hypothesis. More complete investigation, however, seems to point to the conclusion that introversion and extroversion, like tallness and shortness, beauty and ugliness, or brightness and stupidity, are not distinct types at all, but merely two opposed ends of a scheme of classification in which the great majority of people rank somewhere near the middle, with a much smaller number at either extreme. In other words, the distribution of introverts and extroverts among the general population appears to follow the normal frequency curve. Most people belong neither to one type or the other, but somewhere in between.

Experiment No. 33

A Scale for Rating Introversion-Extroversion in Young Children

In this experiment the rating scale devised by Dr. L. R. Marston at the State University of Iowa (176) is to be used.* This scale forms part of a study of the extent to which the emotional and social behavior of young children becomes organized into the habitual modes of reaction which we call "personality traits." Although the scale was constructed upon the hypothesis that introverts and extroverts are distinct personality "types" rather than opposite ends of a continuous series, the fact that it was devised particularly for use with children under the age of six makes it an extremely useful device for studying certain aspects of the emotional behavior of young children. When ratings from several competent judges are secured for the same children and combined to give a single score, the reliability of the scale is usually found to be very high. If repeated ratings are made for the same children year after year, a valuable record of changes in personality can be secured. Although the scale was originally designed for use with children of preschool age it may also be used with children in the primary grades.

Procedure: Select the experimental group with whom the students are most familiar, and have a copy of the Marston scale filled out by each student for each child. If standard blanks are not available, a test sheet may be prepared for each child in the following manner. At the top of the sheet should be placed the child's name, sex, date of birth, name of school, and grade. The date of making the rating and the name of the rater should be added, with a statement as

* Copies of this scale can be obtained from the University of Iowa Child Welfare Research Station, Iowa City, Iowa.

to how long and under what circumstances the rater has been acquainted with the child. Below this the numbers from 1 to 20 should be arranged in parallel columns. The rater should read the descriptions for each trait carefully, and decide upon the score to be given the child in question. This score may then be entered in a second column opposite the number of the trait to which it applies. The sum of the ratings on all the traits should then be found, and entered as the child's total score. According to Marston, ratings above 60 indicate some tendency toward extroversion, while those below 60 show a tendency toward introversion. A somewhat more cautious method of interpretation would be to say that children who rate below 50 tend toward the introvert type, and those rating above 70 toward the extrovert type; while those who rate between 50 and 70 are not definitely classifiable within either group. It should be noted that this statement applies only when the scores are based upon the average ratings of several competent judges. When only one or two judges participate in the rating, personal bias is likely to enter in to such an extent as to make any attempt at individual comparison or classification unsafe.

Problems: 1. Combine all the ratings for each child and prepare a list of the sums. Let each student first subtract his own series of scores from this sum and then find the correlation between his own ratings for the different children and the average given by all the other members of the class, excluding himself. Each student should also find the correlation between his own ratings, and those given by at least three of the other members of the class taken separately. If there are as many as 20 children in the group rated, the Pearson product moment method of computing the correlations should be used, in order to give the students additional facility in the use of this method.

2. Find the mean rating for each child on the introversion-

Introversion and Extroversion   295

extroversion scale as given by all the judges. What is its correlation with chronological age? with mental age if mental tests have been given the children? with IQ?

3. Compare the sexes with regard to introversion-extroversion as indicated by the mean ratings on this scale? How reliable is the difference found?

4. Find the reliability of the combined series of ratings given by all the judges by first dividing the raters into two random halves and then correlating the sums of the ratings given by the first group against the corresponding sums given by the second group. What further procedure is necessary in order to secure an estimate of the reliability of the total? Apply this procedure and compare the result thus obtained with the reliability of other tests and measurements which have been found in previous studies carried out by the class.

5. Draw a frequency polygon showing the distribution of the total ratings for all the children as given by all the members of the class. Does the form of this distribution suggest that two distinct types are present?

REFERENCES

The student is referred to the following titles in the bibliography at the end of this book:

111, 176*, 210, 245, 296*, 302*, 333.

Chapter 33

LAUGHTER

BECAUSE of its universality among human beings at all ages and in all levels of culture, laughter affords a means of studying certain aspects of the personal-social relations of the individual, which has an unusually wide range of applicability. Individuals differ both in respect to the frequency with which they laugh and the nature of the stimuli which cause them to do so. Some stimuli are quite generally laughter provoking while others acquire this quality by virtue of individual experience or the traditions of a particular group. Laughter in children is so easily observed and occurs so frequently that it furnishes excellent material for the study of individual differences in social and emotional behavior.

Experiment No. 34

Individual Differences in Frequency of Laughter, and Their Relationship to Other Personality Characteristics

Procedure: The method of the short time sample described in Chapter 28 (Social behavior) is to be used. The construction of a graded series of categories for laughter is left as an exercise for the class. The series should range from complete soberness of expression to loud boisterous shouts of laughter. Each step should be clearly defined. It is best to work out a series of tentative definitions in class, then have one or more observational periods devoted to testing the objectivity of the descriptions by simultaneous observations of the same children by paired observers who make their records independently of each other. At the end of the period the results of the simultaneous observations should be compared, and the definitions revised at any points where there is much disagreement in classification. At least 95 per cent of the records should agree exactly, and disagreements greater in amount than one step on the scale should not occur.

After a satisfactory series of definitions has been devised, a series of observational samples should be secured for each child by each student in the manner described in Chapter 28. A one minute sample is used as before, but in this case, since laughter is a form of behavior which is relatively transient and which requires but an instant to observe and classify, it will be well to divide the minute of observation into six ten second periods, and to record the behavior separately for each of these intervals.

At the end of the minute make a note of (a) the child's occupation during the period of observation, (b) whether he was alone or in a group, and (c) the apparent cause of the laughter.

Subjects: Children of any age may be used.

Problems: 1. Find the amount of observational error by calculating the per cent of the total number of records in which there was disagreement between simultaneous observers amounting to one, two, or more steps on the scale used for recording the behavior.

2. Calculate a "laughter score" for each child. Weight the various steps on the scale from zero (for absence of laughter or smiling) by progressive increases of 1 up to the highest category used. Then multiply the number of times the child's behavior was classified under each category by the weight

given to that category, add the results and divide by the total number of observations * for that child. If the same number of observations is secured for each subject the weighted sums may be used instead of the means.

3. Find the reliability of the laughter scores by correlating the mean score earned on the even-numbered observations with those earned on the odd numbered observations and correcting by the Spearman-Brown prophecy formula as described in Chapter 15.

4. What is the correlation of the laughter scores with (a) chronological age? (b) mental age and IQ if mental test scores are available? (c) with extroversion if the same children were used for the Marston ratings described in the last experiment? (d) with other measurements or ratings which may have been secured for these children?

5. Analyze the data on the children's occupations at the time the observations were made to see which kinds of occupation are most likely to be accompanied by laughter. What occupations are rarely accompanied by laughter?

6. Is laughter more frequent during solitary or group play? What is the reliability of the difference found?

7. Classify the apparent causes of laughter for this group and arrange in order of frequency.

8. Make a comparative case study of the two children with the highest and the lowest laughter scores. Arrange the data in parallel columns, showing how the children compare in as many characteristics as possible. Include such facts from the home and family background as are available. Add a short descriptive summary, pointing out the facts which seem most significant.

---

* A more exact system of weighting is described in Kelley (390), pp. 99-102. If there are as many as thirty children in the group studied and the class is sufficiently advanced it is well to use this method instead of the arbitrary system of weighting described here.

REFERENCES

The student is referred to the following titles in the bibliography at the end of this book:

34, 35, 68, 70*, 71, 108*, 153, 245, 265*, 290, 302.

Chapter 34

JUDGING EMOTION FROM FACIAL EXPRESSION

FOR many years it was rather generally assumed that each emotion carries with it a characteristic facial expression by which it may be recognized. Books and articles have described in detail the contractions of the facial muscles which were believed to accompany each emotion, and apparatus has been constructed for the purpose of demonstrating in the laboratory the facial expression of emotion. More recent experiments, however, have cast some doubt upon the assumption that the emotional states of others can always or even usually be identified from outward appearance. It has been pointed out that much of the apparent uniformity in the drawings and photographs used as examples of emotional expression may have its origin in mere tradition rather than in fact. Moreover since these illustrations are commonly labeled with the name of the emotion which they have been intended to portray, the observer acquires a "mental set" which leads him to read into the expression a degree of specificity which is not there. Often when a given expression would serve equally well for any one of several emotional states, if the observer is told in advance that a particular one of these, as anger, fear, or jealousy is depicted he will see the expression in the light of this "set" and ignore the other possibilities. Under the influence of the stage, art, and literature, custom has decreed that certain conventional expressions shall be used to indicate the various emotions. Accordingly when one wishes to convey the idea of a certain emotional state he endeavors to arrange his features according to the pattern which convention has set for the portrayal of that emotion.

For these reasons, the practice which has been common in the past of using specially posed photographs of actors or trained adults to illustrate the facial expression of emotion has been justly criticized. These criticisms may be avoided by making use of photographs of young children. The children should be old enough to have developed a fair degree of muscular control * but should not have reached a stage of development at which their general behavior or facial expression is likely to have been affected by a knowledge of traditional standards, and they should be unacquainted with the function of a camera. It is of course true that children of these ages cannot furnish introspective accounts of their emotional states; hence the existence of an emotion must be judged purely from the child's behavior and from a knowledge of the emotional potentialities of the situation. If, however, it turns out that persons ignorant of the nature of the stimulus given are able to judge its general character from observation of the behavior alone, strong evidence for the existence of native or untaught emotional reaction patterns is afforded. If this can be done with fair success from observations of photographs alone, the evidence will be still stronger, since the photograph shows only a single brief stage in the reaction and tells nothing of the sequences of movement or of the vocalizations which accompany it. The task of identifying the total behavior pattern by means of such a small portion of it is far from easy. Whatever success

---

* Sherman (221) has shown that the responses of new-born infants to situations such as dropping, loud noises, pricking with a pin, or restrained movements are so undifferentiated that trained adults cannot distinguish one from another unless the stimulus is known.

occurs takes on added significance because of the small number of clues provided.

Experiment No. 35

Judging Emotion from Photographs

Material: In Figure 29 there will be found a series of photographs of a ten-months-old infant. These photographs were taken under conditions likely to be provocative of mild emotional states at an instant when the child's behavior suggested to the observer that the anticipated emotion had been aroused. Since the youth of the child makes it practically certain that the character of the emotional expression has not been affected by social tradition, and "camera consciousness" is for the same reason ruled out, these photographs have decided advantages over such pictures of adults posed to simulate emotions of various kinds as have generally been used in studies on the judgment of emotional expression.

On the following page will be found descriptions of the situations under which the photographs were taken. In some instances the emotion which the child was believed to be experiencing is also indicated.* Descriptions of four additional situations have been added in order that the matching of the last picture will not be determined automatically by a process of elimination.

Subjects. The members of the class will act as judges.

Procedure. On a separate sheet of paper write in a column the numbers from 1 to 12. These numbers correspond to the situations described on page 303.

* The photographs with their descriptions have been reproduced by permission of the publishers from "Die Entwicklung der Gemütsbewegungen im ersten Lebensjahre" by Martin Buchner, *Beiträge zur Kinderforschung und Heilerziehung*, 1909, 60, pp. 19. The descriptions have been

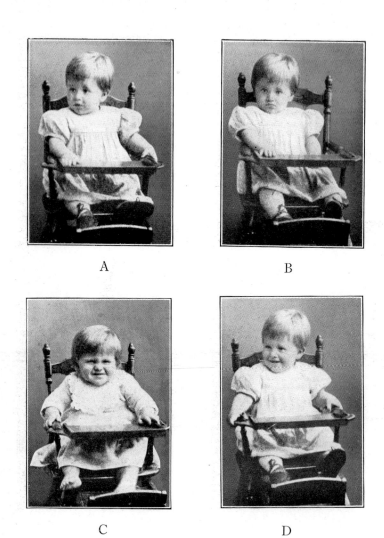

A   B

C   D

FIGURE 29 (From Buchner)

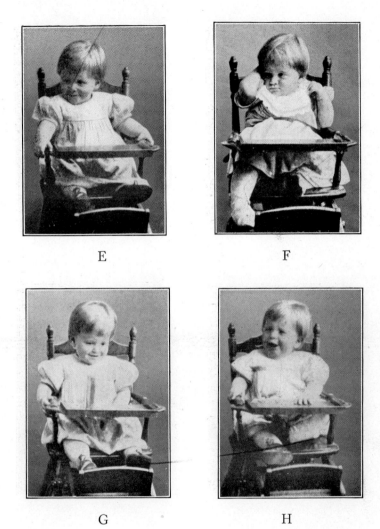

E

F

G

H

Expression of the emotions in a ten-months-old infant.

Now look at the first picture (labeled A) facing page 302. Note the child's facial expression and bodily posture carefully, then read through the descriptions of all the situations in which the child was photographed. One of these

Situations corresponding to photographs facing pages 302 and 304.

(Translated from Buchner with minor adaptations)

1. Satisfied smiling (with affection). He was looking at his mother, who talked to him in a friendly manner.

2. Astonishment (with slight displeasure). I counted loudly and emphatically as I walked toward him—"twenty, twenty-one, twenty-two, *etc.*" He looked me uncomprehendingly in the face.

3. Fear (perhaps with dislike). A strange woman struck two blocks together, growled, and rushed suddenly up to him, frowning darkly.

4. Dissatisfaction (with slight obstinacy). I had taken him up in my arms and then put him back in the chair. He wanted to come to my arms again.

5. Astonishment (with auditory attention). He is listening to the ticking of a watch.

6. Slight obstinacy. His mother wanted him to give her his hands, but he would not because she had just taken a toy away from him.

7. Crying. He was tired of sitting and wanted to come out of his high chair into my arms.

8. Astonishment (with ocular attention). A bright-colored new toy clown was shown to him.

9. Grimacing. The rogue is trying to wink.

10. Pleasure. I rolled a shining tin can on the tray. He said softly, "dai."

11. Roguish smiling (with affection and tense expectation). His mother was teasing him, "Only wait, now, I'm going to catch you!"

12. Anger (and displeasure). A toy has been taken away from him.

translated literally except for the omission of certain specific references which might serve as a guide to the matching.

corresponds to Picture A. When you have decided which one of the situations described would be most likely to elicit the expression shown in this picture, write the letter A after the number of this description on your list. Do the same for Picture B, then for Picture C, and so on until all the pictures have been matched. Four unmatched situations will of course be left over. Turn now to page 517 where you will find a key showing the correct matching. How many of your judgments were correct?

Problems: 1. With eight pictures and twelve situations what is the theoretical probability of correct matching by chance alone? Find the total number of correct matchings for the entire class and subtract from this the number which may fairly be attributed to chance. What is the average number of correct judgments after the correction for chance has been made?

2. Tabulate the number of successes and failures made by the group for each picture separately. Which picture shows the highest percentage of correct judgments? Which has the lowest percentage?

3. Is any picture associated with any one incorrect situation more frequently than with the correct situation? What would you infer from this?

4. Compare the results obtained in this experiment with those reported in the literature.

5. Have the pictures judged by a group of nurses or mothers of young children, and compare with the class results in order to see whether daily experience with infants increases the ability to interpret their emotional behavior correctly.

REFERENCES

The student is referred to the following titles in the bibliography at the end of this book:

40, 80, 91*, 158*, 159*, 161, 220*, 221*, 222, 299.

Chapter 35

MENTAL HYGIENE

A **MAJOR** problem confronting the student of mental health in children is that of recognizing the early symptoms of social and emotional maladjustment and of distinguishing between those forms of behavior which indicate serious difficulties on the part of the child and those which are merely irritating to the adult. A recent study by Wickman (270) shows that teachers and psychiatrists differ considerably in their judgments as to the comparative seriousness of various kinds of misdemeanors shown by children. We cannot say that either the teachers or the psychiatrists were right in their estimates. In a sense both may have been. Undoubtedly all of us are influenced in our judgments by experience and training. Accordingly, when an undescribed list of misdemeanors is given out to be rated, it is improbable that the terms used will convey the same meaning to all the raters. "Stealing" for example is not a simple "all-or-none" phenomenon but ranges all the way from the petty pilferings, of which most children are occasionally guilty, to major thefts. If one rater thinks of stealing in terms of a casual theft of apples from a neighbor's tree, and another in terms of breaking into a store and robbing the cash register, it is not surprising if their ratings differ. It is therefore quite possible for two groups whose daily contacts with children and their problems differ so greatly as do those of teachers and psychiatrists to envisage the problems at such different levels that agreement in rating would hardly be possible.

A knowledge of the attitudes of different groups toward the so-called "problems" of childhood is, however, well worth securing, if we remember that we are dealing with attitudes, rather than with a true measure of the "seriousness" of the behavior under consideration. We may assume, however, that if opinions have been honestly given, the reactions of the group toward behavior of the kind described will vary somewhat in accordance with these opinions. Since social pressure is likely to be strongest when coming from immediate associates, the opinions of children regarding child misdemeanors are of particular interest.

Experiment No. 36

A Comparison of Standards of Behavior at Different Ages

From the literature on behavior problems in children, select from ten to fifteen cases illustrating various forms of maladjusted behavior. Prepare very brief abstracts of these case histories describing the essential features in each case in as simple language as possible. Ages and sex of the children should always be noted. Type each description on a separate slip of paper and have these slips arranged in order from the one judged to be least serious to that judged to be most serious by each of three groups of subjects as follows:

a. A group of elementary school children.

b. The members of the class each working independently.

c. Their parents or a similar group of middle-aged men and women.

Problems: 1. Compare the mean rank order of the various problems as judged by each of the three groups named above. If the number of judges in each group is sufficiently great the sexes should be kept separate, making six groups in place of three. What is the correlation between the mean rank given to each problem by the children and that given by the college students? Between the mean ranks of the students and those of the older adults? Between the ranks of the children and those of the older adults? Which problems show the greatest discrepancies in rank as rated by the different groups? Can you suggest any explanation?

2. It is interesting to note whether with increasing age and experience there is any tendency for opinion among the different members of a group to become more similar or more widely divergent. Do the children or the adults resemble each other more closely in the evaluations which they place upon problems such as those just described? Conclusions from data such as these must be very tentative, since the possibility of important differences in sampling is not excluded. If, however, we should find that the difference in the average intercorrelation of the judgments made by the individual members of each group is fairly marked, the findings would be at least suggestive. Kelley (390) has developed a short method for finding the average intercorrelation between series of scores whose means and standard deviations are equal. When, as in the present instance, scores are expressed in terms of *rank* these conditions are fulfilled. The formula appears intricate, but is really very simple. It will be found to save much labor when the number of intercorrelations to be computed is large.

$$\overline{r}_{11} = 1 - \frac{a\,(4\,N + 2)}{(a - 1)\,(N - 1)} + \frac{12\,\Sigma S^2}{a\,(a - 1)\,N\,(N^2 - 1)} \quad (21)$$

In this formula $\overline{r}_{11}$ is the average intercorrelation between the rank order of the separate judges in the group, a is the number of judges and N is the number of items ranked, in this case the number of problems listed. Σ as usual means *the sum of,* and S is the sum of the ranks given to each problem by all the judges.

A convenient method of tabulating the material is first to list the problems (identified by number or letter) in a column down the left hand side of the paper. The rank orders given by each judge to each problem are then listed in parallel columns to the right. The sum of all the ranks given to each problem is then found and entered in a column labeled S. Each of the S values is then to be squared and the squared values entered in a final column labeled S^2. (A table of squares should be used for this purpose.) The sum of the S^2 column is the value required for the second part of Formula 21.

Using the method just described find the average inter-correlation between the judges in each age and sex group. Do the results suggest that one sex is more uniform in its judgment of conduct disorders than the other? Upon the whole, do the children or members of the older and the younger group of adults show greater uniformity among themselves in attitudes toward these problems? Can you suggest a reason for this greater uniformity?

Experiment No. 37

Individual Differences in "Problem Tendencies" among Young Children

Prepare a list of twenty traits or characteristics shown by kindergarten children which are commonly regarded as desirable. Prepare a second list of twenty traits commonly regarded as undesirable. Be careful that the two lists include no terms which are the exact opposites of each other. Each trait should be defined in as objective terms as possible. Have each member of the class grade each child in the experimental group on each of the twenty traits in the two lists on a three-point scale, in which a grading of 1 indicates little or no manifestation of the trait in question, 2 shows a moderate degree of the trait and 3 a marked degree. Divide the class into two random halves and sum the scores for each child given by the first group of students on the list of desirable traits and also on the list of undesirable traits considered separately. Do the same for the scores given by the second group of students. Then secure a final score for each child on the desirable traits and the undesirable traits separately by combining the ratings given by both groups.

Problems: 1. Find the reliability of the scores of the undesirable traits through correlating the sum of the scores given to each child by the first group of students against the corresponding sum given by the second group. Do the same for the desirable traits. Using the Spearman-Brown formula find the reliability of the total scores given by all the students on each group of traits. Do individuals on the whole seem to agree more closely in their judgments of desirable or of undesirable characteristics?

2. Using the summed scores given by all the students, find the quartiles for the desirable and the undesirable traits separately. The quartiles are the dividing points which separate the groups into four divisions, with an equal number of cases in each division. The top 25 per cent or the upper quartile would then contain the 25 per cent of the cases who received the highest rating; the bottom quartile would include the 25 per cent of cases receiving the lower rating; the two middle quartiles would contain the 25 per cent immediately above and below the median.

3. On the basis of the above division classify the children into four groups as follows:

(a) The children who are classified in the top quartile on the list of desirable traits and in the bottom quartile on the list of undesirable traits. These children may be considered as in general a well-adjusted group, at least so far as the traits included in this list are concerned.

(b) The children who fall within the lowest 25 per cent on the list of desirable traits, and in the highest 25 per cent on the list of undesirable traits. In comparison to other members of the group, these children may be regarded as somewhat poorly adjusted.

(c) Children who seem to show rather negative personalities in that they rank low both in regard to desirable and undesirable qualities. It would probably be well to use the 50 percentile rather than the 25 percentile in classifying this group.

(d) Children whose personality traits are very pronounced both on the negative and the positive side, that is, those who rank in the highest 25 per cent on the list of desirable traits and the highest 25 per cent on the list of undesirable traits.

(e) Classify the remaining children according to the group which they most nearly resemble.

4. If time permits it will be well worth while to have each student make a comparative case study of one child in each of the above groups. All of the data available in the school records should be used, also other material which has been collected by the class in the course of other experiments. If possible this information should be supplemented by a visit to the home for the purpose of getting such information on family relationships and the general home environment as it seems desirable and feasible to secure. In case the home interview is made, the facts to be secured in the course of the visit should be discussed in class, and a standard record form prepared which is to be used by all the students for recording this information. The results obtained by all the students on all the subjects studied in this manner may then be combined in order to show what characteristic differences in home background appear between the groups.

REFERENCES

The student is referred to the following titles in the bibliography at the end of this book:

21, 23, 40, 42, 76*, 114, 120*, 121*, 145, 178, 199*, 200*, 210, 216*, 231, 240, 252, 264, 267, 270*, 274, 277, 279, 337, 390.

Chapter 36

CHILDREN'S PREFERENCES FOR THE DIFFERENT SCHOOL SUBJECTS

A NUMBER of investigations have dealt with children's interests in the various subjects of the school curriculum. In general these investigations have shown that in any school system certain subjects tend to be relatively unpopular while others are quite generally liked. A few subjects, usually those of a comparatively formal nature such as spelling, seem to have rather neutral interest value since the majority of children fail to express either positive liking or definite dislike for them. Still others may be described as ambivalent. While few children are indifferent toward them, they are about equally often liked and disliked.

Unquestionably, methods of teaching the different subjects have some bearing upon the children's comparative interest in them. Interests also vary with sex and with the mental level of the children. In the Stanford University study of gifted children (244), for example, it was found that when both the exceptionally bright children and a control group of unselected children from the same schools were asked to indicate their interests in the subjects studied, the rank orders shown on the following page were obtained:

Reading is popular with all the children, especially with the gifted group. Penmanship is generally disliked, especially by the brighter children. History is better liked by the boys than by the girls, spelling and singing are more liked by the girls, particularly in the control group. In this

	Gifted		Control	
	Boys	Girls	Boys	Girls
Reading	1	1	2	4
History (U. S.)	2	3	1	9
Physical training	3	4	4	3
Spelling	4	2	5	1
Arithmetic	5	8	7	5
Geography	6	5	3	7
Drawing	7	6	6	6
Singing	8	7	9	2
Penmanship	9	9	8	8

group of cases the rank orders given by the gifted boys and the gifted girls to the nine subjects listed here correlate with each other to the extent of +.85; the rank orders given by the gifted and control boys have a correlation of +.83, but those of the gifted and control girls show a small negative correlation of —.13. When a much larger number of school subjects, including many which were studied by only a small proportion of the children (such as instrumental music, clay modeling, civics and agriculture), the corresponding correlations were as follows: gifted boys *vs.* control boys +.717; gifted boys *vs.* gifted girls, +.593; gifted girls *vs.* control girls +.165. These correlations are probably somewhat less reliable since the mean ranks in many instances were based on small numbers of cases. While the findings need confirmation from other groups, they suggest that the academic interests of boys resemble each other rather closely regardless of intellectual level, while those of girls are differentiated along intellectual lines rather than sex lines.

Experiment No. 38

School-Room Interests of Primary Grade Children

Subjects: This investigation is suitable for use with children above the second grade. If desired, a similar investigation may be carried out in the first and second grade by individual questioning, but children of these ages are so likely to be guided in their replies only by their most recent experiences that the results will have considerably less value than those obtained in the upper grades where the children are more able to make their judgments upon the basis of experience extending over a period of time. If carried on throughout an entire school system, the results obtained should have considerable practical value, since if, as is usually the case, it is found that there are certain subjects rather universally disliked while others are popular it at least suggests that some modification in the teaching method used for the unpopular subjects is desirable.

Procedure: Supply each child in the class with a sheet of paper upon which he is to write his name, age at last birthday, name of school and grade. Place on the board a list of the names of all the school subjects taught in that grade and have the children copy it on their papers. When sufficient time has been allowed for the copying of the list give the following instructions.

"We are trying to find out which of the subjects children study in school are liked best. It is really a sort of contest in which we vote for the best school subjects just as we might vote for the person who is to be president of the class. This is a secret ballot, so no one must look to see how anybody else is voting. Vote for the subject which you, yourself, like best. Read through the list on your paper and put a figure 1 in front of the subject which you like best of all. Choose just one subject and mark it No. 1. Do it as quickly as you can." Allow thirty seconds and then say, "Now we are going to vote for the subject which you like next best. Look over the others on the list and decide which one you like second best. Mark it No. 2. Do it as quickly as you can." Allow thirty seconds then say, "Now we will choose the third best.

Look over the names of the other subjects and decide which you like third best. Mark it with a 3." Continue in the same way until all the subjects have been ranked. Collect the papers and give out fresh sheets. After making sure that each child's name is on the paper, have the same list of subjects copied again. Then say, "Some of you had a hard time making up your mind before. Now we are going to mark the subjects again in a different way. This time we shall only say whether you like the subject or whether you don't. Look over the subjects again and mark each one that you really and truly *like* with a capital L. Mark all those that you *don't like* with a capital D. But there may be some subjects which you neither like nor dislike, which you don't mind one way or the other. Mark those with an X. Be sure to write plainly. Do you understand? Mark all the subjects that you really like with a capital L, those that you don't like with a capital D, and those that you neither like nor dislike with an X. All right, go ahead."

If data from as many as fifty children in each grade or at each age are obtained, the results may be scaled according to the method of equally often noticed differences (396, 397). With smaller groups, the error of scaling is likely to be too large to make this method feasible. In such cases a simpler treatment in terms of mean rank for the first set of data and in terms of percentage of each type of reaction for the second set is all that can be obtained.

Problems: 1. Find the order of popularity of the different subjects in each grade in which the investigation is carried out by summing all the ranks given to each subject and dividing by the number of cases in the group. Compare the rank orders of the subjects from grade to grade. Which is the favorite subject in each grade? The least favored subject in each grade?

2. Using the second set of data find for each subject

separately in each grade the percentage of (a) liking, (b) disliking, (c) indifference. Classify the subjects according to the following heads:

a. Usually liked, rarely disliked. At least 75 per cent of the ratings within this grade should be L, not more than 10 per cent D.

b. Usually disliked, rarely liked. More than 50 per cent of the ratings for this group should be D, not more than 25 per cent L. If there is no subject which meets this criterion the limits can be made somewhat less severe and *frequently* substituted for *usually* in the caption, as, "frequently disliked, rarely liked."

c. Subjects with indifferent interest value. 50 per cent or more of the ratings X, with the remainder about equally divided between L's and D's.

d. Ambivalent subjects. Ratings of L and D about equally frequent and making up at least 75 per cent of the entire number.

e. Place any subjects which do not clearly fall into any of the above heads in the group which they most nearly resemble.

Does a given subject tend to keep the same classification from grade to grade? What are the chief shifts in subject preference from grade to grade?

3. Divide the children in each grade into two groups on the basis of chronological age, placing in one group the older 50 per cent of the class, and in the other group the younger 50 per cent. Compare these two groups with regard to (a) the percentage of subjects which are liked, (b) the percentage of subjects which are disliked, (c) the percentage of subjects rated as indifferent. Find the reliability of the difference between these percentages. What conclusions would you draw?

The principle involved in finding the standard error of a difference between percentages is identical with that of finding the standard error of a difference between two means and therefore need not be gone into in detail. The difference formulas are identical with those previously presented, *i.e.*:

$$\sigma_{diff.} = \sqrt{\sigma_1{}^2 + \sigma_2{}^2 - 2r\sigma_1\,\sigma_2} \text{ (for correlated measures)}$$
$$\sigma_{diff.} = \sqrt{\sigma_1{}^2 + \sigma_2{}^2} \qquad \text{(for independent measures)}$$

We need only a method for determining the standard error of a percentage, that is, a formula which will indicate the probability that in other samplings from the same population the percentages obtained would differ by any stated amount. This method is given by the following formula:

$$\sigma_{percentage} = \sqrt{\frac{p.q.}{N}} \tag{22}$$

where p is the percentage of cases within a given category, q is the percentage outside the category (100 per cent $- p$), and N is the number of cases in the entire group.[*]

4. In like manner divide each grade into two groups on the basis of average class standing in all subjects combined. This division may be made either upon the basis of the monthly report cards, or upon the basis of teacher's judgment. Make the same comparisons as were outlined in the previous question and find the reliability of the differences obtained.

5. Find the mean class standing in each subject for all the children who say that they like that subject. Compare with the mean standing of those who dislike it and of those who are indifferent toward it. Have these results any bearing upon the relationship between attitude and success?

6. If mental test results are available for these children make a division upon the basis of IQ. Compare the upper

[*] Time may be economized by the use of a series of tables to facilitate the computation of the reliability of differences between percentages which have been worked out by Edgerton and Paterson, *J. Appl. Psychol.*, 1926, 10, 378-391.

and lower halves with reference to subject preference in the same way as was done previously, and find the reliability of the differences.

7. Which subjects are, on the whole, better liked by the older than by the younger children in each grade? Which tend to be preferred by the younger children?

8. Do the results of Questions 3, 4, 5 and 6 throw any light upon the reason for the apparent ambivalence in preference for certain subjects? Explain.

9. Are there any sex differences in subject preference which tend to remain similar from grade to grade? If so, what are they?

10. Compare the results of this study with the subject preferences of gifted and average children described in *Genetic Studies of Genius* (244).

REFERENCES

The student is referred to the following titles in the bibliography at the end of this book:

184, 244*, 396, 397, 400.

Chapter 37

SPECIAL ABILITIES

HOW early in life does special talent show itself? Is it possible to select from the group of the five-year-olds who enter our kindergartens each year the artists, the musicians, the poets and novelists of a quarter of a century later? Do "special abilities" keep the same pattern from childhood to maturity, or is special talent in reality little more than specialized *interest* which determines the particular channel into which general ability shall be directed? If we examine the childhood biographies of men of genius we find that in many cases there is little evidence of early specialization along the lines for which the individual later became famous, though indications of unusually high general ability are present in most cases. Frequently there is shifting of interest from one field to another, as in the case of de Candolle, the botanist, who "in his early youth was more interested in literature and particularly in poetry and the drama than in the scientific studies which later claimed his attention" and "was distinguished in his boyhood for his facility in writing elegant verse" (53). In other cases, such as Beethoven and Mozart, special talent of an exceptionally high order along the line of later accomplishment seems to have been present from very early childhood.

The most clean-cut evidence for the existence of a special talent which is apparent from childhood is to be found in the case of musical ability. By far the greater number of famous musicians showed decided musical talent at an early age. It is quite possible, however, that the fact that musical ability is so clearly set off from other kinds of performance makes it more likely to be noticed than other forms of special aptitude, such as scientific or literary ability. The latter may be quite as apparent in early life if we only knew what to look for.

The early detection of special talent is one of the most important practical problems in the entire field of individual differences. Presumably there are certain niches into which a given individual will "fit" most satisfactorily; the problem is to know what these niches are. As yet, few measures of special aptitudes have been developed. Of those available, the greater number are suitable for use only with older children or adults. Recently, however, McGinnis (172) has developed a technique by which at least three of the Seashore tests for musical talent may be used with children as young as four years of age.

Experiment No. 39

The Seashore Tests for Musical Ability

These tests are prepared in the form of phonograph records which may be secured from the Columbia Phonograph Company. The series consists of six tests, each measuring a special aspect of the kind of sensory discrimination which seems to be necessary for a musician. When given individually, three of these tests have been found suitable for use with children as young as four years. Children above the fourth grade may be tested in groups.

In the study by McGinnis which was carried out with nursery-school children, the following modification in method was used:

Only the tests of pitch discrimination, intensity, and consonance were used. Each of these requires only a comparison between the two members of a pair of notes sounded in immediate succession. For example, in the pitch test the subject is required to say whether the second of the two notes is higher or lower than the first; in the test of intensity, he must state whether the second is louder or softer, and in the consonance test whether the second tone is better or worse, that is, more consonant or more dissonant than the first. The remaining three tests (tonal memory, time, and rhythm) call for more complex judgments which are not well suited to the early ages since little children have difficulty in understanding what is to be done.

Because of the limited verbal comprehension of young children it is desirable to substitute other terms in place of Seashore's *weak* and *strong, high* and *low, better* and *worse.* In place of the words *weak* and *strong, loud* and *soft* are used. The terms *high* and *low* are explained by reference to the story of the three bears. The child is asked to tell whether the baby bear (high note) or the daddy bear (low note) is singing. In place of the terms *better* and *worse* the expressions *pretty* and *ugly* are substituted in the consonance test. Preliminary practice is given with a mouth organ and with the victrola until it is certain that the child understands what is wanted in each instance. In order to allow for occasional omitted responses due to fluctuations in attention, the percentage of correct responses is calculated upon the basis of the total number of answers rather than the total number of tones. If as many as twenty per cent of the notes are omitted the record is repeated.

Procedure: The student should first familiarize himself with the general procedure for giving the Seashore tests together with the form for recording the results as described in the manual which accompanies the records. Before undertaking to give the tests to young children he should try out the procedure as modified by McGinnis with one or more adults. When the method has been well mastered, the tests for discrimination of pitch, intensity, and consonance should be given individually to each of a group of kindergarten or first grade children, or to a group of four-year-old nursery school children. Each student should give each of the three tests to at least one child. Children from kindergarten or first grade can usually be given an entire side of a record at a single sitting, but if four-year-olds are used the record should be divided as follows: Scratch the records with a pin immediately after the thirtieth pair in order to establish a uniform division point. There is enough space between the end of the thirtieth and the beginning of the thirty-first judgments so that the needle can be placed in the proper groove, the victrola started, and the drag in speed taken up by the time the first of the next pair of tones is sounded.

Record forms of the kind described by Seashore should be prepared in advance, and the child's responses noted by the examiner as they are given. In case the child changes his mind, that is, gives a second response as a correction to his first response, the second response should be recorded, regardless of whether it is right or wrong. Both sides of each record should be used. The entire record should be repeated after an interval not greater than two weeks in order to determine reliability.

Problems: 1. Find the reliability of each test by correlating the scores on the first trial with the scores on the second trial. Compare these results with those obtained by McGinnis for nursery school children and with one or more of the studies carried out on children of school age.

2. Seashore considers that the tests measure aspects of sensory discrimination which are basic and for the most part independent of each other. Most investigators, however, have found an appreciable intercorrelation between the tests, which suggests that the abilities measured are less completely

independent than Seashore supposed. Using the sum of the scores on the two trials find the intercorrelations between the separate tests. Compare these results with those found by other investigators.

3. Find the correlations for each of the three tests separately with teachers' judgments of musical ability or with the average grade in music given on the school report cards for a period of two or three months. Which of the three tests shows the highest correlation with the teachers' judgments or with school standing in music?

4. Combine the results of the three tests into a single score. Compare this score with the teachers' judgments or the school standing. Does one secure a better estimate of the child's musical performance in school by the use of the individual tests separately or by combining them into a total score?

Experiment No. 40

A Study of Special Ability in Drawing

Require all the children in the kindergarten and the first and second grades of the experimental school to make two drawings, each on a separate sheet of paper. The first drawing is to represent the human figure, a man, a woman or a child. The second is to be a drawing of a house. As much time as necessary is permitted for making these drawings. Children should be encouraged to do their best, but no instructions as to how the drawing is to be made should be given. Copying, either from other children or from pictures in books should be prevented. The two drawings may be made on the same day in immediate succession. On the following day two more drawings using the same subjects should be secured from each child. Each drawing should be indorsed with the child's name, age, grade and any other facts thought to be of interest. Each drawing should be scored independently by two members of the class working in ignorance of each others results, using the method described by McCarty (171).

Problems: 1. Find the reliability of the scoring method by correlating for each grade separately the scores given to each drawing by the first scorer against those given by the second scorer. The method of interchangeable variables should be used. For which grade is the scoring most reliable? On the average do the drawings of houses or the drawings of the human figure show the higher reliability of scoring?

2. Find the reliability of the child's performance from day to day by correlating for each grade and each subject separately the scores earned on the first day with those earned on the second day. The average of the scores given by the two judges should be used as the child's score for each occasion. Should the double entry or the single entry method be used for this correlation? Which of the two subjects, on the average, gives the more reliable indication of the child's drawing ability? Is there any grade differences in the relative desirability of the two subjects as a measure of drawing ability?

3. Find the correlations for each grade separately between the scores earned on the drawings of the house and those on the drawings of the human figure. What does this result suggest with regard to the extent to which skill in drawing is independent of the particular subject selected for drawing?

4. Find the correlation between scores earned on each of the two subjects and either the teacher's estimates of drawing ability or the mean class mark in drawing over a period of two or three months. Do the drawings of the house or those of the human figure agree more closely with general school performance in drawing?

5. Many people believe that certain types of artistic ability

tend to go together and thus constitute what may be called an "aesthetic type" as contrasted with other combinations of ability which result in a "scientific type," "a practical type," *etc*. According to this theory we should expect to find a relationship between musical ability as measured by the Seashore tests, and artistic ability as measured by the McCarty tests. If the same children were given both these tests, find the correlation between the total scores on the Seashore test and the total scores on all four drawings according to the McCarty scale. Is the resultant correlation greater than that which would be expected upon the basis of age? The question can be answered more precisely if age differences are rendered constant by partial correlation treatment. For this method the student is referred to the standard textbooks on statistical methods listed in Section IV of the bibliography.

REFERENCES

The student is referred to the following titles in the bibliography at the end of this book:

39, 133, 171*, 172*, 236, 244, 259, 260, 319, 361.

Chapter 38

EDUCATIONAL METHOD

EDUCATIONAL experimentation has pointed the way to many improvements in teaching methods by means of which children's learning can be facilitated. We know, for example, that more will be learned in a number of short daily practice periods than in an equal amount of time spent in practice on a single day; that a certain amount of "over-learning"—*i.e.*, of continued practice after a perfect level of performance has been reached—is desirable for good retention; that the learning of a specific skill such as handwriting is best approached directly, rather than through such formal exercises as tracing sandpaper letters or following the pattern of a groove, and so on. There is undoubtedly much room for improvement in present methods of teaching, toward which well-controlled experimentation might point the way. The following examples are suggestive of the kind of investigation which is likely to be useful.

Experiment No. 41

A Comparison of Two Methods of Teaching by the Use of Paired Groups

Procedure: Divide the children of the experimental kindergarten, or of the first and second grades into two groups, pairing for age, sex, and intelligence test score. Prepare the same nature study lesson in two ways, the first method involving an interesting story which brings in the facts to be taught in dramatic style; the second making use of a descriptive outline in which all the main points are illustrated by attractive pictures without the accompanying story. Teach the lesson to one-half the class by the first method, to the other half by the second method. On the day following the lesson, test each child individually by means of a short list of questions covering the main points of the lesson, and compare the two groups as to amount retained.

Problems: 1. Which method seems to have been the more effective? Is the difference reliable according to the usual test for the reliability of a difference? Note that since paired groups have been used, the formula for the reliability of a difference between correlated measures should be used.

2. Check the results just obtained by preparing two forms of another lesson in the same way and repeating the experiment but reversing the groups, so that the children who were taught by the story method the first time are now taught by the illustrated outline method and *vice versa*. Is the difference in the same direction as that previously found? What is the reliability of the difference on this second test? Would it be safe to assume that similar results would be obtained for all subjects regardless of age or grade?

Experiment No. 42

The "Whole" vs. the "Part" Method in Memorizing Poetry

Procedure: Select a short poem (eight to twelve lines) of a level of difficulty suitable for the experimental group with which it is to be used, making sure that the poem is one which none of the children have heard before. Divide the children into two paired groups as described in the previous experiment. One group of children is to be taught the poem by the "part" method, in which drill is given on two lines at a time until the entire poem has been learned. The second is to be taught by the "whole" method, in which drill is given on the entire poem as a unit until it has been completely memorized. The criterion of perfect learning is to be a perfect repetition of the poem on the day following the last practice.

Problems: 1. Compare the two groups as to the number of trials necessary for complete learning by each method, and find the reliability of the difference.

2. Select a second poem of about equal difficulty to the first, and repeat the experiment, reversing the two groups as was done in the nature study lesson just described. Does the advantage lie with the same method on each of the two occasions? How do these results compare with those reported in the references given at the end of this chapter?

REFERENCES

The student is referred to the following titles in the bibliography at the end of this book:

87*, 88*, 89*, 90*, 97, 110, 127*, 128, 142*, 179, 190*, 238.

Chapter 39

THE DISTRIBUTION OF TEACHERS' TIME

A PROBLEM of decided practical importance in school administration is the determination of the manner in which a teacher's time is distributed among the many activities which have a place in the school day. Certain broad groupings in the schedules as they are planned can of course be easily determined. The grade school teacher plans to devote so many minutes daily to arithmetic, so many to reading, so many to music, and so on. Many investigations have been made to determine not only how teachers actually do divide their time among the various topics of the school curriculum, but also what division of time seems to be optimum for any given grade or curricular requirement.

But there is another aspect of the matter which likewise has great practical significance for the school administrator and also has important bearing on problems of child development and behavior. This is the division of the teacher's time among the different children in her class. Every experienced teacher knows that certain children demand much more of her time than others. While she is probably less keenly aware of the fact, it is also likely to be true that most if not all teachers voluntarily devote much more time to certain children than to others. What are the factors determining how this division of time shall be made? What are the typical characteristics of the children to whom teachers spontaneously give most time, as contrasted with children who demand an unusual amount of time from their teachers? How is the division of teachers' time related to such factors as age, sex, intellectual level, and the personality traits of the children? What proportion of the time devoted to each child goes to problems of general discipline, to helping with work, to answering questions not immediately related to school room tasks, *etc.*? A study of the amount and kind of attention given by the teacher to each child should provide much valuable data on child behavior, while a comparison of the relative frequency of teacher-child contacts for different teachers will furnish evidence with regard to the more personal factors in teaching which are often difficult to determine by the more conventional methods. A method of carrying out an investigation of this kind is described in the following experiment modeled after a study by Foster (75).

Experiment No. 43

The Proportion of the Teacher's Time Taken by Each Individual Member of a Group of Nursery-School, Kindergarten, or Primary Grade Children

Prepare a mimeographed record form similar to the one shown on page 332. Take up an inconspicuous position in the class-room near enough to the teacher whom you are observing so that you will be able to note all that is said and done. Each time that any child initiates any contact with the teacher by questions, requests for help, volunteering information, displaying his work for approbation, *etc.*, record the child's name and the nature of the contact, also the fact that the child took the initiative. By the use of a stop-watch, record the time consumed as exactly as possible. In a similar fashion, record each contact which the teacher initiates with any child. For later convenience in tabulating it is well to list and define in advance a number of broad categories in terms of which records of at least the most frequent types of contact can be made, such as helping with handwork, getting materials, suggesting activities, settling quarrels between children, helping with wraps, *etc.* Time devoted to the entire group, as in story-telling, should not be accredited to any individual child, neither should time which the teacher spends in general supervision of the class without making or receiving any contacts with individuals; * but every individual contact, no matter how brief, should be recorded. Time which the teacher spends with small groups, *e.g.,* in settling difficulties between two or more individual children, should be apportioned equally among the children concerned.

In order to secure an adequate and representative sample of behavior which varies as much from day to day as this is likely to do, a rather prolonged period of observation will be found necessary. Ordinarily a total of at least one hundred hours distributed evenly over the school day will be needed for a class of twenty-five to forty children. With smaller classes a somewhat shorter period may be used. The amount of data needed will vary with the nature of the facts to be determined from it. If it is desired to secure reliable data on individual differences among the children with regard to the *type* of attention which they receive from the teacher, more protracted observation will be necessary than if only individual differences in *amount* of attention are to be studied. A still shorter period of observation will suffice if only group factors, such as age differences, sex differences, or differences between contrasted intellectual levels, are to be studied. Whether or not a given amount of data may be considered adequate for its purpose can be determined by

* The amount of the teacher's time which is not taken up by individual children can readily be determined by subtracting the sum of all the periods spent with individuals from the total length of time the teacher was observed.

FORM FOR RECORDING OBSERVATIONS ON THE DISTRIBUTION OF
TEACHERS' TIME.

Observer.. Date.. Hour observed, from .. to .. Place..
Name of teacher...... Grade or class...... School......
Activity observed ....
(Music period, free-play period, lunch hour, etc. If more
than one activity is observed note time-limits of each.)

Names of children with whom teacher has contact	Contact initiated by	Type of contact	Time consumed

applying the usual statistical tests for reliability, using the correlational technique if individual differences are to be studied, and the test for the reliability of a difference if only group comparisons are to be made.

The treatment of the data obtained in this experiment is left as an exercise for the student. The number of interesting comparisons which can be made is very great and affords a most favorable opportunity for the display of initiative and originality. The data should be analyzed as completely as possible, and both the practical and the scientific implications of the findings should be pointed out.

REFERENCES

The student is referred to the following titles in the bibliography at the end of this book:

31, 32, 75*, 138.

Chapter 40

PROBLEMS FOR MORE ADVANCED STUDENTS

IN this chapter will be found a number of concrete suggestions for problems to be carried out by students who have had some training and experience in research work. Many of the problems are suitable for theses.

In general, the problems selected are such as may be carried out by a single student within the period usually devoted to graduate study. Problems requiring observation of the same subjects over many years or necessitating the cooperation of an entire organization have not been included.

The topical arrangement of the problems is merely suggestive. There is much overlapping from one topic to another, and a number of the problems might with equal appropriateness have been classified under some other head. It is therefore recommended that the student read through the entire list of problems.

A. Physical Activity

1. A study of the comparative reliability of different methods of measuring physical activity in children and adults. For the same group of subjects and over the same period of time (in order to guard against intrinsic and extrinsic errors in sampling) compare the reliability coefficients obtained by the use of pedometers, ratings, systematic observations, measurements of distance traversed in a given period of time, *etc.* Children of any age may be used.

2. The relationship between physical activity during the day and other factors. Using the method of measuring physical activity previously found to be most reliable (Problem 1) find the relationship between activity during the day and frequency of movement during the night (measured by use of recording beds); physical measurements such as height, weight, height-weight index, *etc.;* personality and social characteristics (determined either by ratings or, preferably, by systematic observations); health (determined either by ratings given by a competent physician or by a record of illnesses including colds, *etc.,* over a period of time), and any other factors thought to be of interest.

If possible, several groups of subjects of different ages and sex should be used, in order to determine not only the differences in the amount of activity shown at successive ages, but also whether or not the relationship of activity to other factors changes with age. Sex differences in relation to age should also be studied.

B. Basic Habits Such as Dressing, Eating and Sleep

3. *A study of factors affecting the learning of the dressing process by preschool children.* Devise a series of simple garments, uniform except for a single factor which it is desired to study, such as type, size, or position of fastening. Using the method of paired groups, compare the learning curves of young children for each type of garment. Nursery-school children should be used as subjects.

4. *The establishment of normative standards for the use of table implements in specified ways* (as knife for cutting meat, for spreading butter on bread, *etc.*). Definitions of levels of attainment for knife, fork and spoon should be worked out and the reliability of scoring determined. Tests should be given at or near the meal time, using foods of known consistency which are generally liked by children. Children between the ages of one and eight years should be used as subjects.

5. *The construction of a scale of food preferences in children.* Prepare a list of twelve to twenty common foods covering the complete range of dietary requirements for children. Using the method of paired comparisons with verbal presentation, derive scale values for each food by the method of equally often noticed differences. The reliability of the values obtained can be ascertained by presenting the list twice to the same group of children, with approximately a one week interval between the two presentations, and by comparing the scale values obtained from each of the two presentations.

Use kindergarten children as subjects. It would be interesting to derive two separate scales, one for children from the upper social classes and one for the lower classes.

6. *Racial differences in food preferences among young children.* Use the method described in Problem 5. Children of different national or racial groups, particularly those having rather distinct customs regarding food and its preparation, may be used as subjects.

7. *To ascertain the relationship of the amount of time spent in outdoor play to the length of the day nap, the length of night sleep and the length of time required to go to sleep on both occasions.* Keep a record of the length of time spent in outdoor play each day by one or more children. Find, for each child separately, the relationship between time out-of-doors and the sleep factors listed above. If it is possible to measure the amount of food eaten daily over the same period and correlate this with the outdoor play it would be interesting to do so. At least a thirty day period of observation should be used at each of the four seasons.

This problem may be carried out on a single child of preschool or kindergarten age. If several children can be studied separately, however, the results will be more conclusive.

C. Development of Motor Coördination and Skills

8. *A study of interference in the acquisition of basic skills during infancy, e.g.,* does rapid progress in the acquisition of speech interfere, temporarily, with progress in walking or in the voluntary control of the bladder? (137)

Systematic records to be kept of progress in the acquisition of speech, walking, and bladder control from the ninth to the eighteenth month. Compare the learning curves of one or more infants who are kept under daily observation.

9. *To establish norms for age of first walking, talking, and the eruption of the first tooth in a representative group of children.* Present standards are inadequate for scientific use because of sampling errors and the small number of cases upon which they have been based, also because of the loose definitions of the terms used.

By means of visits to "well baby clinics," state and county fairs, *etc.,* secure a series of actual observations on children at each month of age from nine to thirty months. Define "walking" and "talking" in very objective terms. Grade each child on each trait as "pass" or "fail" according to the criterion used. Draw ogive (percentile) curves for each sex, and read the median age at which the ability is present in 50 per cent of the cases directly from the curves. At least 50 children of each age and sex selected to include a representative sampling of the population (103) should be included. Larger groups would be preferable.

10. *The reliability of questionnaire data obtained for children of school age on the age of first walking, talking, and the eruption of the first tooth.* For an unselected group of school children from the same locality as was used for Problem No. 9, secure from parents data on above phenomena by the use of a questionnaire. Compare the mean age reported

by parents with the standards obtained by actual observation of a presumably comparable group.

11. The learning of balancing and steering by young children. Select one or more children who have had no previous practice in riding a tricycle or a kiddie car with pedals. Choose a clear space at least 20 feet long, put the child on a tricycle if he is unable to get on by himself, and tell him to ride straight across the room to some specified point at the opposite side. Count the number of times each foot slips off the pedal, the number of times the pedals lock, the number of backward starts, the number of definite turns to the right or left, and the number of falls if any. Record also the time required for each trial. Allow a definite number of trials per day until errors of the kind indicated above have become rare.

With older children who have gained some skill in riding, the following method may be used. Lay out a path 25 or more feet long similar to that described in Chapter 15, Experiment No. 7. Draw cross-lines at regular intervals throughout the length of the path so as to divide the course into sections of equal length. The optimum length of the sections should be determined by experimentation. They should be as short as is consistent with accurate observation. The child's performance should be scored in terms of the number of sections in which the front wheel of the tricycle does not leave the path. Partial credits may also be allowed if higher reliability is obtained by so doing. The exact method of scoring should be worked out by the student on the basis of preliminary trial.

The problem can be extended to include children of a higher level of skill by requiring them to ride backward or by using a bicycle on a longer path.

12. The development of breath control in young children and its relationship to other functions. A series of tests involving breath control should be devised and standardized for successive ages. Suggested devices are horn blowing, soap bubbles, the spirometer, *etc*. Correlations with the control of other muscle groups, such as uniocular winking, should be determined, also the relationship to intelligence test scores, personality traits, *etc*.

13. The relationship between muscular coördinations in different parts of the body. Devise a series of coördination tests such as needle threading, standing on one foot, kicking at a moving target, *etc.*, involving as many different muscle groups as possible. The difficulty of the tasks should be adapted to the age of the subjects. Find intercorrelations and test for the presence of a "general" factor by the method of tetrad differences (334). Children of five years or above or adults may be used.

D. Learning

14. A study of age differences in the amount of transfer from learning to run a general bodily maze to a stylus maze of the same pattern, and vice versa. Paired groups at each age to be used, one of which learns the stylus maze first and then transfers to the bodily maze, while the other group reverses the order, so that each acts as a control for the other. As subjects, children of five and ten years and college students are suggested.

15. A comparative study of backward association in maze learning in children and white rats. The same maze pattern should be used for both groups of subjects. Each group to be divided into two paired subgroups, similar in age, sex, and maze learning ability as demonstrated in a simpler practice maze. One of the subgroups should learn the maze in the forward direction and then transfer to the backward direction; the other group reverses the order so that each acts as a control for the other. The same procedure should be followed for both young children and animals, and the amount of transfer compared.

16. A comparison of the rate of learning to discriminate forms in monkeys and infants or young children. A series of geometrical forms cut from slices of orange to be used. Forms which the subject is to be taught to select can be sprinkled with a little powdered sugar; those which he is to avoid with a small amount of quinine. Identical training procedure should be used.

The method can be used with infants as soon as the reaching and grasping response has become well established. A comparison of the rate of learning in infants of different ages up to two or three years would be worth making.

17. A comparison of different types of learning ability among white and negro children. A number of different learning problems should be employed, such as paired associates (words), digit symbol substitution, maze tracing, ball tossing, *etc.*

At least two fairly widely separated age groups of children (as six and twelve years) should be used as subjects.

E. Emotions

18. The expression of the emotions in young children. By setting up special situations designed to elicit the behavior desired, obtain a series of photographs of one or more children during emotional behavior. Suggested emotions are joy, anger, fear, affection, disappointment, shyness. Full length photographs of fair size should be used in order to show bodily posture as well as facial expression. If moving pictures can be secured, so much the better. Have the pictures judged by competent observers as to the emotion displayed (a) when pictures of the response alone are shown, (b) when both the pictures and the stimuli arousing the behavior are shown (if still photographs are used the situations can be described), and (c) when the pictures or the descriptions of the stimuli are attached to the wrong responses.

This is essentially the method employed by Sherman (221), who used new-born infants as subjects. It is well worth while to see whether Sherman's results will be duplicated if somewhat older children are used.

19. A comparative observational study of anger outbursts in young children at home and in the nursery school. Records of all outbursts occurring in each situation should be kept by parents and teachers according to a uniform plan (109). Results should be compared according to the total number of waking hours spent in each situation. At least a month's record should be secured for each child. Nursery-school or kindergarten children may be used as subjects.

20. A comparative study of Watson's and Valentine's theories on the "instinctiveness" of fear behavior and the circumstances under which conditioned fear reactions appear. See References 257 and 266. Contrive test situations similar to those described, making sure that no fear response is present before the experiment is carried out. Use both "neutral" and "potentially fear arousing" stimuli, all of which must be unfamiliar to the subjects. Infants of nine to eighteen months of age are suggested.

21. Age and sex differences with regard to the stimuli occasioning laughter under certain specified conditions of everyday life. Select one or more fairly distinct types of situation, as the school playground, the movies, a public playground, *etc.* Keep notes over a period of time of the stimuli arousing laughter in the individuals nearest you (including as many individuals on each occasion as you are able to observe accurately). Note sex and estimate age as closely as possible. Describe the stimuli as accurately as you can at the time, and classify into broader groups when the data are completed. The age and sex composition of the group within which the laughter takes place should always be described, and failure of certain individuals to laugh when others do so should also be noted.

The study may be confined to children or may be extended to include adults if the situation chosen is one in which both adults and children are commonly found.

22. *A comparative study of the responses of normal, feeble-minded (high grade) and physically handicapped children on the Woodworth-Cady or the Woodworth-Matthews questionnaire for determining emotional stability.* Have the questionnaire filled out by several groups of subjects as suggested and compare the results both on the individual items of the questionnaire and on the average number of undesirable responses made by each group.

The questionnaire is best suited to children of the fifth to the eighth school grades, though it may be used as far down as the third grade. The physically handicapped groups may include crippled children, blind children, deaf children, cardiac cases, tubercular children, *etc.*

F. Reaction Time

23. *Changes in reaction time with age. The establishment of norms for successive ages.* Any of the standard methods and apparatus may be used, but procedure must be uniform from age to age. With suitable management and incentives, simple reaction time may be studied with children as young as two years.

24. *The relationship between simple reaction time and other factors among children of preschool age.* Reaction time scores to be correlated with intelligence test scores, introversion-extroversion ratings or experimental scores (176), birth order, speed of tapping, *etc.* By the use of suitable apparatus comparisons may also be made between reaction times of right and left hand, between hand and foot, *etc.*

G. Perception

25. Intercorrelations of sensory acuity among children. Tests of sensory acuity involving taste and smell, tactual acuity in distinguishing different grades of sandpaper, comparison of weights, lengths of lines, *etc.*, should be used and their intercorrelations established. Children above the age of five may be used as subjects and their performance compared with that of adults.

26. The effect of arrangement on the span of visual apprehension. Tachistoscopic study using dots arranged in different patterns involving horizontal, vertical, and oblique lines of different slopes. Such a study might throw light on the late appearance of the ability to copy a diamond as compared to a square.

For subjects, children of different ages from six years on may be used. A group of adults might also be included for purposes of comparison.

27. A comparison of the two point threshold in corresponding points of the body in children and adults. An aesthesiometer should be used. Since the surface area of the body is considerably smaller in children than in adults, if all touch spots are present and active in childhood two point discrimination should be correspondingly finer during the early years than it is among adults.

Inasmuch as intellectual level as well as the distribution of the touch spots may affect the results, at least three groups of subjects should be employed, (1) a group of six-year-old children, (2) a group of adult imbeciles with mental ages of six, (3) a group of normal adults. If possible two additional groups should be used as checks: (4) a group of nine-year-old children, and (5) a group of mentally defective adults with mental ages of nine. The groups should also be compared with respect to their relative improvement with practice.

28. A qualitative comparison of the drawings made by congenitally blind subjects of normal intelligence with those of seeing children. Line drawings made with stylus on wax tablets should be used. Because of the large amount of comparative data available subjects of particular interest would be the human figure, houses, and common animals.

29. A qualitative analysis of the difficulties commonly experienced by young children in copying a diamond. Experimentation with diagonal lines of different slope, with diamonds of different proportions placed at various angles, and with mirror drawing. The effect of practice with and without coaching should also be studied. Children should be encouraged to describe and discuss their difficulties freely. Children from five to eight years of age are suggested as subjects.

H. Language and Meaning

30. To ascertain the relation of the length and function of the sentence to the situation in which it is used. Secure a series of at least 50 consecutive remarks from each of a group of subjects in a number of different situations, such as the school playground, the indoor playroom, the lunch hour, taking off or putting on wraps, *etc.* Analyze the sentences used in each situation according to the method used by McCarthy (169), (170), and compare the general trends. The same group of subjects should be used throughout in order to cancel out sampling errors. Children from 18 to 54 months of age are most suitable.

31. A study of sex differences in the content of conversation among children of different ages. A method similar to that used by Moore (187) may be employed, except that the hours when children are going to or returning from school would be preferable. The main purpose of the problem is to determine the approximate age at which the sex differences found by Moore first become clearly apparent. School children, ranging in age from the primary grades through the high school period are suitable subjects.

32. A study of age and sex differences in children's requests for information. Either a longitudinal study of one or more single children, or a cross-section study of groups of children observed for shorter periods may be used. All questions dealing with matters of information (what, why, where, how, *etc.*) should be recorded verbatim and classified according to type and content. Simple requests for permission, *etc.*, need not be recorded.

As wide an age range of subjects as possible should be studied. If the cross-section method is used, care should be taken to see that the social composition of the groups is similar from age to age, though it need not be representative of the total population.

33. The establishment of norms of development for certain specific intellectual concepts, such as ideas of time, space, and number. A series of tests which stress the type of information gained incidentally rather than that ordinarily taught in school should be worked out and normative standards obtained by administering the tests to representative groups of children at each age. A separate test should be constructed for each type of concept.

34. Age and sex differences in the meanings assigned by children to familiar social concepts. The subjects are to be asked to define such terms as home, mother, father, friend, teacher, school, *etc.* Definitions to be classified in terms of content rather than form. If opportunity permits, correlations between certain fairly well defined types of definitions and the personality traits of the children may be considered: *i.e.*, how do the children who define *home* in terms of material possessions (where my toys are) compare with those who define it only with reference to themselves (where

I live) or with those who refer it to the family and its members (where my father and mother are), *etc.*

As subjects, children from five to fifteen years of age may be used.

35. A study of the relative difficulty of noting similarities and differences in paired objects with reference to the degree of overt resemblance between them. Prepare a list of paired objects which, in the judgment of adults, vary from those which are very similar to those which have but little in common. On one day have half the subjects state a difference between the members of each pair; on the following day have them state in what respects the objects are alike. The remaining half of the subjects should reverse the order, giving first similarities and then differences. The results for the pairs which are judged to be most similar are then to be compared with those thought to be most unlike, to see whether the apparent tendency for less mature subjects to note differences rather than similarities can be reversed by changing the degree of apparent resemblance between objects to be compared. A representative sampling of children at each age from six to twelve years should be used.

36. The rôle of meaning in immediate recall. Prepare six series of ink blots, sixteen blots in each series, each blot on a separate card. The subjects are to be tested individually, in three sittings. At the first sitting say: "Here I have some funny pictures for you to see. Some of the pictures have names and some have not. I will tell you their names if they have any." Show the cards in the first series one at a time. For eight of the blots chosen at random give names roughly appropriate to their contour; the other eight are to be shown without comment. Each card should be exposed for ten seconds with the named and the unnamed distributed in irregular order. When the entire series has been shown, add the second series of sixteen to the pack, shuffle thoroughly, then show to the child one at a time and ask, for each card in turn, whether or not it was seen before. Compare the percentages of right and wrong responses for the named and the unnamed cards.

At the second sitting the third series of cards should be shown. Say to the child, "Today I have some new cards. Some have names and some have not. This time I am going to have you tell me their names." Show the cards one at a time as before. As each card is shown, say, "What is this one's name?" If child does not respond, or says it has no name, pass on to the next after a ten second exposure. Cards named by the child should also be exposed for ten seconds. At the end of the series add the fourth set of sixteen cards, shuffle and proceed as at the preceding sitting.

At the third sitting the fifth set of cards is used. Procedure is the same as that of the first sitting except that the names applied by the experimenter should bear no apparent relationship to the appearance of the blots.

The results obtained by the three methods should be compared with each other. The relative performances of the individual children may also be compared with other factors such as age, sex, intelligence test scores, *etc.*

Children from four to eight years of age may be used as subjects.

I. Reasoning, Problem Solving, and Insight

37. A study of age and sex differences in the solution of simple mechanical puzzles by children, with special reference to the question of "insight." A series of simple mechanical puzzles to be presented to the subjects individually. Each problem to be solved ten times in immediate succession before another is presented. Time required for each trial to be recorded. After each solution the child should be asked, "How did you find out the way?" Answers, as well as all incidental comments occurring in the course of the solution should be recorded verbatim, and classified later according to type (122). Age and sex differences in time required for solution of the puzzles, the form of the learning curves, verbal reports, *etc.*, to be determined. As subjects, children from four to twelve years of age are suggested.

38. A comparative study of the methods employed in solving arithmetic problems by children of high and low intelligence quotients but corresponding mental ages. The problems should be framed to combine a minimum degree of difficulty in computation with a variety of principles of reasoning. The subjects should be required to solve the problems orally, "thinking aloud," and the methods employed for solution should be recorded verbatim. If possible, two groups of subjects should be used; one with mental ages of about eight, the other with mental ages of about twelve.

J. Speech

39. The validity of questionnaire data on the incidence of speech defects among school children. A questionnaire on the frequency and type of speech defects among the children in their classes is to be filled out by teachers. Speech tests are then to be given to all children in the schools covered by the questionnaire, and the results compared with the questionnaire data. Since teachers are likely to overlook minor defects, the study should result in a closer definition of the *degree* of defect of a given kind which may be assumed to be present on the basis of a positive report from the teacher.

40. The incidence of speech defects among school children as related to age, sex, intelligence test standing, socio-economic status, birth order and size of family, urban or rural residence, etc. If the questionnaire method has been evaluated as suggested in Problem No. 39 it may be used in this study; thus making it possible to secure data on large numbers of cases in a relatively short time. If speech tests can be given, however, the results will be somewhat more accurate. School children of any age may be used as subjects.

41. Familial resemblance in speech defects. Give speech tests to as many members of the same families as possible (including both parents and all children where this can be done). Reduce the results to standard scores on the basis of norms derived from Problems 39 and 40, so as to equalize the age factor. Find marital, parent-child and fraternal correlations. Compare also types of defect. If a group of foster children and one of siblings reared apart can be included, the study will have greater value. It is worth doing even if children reared by their own parents are used.

42. Age and sex differences in the responsiveness of children to training for articulatory defects. Paired groups of children with articulatory defects at each of several distinct ages (as three, six, nine, and twelve years) are to be selected. One group at each age is to be given speech training; the other serves as a control. Compare the gross improvement and the per cent of improvement of each trained group over its control group. At which age is training most effective?

K. Memory

43. The development of a comprehensive series of tests of immediate memory. Digit-span, nonsense syllables, logical prose, reproduction of movements as in the Knox Cube Test, memory for pictures, *etc.*, should be used. If time permits it would be well to develop two independent tests; one for recall or reproduction, the other for recognition.

The test should be standardized over as wide an age

range as possible. However, if time is limited it is better to use fewer ages and secure adequate samplings at each age within the range covered.

44. A study of obliviscence, reminiscence, and the effect of verbal recitation in the recall of visually perceived objects among children. Select four groups of subjects matched for age, sex, and intelligence test scores. Prepare four groups of common objects and familiar toys. By means of a preliminary test, make sure that each subject knows the names of all objects used.

Experiment 1: Arrange first set of objects in a predetermined order behind a screen. Instruct the subject to look carefully so that he will know what is there. Remove the screen. Allow a definite exposure period, say 20 seconds, then replace the screen and send the child back to his class-room. On the following day, recall him and ask him to state what he saw yesterday.

Experiment 2: Same as Experiment 1, except that a different set of objects is used and the child is asked to name the objects immediately after the screen is replaced (immediate recall) and again after an interval of one day (delayed recall).

Experiment 3: Same as before, but using a third set of objects and requiring the child to name them from sight as soon as the screen is removed. Delayed recall only.

Experiment 4: Same as 3, using the fourth set of objects with both immediate and delayed recall.

All four experiments to be tried with each group of subjects in following order: Group I in order 1, 2, 3, 4; Group II in order 2, 4, 1, 3; Group III, 3, 1, 4, 2; and Group IV, 4, 3, 2, 1.

Compare amount of obliviscence (forgetting) in immediate and delayed recall with and without naming from sight. Compare amount of reminiscence (naming objects in delayed recall which were omitted in preceding immediate recall) under both conditions, *etc.* Find relationship of both obliviscence and reminiscence to other factors, such as age, sex, intelligence test scores, *etc.*

Children of four or older should be used as subjects. If possible, several age groups should be used for comparison.

L. Intelligence

45. To determine the effect of similarity of environmental stimulation upon the test performance of children. Orphanage children to be used as subjects. A series of intelligence tests and educational tests should be given, and the standard deviations of the distributions of scores made by children of like age but different periods of residence in the orphanage compared. The study should be carried out in an orphanage which does not aim to place children for adoption, otherwise selective elimination of the brighter children may affect the results.

46. To determine the effect of practice upon the mental test scores of children. Two groups of subjects should be used, paired for age, sex, social status, and test score at the beginning of the experiment. The experimental group should be given the test selected for study at bi-weekly intervals for a period of three months. The control group should be given no further practice after the initial test until the end of the experimental period, when both groups are to be retested and their relative amounts of gain computed. The problem can be extended and made more valuable if several tests of different content (*e.g.,* language tests and those not employing language) are studied in this way. Since the effect of practice may vary with age, it is worth while to use two age groups, one of preschool children and the other of elementary school children. The range of ages in each group should be restricted to one year or less.

47. *A study of national and racial differences in intelligence test scores among children of preschool age.* A nonlanguage test should be used or, preferably, two tests in order that one may serve as a check upon the other. The Atkins Object Fitting Test (7) and the Merrill-Palmer Test (376), omitting the verbal items, are suggested.

As subjects immigrant children arriving at Ellis Island would be preferable, but if this is not feasible, the children of first generation immigrants may be used. Negro children should also be included.

48. *The relation of adenoids and diseased tonsils to mental development in preschool children.* Procedure similar to that used by Rogers (211) but using preschool children as subjects. It is conceivable that the negative results obtained in the former study might not hold good with very young children. At least the question is worth investigation.

M. Special Abilities

49. *The relationship between auditory acuity and performance on the Seashore Tests of Musical Ability.* Audiometer tests to be compared with each of the six Seashore tests. Children and adults may be used.

50. *A comparison of the degree of resemblance in special aptitudes of identical and like-sex fraternal twins.* Suggested tests are the Seashore Tests of Musical Ability, the McCarty or the Kline and Carey Tests for Drawing Ability, the Minnesota Mechanical Ability Tests, *etc.* Twins of any age may be used.

51. *A measuring scale for constructive ability at the nursery-school and kindergarten levels.* Select and photograph from at least two angles a graded series of specimens of block constructions of young children. Include one or two models built by older children in order that the scale may provide for cases of exceptional talent. Have the photo-

graphs ranked in order of merit by at least 100 judges and compute scale values for each model.

52. A comparison of the values assigned to photographs of block construction models by adults and by children of the ages to whom the scale is supposed to apply. Using the same series of photographs as in Problem No. 51, construct a scale based upon the judgments of kindergarten and first grade children and compare the values with those given by adults.

N. Social Behavior and Play

53. A comparative study of the free play of children. Systematic observation and comparison of the kind and variety of play behavior of children from different parts of the city (superior residential districts *vs.* slums, rural *vs.* city children, *etc.*). Age and sex differences should be compared for all groups. Unselected children found playing in city streets, vacant lots, unsupervised playgrounds and parks, *etc.*, may be used as subjects. Ages are to be estimated as closely as possible.

54. A study of the methods employed by children of different ages and social groups in order to secure leadership. Observational study of children found playing without adult supervision in streets, vacant lots, *etc.*

55. Individual vs. coöperative activity in nursery-school or kindergarten children. Using the scale of constructive ability (Problem No. 51), compare the relative merit of the productions of each of a group of kindergarten or nursery-school children when working alone with the coöperative product of the entire group or of selected smaller groups when working together. Various experimental combinations of children may be used, as groups composed only of good individual builders, those composed only of poor builders, groups of different sizes, *etc.* The coöperative products of children who usually play together may be compared with those of other groups of equal size, made up of equally good builders who rarely associate with each other, *etc.*

56. A study of the self-estimates of children, compared with their estimates of associates. Each child is to rate himself and at least two of his classmates on a series of personality traits. The associates to be rated should be selected by the experimenter to insure that all children will be equally represented.

Children from the fourth grade through the high school may be used.

O. Educational Method

57. A comparative study of the educational progress of children taught typewriting in place of longhand with that of children taught to write in longhand. Two groups of first grade children paired for age, sex, and intelligence test scores to be used. One group is to use the typewriter for all written work from the beginning; the other taught to write in longhand. To be reasonably conclusive, the study should be carried out over a period of at least three years. During the first two years the experimental group should continue to use only the typewriter for all written work. During the third year they should be taught longhand as well. At the end of the third year, both groups should be given a series of comprehensive tests in reading, penmanship, spelling and written composition for comparison of their relative standing.

58. A comparative study of the relative advantages of formal vs. informal training in spelling. Two groups of subjects, paired for age, sex, and intelligence test standing should be used. One group is to be given daily lessons in spelling; the other group to have no formal instruction in spelling other than correcting misspelled words in their written work in other subjects. Compare the spelling ability of the two groups after two years of training. This study should be begun in the second or third grade.

P. Training and Adjustment

59. A study of age and sex differences in the incidence of specific behavior problems in children. Data can be obtained from records of preschool and school behavior clinics if these have been carefully kept. However, since these records are likely to include many systematic omissions resulting from differences in opinion as to what constitutes a "behavior problem" it is better to use a standardized interview record and secure the data separately from home and school. If possible, both parents and at least two teachers (the child's present teacher and the one whose class he last attended) should be interviewed separately. In addition to information on the frequency and intensity with which the specified behavior problems are manifested, data should be secured on the education and occupation of the parents, size of family, birth order of child, and any other factors thought to have a bearing on the question.

The two sexes should be studied separately. Since a fairly large sample (at least 50 cases in each group) will be needed, results will be most significant if rather widely separated discrete age groups are used. Suggested ages are five, ten, and fifteen years. If possible a representative sample of the population should be obtained at each age, using paternal occupation as a criterion. If this cannot be done, the social composition of the groups studied should at least be ascertained and reported.

60. To derive a scale for measuring the seriousness of offenses as judged from the standpoint of their symptomatic importance for the social and emotional adjustment of the individual. Prepare a list of representative offenses or "behavior problems." Define each in terms of degree and frequency of manifestation, and the circumstances under which it is commonly shown. Have the offenses ranked by at least 100 individuals who have had some experience or training in dealing with "problem children." These persons should either be definitely selected to represent a composite of opinions (in which case it should include psychiatrists, psychologists, teachers, social workers, physicians, juvenile court officials, *etc.*) or else the group should be made up exclusively of one of these classes. If the latter method is used, it would be desirable to work out several scales, each based upon the opinions of a different class of judges. Scaling should be done by the method of equally often noticed differences. Separate scales should be prepared for each sex and for at least three ages: early childhood (*e.g.*, four years), middle childhood (eight or nine years), and adolescence (fourteen or fifteen years). A scale for college students might also be constructed.

61. To derive a scale for measuring the seriousness of offenses as judged from the standpoint of their interference with reasonable standards of social order. The same method and the same list of offenses as were used in Problem 58 should be used here in order that the scales may be compared with each other. A similar selection of subjects should be used.

62. A historical survey of points of view with regard to child training. Compare the opinions of early writers on child training with those of the present day. See especially Seneca, Plutarch, Plato, and later, Locke, Comenius, Rousseau, *etc.* The study demands a careful search of the literature, as but little of the material will be found under titles which suggest its character.

63. A study of individual and group differences in opinions regarding methods of handling problem situations aris-

ing in connection with child training. Prepare a series of descriptions of situations illustrating various types of problems arising in connection with child management. The age and sex of the child concerned should be stated, and the difficulty described as concretely as possible. Each description should be followed by a multiple choice question, "What should be done?" followed by several alternatives. Secure opinions from parents of both sexes and of varying degrees of education and training. Compare the opinions of fathers and those of mothers, of college trained parents with those having only grade school education, of rural *vs.* urban groups, *etc.* If a sufficient number of judgments are obtained for each group studied, the data may be scaled by the method of equally often noticed differences.

64. A study of individual and group differences in opinions regarding the level of obedience to be expected from children of different ages, and the amount of freedom, advice (solicited or unsolicited), coercion or restraint which is considered desirable. Use methods similar to those employed for the corresponding study on methods of handling problem situations described in Problem 61.

65. The relation of intelligence to type of problem shown by preschool children registered at a habit clinic. An individual intelligence test should be used. Age, sex, and socio-economic status should be controlled.

Q. Case Histories

66. To find the reliability of social case history data. Two or more social workers are to secure case histories of each of a group of subjects through independent interviews with parents and teachers. The amount of agreement in (a) the kind of facts secured by each, (b) the quantitative aspects of the data, and (c) the interpretative statements made by each is to be compared. The study may be extended by comparing the amount of agreement between case histories taken with and without formal outlines. Children from a behavior clinic or school children who are regarded as behavior problems may be used as subjects.

67. *To ascertain the amount of agreement between psychiatrists, psychologists, social workers, and pediatricians in their interpretation of the causative factors determining the behavior of children referred to behavior clinics and in their recommendations for treatment.* Submit the completed histories of several cases including records of the psychiatric, medical, and psychological examinations and the reports of the social worker to at least ten judges in each of the above classes. Prepare a list of possible causative factors, such as "unwise treatment on part of mother," "unwise treatment on part of father," "intellectual retardation," "undesirable companionship," *etc.* This list should aim at covering a great number of the possible causative factors suggested in the histories. Request the judges to rank the various causes listed in order of their respective importance for each case. Allow space for adding other causes if desired. Compare the results to show (a) the average amount of agreement between the individual members of each group of judges, and (b) constant tendencies in opinion characteristic of the several groups.

In like manner compare the groups with reference to recommendations for treatment.

The number of cases should not exceed twenty or twenty-five, in order to guard as far as possible against too hasty judgment. Fifteen is probably a reasonable number. The cases should constitute a fair sample of the clinic population. All identifying data should be removed from the records before submitting them to the judges. Because of the possibility of identifying the cases from the descriptions alone, no persons who have had any previous acquaintance with the case should be included in the group of judges used.

R. Resemblances in Siblings and Twins

68. The relationship of mental to physical resemblance among non-twin siblings. Either of two methods might be used. The preferable method would be to make use of the same criteria of physical resemblance which have commonly been employed for the study of twins (height, weight, hair and eye color, hand and foot prints, *etc.*) using standard scores or percentile ranks to correct for the age factor in the case of those measurements which are changing with age. If the use of measurements is not feasible, ratings of the general degree of physical resemblance may be used, but as these would presumably be less reliable than measurements, the results obtained would therefore be less clean-cut. At least two standard intelligence tests, a battery of educational tests, and possibly one or more of the better standardized tests of emotional and social traits should be employed for the study of mental resemblance. On the basis of the physical resemblance, arrange the sibling pairs in order from the most like to the most unlike. For each of the mental traits separately find the correlation between the pairs for the upper and lower quartiles of the grouping according to physical resemblance, and for the middle 50 per cent. A check on these results may be obtained by reducing the entire group of physical traits to a single standard score value, giving equal weight to each (402) or weighting by the method of internal consistency (45) and thus by simple subtraction obtaining a single measure of physical similarity or resemblance for each pair. In like manner a general measure of mental resemblance may be obtained by reducing the results of the mental tests to standard score values and subtracting. If the correlation between the measure of physical resemblance and that of mental resemblance on a given test for the entire series of pairs is zero, the genetic factors determining the physical and mental characteristics in question would appear to be independent of each other, *i.e.*, non-linked. If, on the other hand, the correlation is significantly positive, some degree of genetic linkage might fairly be assumed.

Siblings of school age, in whom the age difference between the members of the pairs in no case exceeds three years, may be used as subjects. In order to avoid irregularities resulting from the preadolescent spurt in physical growth, it is recommended that the study be confined to children between the ages of six and ten years.

69. The relationship between physical and mental traits studied by the method of sibling control.

Secure a series of mental and physical measurements on a group of siblings between the ages of five and ten years, using only pairs of like sex who differ from each other in age by not over three years. Reduce all measurements to percentiles or to standard scores unless previous records are available from which comparisons can be made on a constant age basis for both members of a pair.

Begin with height. Separate the siblings into two groups, placing in one group the taller member of each pair, in the other the shorter member. Compare the mean IQ's of the two groups and find the reliability of the difference. Then reverse the process. Separate the children on the basis of IQ and compare their heights. Do the same for the other measures considered. Keep sexes separate throughout.

70. A study of the comparative resemblance in learning ability among identical and fraternal twins. Any of the standard learning situations may be used, as digit-symbol substitution, maze learning, *etc.* Preferably two or more kinds of learning should be considered.

PART III

METHODS FOR THE COLLECTION
OF DATA

In the following chapters, the general principles involved in the use of different methods of collecting data have been brought together for convenient reference. It is suggested that the chapters be assigned for the student's reading in connection with the particular experiments to which they apply. No single experiment carried out by the student can in itself give him adequate acquaintance with a method in all its implications. The use of any method involves an understanding of certain fundamental principles which are wider in their scope than the relatively brief and simple experiments which are suitable for class use. The purpose of a course in experimental child study is not simply to train the student to carry out a number of prescribed exercises, but rather to provide him with a general grounding in method, on the basis of which he may proceed to more extensive investigations of his own.

Chapter 41

INCIDENTAL OBSERVATIONS AND CASE HISTORIES

INCIDENTAL observation as a guide to scientific investigation. The place of the incidental observation in the advancement of knowledge is likely to be misunderstood both by the layman and the scientific worker. The layman is far too likely to ignore the possibility of chance exceptions to the general rule and to make sweeping generalizations from any event or sequence of occurrences which happens to fall within his own personal experience. "I know that to walk under a ladder brings bad luck because my house burned down the day after I did so." "I bathed twice a day all the time I was pregnant and that is why my baby has such a lovely skin." "Children should never be allowed to skip grades in school. Mrs. Brown's boy skipped a grade and now he stutters," and so on. On the other hand, many scientific workers fall into the opposite error of "pooh-poohing" all reports of individual observations and of regarding as necessarily worthless any fact whose generality has not been proved.

While it is true that incidental observations do not warrant general conclusions, they nevertheless constitute the leading source of material for the formulation of scientific hypotheses. Through incidental observations, questions are raised and problems are defined which may eventually lead to the most significant scientific discoveries. Any observation if carefully and accurately made has potential importance for the advancement of knowledge. How is it, then, that the proportion actually resulting in significant discoveries is so small?

New observations must be related to present knowledge. Since the number of events observed by any individual during even a short period of time is so great, it would clearly be impossible to conduct extended investigations regarding more than a very small percentage of them. Selection is necessary. On what basis shall this selection be made? How shall we determine which of the many hypotheses which might be formulated in this way are sufficiently reasonable and important to warrant further study?

It is here that the importance of a thoroughgoing knowledge of the work of previous investigators in the field is most clearly apparent. To a visitor from Mars, the sight of a pink haired Chinaman might be far less amazing than that of a trolley car; and the appearance of an ant-eater or a kangaroo on the streets of New York might easily fail to arouse notice. The botanist may find a rare plant on the very spot which has just been passed over by a dozen unthinking tourists. To the bacteriologist, each of the myriad wriggling specks which he views through his microscope has an identity and a meaning, though the layman finds them well-nigh indistinguishable. So in the study of child behavior and development, an acquaintance with what is already known is necessary in order to distinguish between the usual and the rare, the significant and the trivial, the possible and the improbable. New as the subject is, and meager as is our stock of information, the time has already passed when the casual observations of the uninformed person are likely to add much to our knowledge. Only when these observations are examined in the light of already established facts and principles are the hypotheses which may result from them likely to have value. The range of the obvious has already been pretty well explored. The value of observation is henceforth dependent upon knowing what to observe.

Longitudinal records of the development of single children. Perhaps nowhere can more striking demonstration of the importance of the principle just stated be found than by examination of the various diary records of the development of single children. Some are made up chiefly of little anecdotes, "clever" sayings and the like, with little consistent attempt at organization or at relating the events recorded to preceding ones. Many of the observations are interpretative rather than descriptive. "Baby missed his father to-day. He fretted almost continually and I am sure that was the trouble." Such a report is meaningless in the absence of a detailed account of the actual behavior which formed the basis for the judgment. In marked contrast are some of the diaries kept by competent psychologists in which the events recorded are described clearly in such a way as to bring developmental sequences into clear relief and to show the changes in behavior which occur in response to specified changes in the conditions. Many of these observations are really accounts of simple experiments. A reaction is observed, and the situation which induced it is purposely repeated, possibly with some predetermined variation intended to check the hypothesis suggested by the first event. The following is an example:

In an attempt to test Watson's well-known studies of conditioned fear behavior, Valentine * reports the following notes from the diary record of his little daughter:

"Test 1. Y (aged 12 months, 2 weeks) was on her mother's knee. The opera glasses were placed on a table in front of her, after she had handled them a moment or two.

* Valentine, C. W., The innate bases of fear, *J. Genet. Psychol.*, 1930, 37, 394-420.

When she stretched out her hands to seize them, and as she touched them, I blew a loud wooden whistle behind her as loudly as I could. She quietly turned around as if to see where the noise came from. The process was repeated with the same result.

She was now put on my knee. I carefully kept the whistle from her sight and blew it again when she touched the glasses, and she again turned around, showing no sign of fear. The tests showed that, in itself, the whistle was inadequate to startle the baby, though I blew on it as loudly as I could. This fact provides us with results of considerable interest in my next test."

"TEST 2. The same afternoon, Y, seated on my knee, was shown a 'woolly' caterpillar on her brother C's hand. She had seen one before but had never touched it or been plagued with one or had fear or disgust of one suggested to her, to the best of my knowledge. She repeatedly turned away with a shrug of the shoulder or slight shudder, 'waggling' her hand from the wrist at it (as she sometimes does when annoyed), but without touching it.

"When she turned again to look at the caterpillar, I loudly blew the wooden whistle. At once Y gave a loud scream and turned away from the caterpillar. This was repeated four times with precisely the same effects."

Valentine comments on this as follows: "It is remarkable that the blowing of the whistle, which that same morning had caused only a slight interest, should now so accentuate the reaction to the caterpillar. It can only be explained, I think, on the assumption that the attitude toward the caterpillar was a very *unstable* one, ready to be changed to great excitement and fear, or to calm acceptance as seen later. The loud whistle, in itself undisturbing, provided just the slight added shock to make the fear of the caterpillar burst forth."

Note how acquaintance with the work of other investigators has served as a guide in the selection of facts to be recorded and in the planning of the checks which were carried out. It is unlikely that Valentine's simple experiments would have occurred to a person unacquainted with Watson's earlier studies.

Statements should always be made in as exact terms as possible. Scupin recorded that his little son once opened and closed the hinged cover of a can seventy-nine times in immediate succession. Such a statement is far more meaningful than would be a general note to the effect that the can was opened and closed "over and over again" or that the activity was persisted in "for a long time." One of the most noticeable differences between the records of trained and untrained observers is seen in the comparative exactness of their statements, and in their tendency to substitute quantitative for descriptive terms wherever possible.

Although the diary record has lost some of its former popularity as a method of studying child development, its possibilities, if kept by a competent person, have by no means been exhausted. Even to-day we turn back to these records for information on many questions of early development. One of the chief difficulties with the method, however, lies in the absence of any general agreement as to what facts shall be recorded, and in what manner the records shall be made. This makes it difficult or impossible to compare the records of different children in anything more than a very crude fashion. Even in the case of behavior which seems thoroughly objective, the failure to define terms frequently renders interpretation difficult. When does a child begin to creep? The infant of two or three months will make some progress if placed in a prone position on a flat surface and suitably stimulated. How shall we define the beginning of speech? Is the child who will repeat certain words on request but who makes no spontaneous use of them to be given credit for these words in a vocabulary count? When counting the vocabularies of children who are slightly older, what shall we do about plurals, irregular verbs, compound words, social phrases such as "thank you," "good morning," and the like which the child learns as units even though they actually include more than single words. Failure to specify what principle has been followed in these and similar matters probably accounts at least in part for many of the apparent discrepancies in the data which have been collected in this way by different workers.

The person who is considering the keeping of a diary record which he desires to have of both scientific and personal value should therefore observe the following general rules:

1. First of all, acquaint yourself as thoroughly as possible with previous investigations. Find out what plans have been followed by other people who have used this method. Also, read as much of the experimental literature on child development as possible, noting the theories which have been put forth and considering what kinds of facts are most likely to yield evidence for or against them.

2. Prepare a definite plan or outline to be followed in making your records. If possible, make some practice observations on other children in order to gain facility in recording.

3. Take all records at the time of observation whenever possible, and in any case do not allow more than a few hours to elapse between the actual observation and the making of the record.

4. Prepare a subject index for your records and keep this index simultaneously with the records. This can most expeditiously be done by means of a card file. A separate card should be used for each topic, on which the pages in the diary record with data bearing on the topic in question can be entered in order as the observations are made. This makes it possible, later on, to trace with a minimum expenditure of time and effort the development of any form of behavior from the earliest records of its occurrence. Cross indexing should be used freely. The making of the index will also help to systematize the taking of the observa-

tions, since it provides a constant reminder of the topics which are to be considered.

5. Records should aim at clear description rather than interpretation. If interpretations are made, be sure that they are not confused with the actual descriptions. Remember that the situation as well as the child's response should always be noted.

6. Keep a glossary or key to the terminology used. This key should state clearly just what rules were followed in such matters as making a vocabulary count, classifying behavior as "imitative," "dramatic," "angry," "fearful" and so on. Whenever a term of this sort is used for the first time, define it as carefully as possible and enter the definition in the front of the diary record. As behavior becomes more complex the original definitions may have to be modified or extended. Be sure to keep them up to date.

7. If time is limited, it may be well to confine the record to the development of a single form of behavior such as speech, emotional reactions, social reactions, or physical growth. A carefully kept record of a single aspect of development will usually be far more valuable than a series of loose notes on a wide variety of topics with insufficient data on any one subject to render conclusions possible.

Origin and development of the case history. The case history, as it is usually obtained, differs from the child biography in two important respects. In the first place, the facts recorded are for the most part retrospective rather than immediate records of events as they occur. Secondly, since the case history method is commonly used for the study of individuals who deviate from the normal standard in regard to some aspect of physical or mental health, the data are likely to be confined rather closely to an account of events and conditions generally believed to have bearing on the particular difficulty under consideration. If existing knowledge on the subject is adequate to explain all the facts, no objection to this limitation can be made. It is evident, however, that such a method is not calculated to enlarge our knowledge of any subject, since the information needed for the development of new hypotheses is not likely to be obtained consistently. Moreover, it is unlikely that the method will lead to the discovery of errors in present theories. The general practice of beginning with a known problem, and investigating only or chiefly those conditions which are believed to have a bearing on it, obviously makes for the perpetuation of existent theories, whether they be right or wrong.

Historically, the case history method is an outgrowth of the physician's case book on the one hand and charitable enterprises on the other. The physician with a large practice early found it desirable to write down the chief facts regarding his cases for reference in later treatment in order to avoid confusion between patients. As charitable work gradually passed from the hands of private individuals to religious and social agencies of various kinds, it became evident that a wise expenditure of funds necessitated some means of distinguishing between the truly needy and impostors. In the beginning the task of investigating applicants for assistance was turned over largely to volunteer workers, frequently known as "district visitors." However, it soon became evident that the best results could not be expected from untrained workers, no matter how well meaning they might be. Courses for the training of social workers have therefore been instituted in many colleges and universities, and as time passes the volunteer worker is gradually disappearing. At present the case history fills an important place in the fields of medicine, psychiatry and clinical psychology, and in organized social work. Recently a subdivision within the field has taken place. In addition to the general social worker we now have the specialized psychiatric social worker and the medical social worker with separate courses of training for each.

Purposes of the case history. From the outset, the case history has been designed to serve a practical rather than a scientific end. It is intended as a means of bringing together in organized form all the available information regarding an individual, in order to have a basis for diagnosis and treatment. A secondary purpose has been to provide illustrative material of a type likely to arouse public interest and to stimulate participation in campaigns for public welfare, or for use in general class-room instruction.

More recently, attempts have been made to utilize the facts reported in case histories as a means of throwing light on general scientific problems. Theoretically, the material should furnish important evidence on the manner in which behavior sequences are built up, the relative importance of hereditary and environmental factors in the production of physical and mental maladjustments of various kinds, the extent to which such conditions respond to treatment, and so on. Actually, when one attempts a statistical treatment of the data from the average case history, many problems arise. Few of the facts are reported consistently for all cases. Do the omissions indicate that the conditions in question were not present, or that the worker failed to investigate them? If the latter, what were the reasons for investigating them in certain cases and not in others? Another source of difficulty is to be found in the loosely descriptive nature of many of the statements. "X is overactive, excitable, and does not like to go to school." "Y is a very active and energetic boy, fond of excitement, and would rather play out of doors than go to school." The impression gained from the two descriptions is very different, yet they may easily represent exactly the same behavior, the difference in emphasis reflecting the personal attitude of the person interviewed or of the social worker herself. It is true that many of the factors with which the case history deals are not as yet subject to measurement and must therefore be handled in general descriptive terms, if at all. More precise definition of the terms used would help to clear away the ambiguities and bring about greater uniformity between the reports of different workers, though much of the difficulty would still remain.

A third source of error is to be found in the errors of memory resulting from the fact that a considerable period of time has elapsed between the taking of the history and the actual occurrence of many of the events reported. This error is likely to be accentuated by reason of the strong emotional associations which have grown up about many of these events because of later occurrences, and which cause them to be regarded in a very different light from that in which they were originally seen. Thus, parents of feeble-minded children are much more prone than others to report early falls and bumps, and similar minor injuries. Yet there is little scientific evidence to show that such occurrences are actually much more frequent among the feeble-minded than among normal children. The reason for their more frequent report is probably to be found in the fact that the subsequent discovery of the child's mental condition set the parents to searching their memories for a cause for the defect, with the result that minor accidents were brought to mind which would otherwise have been forgotten. In like manner, juvenile delinquencies of all kinds are recalled for the child who later receives a court sentence, although in the absence of later behavior difficulties many of these childish escapades would have been regarded as trivial. Forgetting is far from being a matter of chance. Because of these systematic errors of memory and report it is likely to be unsafe to make comparisons between groups or individuals on the basis of case history data unless the latter have been carefully checked. Nevertheless, because of the immense amount of material of this kind which is collected annually for practical purposes, it is worth while to consider by what means, if any, this great body of source material can be utilized for purposes of scientific research with a minimum probability of error.

Principles of collecting case histories. While the principles here enumerated have been drawn up primarily from the standpoint of the research worker, it is believed that to the extent that they improve the accuracy of the facts elicited they will also improve the usefulness of the history from the standpoint of its service function. Accuracy of diagnosis is not facilitated by an inaccurate presentation of the basic facts. If, for purposes of instruction or social propaganda it is desired to have a colorful descriptive account of the case in addition to the factual data, the securing of the latter in no way interferes with this requirement. Indeed the descriptive account will often be needed as a means of qualifying or explaining unusual features in the more formal arraignment of facts and figures.

1. The first principle may be stated thus: *A uniform procedure must be followed as regards the basic facts to be ascertained and the manner in which they are elicited.* This does not mean that every case must be approached in exactly the same way without allowance for differences in intelligence, social background, cooperativeness or antagonism, emotional stress and the like, which make the establishment of the necessary *rapport* between interviewer and interviewed so delicate a problem. To insist upon this would inevitably lead to gross inaccuracies in many instances, due to failure to establish confidence or to misunderstanding of questions. Neither does it mean that when information not called for in the formal outline seems to have an important bearing on the case in question, such in-

formation is to be regarded as superfluous. It does mean, however, that a certain *minimum* amount of information is to be obtained for all subjects regardless of whether the facts included seem to the investigator to be pertinent to the individual case, and that this information is to be recorded in a uniform manner in terms whose meaning has been defined as precisely as possible. Additional data should be obtained whenever, in the judgment of the worker, such facts will be helpful in the practical treatment of the individual case, or when special circumstances are present which would modify the interpretation of certain items in the formal summary.

2. In the selection of items to be included in the uniform record, *care must be taken to choose the facts most likely to be of service both for the understanding of the individual case and for the scientific study of physical, mental, and social problems.* Unless great care is taken, there is always likely to be a tendency to make this part of the record so long and involved that its use becomes very burdensome. Such records are likely either to be discontinued after a brief trial or to be very incompletely filled out. They thus defeat their own ends. A dozen wisely selected facts, consistently and uniformly obtained for all subjects are more valuable for scientific purposes than a hundred items less carefully chosen and incompletely recorded in terms whose meaning may be ambiguous. The selection of the basic data is a question of major importance and should not be left to the hasty judgment of one or two individuals.

3. *In order to make sure that the basic data are obtained in all instances, the use of a printed summary form is essential.* This form should be carefully planned, the terminology to be used should be specified and defined, and wherever possible should be listed in such a way that the facts can be supplied by underlining or checking. Ample space should be allowed wherever a written statement is called for, in order to avoid illegibility from overcrowding.

This sheet should be planned to include only the

most essential facts. It is expected that it will be supplemented by a descriptive account of the home situation in which information not readily reduced to tabular form will be presented for the guidance of those handling the individual case; by the original records of the psychological and medical examinations and any other data obtained by the psychologist or the pediatrician; by the report of the psychiatric interviews if any are given and by a more detailed statement of the recommendations made. Follow-up records should be added at stated intervals.

The sheet should contain brief instructions as to the manner of recording each item, thus making recourse to a key sheet unnecessary. There is always a temptation for the busy worker to guess at the meaning of a term, or at the manner in which an item is to be recorded when the instructions are not at hand.

No identifying data except the serial number of the case should be placed on this sheet. This makes it possible for the records to be turned over to statistical workers without fear of confidential material being misused. Reference to a master file will identify the cases when necessary.

4. *Always distinguish between negative items and omissions*. Failure to make this distinction, and to record in general only positive items is one of the most serious sources of error in case history material. In a recent comparative study, based upon behavior clinic case histories which shall remain unnamed, conclusions were drawn regarding traits for which information had been recorded in fewer than 10 per cent of the cases! Yet these were traits which every one shows to some extent, the only differences being those of degree. Such material is worthless for scientific analysis. However, because of the great amount of time required to secure for every case all the facts which at times seem important for the individual, some modification of the rule occasionally suggested, *viz.*, that if any fact is reported for one case it must therefore be ascertained for all, seems a practical necessity. If the following conditions are met, the case history need lose none of

its diagnostic value for the individual, while its possibilities for research will be adequately fulfilled.

(a) Every item called for on the general summary sheet must be completely supplied for all cases. Additional material which seems pertinent to the individual case will be included in the descriptive case history. There is no requirement that material of this kind shall be uniform.

(b) If, for any reason whatever, one or more of the items in the general summary cannot be ascertained, the space *should not be left blank* (which might mean that it had been inadvertently overlooked) but a special symbol should be used to indicate that the facts were not obtainable. The reasons for each omission should be written out completely in a space provided for that purpose. If this is done consistently, such unavoidable omissions need introduce no systematic error when the results are worked up, since the reasons given will usually provide a basis for determining how the remaining data in the history should be handled.

5. *Data should be verified wherever possible.* Dates of birth can be checked against official records. Family income can frequently be verified from employers. Where a central clearing agency for social service exists, it is possible to ascertain whether the family has previously been in touch with other agencies and if so, to what extent the information obtained checks with previous reports.

Since much of the data in the usual social history consists of subjective judgments or opinions, which vary considerably from one person to another, it is highly desirable that information of this kind should be checked by comparison of the opinions of two or more competent persons wherever this is possible. For example, data on behavior problems should be obtained from both parent and teacher.

The evaluation of case history data. It is always difficult to determine how much confidence may reasonably be placed in material of this kind. Assuming, however, that the workers are adequately trained, and that the demands upon their time are not unreasonable, it seems fair to expect that information obtained in this way (provided that the principles outlined in the last section have been followed) is at least sufficiently accurate to warrant comparison between groups. However it is highly improbable that all such material is equally accurate, and it would be an important contribution to research technique to ascertain which kinds of facts are most reliably reported and what are the best sources, on the average, from which to obtain specific kinds of information. For example, on which problems do parents and teachers agree most closely in their ratings of individual children? On the whole, do parents or teachers agree more closely with the judgments of trained experts? (Remember that this may vary with the problem.) If opportunity permits, it is worth while to have two social workers secure histories on a number of cases independently, and compare the results. It would also be desirable to have a number of experts go over the records of a group of cases independently, and write down their opinions of the main causative factors for the problems, and their recommendations for treatment, all, of course, without consultation with each other.

The methods suggested above have to do with what is commonly known as the *reliability* of the method, that is, the extent to which the obtained facts can be depended upon as measures of whatever they happen to be. But we are also concerned with the *validity* of the data; the extent to which the various facts obtained help us to understand the child and his problems. Suppose that a child is brought to a behavior clinic because of persistent stealing. What facts in the child's personal history or home background are most likely to be related to stealing, and hence most likely to repay investigation? Conversely, which of the facts commonly collected in social case histories most frequently contribute to the understanding of the problems at hand, and which are irrelevant? A careful study of factors such as these would do much to improve the effectiveness of the case study technique in its practical as well as its scientific aspects. The problem is a very large one and there are many difficulties in the way, but the general method of attack seems fairly clear. It is greatly to be hoped that in the near future concerted efforts may improve the present methods and make the great mass of material which is being collected in this way more amenable to scientific investigation.

Chapter 42

THE QUESTIONNAIRE

DEFINITION and classification of questionnaires. The questionnaire may be roughly characterized as a method of securing information from others through verbal responses alone. Although we are accustomed to think of it purely in terms of the forms encountered in our daily mail, the actual scope of the questionnaire is far wider than most people realize. The United States Census is a questionnaire; so also is the medical history taken by the physician, and the personal data called for on an application or registration blank. Any formally organized list of questions which are presented in a uniform manner to a number of persons is a questionnaire. The responses may be either oral or written; they may be obtained by personal interview, from supervised groups, or through the use of the mails. The data requested are of many kinds and vary greatly in objectivity and in the amount of confidence which they warrant. Sometimes they call for information regarding past events, concerning which many, perhaps most of the subjects, will have kept no written record. For example, parents may be asked to state the birth weights of elementary school children, or college students may be asked the grades which they received in certain subjects studied in the elementary school. Some parents, it is true, may have kept "baby books" in which the birth weights of their children were recorded, and some students may have preserved their school report cards, but there is little chance that many will have done so, or

379

that all who have records will go to the trouble of consulting them.

A second type of information often asked for has to do with present facts or conditions with which the subject is presumed to be familiar, though he is not likely to have made them the subject of formal records. The number of rooms in the present dwelling, the eye and hair color of certain members of the family, the number of living children in the family are examples.

A third type deals either with past events or present conditions for which formal records have been made which are available to the respondents but not to the investigator. A social service agency may be asked for a report on the number of persons applying for assistance during the past year, the number of these which were investigated, the number given assistance, the number who were refused, the number transferred to other agencies, *etc.*

The three types of questionnaire thus far described have dealt with material which is presumed to be objective in the sense that the facts asked for are or have been verifiable by other persons. A fourth and very important use of the questionnaire is to secure data on facts which are admittedly subjective in the sense that they are at no time open to observation by any one except the respondent himself. Questionnaires calling for personal opinions, judgments, beliefs, interests and preferences, feelings and emotions, and so on, belong to this class. It is important to distinguish here between two fairly common ways of interpreting material of this kind. Sometimes it is looked upon as an imperfect substitute for objective measurement, tolerated merely because no other method is available. The judgments of supposedly competent individuals are frequently employed as a means of validating tests designed to measure intelligence, special abilities, character and personality traits and

the like. Here it is assumed that such judgments contain
some measure of objective truth, although, since the judgments of two equally competent persons rarely agree very
closely with each other, it is apparent that they also contain a rather large element of objective error, or that at
least one of them must do so.

Another way of interpreting such material which is rather
less hazardous and frequently more useful is to take them
simply for what they are, that is, as expressions of opinions.
In this case we are not for the time being interested in the
"real" facts, so much as we are interested in knowing what
some particular person thinks the facts are. Often such
knowledge throws much light on the behavior of the person
in question or of others with whom he is associated. The
fact that a given individual *believes* himself to be unfairly
treated by most of his associates may be a much more
significant index to his behavior than could possibly be obtained by an objective study of the treatment which he
actually receives. Likewise, if a certain father *believes* his
boy to be very stupid, his resultant behavior may affect the
personality of the boy much more seriously in case the boy is
truly bright, than if he is truly as stupid as his father
thinks. Beliefs, attitudes, desires and the like are thus very
real facts, of dynamic and vital importance, concerning which
far too little is known.

The reliability of questionnaire data. Since the questionnaire method permits only verbal responses, its use should,
in general, be restricted to material for which a verbal
reaction is usually accepted as adequate, or to situations
for which no other type of reaction can readily be secured.
It is evident that the "adequacy" of a verbal response is
not a hard and fast category but will vary according to the
degree of precision required in the response, and the extent
to which the responses are likely to be modified in accord-

ance with social standards, unwillingness to admit personal deficiencies, desire for personal aggrandizement, or similar reasons of expediency. Under certain circumstances, therefore, a verbal response may reasonably be considered adequate which under other circumstances would be quite inadequate. For example, when it is desired to know the ages of a group of children who are to be given a certain test, it is ordinarily sufficient to obtain this information from the parents, or, in the case of older children, from the subjects themselves. If, however, the information regarding age is needed as evidence for the granting of working papers, a birth certificate is usually required, not only because of the greater importance of the occasion, but also because of the possible temptation to give a false report.

In considering whether or not any given piece of information may safely be secured through verbal report alone, it is necessary to consider both the use which is to be made of the results and the nature and extent of the errors which are likely to enter into the data obtained. These errors may be either *variable* (as likely to take one direction as the other) or *constant* (tending to take a constant direction or to show a consistent trend). Suppose that a group of unselected adults are asked to state their heights. Offhand, it might seem that the only errors in response would be occasioned by the fact that some individuals would not know their exact height and would therefore have to make an estimate, and that these estimates would, on the whole, be as likely to be too high as too low. Actually, however, the errors are likely to show a systematic trend in the direction of conventional standards of physical attractiveness. The very short men will be likely to overstate their height, the very tall women to understate it. Likewise, if mothers are asked to state the birth-weights of their children some years afterward, it is probable that there will be a slight general tendency to exaggerate the weights somewhat, in line with the feeling current among many women that it is an achievement to give birth to a "big, bouncing baby." Exceptionally tiny infants, on the other hand, may become even smaller in retrospect than they were in fact, since in this case it is their smallness which contributes to their remarkableness as babies. Persons applying to a welfare agency for financial aid are more likely to understate the amount of the family income than to exaggerate it, while in discussing their affairs with people of their own station the reverse may be true. Examples might be multiplied almost indefinitely, but the foregoing are probably sufficient to show the need of scrutinizing the data obtained in this way with especial care and of keeping constantly in mind the conditions under which the information was obtained and the direction which the errors of report are most likely to take. This is particularly true when the questionnaires deal with past events for which no records were kept, so that reliance upon memory is necessary. Memory, it must be emphasized, is not a simple mechanical process of reproduction, but always involves a considerable degree of reorganization of the original experience, in the course of which some elements are dropped out, others are modified or elaborated, while still others may be transferred bodily from one context or setting to another.* The greater the lapse of time between the occurrence of the event and its report, the more complex and involved does this process of organization become, and the more difficult it is to make a fair interpretation of the results.

Since questionnaires which require the recall of past events are particularly liable to inaccuracies, they should never be

---

* In investigating cases of mental deficiency, it is not uncommon to find that parents or relatives have ascribed to the mentally defective child, accidents which actually happened to other members of the family.

used when it is possible to substitute actual records of events as they occur. There is no excuse for resorting to such a method for the purpose of securing general normative data, such as age at walking, age at talking, birth weights, *etc.*, for an unselected population. However, it is sometimes desirable to compare the early development of a selected group of individuals with that of children in general. The ideal method, of course, would be to begin the study during the infancy of the subjects and thus secure direct observation from the beginning. This method, however, is not always feasible, particularly when the study has to do with cases whose incidence in the general population is small and who cannot be selected at the outset (famous men, criminals, the insane, *etc.*). The number of cases which it would be necessary to include in the original sampling in order to make sure of a sufficient number of the special cases which it is desired to study would in such cases be prohibitive. If their early development is to be studied at all, a written questionnaire or a standardized interview seems to be about the only practical alternative.

With what should the results of such a study of a selected group be compared? Very often, excellent normative standards based upon direct observations or actual measurements of an unselected sample of the population are available. These data are undoubtedly nearer the facts than similar standards derived from a recall questionnaire are likely to be. Should they not then be used, in order that the standard of reference may be as accurate as possible, even though errors are known or presumed to exist in the questionnaire data obtained for the selected group?

If it could be assumed that the errors in the questionnaire data would distribute themselves at random, that is, would be as likely to take one direction as the other so that they would tend to cancel each other for the group as a whole, the answer to this question would undoubtedly be in the affirmative. If, as is usually the case, the recall data are likely to include certain constant errors, the nature of which will be fairly similar for both the selected and the control group, then the comparison will be more accurate if both sets of data are obtained in the same manner. For example, very accurate standards of birth weight, based upon hospital weighings of large numbers of cases, have been reported in the literature. These standards should unquestionably be used in the comparison of actually measured weights of individuals or of groups. But it has been pointed out that when birth weights are reported by parents at some later date there is likely to be a slight tendency to exaggerate size, except possibly in the case of the exceptionally small infant. This will result in raising the mean of the group for whom the report is made somewhat above its true value. If the mean thus obtained is compared with that of another group for whom the data were obtained through hospital weighings, an apparent difference in favor of the selected group will appear even if the two groups are in fact closely similar. But if the questionnaire data from the selected group are compared, not with hospital weighings but with corresponding data obtained by the questionnaire method from another group, similar except for the fact which has formed the basis for the selection, the size and direction of the error is likely to be approximately the same in both instances. A comparison of the mean birth weights of the two groups may therefore be quite valid, even though each of the means entering into the comparison is in error by an undetermined amount. Since the questionnaire method is so frequently employed for studies of the early development of special groups, it would appear to be well worth while to conduct a special study for the ascertainment of standards of development in an unselected group *as they are reported by parents.* Because of the probability that on the whole the constant errors would tend to follow the same direction, such standards are likely to be a more suitable basis for comparison with results secured in a similar manner for selected groups than the more accurate standards derived from exact measurement. If the latter also can be secured or are already available, the amount of the constant error likely to be inherent in the questionnaire data can be ascertained at least within rough limits, and an appropriate correction can thereafter be made.

The foregoing statements are true only in case the factors determining the selection of the special group are unrelated to the factors responsible for the constant error. If such a relationship exists, the error will not be minimized by the use of standards derived in a similar manner, since it has its roots in the same facts which caused the special group to be selected. In the case of the relationship of childhood accidents to mental deficiency, it is this very fact of mental defectiveness which causes the parents of the defective children to remember and report minor accidents which other parents overlook. Putting it conversely, it is the absence of any subsequent difficulties which causes a large proportion of such accidents to be forgotten by the average parent whose children have developed normally. The use of the questionnaire method for both groups will not do away with the error in such cases.

In the case of questionnaires of the fourth type, when the responses are taken to represent feelings or attitudes and not as expressions of objective fact, the question of reliability or accuracy of statement still enters in, though in a somewhat different way. Here we are not concerned with the question of how closely the statements as reported agree with the objective facts, but rather with their accuracy as frank expressions of opinion. How great is the likelihood that a knowledge of conventional standards of true and false, desirable and undesirable, good taste and poor taste, will cause the average person to modify his statements to some extent in the direction of social acceptability? If asked to state her method of controlling her children, will the mother who is acquainted with modern ideas of child training be as free to admit her use of "scolding," "threatening," or "slapping," as she will be to admit "ignoring," "reasoning," or "depriving of privileges"? Can the child who has been ridiculed for his fear of the dark be depended upon to admit that fear when asked the question in a test of "emotional stability," particularly if he knows or at least surmises that there will be no way of checking up on his response?

It would be possible, though not always easy, to arrange at least partial checks for the purpose of determining the *average* amount of the constant error in statements of this kind for groups of known composition. Of course this error would not be the same for all individuals, but since material of this kind is rarely suitable for the study of individuals and is used chiefly for the comparison of groups, individual differences are of small concern. Thus, in the example just given, if a smaller group of children were actually observed for a short time in order to determine their tendency to avoid dark places, and the results of these observations were compared with the children's own statements about fear of the dark, at least a rough measure of the extent to which the group as a whole tends to deny its fears might be obtained. While it would not be correct to assume that other groups, similar to the one actually studied in age, sex, and social background would behave in an exactly similar fashion when given the same questionnaire, such an assumption would almost certainly be more nearly correct than would be the acceptance of the statements at their face value.

A question having very important bearing on the amount

of confidence which can be placed in the results obtained from questionnaires has to do with the character of the *sampling,* that is, the group from whom replies are received. It is only rarely that our interest in the facts obtained is confined to this particular group. As a rule, we wish to look upon these persons as representative *samples* of a larger population, and hence to assume that what is found to be true for them will also, within certain limits of accuracy, be true for the larger group who were not studied. Under what conditions are we warranted in making such an assumption?

In order to answer this question, two things must be known. First, what were the general characteristics of the group from whom the information was solicited? If the subjects were all city dwellers, it would not be safe to extend the findings to rural districts unless it is certain that the information is of a kind which is unrelated to place of residence. If the respondents were all or chiefly persons with college educations, it would be unwise to assume that the same facts would hold true for persons of little schooling. For these, and for another reason which will be brought out presently, it is always wise to secure some basic information regarding the composition of the group to whom the questionnaire is to be given *before the request for information is actually made.* By this means it is possible to select in advance a group which resembles the larger population to whom the findings are expected to apply, and to avoid overweighting the sample with a disproportionate number of certain types of cases to the neglect of others.

But suppose, as frequently happens when a questionnaire is sent out by mail, a large number of persons fail to reply? Can we assume that the number who do reply constitute a fair sample of the total number to whom the request was addressed and that the results therefore suffer no other defect than having their reliability somewhat reduced by reason of smaller numbers? Should special effort be made to secure returns from the particular cases first approached, or may a deficiency in numbers be made up from other sources without loss of accuracy?

It is here that a knowledge of the composition of the original group will be of most service. If educational status is known, a comparison of the average amount of schooling among the actual respondents with that of the total group from whom the replies were solicited will show whether or not there was a selective tendency for the less educated to fail to reply, or *vice versa*. Similar comparisons can be made with place of residence, occupation, size of family, possession of a telephone, and a number of other facts of this kind; provided always that the necessary data are obtained *before* the questionnaires are mailed. The comparisons will then show how the group of respondents differ from the group of non-respondents in respect to these factors at least, and further inferences can often be made therefrom with fair assurance.

Unfortunately, there are often present other factors not likely to be ascertainable in advance, which may seriously affect the representativeness of the returns in cases where there are many failures to reply. Suppose, for example, that the questionnaire includes a number of questions on the religious training of children, and that persons not giving religious training to their children commonly failed to answer at all, while those particularly interested in religious subjects did so almost without exception. If taken at their face value the results would seem to indicate a keen interest in religious training throughout the community, whereas actually it might be that only a small proportion possessed such an interest.

Because of the impossibility of knowing all the reasons which may operate in a selective fashion to cause persons for whom one series of conditions exists to reply to a given questionnaire in greater proportion than do those for whom the opposite conditions are true, it is always of great importance to secure as complete a percentage of returns as possible. To this end, as well as for reasons of courtesy, a questionnaire should always be accompanied by a letter of explanation in which the purposes of the investigation are set forth in an interesting fashion, and the reasons why the study is deemed of importance are stated. A report of findings should also be promised, and the promise should be kept. A stamped and addressed envelope for the return of the questionnaire should always be enclosed. At least one follow-up letter should be sent to those failing to reply.

The construction of a questionnaire. Unless great care is taken when a questionnaire is first drawn up to foresee sources of ambiguity in phrasing and difficulties likely to arise in the tabulation and interpretation of the results, disappointment is practically certain to ensue. The construction of a good questionnaire is a problem of major difficulty, calling for the best efforts of even thoroughly trained and experienced people. Much of the general criticism of the questionnaire as a method is a result of the fact that a considerable proportion of those sent out violate most of the established principles of questionnaire construction. This is inexcusable. The filling out of a questionnaire is a courtesy which should not be asked unless the person making the request is willing to go to the trouble of making sure that the questionnaire has been formulated in such a way that the results secured will require a minimal expenditure of the respondent's time, and yield a maximal amount of usable data for the time expended. The questionnaire has been traditionally looked upon as a "lazy man's way" of collecting data. It might be added that the lazy man's reward is in this case usually commensurate with his effort.

It is impossible to formulate a set of rules for question-naire construction which will cover all the conditions or topics for which the method might conceivably be used. However, the following suggestions, if consistently carried out, will be found to add materially to the accuracy of the facts obtained and to the ease with which results may be summarized. Well-constructed questionnaires, moreover, will usually yield a higher percentage of returns, thus reducing the sampling error, which is a matter of much importance in interpreting the data.

1. *The information asked for should be simple, concrete, and objective.* It should deal only with facts which the respondents will be able to supply without going to the trouble of looking them up. Respondents should not be asked to take measurements, count minor items of clothing or books, or perform similar tasks when the investigator has no way of knowing whether the instructions are fulfilled. Unless the members of the group are known to be exceptionally conscientious and coöperative it is safe to assume that when such counts or measurements are asked for, a fairly large percent-age of the replies will be estimates rather than actual measurements. If an estimate is all that is required, it is better to word the request in that way and to inter-pret the results accordingly; bearing in mind that such estimates are likely to be somewhat more favorable than the actual facts. If precise facts of this kind are needed, some other method must be employed to secure them.

2. *Questionnaires should be brief and should look so.* Through careless arrangement or unnecessary verbiage questionnaires which actually require but a few minutes to fill out may take on so formidable an appearance as to discourage many respondents at the outset. In planning questionnaire forms it is well worth while to devote thought to arranging the sheet in such a way as to minimize the apparent as well as the actual labor required to supply the data.

3. *Questions should be so phrased as to call for a minimum of writing in reply, and to facilitate tabulating.*
   Whenever possible, answers should be classified in advance and presented in the form of a "multiple-choice"
   series of responses. The respondent can then indicate
   his response by underlining or encircling the correct
   word or phrase. Encircling is to be preferred to underlining whenever the responses are so short that confusion is likely to result from underlinings which are
   not accurately placed. The method to be used should
   always be specified. When the answers are to be regarded as mutually exclusive, ambiguities will be
   avoided by specifying that only one response should be
   underlined.

   If the number of possible responses exceeds four or
   five, a double- or triple-column arrangement is to be
   preferred. Each response should then be followed by a
   "box" (see p. 400) in which a check mark can be
   placed to indicate the choice. Some questionnaires also
   employ the box method for multiple choice responses
   arranged in the form of a running text. This method
   has been used in the sample questionnaire given on
   p. 400. Note that when the box method is used in this
   way, care must be taken to insure that each of the
   responses with its accompanying box is clearly separated from those preceding and following it. Unless
   this is done, confusion and inaccuracy are almost certain to result, since some respondents will place their
   check in the box preceding an item, others in the one
   following it, so that it is impossible to know which was
   intended. In the example given, a semicolon has been
   used for this purpose. An even better method is to
   group the items in such a way as to leave an appreciable space between them. This catches the eye and
   admits of no possible confusion, but has the disadvantage of requiring more space.

4. *Each question should be complete in itself, that is, it
   should be in no way dependent upon the response to
   any other question.* In a certain questionnaire sent to
   public school teachers the following questions designed
   to throw light on the extent to which specialization of

ability among children is recognized by their teachers were included:

A. "Is this child's mental ability very even, fairly even, rather uneven, very uneven? (Underline.)"

B. "If child's ability is uneven, in what respects is he
   (1) Very superior as compared to the average child of his own age?.....................
   (2) Very inferior as compared to the average child of his own age?........................"

Regardless of how the first question was answered, considerably more than 50 per cent of the teachers who filled out the questionnaire answered the second question in simple terms of "yes" or "no." This is not surprising when we note that this question is doubly dependent. As a whole, it is to be answered only in case one of the last two alternatives is underlined in the preceding question. In addition to this, the question is divided into two parallel sections with the significant phrase *in what respects* effectively separated from both by being placed in a different line, which suggests that it belongs to a different question. As a result, the great majority of the respondents looked upon the two dependent sections as independent questions referring to the child's general ability, and thus the entire force of the question was lost.

The double question is open to the same hazard as the dependent question; that is, the likelihood that only half the question will be read. Such a question, for example, as "Are the children in your nursery-school kept in a single group, or is there separation into groups or classes on the basis of age?" is likely to bring forth a discouragingly high percentage of "yes" and "no" answers from obliging but busy respondents. The statement of both alternatives is intended to clarify the meaning of the question but actually introduces a worse confusion than that which it is designed to correct. In most cases such questions can be rephrased in such a way as to state one alternative only, with space for an affirmative or negative response. When this is done, however, care must be taken to insure that the categorical "yes" or "no" really provides for all possibilities with no need for intermediate or qualified responses. In the example just cited, no provision is made for a condition commonly found in nursery-schools, where the children are separated into classes or groups for parts of the day or for certain activities, but otherwise mingle freely. This illustrates another important principle of questionnaire construction, namely, that in order to plan a questionnaire properly the investigator must have a thorough acquaintance with the field which he proposes to investigate.

5. *Questions should be so formulated as not to suggest or favor one type of response more than another.* Such a question as "Does child usually take a daily nap?" is likely to elicit positive responses from many parents when as a matter of fact the nap is an occasional rather than a customary event. When an estimate rather than an exact record is requested, the terms of the estimate should always be defined as precisely as possible. The foregoing question might better read: "About how often does the child take a daytime nap: more than twice a day; twice a day; once or twice a day; once a day; from four to six times a week; from one to three times a week; rarely or not at all."

Not only the wording of a question, but the context in which it occurs may affect the responses likely to be given to it. If it is desired to test the truth of a theory with which some of the respondents may be familiar or which they may infer from the nature of the questions asked, it is usually well to separate the critical items from each other by intervening questions which will lessen the probability that the replies will be affected by a knowledge of the general theory. Thus, a rather well-known but unsubstantiated hypothesis regarding the origin of stuttering ascribes this difficulty to an early enforced change in handedness, *e.g.*, when a normally left-handed child is consistently required to use his right hand for such tasks as writing, eating, etc. If the question regarding stuttering is immediately preceded or followed by a question concerning attempts to modify hand preference, persons familiar with the hypothesis just mentioned may be influenced by this knowledge in making their responses. Again, this does not necessarily involve deliberate or conscious falsification. Most children sometimes use the left hand for purposes which are conventionally carried out with the right. Most parents train their children to use the right hand for such activities, either deliberately by use of verbal precept, or unconsciously by putting the spoon into the right hand rather than the left, and so on. The question at issue is, whether or not tendencies to use the left hand were on the average more definite, and met with more insistent attempts at modification in the case of children who stutter than with those who do not. Apparent support for the hypothesis would be found if a significantly greater proportion of the parents of the stutterers reported an early left-hand preference which was corrected or interfered with by training than did the parents of the non-stutterers. But if it should happen that in a large proportion of the cases the parents had this particular hypothesis in mind at the time of answering the questions, it might readily come about that their very desire to respond truthfully would cause the parents of the stutterers to search their memories more carefully for evidence of an original left-hand preference in their children, and to interpret their attempts at training more rigidly than they would otherwise do. Parents of the non-stutterers, on the other hand, would be more inclined to take the absence of stuttering as evidence that whatever tendencies toward use of the left hand in early childhood might have been observed were merely "passing phases" not worthy of record, since no disturbances of speech were consequent upon their correction. While separation of the two questions by placing them in different parts of the questionnaire does not make it certain that each will be answered on its own merits, it does lessen the probability that such distorting associations will arise.

6. *Questions dealing with matters likely to have strong emotional associations, or those which convey definite implications of social or moral values for many or all*

of the respondents should be avoided. At best the responses to such questions are of doubtful significance.
Many respondents will fail to answer, or will qualify
their responses in such a way that interpretation is
difficult. Others may rationalize concerning the question or the situation with which it deals until they find
warrant for a favorable response. Thus, a mother who
is asked to reply to the question, "Do you criticize the
school or teachers unfavorably in the presence of your
children—frequently, occasionally, never?" may argue
something as follows. "I don't make unfavorable
criticisms of the school or teachers. But when something happens at school that I consider wrong, or when
the teacher does something that I should not want my
children to imitate, I do express my opinion. That is not
criticism, it is merely setting a high standard of conduct." This mother thus justifies herself in underlining
the word *never.* Or a negative reply may be made to
such a question as "Have you ever intentionally induced an abortion or miscarriage?" with the mental
reservation, "It is true that I took the medicine that
Mrs. Smith told me about. But Mrs. Jones took it too
and it had no effect on her, so I probably would have
had the miscarriage anyway. And besides it's none of
their business."

If questions of this kind are asked at all, the requirement of affixing signatures should be waived, the purpose and significance of the investigation explained
with even more than the usual care, and the need for
absolute frankness stressed. With adequate assurance
of anonymity fairly satisfactory returns may sometimes be obtained even from questionnaires dealing
with highly personal matters. Dr. Katherine B. Davis'
study of the sex life of college women (59) is an example. It may be well to add the caution that serious
difficulties are likely to arise from the circulation of
questionnaires containing items on tabooed subjects, or
even on subjects which some respondents may regard
as personal. For this reason it is usually unwise to
attempt to distribute such questionnaires within a
school or college group, even though signatures are not

requested. Such information may better be obtained through other methods.

7. *In questionnaires of the third type which involve a transcription of written records, errors may be made in tabulating or copying the data as well as in the original records. The copy should therefore always be proof-read carefully.* Copying will be easier and errors less frequent if the form of the questionnaire is made to correspond as nearly as possible to that of the original records. If printed forms have been used, copies of these should be secured for reference in preparing the questionnaire. If all the data are to be obtained from a single source the questionnaire may simply duplicate the form of the original record, but when the information is to be secured from a number of different organizations or communities whose records have been kept in various ways, considerable ingenuity is sometimes needed in order to construct the questionnaire form in such a way that errors in transcription due to the confusion or misplacement of items are least likely to occur. If much copying is asked for, arrangements should be made to defray the clerical expenses involved.

On pages 400 ff. are reproduced certain sections of a questionnaire used by the *Committee on The Infant and Pre-School Child* of the *Section on Education and Training* of the *White House Conference on Child Health and Protection.* The purpose of this questionnaire was to obtain general information with regard to the conditions under which children the country over are being reared. The data were obtained by interviews secured by field workers connected with many different organizations throughout the country. It was thus used as an oral rather than a written questionnaire, though it is evident that with the omission of certain items to be noted directly by the field worker, and with suitable changes in the instructions, it could be filled out directly by the respondents. The method used in constructing this questionnaire is a good example of the care which is needed in preparing forms of this kind.

First it was decided what general topics were to be covered in the investigation and the manner in which the data would be obtained. These topics, together with notes as to the range of information to be considered under each, were listed as a means of guiding the discussion of the subcommittee who were to draw up the questionnaire. The subcommittee was then assembled for a two day meeting, at the end of which a long list of questions had been roughly formulated, and the general arrangement of the material decided upon.

After the committee meeting, the questions were put into tentative form and blanks were mimeographed for use in a practical tryout.

Letters were then sent to about forty directors of nursery-schools and workers in child welfare organizations of various kinds, describing the project and asking if they would be willing to give the forms which had been prepared a preliminary tryout. They were asked to secure from five to ten interviews each and to make a critical report of their experiences, stressing any practical difficulties encountered such as antagonism toward answering certain questions, ambiguities in the instructions, conditions not provided for in the list of answers to certain questions, questions for which information was frequently lacking, *etc*. The responses to this request were very gratifying. A total of 175 trial interviews were secured together with many valuable criticisms, comments and suggestions. The findings and the criticisms were then tabulated for each question separately. A tabulation was also made of the criticisms of the blank as a whole. This concrete trial of the procedure revealed many sources of error which would otherwise have crept into the data in spite of the care which had been exercised in the preparation of the forms up to this point.

Each item in the questionnaire was then gone over with the utmost care, the criticisms which had been sent in were compared and the doubtful questions were either thrown out completely or were reformulated in such a way as to obviate the difficulties which had been found. Much of the material was rearranged, and the instructions to the field worker were revised at the points where they had been found unsatisfactory or incomplete. Before submitting the final copy to the printer it was gone over independently by three members of the original committee, each of whom, it is interesting to note, had one or two minor improvements to suggest even after the extremely careful editing which the forms had already received.

If persons with extensive training and experience find it necessary to spend so much time and effort in the preparation of a questionnaire, how much more necessary it is for the beginner to do so. Perhaps one of the surest ways of overcoming the "plague of the questionnaire," as it is sometimes called by those who sort out the bulky envelopes in their daily mail with one disillusioned eye on the wastebasket, would be to start a determined crusade against the answering of any which do not bear evidence of at least reasonably careful planning. The time thus saved could then be expended upon more careful replies to those which merit it. If this plan were uniformly adhered to, many of our present aspirants to easy fame would be forced to adopt some other and perhaps less troublesome road, while the questionnaire, which has long been regarded as a changeling in the lap of science, might take its rightful place among its methodological brothers and sisters.

WHITE HOUSE CONFERENCE ON CHILD HEALTH AND PROTECTION *

COMMITTEE III, B, EDUCATION AND TRAINING OF THE INFANT AND PRESCHOOL CHILD

John E. Anderson, Chairman

THE YOUNG CHILD—FROM I TO 5 YEARS, INCLUSIVE

(Check small square to indicate answer where choice is given, thus [✓])

1. Name of child ....
2. Sex   *Male* □; *Female* □;
3. Age ....*yrs.* 4. Date of birth ....
5. Was he breastfed?   *Yes* □; *No* □
6. If so, how many months was he entirely breastfed? ....
7. Height ....
8. Was height obtained by measuring?   *Yes* □; *No* □
9. If not, was height estimated?   *Yes* □; *No* □
10. Weight: ....
11. Was weight obtained by use of scale? *Yes* □; *No* □
12. If not, was weight estimated?   *Yes* □; *No* □
13. Does this weight include clothes?   *Yes* □; *No* □
14. Is he weighed regularly?   *Yes* □; *No* □
15. If so, how often is he weighed? weekly □; monthly □; half yearly □; yearly □; other ....

SLEEP

16. At what time did he retire last night?............*P.M.*
17. At what time did he arise this morning?..........*A.M.*
18. Did he take a nap yesterday morning?   *Yes* □; *No* □
19. If so, *from* .... *to* ....
20. Did he nap yesterday afternoon?   *Yes* □; *No* □
21. If so, *from* .... *to* ....
22. How many others sleep in his bedroom?..............
    men........ *women*........ *boys*...... *girls*.......
    infants........ *If none, check here* □

* Published by permission of the Director of the Conference.

23. How many others sleep in his bed?...................
men........ women........ boys....... girls.......
infants........ *If none, check here* ☐

INTELLECTUAL LIFE

102. Does he have a favorite book or story?
Yes ☐; *No* ☐
103. If so, name and author ....·····
104. Did mother tell or read stories to child yesterday?
Yes ☐; *No* ☐
105. Did father tell or read stories to child yesterday?
Yes ☐; *No* ☐
106. Has he learned or is he learning—*to read* ☐; *to count* ☐; *rhymes* ☐; *prayers* ☐; *songs* ☐; *alphabet* ☐; *other* ....
107. Has he asked where babies come from?
Yes ☐; *No* ☐
108. How old was he when he first asked this?........*yrs.*
109. Did mother answer? *Yes* ☐; *No* ☐
110. If so, what did she say? ....
....
....

SOCIAL LIFE

111. Is he restricted when unsupervised—*to the home* ☐; *to the home yard* ☐; *to the block* ☐; *to neighborhood* ☐; *If not restricted, check here* ☐
112. Does he play with other children
in his home? *Yes* ☐; *No* ☐
elsewhere? *Yes* ☐; *No* ☐
113. Does he have a favorite playmate outside of family?
Yes ☐; *No* ☐
114. If so, how old is favorite playmate?..............*yrs.*
115. Did child play outdoors yesterday? *Yes* ☐; *No* ☐
116. If so, about how many hours?...................*hrs.*
117. Where does he play away from home? *in street* ☐; *park* ☐; *vacant lot* ☐; *neighbors' yards or homes* ☐; *playground* ☐; *other* ....
118. Has he ever attended the movies? *Yes* ☐; *No* ☐

119. How many times has he attended movies in last month?
....

120. Has he ever attended Sunday School? *Yes* ☐; *No* ☐
121. Times attended Sunday School in last month?........
122. At what age did he begin Sunday School?............
123. Does he attend— *nursery school* ☐; *kindergarten* ☐; *junior kindergarten* ☐; *day nursery* ☐; *play school* ☐; *other of similar nature*............................

Chapter 43

DIRECT MEASUREMENTS

THE purposes of measurement. The uses of measurement in everyday life are so many and so obvious that it is hardly necessary to mention them. No housewife would think of asking her grocer to send her "a moderate amount" of sugar, or "several" eggs; nor does the carpenter plan the building of a house in terms of "so many piles of lumber." In the physical sciences, measurement is so important that instruments of almost unbelievable delicacy have been devised. Scales exist which literally weigh the dot on the letter i; there are micrometers which measure accurately the differences in the diameters of two hairs. Advance of knowledge in the physical world has been accomplished very largely through the development of such instruments of precision.

In the social sciences such as education, psychology, and sociology, measurement is hardly less important though as yet it is far less precise. This is not surprising when we recall that while measurement in the physical world reaches back over thousands of years into the unknown past, measurement in the study of human behavior has been used even crudely for hardly more than a century. Yet it is to the use of measurement that psychology owes its emergence from a matrix predominantly philosophical to the status of a definite science. By the use of measurements education has developed a body of scientific knowledge upon which to base its practices, and sociology is finding a way to put its numerous theories to empirical test. No science can progress far without measurement.

In the study of child development, measurements of many kinds are employed. The child's physical growth is measured not only in gross terms of height and weight, but the various parts of the body are measured separately and their individual growth curves studied. In this way it has been found that different parts grow at different rates and reach their maxima at different periods. Not only does the body change in size with advancing age, but the composition of its tissues also changes. The infant's body has a much higher percentage of water than the body of the adult; its bones have a smaller mineral content, and there are many other measurable differences.

But the use of measurement is not confined to the study of body structure. It is also our chief source of information regarding bodily and mental function. To measure function is commonly more difficult than to measure structure, not only because of the rapidity with which the various acts are carried out, but also because of the varying and frequently obscure factors by which they are affected from one instant to the next. Thus we may measure the time required for an individual to react to a given stimulus by pressing a telegraph key. This is known as the "simple reaction time." But the reaction time is not as "simple" as the name might indicate, since experiment has shown that it varies according to a number of factors. It is shorter when the stimulus is auditory than when it is visual; shorter when the subject concentrates his attention upon the movement to be made than when he directs it chiefly toward watching for the stimulus to be given, and so on. Even when all factors known to affect the results are held constant, the reaction time of any individual will still vary appreciably from one trial to another, so that it is necessary to take the average of a large number of trials in order to get a reliable measure. When this is done it will be found that under the same conditions

subjects differ appreciably from each other in average reaction time. This shows that reaction time is determined not
only by the conditions under which it is taken, but that even
when conditions are the same, people differ from each other
in the speed with which they can react. Although little work
has thus far been done upon the reaction time of young
children, such data as have been obtained show that on the
average it is slower than the reaction time of adults, and that
differences between individual children are at least equally as
great as those among adults. In like manner we make use of
measurement to determine the extent of the differences
which are associated with age, sex, conditions of experiment,
and so on in practically all types of mental and motor performances and physiological processes. In the absence of
measurement we can sometimes give crude descriptions of
facts as they take place. However, such descriptions are too
inexact and too subject to varying interpretation to be of
great service in the advancement of scientific knowledge.

What can be measured? Strictly speaking, the term *measurement* should be confined to facts or processes which can
be observed directly and which can be expressed in terms of
space, time, or number. Thus we say that Johnny Brown is
46 inches tall; that he ran 25 yards in 20 seconds; and that
he repeated 5 digits after a single hearing. All these are
simple facts, observed and measured in terms which have
universal meaning. An inch is a unit of space which may be
applied indiscriminately to all physical structures whether
animate or inanimate. Its use is not confined to any single
purpose. Likewise time and number are universal measures.
But there are other ways of describing individuals, sometimes spoken of as measurements, which lack this feature
of universality and whose meaning is therefore limited in
ways which it is important for the student to understand.
These methods will be described in more detail in Chapter

46, *Standardized Tests of General Traits or Characteristics.*
To avoid confusion for the present, it is sufficient for the
student to note that the ordinary mental test is not a measurement of intelligence in the same sense that the time intervening between stimulus and response is a measurement of
reaction time, or that the distance from head to foot is a
measure of height. For the latter we have units of measurement which have meaning apart from the individuals to
which they are applied. For the "mental test," on the other
hand, we have no units except those derived from applying
the test to many different persons and noting their responses.
On the basis of this experience we can say that a given child
has a "mental age" of so many years; that is, his performance on this test is equal to that of the average child of the
age specified. Or we can say that he ranks in the seventy-
fifth percentile for his age; meaning that out of a hundred
children of his age he would rank seventy-fifth from the bottom (or twenty-fifth from the top). Strictly speaking this is
classification rather than *measurement,* even though some
sort of a quantitative comparison which has many features
in common with measurement must be made before the classification becomes possible.

The reliability of measurement. The inexperienced person is inclined to think that any measurement of an object
or process which can be observed directly is for that very
reason a "true" measurement, whose reliability can be taken
for granted. Further consideration will usually cause such
persons to admit that carelessness may cause errors in
measurement, but it is less easy for them to see that every
measurement, no matter how carefully taken, has its limits
of accuracy. It is highly important that these limits be determined, since in some cases they may be so great as to
render conclusions very doubtful unless methods can be improved.

How can the accuracy of a measurement be determined? In the case of physical structures such as the human body in which changes take place so slowly that a brief time interval can be ignored, accuracy can be tested by consecutive measurements of a number of cases by two or more competent persons working in complete ignorance of each other's results. In the case of processes or activities which are likely to vary somewhat from trial to trial, both simultaneous and consecutive measurements by two or more investigators are needed as a rule, in order to ascertain both the amount of error in the individual measurements, and the extent of the variation which takes place from time to time in the same individual. By this means we are able to determine how many measurements it is necessary to take in order to secure a dependable measure of the subject's average or most typical performance.

It is customary among many people to speak of the *reliability* of a measurement as a sort of final determination of which no further analysis is possible. This is an unfortunate point of view. By *reliability*, let us remember, we mean the *accuracy* with which objects or processes are measured by means of the procedure under consideration. Expressed somewhat differently, it refers to the *consistency* of the results obtained by a measuring process applied repeatedly to the same individuals under similar conditions. There are a number of factors which make for inconsistency in results. These may be classified as follows:

1. *The measuring instrument may vary*. If lengths are measured with a damp cotton tape which stretches when it is drawn tight, consistent results can hardly be expected. Or if "digit span" (the number of digits which can be repeated correctly after a single hearing) is tested by an examiner who sometimes repeats the digits rapidly, sometimes slowly; sometimes rhythmically, at other times monotonously; inconsist-

encies due to variation in the instrument (which in this case consists of the verbal recitation of the digits by the examiner) are almost certain to occur.

2. *The instrument may register correctly, but the observer who makes the record may make it imperfectly or without sufficient precision.* To a certain extent imperfect observation is inevitable. Human perception has its final limits of exactness, which no amount of care or training will overcome. As two lines are made more and more nearly alike in length, a point is reached at which no amount of effort will enable the unaided human eye to distinguish between them. By the use of special instruments greater precision can be attained. However, no matter how delicate the instrument finer distinction is always theoretically possible, though it may be unnecessary for the purpose at hand.

But errors due to limits of precision are far from being the most vicious to which the observer is subject. If his method or his standards vary from time to time more serious distortions may arise. In taking measures of length the observer may fail to change his own position when the measurements fall at different points on the scale, and thus read the extremes always from an acute visual angle which tends to distort the results. In trying to determine the average size of the group within which a given child is most commonly found during his play-hours the observer's ideas as to what constitutes a "group" may vary somewhat from time to time in spite of careful definition, and are practically certain to do so if no formal definitions have been drawn up.

3. *In addition to instrumental and observational errors true variations may take place within the subjects themselves from one occasion to another even when the trials take place in immediate succession.* This is sometimes true even in the case of physical dimensions. For example, chest girth is affected by changes in respiration rarely susceptible to exact control. In measurements of physical, mental, and motor processes or activities such changes almost always occur, since only

occasionally will an act be repeated in exactly the same way. Since most of these changes are due to factors which the experimenter is unable to ascertain or control, it is usually necessary to repeat these measurements many times and to take the average of all the repetitions as the subject's measurement or score. The number of repetitions necessary will vary with the degree of precision needed and the amount of variation in the responses. A good rule is to continue until the addition of more measurements will not affect the average to an extent which would interfere with the conclusions which are to be drawn. Inaccuracy of measurement resulting from true but uncontrollable variations in the subjects measured is known as the *intrinsic error.*

4. *A fourth source of error which is always present in some degree but which is likely to be greatest when the number of subjects used is small, is the sampling error.* Reference was made to this in the chapter on the questionnaire. One of the most important uses of measurement in the study of child development is the establishment of *norms* or standards of reference with which other individuals can be compared. If we know the average height of four-year-old girls, we can thereafter measure any girl of that age and say at once whether she is taller or shorter than the average. If we know the average weight of children of certain ages and heights we are able to ascertain whether other children are above or below the usual standards in weight. If properly interpreted, this may afford a useful indication of their state of health. It is necessary, however, if such norms are not to be misleading, that the composition of the group measured in establishing these norms be carefully described or defined. It would be foolish to use norms derived from measuring the height of a group of Scotch children as standards for Japanese children of the same age. Errors as gross as this, to be sure, are not likely to occur, but others which are less obvious may be quite as serious. To assume that findings for a particular group which has been measured

will on the average be true for other groups who have
not been measured is warranted only if (a) the group
measured is large enough so that the addition of more
cases does not materially change the value of the
averages obtained, and if (b) its composition is sufficiently well-known to make it possible to state with
reasonable accuracy to what other groups these standards may safely be applied. This means that it is not
safe to measure a group of children chosen at random
from one community and to assume without further
investigation that the same findings will hold for another group selected at random from another community. It is necessary first to consider what facts
(such as age, sex, racial composition, social or cultural
background, *etc.*) may reasonably be expected to affect
the results and then to find out how the group in question is made up with respect to these facts. Are the
children predominately Irish, German, Jewish, or
Italian? Do they come from poor or wealthy neighbor-
hoods? About how much education have the parents?
and so on. The facts which should be ascertained vary
with the type of measurement which is being made
and it may sometimes be impossible to secure all the
data exactly, but the more carefully the sampling is
defined the more useful and accurate will be the results
obtained, and the smaller will be the likelihood of
serious errors in interpretation.

The reliability of a measurement should therefore be
stated not merely in gross terms without attempt at
analysis into the separate factors which make for error,
but each possible source of unreliability should be
examined separately. This takes more time, to be
sure, but is necessary if accuracy of measurement is to
be improved. If we know that the instrument is imperfect we can often find means to improve it. If we
know that the observer is inconsistent in his methods,
more precise regulations can be laid down. If we know
that the subjects vary in their responses from one trial
to another, two lines of attack are open. The first is
to make sure that the situation remains uniform and

that the instructions given are sufficiently exact to insure a uniform method and effort. Particularly in the case of young children, such matters as attention, fatigue, interest, boredom, shyness, and the like must be watched carefully. When all these factors have been controlled as completely as possible, a sufficient number of trials must be made to secure a stable average. Care in controlling the factors which make for variability in the subjects' performances will greatly reduce the number of trials needed. And finally, the composition of the group actually measured must be carefully described in such a way as to lessen the dangers of serious errors of sampling which may result from attempting to apply standards derived from one group to another which is widely different.

The importance of norms in child study. Since one of the most important aspects of child study is the study of *development,* of the changes which take place with advancing age, the establishment of a wide variety of norms or standards by which development can be measured is a task of first importance. On the physical side we need to extend our present norms for the growth of gross portions of the body to include finer units. We need to define all standards more clearly in terms of racial background, perhaps even in terms of immediate family history. Should the same weight norms calculated on the basis of age and height be applied to the child whose parents and grandparents are tall and lean as to the one whose ancestors are short and tubby? We also need more adequate standards for physiological processes and body chemistry. On the mental side as well, more analytic standards are needed. We need to supplement our general norms of mental development as a whole by more specific knowledge of the development of its different aspects or processes. Norms of social and emotional development and of the development of special habits, and the like, are at present almost wholly lacking.

With the establishment of a greater variety of accurate norms we shall not only be able to study and describe the individual child in a more truthful fashion and thus be in a better position to determine his particular needs, but the entire growth process will be brought into stronger relief, and its interrelationships more clearly understood.

Chapter 44

RATING SCALES AND RANKING METHODS

DEFINITIONS **and descriptions.** In addition to such properties or qualities as height, weight, speed of movement, and so on, which can be measured directly, human beings have many other characteristics which can be observed in a general way but for which no measuring devices are as yet available. Nevertheless, such qualities or *traits* as persistence, aggressiveness, emotional stability, truthfulness, optimism, and social adaptability are often more important factors in the life of a child or an adult than the more objective factors which are subject to measurement. For this reason it is worth while to examine the methods which have been developed for reducing the incidental observations and judgments of characteristics such as those just mentioned to a form which renders them suitable for quantitative treatment.

Judgments of this kind, made in an informal way and couched in varying terms, are heard daily. "Mary Smith is the *most tactless* creature!" "Henry Jones is *rather clever,* but *unbearably conceited.*" "Johnny is a *born leader,*" and so on. Such comments are often illuminating, but they do not lend themselves to formal study because of the many different ways in which the same fact is expressed and the fact that they are often made hastily or with a single instance in mind which may be quite different from the subject's usual behavior.

Two methods of organizing unsystematized opinions which

have been formed through everyday acquaintance with the subjects judged are in common use. The first is the *ranking method* in which the judge is asked to arrange the subjects in order of merit, placing at one extreme the subject who, in his opinion, possesses the trait in question to the most marked degree and at the other extreme the one who is most lacking in it, with the remaining cases arranged in order between the extremes. The second is the method of *rating*, in which the judge is asked to classify each subject with regard to the trait in question according to a series of graded categories formulated by the investigator, such as *"very superior," "somewhat inferior"* or *"average."* Sometimes, in order to give these terms a more concrete meaning, the investigator adds a series of descriptive notes, such as *"Very marked qualities of leadership. His advice is sought by most of his associates, and his opinions and authority are rarely questioned,"* or on the other hand, *"Conspicuously lacking in leadership. Yields to the wishes and opinions of others without question, often to his own disadvantage. Rarely proffers a suggestion, and when he does so it is commonly disregarded by the group."*

Whether the ranking or the rating method is to be regarded as preferable depends upon the circumstances under which the data are to be obtained. Each has certain points in its favor as well as certain disadvantages or limitations.

The ranking method is generally to be preferred when the number of subjects or samples to be ranked does not exceed forty or fifty, and when the judge or judges have sufficient acquaintance with all of them so that the method is feasible. It evidently cannot be used if the individual judges are acquainted with only part of the subjects. With large numbers of subjects its use becomes so laborious as to be impractical. Its advantages lie chiefly in the fact that it can be used with judges whose experience is too limited to make their concepts of "average" or "inferior" of much value, since it requires only the comparison of one concrete person or object with another. This is always easier than comparison with an abstract standard. It is particularly useful when the subjects to be judged are not persons but work products, such as samples of handwriting, sewing, woodwork, drawing, *etc.*, where the samples to be ranked can be examined at leisure and arranged in order of merit by as many judges as it seems desirable to consult. This is the method commonly used in the construction of handwriting scales, drawing scales, and the like. The same method can be used for written descriptions of acts or events concerning which the combined judgments of competent persons are desired. Such a method, for example, might very profitably be employed in the study of behavior problems, or in evaluating the importance for child welfare of certain defined conditions in the home or in the family relationships.

The rating method has a somewhat wider range of application than the ranking method, since it does not necessitate that the ratings of all the subjects be made by the same judges. It can therefore be used when selected subjects from many localities are being studied (as in investigations of the behavior of foster children, of the feeble-minded or the specially gifted). Since comparison is made with a general standard rather than between concrete individuals there is danger that, unless careful definitions are given, different judges will vary in their concepts of what that standard should be. Thus, a teacher whose experience has been largely with children from highly cultured homes may rank a child as "inferior" whom another teacher accustomed chiefly to children of very limited cultural background may consider "superior." Their actual opinions of the child if made without reference to others may be much the same, but the first teacher is comparing him with a very high standard, the

second with one which is much lower. He excels the latter
standard but does not quite measure up to the first. This
danger may be in part overcome by describing as exactly as
possible just what degree of excellence is to be understood
by each step on the scale. The rating method has the
further advantage of requiring less time except when the
number of subjects to be judged is very small, and of permitting easy combination of ratings on a number of specific
traits into a more generalized scale. This method is described on page 421.

Methods of securing rankings. Three ways of securing an
order-of-merit arrangement of a group of subjects have been
used. The first method, which is probably the most accurate,
is known as the *method of paired comparisons*. A written
check list is prepared in which each subject is compared with
every other subject. The judge is asked to state in each case
which member of the pair he considers superior in the trait
in question. Thus, if the task is that of arranging the children
in a certain kindergarten in order of physical beauty, the
judge is given a prepared list in which each child's name is
presented for comparison with that of every other child, and
is required to check the member of the pair whom he regards as the more beautiful. This will necessitate $\dfrac{n^2 - n}{2}$
comparisons, or 435 judgments if there are 30 children in the
class and position within the pair is disregarded. If, as is
sometimes recommended, each comparison is repeated so
that the name of each child occurs once in the initial and
once in the final position in each comparison, 870 judgments
will be required for a class of 30. Because of the amount of
time required, this method is rarely used except for problems
of scale construction where the results are expected to have
general significance (as, for example, in the construction of a
handwriting scale with which other specimens may be com-

pared, or in the development of a scale for rating the seriousness of certain "behavior problems").

A method which retains most of the advantages of the
method of paired comparisons, but which requires less time
and appears far less formidable, may for convenience be
called the *method of comparative arrangement*. Each judge
is given a set of the samples or descriptions to be ranked,
or if the comparison is to be made between human beings as
in the example just cited, he is given a set of cards or paper
slips each of which bears the name of a single subject. He is
told to select any two slips at random, compare them with
each other and place the one which he regards as superior
on the right, the other on the left, as shown below:

A   B

He then selects another card at random, and compares it
with A. If he thinks it inferior to A, he places it still further
to the left. If he thinks it better than A, he compares it with
B, and places it to the right or left according as it is judged
to be superior or inferior to B. Suppose that he considers
it to be superior to A but inferior to B. He would then place
it in an intermediate position, as shown below:

A   C   B

A fourth card, D, is then selected and the successive comparisons made as before. If it is judged to be better than A
or C but inferior to B the arrangement would then be:

A   C   D   B

The process is continued in the same way until all the
cards or samples have been arranged in order. The arrangement should then be checked through by reading the successive cards in order first from left to right, that is from

lowest to highest, and then backward from right to left (highest to lowest) and any changes in order which seem warranted should be made. The arrangement is then copied and the list turned over to the investigator. This method has the advantage of simplifying and objectifying the task through requiring comparison between only two subjects at a time, and takes little more time than the method next to be described, which is usually much less accurate.

The third method consists in *ranking from a random list* without formal rearrangement. The subjects are listed in random order, and the judge is asked to write before each name (or each description) a number corresponding to the rank-order which he thinks it should take. Thus the best subject is numbered 1; the second best 2; and so on. If the list is short the method may be fairly accurate, but with longer lists the difficulty of keeping the attention fixed on the subject last ranked while rereading the names of so many others is very great, and confusions and inaccuracies are extremely likely to result.

Methods of securing ratings. In the making of ratings as well as in ranking, a number of different devices are used. The oldest and least adequate method was referred to in a previous paragraph. It consists in asking each judge to indicate the general degree of superiority or inferiority of the subject rated, without specifying how the various grades are to be defined, as in the example shown below:

"Is this child's general health—very superior, somewhat above average, average, somewhat inferior, very inferior? (Underline.)"

A method very similar to this is that in which the judges are requested to refer their judgments to a definite standard within their own experience. For example, if they are to rate a group of children with regard to beauty, the instructions would be given somewhat as follows:

"Think of the most beautiful child you ever saw. Write that child's name on a separate sheet of paper and mark it 1.

"Now think of the ugliest child you ever saw. Write that child's name on the paper and mark it 5.

"Now try to think of some child whom you would judge to be just about half-way between these two in beauty. Write his name and mark it 3.

"Here is a list of the children in your class. You are to rate each one for beauty by comparing them with the children whose names you have just written. Take the first child on the list. If you think he is as beautiful as the child whom you rated 1, write the number 1 after his name. If he is less beautiful than that child but more beautiful than the one you rated 3, write a 2 after his name; if he is about equally as beautiful as the child you rated 3, write 3 after his name. If he is less beautiful than 3, but more beautiful than 5, rate him 4, and if he is no more beautiful than 5, rate him 5. Do the same with each of the others."

This method has some advantage over the former in that it provides each judge with a fairly constant standard for making his ratings, and thus makes it improbable that he will become progressively more lenient or more critical in rating the children at the end of the list than he was at the beginning, but it does not guard against the probability that different judges will have different standards. It works fairly well when all the ratings are made by a single judge, but does not provide a good basis for combining the ratings from several judges.

A better method is for the investigator to prepare a set of definitions for each step on the scale in advance, and to ask the judges to rate the subjects according to these definitions rather than according to any standards within their own personal experience. If the judges have had some experience in making ratings of this kind, it will usually be sufficient to give each one a copy of the definitions and a list of the subjects to be rated, and to ask him to write after the name of each subject the number of the definition which he thinks best describes that person. With inexperienced judges it is often better to make use of what is known as the *graphic rating scale*.

In the graphic rating scale, a line several inches in length is drawn across the sheet with division points at regular intervals. Above each division point is a definition or description indicating the degree of the trait in question to which the division point is supposed to correspond. An example is given below:

Instructions: Read through each of the descriptive phrases above the line. Decide which one best describes this child, or between which two he seems to fall; then place a cross (X) on the line at the point where you think he belongs. Note that you do not have to make the cross correspond exactly to any one of the descriptive phrases. If you think the child falls between two of these points, make the cross as far to the right or left of one of them as you think it should be placed.

Physical courage.

Exceedingly cowardly, afraid to take slightest risk.	Timid but making effort to overcome it.	Reasonably cautious in face of danger but fearless under ordinary conditions.	Inclined to be over-bold, often takes unwise chances.	Foolhardy. No recognition of danger. A dare-devil.

Since the definitions in the graphic rating scale are placed directly above the line on which the ratings are to be made, the likelihood that the judges will fail to make the necessary reference to them is considerably lessened. The method also makes allowance for intermediate ratings of any desired degree of fineness. As a matter of fact, however, the number of people who make use of intermediate ratings is usually rather small. Actually, since few people seem able to distinguish more than five or at most seven degrees of difference in traits for which measuring devices are lacking, the provision of opportunities to make finely graduated judgments is a useless refinement of method.

The graphic rating scale is most frequently used when it is desired to secure ratings on a large number of different traits for the same individual. The scales for the different traits, with their definitions, are printed on a single sheet or folder, together with the instructions for rating, and the judges are requested to rate each subject on each trait listed.

A recent development of the trait rating method is the *composite scale*. A general trait is selected which it is desired to study more carefully. This trait is then analyzed into a number of finer elements or subtraits, of which it may be said to be composed. Ratings are then made on each of the subtraits independently; and numerical values, say from 1 to 5, are assigned to each step on each of the scales. The sum of all the ratings on the subtraits is then taken as the individual's "score" on the more general trait. Thus, beauty might be subdivided into beauty of eyes, of hair, complexion, bodily proportions, and so on, and ratings on each of these separate features be combined to give a single score. Olson (200) has used this method in a series of ratings designed to predict the likelihood that a given child will be a "behavior problem"; Furfey (82) uses it in rating "developmental age," and Marston (176) in rating introversion-extroversion. The ratings given by different judges on these combined scales usually show much closer agreement with each other than do ordinary undifferentiated ratings. In this sense the scales may be said to be more reliable.

Reference should also be made here to ratings made by comparing actual specimens of children's work (drawing, handwriting, *etc.*) with standardized scales of excellence. These scales may be considered somewhat analogous to the

printed descriptions of the successive steps on the ordinary
rating scale, except that their numerical values have been
worked out statistically instead of being arbitrarily assigned.
Since they represent the same kind of product as that with
which they are compared they permit more exact comparisons than can possibly be made by means of a verbal description alone.

Methods of scaling. The assignment of arbitrary numerical
values to the successive steps on a rating scale is frequently
all that can be done, since the determination of the true
values of these steps requires more data than are obtained
in the majority of investigations. The student should realize,
however, that these arbitrary values may be quite wide of
the mark, and that much more precise methods exist which
should be used whenever the data warrant it. It is impossible
to set any hard and fast rule as to the amount of data
required for scaling to be worth while, since it depends in
part on the extent of agreement between the judges. With
the agreement commonly found, if rankings are made by as
many as twenty-five different judges or if ratings are available on a hundred or more different subjects regardless of
the number of judges, the statistical determination of more
exact scale values is usually to be preferred to the simple
averaging of ranks or the assignment of arbitrary values to
ratings. For methods of determining scale values the reader
is referred to Section IV of the bibliography.

The reliability of ratings and rankings. The problem of
determining the reliability of judgments of this kind is a
very difficult one. It is complicated first of all by the fact that
judges differ in their ability to appraise others, and that their
opportunities for acquaintance with the subjects usually differ
not only in amount but in kind. One would hardly expect
even an unbiased parent to rate the behavior of her child exactly the same as an equally unbiased teacher, since they

have been accustomed to observe him in such very different situations, and since few children behave in quite the same way at home as they do in school. Not only are some people better judges than others, but the same person will usually be a better judge of some traits than he is of others. It is impossible, therefore, to speak of the reliability of a rating scale in the same way in which we speak of the reliability of a measurement. If two well-trained persons make a certain measurement independently of each other, we are fairly safe in taking the amount of disagreement between their results as an indication of the amount of disagreement likely to be found between the measurements of any other two equally well-trained persons. In other words, we can make generalized statements as to the reliability of the measurement in question without reference to the particular persons who happen to make it, since the difference in the ability of well-trained persons to take measurements is usually so small. In the case of ratings or rankings given by persons of equal training and equal acquaintance with the subjects, differences in the ability of the different judges is usually so great that statements as to their reliability must either be made separately for each individual judge, or must be based upon averages for large numbers of judges whose experience with the subjects is similar.

Methods of calculating the reliability of ratings are somewhat complex and will not be taken up here. The student who contemplates making much use of these methods should consult Kelley (390) and Shen (220). The article by Shen is particularly important since it calls attention to a systematic error which arises in correlating the ratings of two judges of unequal reliability with each other. It also gives a method for weighting the ratings given by a number of different judges for the same subjects in accordance with their respective reliabilities. By this method the ratings given by the poor judges play a much smaller part in determining the total or average score than do those of the good judges, which is as it should be.

The uses of rating scales. In addition to securing quantitative data in fields for which no formal measuring devices have been devised, rating scales furnish one of our chief methods of determining how well the results of newly devised tests agree with the judgments of reasonably competent individuals as to the personal qualities of others who are given these tests. The mere fact that a certain set of tasks has been called a test of "character," "persistence," "will power," or what not does not mean that it is necessarily a good test of these qualities. Unless the results of the tests correspond fairly well with the judgments of competent persons it is usually unwise to place much confidence in them.

A third and very important use of rating scales is in the study of self-estimates, particularly in comparison with the estimates of associates. To what extent do we "see ourselves as others see us" and, conversely, how does the way in which we regard ourselves affect our opinions of others? Does the person who regards himself as exceptionally free from conceit tend to see others as more or less conceited than they are judged by their other associates? Is the person who admits that he is sometimes untruthful more or less likely to impute untruthfulness to his acquaintances than the one who claims impeccable honesty? In what kinds of traits are self-ratings commonly more favorable than the ratings of associates, and *vice versa?* The possibilities for the investigation of human behavior to be found in studies of this kind are almost endless, and while a small amount of work has been done with adults, practically no such studies have been carried out with children. The method is nevertheless entirely feasible for children who have reached the third or fourth grade in school if the traits selected are such as fall within the range of childish vocabulary and experience, are simply and clearly defined, and only rather coarse distinctions are required.

Chapter 45

SYSTEMATIC OBSERVATIONS WITHOUT CONTROL OF CONDITIONS

THE difference between systematic and incidental observation. Although incidental observation of facts as they chance to occur forms the starting point of most scientific investigation, it is not of equal service in the solution of specific problems or in the determination of general principles of behavior. When there is no attempt to introduce experimental control of conditions, the possibilities of variation are so great that unless some method of limiting and defining the facts to be observed can be devised, the drawing of general conclusions becomes extremely hazardous. The single incident may be a useful point of departure but it is an unsafe terminal point.

There are, however, a number of ways by which observations taken under "natural" conditions, *i.e.*, without the setting up of a formal laboratory situation, may be rendered suitable for scientific study. These methods are especially important since there are many forms of behavior which it is desirable to study that cannot readily be induced at will. We may take a child into a laboratory and instruct him to tap as rapidly as he can on a brass plate with a metal stylus. In this way we may secure a fair index of his manual speed. But we shall be less successful if we bring two children together into the laboratory and say to them, "Now let us see how sociable you can be." Moreover, we are rightly hesitant about subjecting children to experiences which might carry undesirable consequences, such as severe frights, unnecessary thwarting of desires, and the like, merely in order to study their reactions. Instead, it is preferable to take advantage of such situations as they naturally and unavoidably occur, and to record the facts in a uniform and systematic fashion which makes it possible to combine the findings from many such episodes for statistical treatment.

The first requirement for this purpose is that the manner of keeping the records be uniform. The terminology must be the same from record to record; the same series of facts must be recorded each time, and every occurrence of the behavior in question which takes place during the period of observation must be set down. None of these conditions are likely to be met without careful planning at the outset. Moreover, unless the facts to be recorded are very simple and few in number, omission of significant items is almost certain to occur from time to time through oversight. For this reason it is highly desirable to prepare a definite record form in advance upon which the facts can be entered. The use of such forms has the further advantage of keeping all records in uniform arrangement, greatly facilitating tabulation. Forms can be printed, mimeographed, or, if the data are not too complex, the items can be entered in ruled columns properly labeled.

The time factor must also be controlled or recorded. This can be done either by having each observational period occupy a definite and predetermined period of time, or by recording the length of time occupied by each event which is recorded. This brings the time factor under the same rules as those used in general laboratory experiments or in mental testing where scoring is done either in terms of the number of tasks per unit of time, as in the ordinary group test, or in terms of the time required to perform a certain task, as in most of the individual performance tests.

The situations under which the behavior takes place must also be recorded. If these situations can be classified in advance into certain broad groups and the records made in terms of this classification, not only will tabulation be easier but less time will be required for recording. However, since it is rarely possible to foresee in advance all the situations that may occur, it is usually well to reserve space on the record blank for the description of unforeseen situations which do not properly fall into any of the original classes. These can be recorded in descriptive terms at the time and classified later when the study is completed.

The differences between the systematic observations which are filling an increasingly important place in modern studies of behavior, and the unsystematized or incidental observations which were popular at an earlier period may be summarized somewhat as follows:

	Systematized	*Unsystematized*
Nature of facts to be recorded	Determined and defined in advance.	Miscellaneous.
Time limits	Either kept uniform for all observations or records made of time required for a specified unit of behavior.	Frequently unrecorded. No uniform system of time limits.
Place or situation	Always recorded. Sometimes partially controlled by selecting a constant time and place favorable to the free display of the behavior in question and taking all observations under these conditions.	Usually recorded, but in such general descriptive terms as to render classification very difficult.

	Systematized	*Unsystematized*
Manner of making records		
(a) Terminology	Uniform, with all terms defined in advance.	Loosely descriptive, varying from record to record.
(b) Arrangement	Uniform, planned to eliminate all unnecessary writing and to facilitate tabulating.	No formal arrangement. Diary plan most common.
Number of records taken	Number required to yield reliable conclusions determined statistically and observations continued until required amount of data has been secured.	Indefinite.
Treatment of results	Quantitative (statistical).	Qualitative (descriptive).
Completeness of information	Selected facts recorded in full, but little or no attempt to note behavior falling outside the predetermined field of investigation.	Entire freedom in selecting kind of facts to be noted but no requirement that any one form of behavior will be recorded consistently.
Chief application	For the solution of problems formulated in advance.	For the setting of new problems.

Definitions and descriptions of methods. An observational technique which has many points in common with the controlled experiment may be called a *situational analysis.* Its purpose is to study the changes in behavior which take place in accordance with known changes in the situation under which the behavior occurs. For example, McCarthy (169) studied the differences between the conversation of nursery-school children with each other during the free play hour, and with an adult who took them into a separate room and showed them toys and pictures. Moore (187) and Landis (160) recorded the snatches of conversation which were overheard on city streets, and classified it according to whether the participants were (a) men only, (b) women only, or (c) of opposite sex. Very characteristic differences were found under these circumstances. It would be well worth while to carry out a corresponding study over a wide age range, in order to determine at about what age modifications in the subject matter of conversation according to sex can first be detected. The situational analysis is suitable for many comparative investigations, such as the differences between indoor and outdoor play, in the amount of activity before and after naps, behavior of the children in the nursery-school as contrasted with that at home, *etc.*

A second method which has been reduced to a high degree of objectivity is known as the *time sample* or the *method of short samples*. This method differs from the situational analysis just described in that it is commonly used for the study of individual differences in behavior, rather than for the study of changes induced by modifying the situation. A considerable amount of data for each subject is therefore needed. The number of observational samples required will vary with the length of the separate time samples, the size of the observational error, the frequency with which the behavior in question is displayed and the variability in the behavior of the same subjects from time to time. The greater the number of observations, the higher will be the reliability.

The use of the time sample was first developed by Olson (199) in a study of so-called nervous habits in school children. Since then, various modifications of the method have been worked out by different investigators. Olson's procedure was devised particularly for use with large groups of children in a situation where the subjects are not moving about and are in close proximity to each other. This makes it possible for the observer to choose a position which will enable him to see the entire group at one time. Since the subjects can be identified by position as well as by appearance, the task of learning to recognize the individual members of the group is reduced to a minimum. An ideal situation of this kind is provided by the ordinary school class-room. A plan of the seating arrangement can be prepared in advance, and the records of the individual subjects entered directly on this plan. Olson's method was to select a very simple form of behavior, such as inserting the finger into the mouth (regardless of the length of time it was kept there) and to record the number of five minute periods out of a total of twenty in which this form of behavior was observed to occur. Since an entire group was being observed simultaneously, it was not found feasible to attempt to record every occurrence of the event in question, but only to indicate for each individual subject whether or not it was observed at least once during a given five minute period. The highest possible score for each child would thus be equal to the number of separate time units included within the total series of observations. If a series of 20 five minute periods was used, as in the case of Olson's study of oral habits, a child who was seen to insert his finger into his mouth at least once during each five minute period would receive a score of 20, while one who did not do so at all would receive a score of 0. This method has the great advantage of being very economical of time, since an entire group of subjects can be observed simultaneously in little more than the time required to secure an equal amount of data for a single subject when the individual method is used. Obviously, however, it is not well suited to the study of complex forms of behavior.

As used by Olson the method has a distinct defect in that all observations were taken in immediate succession thus making it possible that temporary conditions may have operated to cause certain subjects to react in a manner not at all characteristic of their usual behavior. Thus in the observations on oral habits, temporary conditions such as the presence of a hangnail or some other minor irritation might well cause certain children to insert the finger into the mouth very frequently throughout the series of observations, although such behavior might be quite contrary to their usual habits. In like manner hirsutal habits (scratching the head, pulling or fingering the hair, *etc.*) might reasonably be expected to be somewhat related to the length of time since the last shampoo. Errors of this sort will be avoided if the precaution is taken of scattering the observations over a number of occasions.

Several modifications of the Olson technique have been worked out by other persons. A method was devised by Parten (201) for studying social behavior at the early ages. At Columbia, Thomas (245) and her assistants have developed a number of procedures of this type. Physical contacts between children are observed and recorded in terms of such units as hit, push, pull, point, *etc.*, and note is also made as to which child initiates the contact and which is subjected to it. Other methods reported by Thomas, in which the time sample is used, include a study of the space covered or distance traversed in a given number of observational samples of known length. Thomas also employed the time sample method in studies of interests and occupations, the composition of social groups, *etc.* At Minnesota (108) a one-minute time sample has been used in studies of laughter, compliance, anger, talkativeness, physical activity, and a number of other characteristics.

It is sometimes desirable to study the behavior either of individual children or of certain groups for considerable periods of time. At Minnesota a number of interested parents kept records on every outburst of anger shown by their children over intervals lasting from one to four months (109). The establishment of bladder control in an infant was studied by Hull (137). Records of the eating habits of nursery-school children at the lunch period are kept in a number of nursery-schools.

The situational analysis and the time sampling method are particularly significant, in the first place because of the readiness with which they lend themselves to quantitative treatment and secondly because of the amount of experimental control which is introduced. Other methods of carrying out observational studies, while they sometimes yield interesting conclusions, are less easy to evaluate. As a rule there is no way of determining the reliability of the records, and because of the descriptive nature of much of the data it is often difficult to distinguish between interpretation and fact. There are of course wide differences in the technical adequacy of the observational methods employed by investigators whose work does not come strictly under either of the two methods just cited. In some cases, particularly those which have dealt with specific developmental traits such as the acquisition of speech or the learning of fundamental habits, a high degree of scientific control has been introduced. It nevertheless remains true that when the behavior to be studied is of a kind which lends itself well to either the time-sampling method or the situational analysis, the use of these methods is likely to result both in a gain in scientific accuracy and in a more efficient use of the observer's time.

In the Yale Psycho Clinic a one way vision screen has been devised which greatly facilitates the use of observational techniques, since it permits the subjects to be seen and heard with perfect clearness while the observer remains invisible to them (95). This screen will be found very useful for indoor observation.

The statistical treatment of data obtained through systematic observations. Several of the experiments outlined in Part II of this book made use of special observational methods. The student is referred to those discussions for an account of the statistical devices most commonly used.

Since the observations are made directly and are recorded in terms of the facts actually observed, their validity may be taken for granted so long as the interpretation is confined to those facts and is not extended to cover more general characteristics for which the observed behavior is taken as an index. For example, in investigations such as Olson's study of "nervous habits," so long as the observer is interested simply in thumb sucking, pulling and fingering the hair and so on, in and for themselves the only question as to the truth of the facts recorded centers about the accuracy of the observations made. But if he is studying "nervousness" and assumes that thumb sucking is a partial or complete sign of a nervous tendency, it is necessary for him to show not only that he has observed the facts correctly but that his interpretation of their significance is correct. As a rule it is better to avoid such assumptions and to interpret the findings in terms of the actual facts as they are observed. When this is done, the accuracy of the findings becomes purely a question of their reliability.

The reliability of the observations should be determined by the same kind of analysis as was described in the chapter on measurements, since in this way improvement in method may often be brought about. In the case of the situational analysis, unreliability may be due to inaccurate classification of the situations, to inaccurate observation and recording of the behavior, to selective factors operating in such a way as to make for different samplings of subjects in the different situations studied * or to failure to secure a sufficient amount of data to bring out the facts. If it can safely be assumed that differential selection of the kind described in the footnote is absent, inadequacies in amount can be made up either by adding to the number of subjects or to the number of observations secured for each subject. The amount of reliance which can safely be placed upon the differences found is expressed in terms of the standard error of these differences.

In studies of individual differences in behavior by the time sampling method, reliability is most conveniently expressed by the coefficient of reliability determined by correlation. The reason for using the coefficient of reliability here and not in the situational analysis is to be found in the different purposes for which the two methods are used. The situational analysis is concerned with the difference in behavior between groups studied under different circumstances. The reliability of the group difference is therefore the fact to be established. The time sampling method is most

* If the subjects observed in the different situations are not the same, care must be taken that they are similar in gross characteristics at least. Otherwise, it may well be that the differences observed are due primarily to differences in individuals which cause them to choose certain situations rather than others, and not to the situations themselves. If, for example, older children tend to prefer Situation A and younger children Situation B, the differences observed in the behavior of subjects observed in the two situations may be really determined by the differences in age rather than by differences in the situations. Ambiguities of this kind may be avoided in either of two ways: by using exactly the same group of subjects in all situations which are to be compared as was done by McCarthy (169), or by securing a considerable amount of supplementary data for each subject observed and analyzing the situations with regard to the characteristics of the subjects most commonly found in each.

commonly used for the study of differences between individuals; hence the question of reliability centers about the accuracy with which the display of these differences on further occasions can be predicted from the behavior actually observed. In computing the reliability coefficient, the odd-even method is commonly employed. The observations are numbered in order as they are taken, and the sum of the scores for each subject on the odd numbered occasions are used as the first variable, those on the even numbered occasions as the second. Since the correlation thus obtained represents the reliability of only one-half the sample actually obtained, the Spearman-Brown prophecy formula should be applied to determine the probable reliability of the total.

A distinction should be made between unreliability due to variability in the behavior of the same subjects from day to day, and unreliability due to observational errors. The latter can be checked by having two simultaneous observers record the behavior of a group of subjects independently of each other.

Another factor which affects the reliability of individual differences as determined by the time sampling method is the frequency with which the form of behavior under consideration is manifested. If the events to be observed rarely occur in any of the subjects, so much of the observer's time is wasted that the number of observations which must be made to secure an adequate sample of behavior will be greatly increased. It is important, therefore, to make the observations under conditions which afford ample opportunity for the display of the behavior in question. Provided that all the observations are made under reasonably similar conditions, the Spearman-Brown prophecy formula will enable one to predict from any given number of observations how many additional observations will be needed to secure a reliability coefficient of any required magnitude.* This is an important property of the method, since if a given total amount of time is available for a particular investigation it is possible after a relatively short tryout to state with fair assurance whether or not the time sampling method is likely to be suitable for the purpose.

When the behavior observed may fairly be regarded as a continuous variable of approximately normal distribution so that the scores recorded constitute successive steps on a linear scale, it is often worth while to combine them in such a way as to yield a single final score for each child. For example, such characteristics as amount of laughter or talkativeness may be scored in terms of a series of graded and defined steps running from absence of the behavior (complete soberness or silence throughout the period of observation) to a very high degree (loud, boisterous laughter or continued chatter) at the upper extreme. If a normal distribution may be assumed, the data for all the subjects may be combined and the scale value of each defined step be determined from the proportion of the total number of observations which fall within each category (108, 390).

Certain unique advantages of the observational method. There are many forms of behavior which cannot be induced satisfactorily in the laboratory or the induction of which might lead either to undesirable consequences for the subjects or lay the investigator open to serious adverse criticism. This is particularly true when the subjects are little children, and overanxious parents or conscientious institution attendants have to be reckoned with. Attempts to arouse such emotions as anger or fear except of an extremely mild degree, and similar experiments dealing with behavior which is generally considered undesirable, are almost certain to arouse antagonism on the part of the general public. Careful

* Within the limits of chance variation.

systematic records based upon observations of such events as they chance to occur have therefore considerable value. Parents and teachers in particular, because of their close contact with children over considerable periods of time, are in a favored position for securing observations on behavior of this kind.

The study of social behavior is another example. There are many aspects of social behavior which cannot well be approached by the experimental method, since most real social reactions arise spontaneously and cannot be evoked at will. Such factors as choice of companions, choice of occupations or activities, and many other similar phenomena must be approached by the observational method if at all, at least during the early years. While the questionnaire method is sometimes resorted to for studies of this kind among older children, questionnaires at best must be regarded as a poor substitute for the observation of actual behavior, since most people have a tendency to rationalize their own conduct along lines commonly regarded as desirable when making self-reports. The fact that observational techniques can be adapted to the solution of so many different problems, for many of which no other direct method of study is at present available, makes the method well worthy of careful study. Although casual and unsystematized observations have been used for many years, attempts to reduce such observations to a more exact and quantitative level are still comparatively new. There can be little doubt that with further use of these methods many improvements in technique will be worked out.

Chapter 46

STANDARDIZED TESTS OF GENERAL TRAITS OR CHARACTERISTICS *

DEFINITIONS **and examples.** As we observe the behavior of those about us, we are frequently impressed by certain consistencies in the patterns of reaction most typical of each individual. We say that this person is "unusually intelligent," that one is "stupid," another is "honest," a fourth is "deceitful," and so on. In making such statements we are unconsciously taking a sort of average of each individual's behavior and comparing these averages one with another. When we say that one person is "unusually intelligent" we do not imply that he invariably displays exceptionally good judgment whatever the circumstances. We do mean that on the average, his judgment is likely to be superior to that of others who have had equal experience with the matter in question. The person who is justly said to be "very deceitful" does not always attempt to deceive, but he does so more frequently than others who are rightfully described as "honest" in spite of the fact that their behavior is not invariably free from traces of deceit. Characteristics of this sort are not displayed in an "all-or-none" fashion, but in varying degrees. The extent of display varies somewhat

* No attempt will be made here to enter into a discussion of the various theories of mental organization as they have been advanced by such men as Spearman, Thorndike, and others, since a useful understanding of these theories demands a statistical knowledge considerably in advance of the requirements of this book. The student who is interested in the subject should consult the references given in the bibliography.

for the same individual according to the situations which call it forth, but the *average* extent of display under all situations capable of arousing the behavior in question will also differ from one individual to another. Our classification of individuals theoretically is based upon the extent to which they differ in their average or most typical reactions to situations of the same general class.

But it is rarely, if ever, that any one person has the opportunity to observe all the behavior of another. Even if he had such opportunity, the chances are that he would notice and remember the behavior shown on certain occasions and ignore or forget that shown at other times. This selective attention, though in part determined by chance factors, is even more likely to be due to the personality characteristics of the observer himself and to his attitude toward the person observed or the kind of behavior displayed. Ratings of children by parents and teachers rarely agree closely with each other, not only because parents and teachers see the children under different circumstances but also because their attitudes toward them are different and their standards of comparison vary.

Factors such as these will continue to set an irreducible limit to the accuracy of rating scales and similar devices for subjective classification of individuals in terms of the casual impressions which they make upon certain of their fellows. Recognition of these limitations has led to many attempts to devise standardized series' of test situations, in which all subjects are given a certain number of tasks to perform, and their relative performance on these tasks is taken as a "measure" or an index of their most probable behavior in other similar situations. This insures that all individuals will be judged from their behavior in the same series of situations, rather than from situations which vary widely from one individual to another as in the case of the rating scale. It insures furthermore that all judges will use exactly the same standards in grading the performances of the different subjects, since the standards of performance are rigidly defined in a way which leaves little or nothing to be decided on the basis of personal opinion. Records are made at the time of observation, thus doing away with errors due to lapses of memory. And finally, since the tasks set are the same for all, the "trait" tested takes on a clearness of definition which is lacking when each judge defines it in his own way. Even scientists who have devoted many years of thought to the matter differ considerably when asked to define such a trait as "intelligence." Terman, who is the author of our best known scale of intelligence tests, defines it as "the power to think in abstract terms"; other leading psychologists have defined it as "the ability to make correct responses from the standpoint of truth or fact," "the ability to adapt adequately to new situations," and so on (340). These definitions, though not exactly the same, obviously have much in common.

If we now turn to the statements made by teachers concerning the factors which they consider in judging the intelligence of their pupils, we find much greater variation. Some emphasize physical characteristics, "the glance of the eye" or the shape of the head. Others think chiefly in terms of the child's daily school work. Still others note particularly the child's apparent response to his immediate environment, his attentiveness or mental alertness or his speed of reaction. If we were to question a group of persons with still less training and with a wider variety of experience and social background—representatives of the hypothetical "man in the street"—we should probably find even less agreement in definition. No single "test" of intelligence can possibly yield results which will accord with all these varying definitions, but the test at least has the advantage of uniformity. It can be described in precise terms, and its results checked up against other criteria with a degree of assurance which can never be felt for the rating scale where the personal factor of the rater is so great as to preclude general evaluation. This does not mean that any test, merely because it is a test, will always yield a better or truer classification of individuals than can be obtained by the use of ratings given by competent persons. It does mean that while ratings will continue to be good or poor according to the capacities of the judges by whom they are made, tests have more constant qualities of goodness or poorness which are relatively independent of the persons who happen to administer them, and which can therefore be determined once and for all. Once their adequacy has been determined, a statistical analyses of the factors making for unreliability will often point the way to improvement. The theoretical and practical limitations of the rating scale method are far greater than those of the test method.

We may then define the standardized general test as a uniform and predetermined series of tasks or situations, the performance of which has been shown to be in some measure diagnostic of an individual's capacities, attainments, or habits in certain general lines. As compared to the rating scale it substitutes a uniform situation for one which varies from individual to individual; definite standards of performance for indefinite standards which vary with the individual rater. Its results can be analyzed and its values and weaknesses determined with a degree of finality impossible for the rating scale whose adequacy is so largely dependent upon the individual rater. In these respects its superiority to the rating scale is unquestioned. If the items of which the test is composed have been well selected from the standpoint of diagnostic value, if they cover a sufficiently wide range to take in all of the traits to be measured, if they are sufficient in number to guard against chance variations in the behavior of the subjects, if the method of administering and scoring has been so carefully defined as to guard against irregularities in technique, and if the test is administered by a trained examiner capable of arousing maximum coöperation on the part of the subjects, the results obtained will commonly permit a much more truthful classification of the subjects tested than can possibly be secured by any other method now available. If any or all of these conditions are not fulfilled, the results may be very misleading. The fact that a certain series of tasks has been *called* a test of "intelligence," of "persistence," of "character" or what not does not in itself mean that individuals can be classified by it in any useful way. However, the amount of reliance which can be placed upon it can be determined. This should always be done before the test is put to practical use.

Units of measurement employed in testing. Suppose that in a certain very primitive tribe who had never developed any methods of measuring length, a mother became concerned about the height of her six-year-old boy. She does not think he is as tall as he should be at his age. She takes him to the chief of the tribe and asks his opinion. The chief is not sure, but assures the mother that he will find out. So he orders all the six-year-old boys in the tribe to be brought before him. One by one he stands them up against a large tree and cuts notches in the bark to show the level of each head. As the notches accumulate it is found that some are higher, some lower, but the great majority cluster around one central region with the others scattered about equally above and below. (See Figure 30.) When the height of each boy has been indicated in this way, the chief calls the anxious mother to him again, and they compare her boy's height with the series of notches on the tree. Since they have no other unit of measurement, they cannot say by *how much* his height differs from that of the most typical boy of his age but they can make a few simple comparisons. By counting the notches, they can say how many boys are taller, how many are shorter, and how many are about the

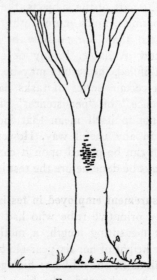

FIGURE 30.

Distribution of heights of six-year-old boys.

same height. Crude as the method is, it at least tells them much more than they knew before.

But other mothers now become interested. They want to know how their children compare with others of their age. Fortunately, there are plenty of trees and the chief is patient. A tree is selected for each year of age, and all the children in the tribe are brought up in turn and their various heights are notched in on the appropriate trees. They now have a series of standards for each age, and the mothers are greatly interested in comparing their children with the notches on the age-trees.

Then one proud mother makes a discovery. Her six-year-old boy's notch shows him to be one of the tallest of his age in the tribe. She takes him over to the "seven-year tree" and finds that he is even taller than the majority of the boys of that age. She takes him to the "eight-year tree" and finds that his head reaches exactly to the point where the notches are most numerous. This gives her great joy. "My boy has eight-year height although he is only six," she boasts. Other mothers follow her example. By trying one tree after another they are able to determine the age to which their children's heights correspond.

In measurements of such general traits as intelligence we are still at much the same level of scientific knowledge as was this tribe in its attempts to measure height. We can determine the average performance of children of different ages on our standardized series of tasks and by comparing other children with the standards thus obtained, we can ascertain the age to which their performances most nearly correspond. In measurements of intelligence we speak of this as the "mental age." Or we may go a step further and obtain a rough measure of the average rate of mental growth by dividing the mental age by the chronological age. Thus, a child of six whose performance on a certain intelligence test was equal to that of the average child of nine years would be said to have a mental age of nine. If we now divide this mental age by his chronological age we get a result of 1.50, which means that on the average his rate of mental growth (in terms of the test in question) has been 1.50 times as great as that of the average child. In expressing these ratios or "intelligence quotients" as they are called, it is customary to omit the decimal point and to write only the initial letters IQ of the words "intelligence quotient." In the example given the child would be said to have an IQ of 150. Another child who at six years did only as well as the average child of five would be said to have an IQ of 83 *; a ten-year-old with a mental age of eight would have an IQ of 80.

Another method of expressing an individual's standing on tests of this kind is in terms of his position with reference to others of his age. Just as by counting the notches on the tree the mothers in the primitive tribe could find how many children of his age were taller or shorter than a given child; so we can find how many, or, more generally speaking, what *percentage* of the children in a certain group equal or exceed the performance of a given member of the group. Thus if 100 six-year-olds are given a certain test and it is found that in this group 59 make a poorer showing than Johnny Smith, while the remainder do as well or better than he, then Johnny would rank as No. 60 in the group of 100. In order to make it possible to compare groups of different sizes it is customary to reduce all ranks to the position which they would presumably occupy in a similar group of 100, and to speak of these as *percentile ranks*. Like the IQ, the percentile rank is a method of expressing an individual's standing in a way which has much the same meaning regardless of age.

All of these methods, however, are methods of classification rather than methods of measurement. They are all based upon a comparison of individuals with each other rather than with some abstract standard which is independent of the individuals who are compared. Even the mental

---

* Mental and chronological ages are commonly taken to the nearest whole month and the quotient carried to two decimal places only. With children under five or six years, however, it may be preferable to calculate ages to the nearest half month; since the small size of the denominator introduces an appreciable shift in the IQ if an entire month is added to the chronological age at one time.

age, which has sometimes been unthinkingly spoken of as an "absolute" measure, is relative in the sense of being derived from the performance of children of the age in question. A mental age of six does not mean an intelligence twice as great as a mental age of three, nor are we warranted in speaking in any general way about "a year of mental growth," since we have no reason whatever for assuming that the average amount of growth is constant from one year to another. If it is useful to do so, we may speak of the amount of gain on a certain test which is made between the third and fourth birthdays, but we have no way of knowing how this compares with the amount gained between the seventh and eighth birthdays. The two amounts cannot be used interchangeably. Many attempts have been made to develop "absolute" units of mental growth, but none has met with universal acceptance.

From the standpoint of scientific investigation, the absence of absolute standards of measurement for such traits frequently imposes a serious handicap upon research. Practically, the limitations resulting from this lack are less serious. Even in such matters as physical size, we use measurement chiefly as a basis for classification. Our problem is not essentially different from that of the women in the primitive tribe. We ask, not "How tall is Johnny?" but "Is Johnny as tall as he should be?", that is, as tall as other children of his age. If we state that a certain seven-year-old is 55 inches in height, the average person will not know whether he is exceptionally tall or exceptionally short, but if we say that he is as tall as the average nine-year-old or that he takes a ten-year size in suits, the statement takes on immediate meaning. Measurement rarely has much significance for the individual until it has been referred to some general standard or norm by which individuals can be classified.

The standardization of tests. In attempting to devise a new series of tests for the classification of individuals a preliminary tryout of the proposed method is usually essential. In making this trial it is wise to select a larger number of tasks or items than will be needed for the final form of the test, since it is probable that a certain number tried will prove worthless and be discarded. In the initial selection of items for trial the following points should be kept in mind:

1. Each item should be diagnostic, that is, should be significantly related to the trait which it is desired to study.

2. The range of difficulty of the items should be great enough to make it highly unlikely that any subject of the ages for which the test is planned will make either a zero or a perfect score. A subject who earns a zero score may truly rank just below another who is able to pass only one item, or he may be so far below the latter that their abilities can hardly be compared. Likewise a perfect score may mean either very much or very little more than a score which is just short of being perfect, and there is no way of knowing which interpretation is true. The possible range of scores should therefore always be greater than the range of abilities among the subjects to be tested.

3. The items should be so selected as to guard against the effect of unequal practice among the subjects as far as possible. If some of the subjects have had much practice in tasks closely similar to those used in the tests, while others are entirely unfamiliar with them, the meaning of the results will be uncertain. There is a question whether new tasks which may be said to test the ability of the subjects to adapt to unfamiliar situations, or familiar tasks which afford an indication of how adequately the subject has profited by his experiences of the past are likely to be more useful. It is not a bad plan to have the test series include some items of each kind.

4. The items should be varied in type, in order to afford as wide a sampling of the field under consideration as possible.

5. Particularly if the test is designed for young children, it is important that all items be interesting and attractive in themselves. It is true that a skilful examiner can often arouse an artificial interest in tasks which would otherwise be unattractive. But since examiners differ greatly in their ability to handle children it is unsafe to rely upon a factor so variable as this is likely to be. Since tests tend to be meaningless unless the coöperation of the subjects is secured, every effort should be made to select material of a kind which will arouse spontaneous interest and effort.

6. The tests should be convenient to administer and should have a limited range of possible responses so that scoring and treatment may be uniform and objective.

When a tentative list of items has been selected which gives promise of meeting these criteria, it should be tried out with a preliminary group of subjects selected to be roughly representative of the group for whom the test is designed. This preliminary group should include representatives of both sexes and of all the ages and social classes with whom it is intended to use the test. Particular care should be taken to include both extremes of ability, in order to make sure that the items cover a sufficiently wide range. The responses of the subjects should be recorded verbatim. Notes should be taken of any difficulties in administration. Any comments made by the subjects upon their attitudes toward the tasks should be recorded. The examiner should also note evidences of apparent interest and effort on the part of the children while performing the tasks. The results obtained for each item should then be carefully examined to see how well they conform to the requirements listed above.

Frequently there will be no single check which is adequate to determine the diagnostic value of the items since no valid measurement of the trait in question exists. In such cases it will be necessary to employ as many partial criteria as are available. For example, if the trait is one such as intelligence or motor ability which is known to show progress with age, the extent of the age progress can be used as a partial sign of the test's diagnostic value. Age is an imperfect criterion, however, since there are many factors which increase with age but are unrelated to the trait which it is desired to measure. In addition to age progress, therefore, other criteria must be employed. Ratings by competent judges, achievement in fields known to be related to the trait in question (such as school-progress in the case of an intelligence test) comparison of sharply contrasted groups (as reform-school boys with boys who have never had a court record in the case of a "character" test) may all be useful. The internal consistency of the test, that is, the extent to which the various items hang together as measures of the same general trait may be determined by the intercorrelations of the different items with each other and with the total. Intercorrelations should be positive but not too high, since high correlations mean that the items are in large measure duplicating each other and are making little independent contribution to the scale as a whole.

Upon the basis of the preliminary tryout, the scale should be reorganized and if a sufficient number of items have stood the test it may be put into final form. Sometimes a number of preliminary trials are needed to yield a sufficient number of useful items to warrant final standardization. The number of items needed will vary with the reliability and diagnostic value of each, and with the degree of precision which is needed. The test as a whole should be sufficiently accurate to make the distinctions which are required without gross misclassification of the subjects.

In the final standardization, care should be taken to secure a group of subjects who may be considered representative of the group to whom the norms or standards are expected to apply. This means that the sexes should be about equally represented at each age. Un-

less it can be shown that the test is one which is un-
affected by differences in social status, the social factor
should also be controlled by having the different social
classes represented in approximately the same proportion as they are found in the general population. A
fairly satisfactory way of doing this is to use paternal
occupation as a rough measure of social status, and
to consult the U. S. Census reports in order to determine the proportion of the total number of adult
males in the community falling within each of certain
general occupational categories, as in the industrial
classification devised by Taussig (336), the Barr scale
values (11), or the combination of the two worked out
at the University of Minnesota. (Appendix A.) If it
is found impossible to control factors such as these by
selection, the composition of the group used for standardization should at least be carefully described in objective terms, to permit persons who wish to use the
test for other groups to determine in advance whether
or not the original norms may be taken as standards
with which their children may be fairly compared.

A discussion of the statistical aspects of test construction would be beyond the scope of this book. A number of
useful references are given in the bibliography. Whatever
the method employed, the standardization should not be considered complete until the adequacy of the method has been
thoroughly investigated. Such an investigation should include
first of all an analysis of the amount of experimental error
in giving and scoring the test. Are the directions so clear
that two persons will always give and score each test in
exactly the same way? The stability of the norms or standards at each age should also be ascertained. If another
person should restandardize the test upon another group
of subjects drawn from the same general population, by
how little would his standards be expected to differ from
those originally obtained? The consistency of the results obtained by the test should be ascertained both by the test-

retest method, in which the results of two successive administrations of the test are compared with each other, and by the split-scale method in which the sum of the scores earned on half the test are compared with those made on the other half. In dividing the scale for this purpose it is customary to include the odd numbered items in the first half and the even numbered items in the second half. By this means such factors as habituation to the test situation, fatigue, *etc.*, are distributed fairly evenly over both halves, permitting more valid comparisons. If more than one form of the test has been devised, the amount of agreement between the two forms should also be determined. The validity of the test, *i.e.*, the extent to which it agrees with other measures or ratings of the trait in question should be checked by the use of as many different criteria as possible, since it is but rarely that any single criterion will be entirely satisfactory. The reliability of the criteria used should also be determined, since even the best test cannot agree very closely with a criterion which is itself unreliable. All the findings should be reported in sufficient detail so that their interpretation will be unmistakable.

The practical use of tests. In the use of standardized tests as instruments for practical diagnosis and guidance of the individual child, two fairly common practices should be guarded against. First, tests whose merit has not been proved should not be adopted for practical use until the necessary evaluation has been made. Merely because a test has been given a certain name, which happens to coincide with a felt need for a particular kind of diagnostic instrument is no evidence that the test in question can be depended upon to make such a diagnosis. The clinical worker must be continually on his guard to see that his critical judgment is not blinded by his desire for making striking or spectacular diagnoses of vocational aptitudes, special talents and defects, character and personality traits and similar factors which always make strong appeal to the popular fancy. Often the demands for such diagnoses become so strong that it is difficult to withstand them. The clinician who begins by trying a certain test "to see how it works" and perhaps finds that in one or two cases it appears to check up fairly well with other observations of the subject, may be tempted to let his investigation stop there and to continue to use the test as a guide to decisions or recommendations which may seriously affect the future welfare of his subjects. The number of new "tests" which appear each year is so great that the problem of selecting those which are most valuable for a given purpose is a serious one. Only when the clinician is thoroughly acquainted with the principles of test construction and evaluation is he in a position to separate the wheat from the chaff.

A second practice, unfortunately common among many clinical workers, is that of modifying the standardized methods of administering tests in order to make them conform more nearly to certain actual or fancied requirements of individual children. To do this not only violates one of the most fundamental rules of scientific technique, but is also likely to defeat its own end, since it makes it impossible to determine at any later time just what the child's true performance on a test properly given would have been. If the clinician's judgment of the child's ability which led him to modify the test conditions was correct, then the test was unnecessary; if it was incorrect, the change in the testing method will have so obscured the source of the error that later correction becomes impossible. This does not mean that in clinical practice all tests should be given in a purely mechanical way and their results interpreted without regard to the past experience of the subject or other factors which may affect their adequacy for the individual. No tests are perfect, and the best of them may on occasion yield a very distorted picture of the facts as they are. In our present state of ignorance with regard to the special factors which underlie behavior, there can be no reasonable criticism of the clinician who, *for reasons which he is willing to put on record,* decides to ignore completely the results of all tests or measurements which have been given and to make a diagnosis and prescribe treatment upon the basis of what he regards as a sensible interpretation of facts obtained through other sources. When this is done, the records of all tests given should be preserved with as great care as if they were to be used, the reasons why they are regarded as inadequate or unreliable should be set down in detail, together with the clinician's diagnosis and a summary of the facts upon which this diagnosis is based. Later follow-up of the case will make it possible to determine whether the clinician or the test was more nearly right. With the accumulation of many such records the foundation may be laid for decided improvement in our present methods of clinical diagnosis. If, on the other hand, the clinician feels it necessary to bolster up his judgment by modifying the tests in such a way that they will give apparent support to opinions which he has already formed, later on there will be absolutely no way by which opinion can be distinguished from fact.

Chapter 47

EXPERIMENTS OR CONTROLLED INVESTIGATIONS

THE characteristics of experiments. The word experiment refers to a method of investigation in which the investigator undertakes to control as many factors as possible in order to bring out the essential relationship between the phenomena studied. By deliberately setting about the creation of situations which can be produced as many times as he sees fit, the investigator secures many more observations than could be obtained if he waited for the events to occur naturally. By eliminating and isolating irrelevant factors, he brings the true relationships into clear relief. The limitation and definition of the conditions under which the experiment is conducted, makes it possible for other investigators to repeat the experiment. By such repetition and verification correct generalization is ultimately established.

The relation between incidental observation and experimentation becomes clear if we consider for a moment how an experiment originates. Observations of certain phenomena are made. On the basis of these observations a question is formulated. A special technique or *experiment* is then set up by means of which the question is answered.

For instance, Day * noticed that occasional pairs of twins showed decided retardation in language development and in rare cases even developed a language of their own. She wondered whether these were sporadic instances or whether

* Unpublished Ph.D. thesis, University of Minnesota.

455

the language development of twins in general is less than that of single children of corresponding age. Her method of answering this question was to parallel with twins the investigation previously done by McCarthy (170) on single children. The results provide evidence not only that there is linguistic retardation in twins, but also that it becomes progressively more marked up to the age of five years. In speculating as to possible causes for this retardation, it was pointed out that twins might not be under the same necessity of learning the language in order to participate in the life of older children and adults as are single children, because of their constant companionship with each other.

This *hypothesis* might be subjected to further test. One possibility is the study of the language development of the surviving member of pairs of twins in cases where one of the children died in infancy. Another possibility is the comparison of the language development of twins before and after their entrance into school. If the retardation is the result of the limited social situation in which twins develop, it should be lessened under the influence of the broader social relations of school. Here, as in many other instances, the solution of one problem forms the starting point for another series of investigations. This is characteristic of all science.

It should be noted that the question to be attacked by an experiment always has reference to human behavior in general rather than to the behavior of a particular individual. Day was interested in the effect of the twin situation upon language development. Her study was neither designed to furnish norms of language development nor to assay individual abilities. In this respect the experiment is sharply set off from the other methods which have been described. Even though in carrying out an experiment the investigator may make use of such devices as tests, ratings, systematic observations and measurements or any other which seems suited to his purpose, he is nevertheless not interested in the particular individuals who are tested, rated or measured. Rather his purpose is to ascertain the effect of certain deliberately introduced or selected factors upon behavior in general.

Control of conditions. Ideally an experiment involves the control of all the factors in the situation and in the subjects except the one factor which is under investigation. As a result of this control the investigator is able to connect a response with the particular situation which has been set up, and thus is able to isolate the significant factor. Theoretically, in setting up an experiment the investigator knows the relative significance of the factors he wishes to control. Otherwise adequate control cannot be set up. When the experiment is completed, its results should answer the question originally put.

Consider an instance. We wish to determine the effect of lapse of time upon memory, *i.e.*, does memory remain at the same level or fall off as time passes? Even though everyday observation indicates that memory decreases as time passes, there remains the problem of the rate of decrease. In order to experiment we must state the problem even more precisely. Do we remember as much at the end of twenty hours as at the end of six hours, as much at the end of forty as at the end of twenty hours?

At first sight this problem appears very simple. But other questions immediately arise. What kind of material shall we give the persons who are going to memorize? Since there are differences in memory for different types of subject matter, it is necessary to control this factor by providing uniform material. If we start out with prose material we shall soon find that certain parts are easier to remember than others, because of the element of meaning. This may bring us to the point of seeking uniform material, such as nonsense syllables in which even the meaning factor is absent.

But the problem of control is not yet solved. Shall we have the subjects read the nonsense syllables silently or aloud, or shall we read the syllables to them? Suppose we decide to have the syllables pronounced as they are seen and thus control the subjects' overt reaction to the syllables. Then we face the question of the rate at which the syllables shall be presented. How shall we make sure that the rate does not vary? Since it is necessary to present the syllables at a constant rate, we devise instruments for the control of this factor. Finally, since the amount of reproduction at the end of a given period of time is related to the length of the list, the lists used should be of the same length.

Although we have controlled four factors: material, rate, manner of reaction, and length of list, we must go still farther. Since we know that memory is related to age, we introduce control of this factor by performing our experiments on children of the same age. Then the problem of determining the time which shall elapse between the learning of the nonsense syllables and their reproduction arises. Obviously, if we are to study the effects of lapse of time upon memory we shall have to vary the length of time between stimulation and reproduction in a systematic fashion. Suppose we decide to test at regular intervals of one hour each after presentation, *i.e.*, at one hour, two hours, three hours, four hours, *etc*. In selecting this series of intervals we are controlling time. But it is far too simple a procedure to give a list of syllables and test on the same list at one hour, two hours, *etc*. We must give a number of lists, testing for the first at one hour, the second at two hours, and so on. Otherwise, the recitation of the lists in the course of the testing will reinforce memory for them and thus distort the results. The foregoing account is an excellent example of the necessity of knowing in advance what factors are most likely to affect the results of a particular experiment if adequate controls are to be set up. These factors will vary with the problem and cannot be determined arbitrarily.

In the instance cited it is necessary to know something about the relationship of memory to age, to amount of material, to manner of presentation, *etc.*, before an effective experiment can be blocked out. In the physical sciences, where the material to be dealt with is inert and lends itself readily to the will of the investigator, the setting up of adequate controls is far more simple than is the case in experimentation with living organisms.

In child psychology the ideal of controlling all the factors save the particular one which is under study and permitting that factor alone to vary, is achieved rarely, if ever. If we could stop human beings from growing and hold them *in statu quo* for a period of time, if we knew how to control their motivation and the amount and quality of their previous incidental practice, if we could eliminate all possible stimulation save that which we ourselves present, we might be able to set up experiments which would be crucial and would answer once and for all the questions originally proposed. Actually in the human situation we seldom have precise knowledge or control of any of these factors. Accordingly we attempt to control all the factors which we know are relevant to the particular experiment, either directly through the experimental set-up or indirectly by the use of control groups.

Experimentation through direct measurements, tests, or ratings of the same individuals. In the carrying out of an experiment, it is necessary to secure some quantitative expression of the changes which take place. In the study of memory previously described, the measure used is the number of nonsense syllables retained after varying intervals of time. In the experiment on color discrimination, the time required for matching the different colors and the number of errors in matching is utilized. In the experiment on sustained attention, the length of time the eyes are fixated on each box is employed as a measure. In the experiment studying the effect of a change in the situation on language behavior, the mean number of words per sentence, the proportion of parts of speech, the number of different words used and a classification of the social function of the different sentences is used.

Often special mechanical devices have been constructed for the purpose of presenting stimuli or recording the responses of the subject in a more precise and uniform fashion than can be done by the unaided human observer. These vary greatly from experiment to experiment in accordance with the problem studied. As a rule, the better planned the experiment and the more precise the instrument, the simpler is the process of measurement. The experimenter may also employ indirect measures or measures of complex functions, where no methods of direct measurement are available for the particular problem at hand. Thus, if he wishes to carry on an experiment on the effect of training upon emotional reactions he may have the emotional reactions of the children rated on a carefully prepared scale, and then subject the children to a particular training method for a period of time. At the end of that period of time the children may be rerated on the same scale. Note that in such an experiment it would be necessary to have the raters on both occasions ignorant of the kind and type of training given in order that no bias might operate to modify their ratings. Where other than direct measures are used in experiment, extra precautions must be taken to secure accurate and impartial data.

The use of control groups in experimentation. The student of child behavior attacks many problems in which it is impossible for him to control, through an experimental set-up, all the factors which may affect the problem studied. For the most part this is due to the fact that in developing organisms various phenomena take as a result of maturation, incidental stimulation or genetic factors rather than as a result of the introduction of an experimental condition. To meet this difficulty the technique of the control group may be used. Suppose we wish to find out whether or not children master material presented for their learning in class better when moving pictures are used for demonstrations than when ordinary still visual aids are used. At first glance this problem appears simple. Why not show moving pictures to a class and record the results? But this procedure would not enable us to draw any conclusion. It is quite possible that if the moving pictures had not been shown to the class, its members would have improved quite as much under the old methods as when the new device is introduced. How are we to solve the problem? One method would be to divide the class in half, giving one half regular instruction along established lines and the other half the moving pictures, testing both groups at the end of the period of time. By comparing the two groups with regard to their mastery of the subject matter some idea would be obtained as to which of the two methods was the better under the circumstances used.

This is known as the *control group* technique. It is widely used in experimental studies on children, whenever factors are present in the life of the child, either as a result of growth, or as a result of outside stimulation beyond the control of the investigator which may make for increased attainment or progress in a particular function independently of any experimental condition which may be introduced. In its original use children were divided at random into two groups. The experimental condition was then introduced into one group but not the other, and measurements were made on both groups at the end of a period of time. But it soon became apparent that unless the groups were extremely large, such differences as were apparent at the end of the experimental period might be nothing more than the effect of the chance results of sampling which would have been equally apparent at the beginning of the period had measurement been taken at that time. Therefore the procedure now followed is to make a test or measurement of all the children at the outset with respect to the function in question, then divide them into two groups of equal size, and subject one to the experimental condition, while keeping the other as a *control group*. At the end of the period, both groups are subjected to the same measurements or tests as were given originally. The change which has resulted in the control group is then subtracted from the change which has resulted in the experimental group and the remainder taken as the effect of the experimentally introduced factor. Various methods of comparison other than those afforded by simple subtraction have been developed for analyzing data furnished by such studies.

An improvement on this procedure is found in some investigations in which, after the second set of tests, nothing is done to the children for a period of time. They are then subjected to a third series of tests or measurements in order to ascertain the permanency of the results. In this way a double check is obtained, since a comparison of the experimental group with the control group is made at the end of the experimental period and a further comparison of both groups is made after a period of time in which the experimental condition is absent.

In modern practice another technique, called *control by pairing*, has arisen. Preliminary tests or measurements are given the children as before. On the basis of these tests or measurements the children are divided into two groups paired one with another with respect to various measurements. Thus if there were two children with IQ's of 140, one child with an IQ of 140 would go into the experimental group and the other would go into the control group. When a number of measurements are to be used in pairing, a practical procedure to facilitate the work is to write the measurements for each child on a separate card. Select as pairs the cases which most nearly resemble each other on all the measurements. One member of each pair goes into the experimental group, the other into the control group. By this process it is insured that the groups will have similar means and similar dispersions for each of the variables on which pairing has been done. Since the use of paired groups insures that the major sources of error resulting from unequal selection are ruled out, small differences in final standing are of far greater significance than is the case where both the control and the experimental groups are selected at random. In determining the reliability of these differences the formula for correlated variables should be used. An interesting example of the use of paired groups is furnished in the Gates and Taylor studies (88, 89).

If a large group of subjects is available from which selection can be made, it is possible to match the subjects much more closely. For instance in a study undertaken by Goodenough (105) on the influence of the nursery-school upon changes in intelligence quotients, children were paired with respect to sex, age, IQ, education of father, education of mother, socio-economic status of the father, and the nativity of parents. The experimental group consisted of 28 children enrolled in a nursery-school. The composition of this group could not be changed. In selecting the control group, the records of some 300 children in the community were examined. In this way it was possible to secure 28 cases which matched the experimental group much more closely than would have been possible if a smaller number had been available.

A modification of the method of control through pairing is furnished through the fact that nature occasionally does an excellent job of pairing through producing what are known to the scientist as identical twins, who can be used for study and observation. Gesell (97) has developed what he calls the *method of co-twin control,* which consists essentially in making a series of measurements and observations on both members of a pair of identical twins, then subjecting one member of the pair to an experimental situation (such as practice in stair-climbing), while the other remains in a natural environment or is prevented from exercising the particular activities in which the other is being given practice. At the end of a given period of time, measurements are made both on the practiced twin and the control twin, and conclusions drawn. Although up to the present, the method has been applied to single pairs, only the relative inaccessibility of identical twins in large numbers prevents its being used on a larger scale.

Comparative studies. In the ordinary course of nature many experiments are performed for us, of which we need only to take advantage. People differ with respect to sex, race, social status, the size of the family from which they come, rural or city residence, order of birth, and so on. The greater number of these factors have existed throughout the lifetime of the individual and therefore have had the maximum opportunity to exert their effects. Although we cannot control these factors in the same way that we can control the temperature of the laboratory, the time of day at which an experiment is performed, the manner of presenting a stimulus, *etc.,* we can control them through selecting as subjects individuals in whom the required conditions are known to have been operative. This is known as the *comparative method*. Thus we may contrast the behavior of only children with that of children who have brothers and sisters in exactly the same way that we can contrast the behavior of children to whom we have intentionally given a particular kind of training with that of children who have not had such training. We may pair the groups for other related variables in the same way as is done in the formal experiment. We can test or measure the effect of the condition in a similar fashion. Inasmuch as the condition studied has commonly existed throughout life, one aspect of complete control is commonly lacking, namely, the measurement of initial status previous to the introduction of the experimental factor. For this reason larger numbers of cases are commonly needed to secure valid results than in experiments where such control is possible.

Control by norms or statistical devices. Another type of control is available when we have accurate norms. For example, if accurate norms on the development of language in children are available it may be possible to introduce a condition into the lives of a group of children which will affect language, and then measure the results by using the norms for control without the necessity of setting up a separate control group. However, the possibilities of this mode of attack are decidedly limited since it is but rarely that the investigator can be certain that the experimental group is similar in composition to the normative group. Further, it is necessary for the investigator who attempts a study of this type to reproduce the exact conditions under which the norms were obtained.

It has been pointed out that in the experiment, an attempt is made to control all the factors except the particular one which is undergoing analysis. By the use of a

statistical technique * known as partial correlation it is possible to secure a result similar to that obtained when experimental control is introduced. The technique is chiefly utilized in the analysis of relations where either an experimental
set-up is impossible because of the nature of the material
to be gathered, or as a substitute method in the handling
of data already collected without experimental control. An
illustration will make the point clear. Suppose that we are
interested in the relation between intelligence test scores and
scholastic success. This relation will be affected by time
spent in study. If we secure a large number of observations
or measurements of children with respect to intelligence,
time spent in study, and scholastic success, we can proceed
by the use of partial correlation to hold time spent in study
constant and determine the relationship between intelligence
and scholastic success. Or we can select two groups of
children who differ with respect to intelligence, pair them
with respect to time spent in study and then find the difference between the two groups with respect to scholastic success. Or we may proceed by the experimental method to take
a group of children who vary with respect to intelligence
and place them under conditions in which we equalize the
amount of time spent in studying for all children and then
study the relation between intelligence and scholastic success.
Although recognizing in the last case the fact that we cannot completely control such factors as the motivation or
energy with which study is carried on by controlling the time
spent in study, nevertheless a clearer picture of the relationship between intelligence and scholastic success would be
obtained with time of study artificially and experimentally
held constant. Here are three techniques for attacking the

* For the method of computing partial correlations the student is
referred to the textbooks on statistics listed in Section IV of the
bibliography.

same problem, ranging from one involving complex statistical treatment, to one in which the statistical treatment necessary is relatively simple, since by deliberate control of one factor, much of the subsequent need for complex analysis is eliminated. This brings us to a rather important point with reference to method. In general, control of conditions in advance is to be preferred to the accumulation of a mass of measurements on a large body of cases without such control, necessitating involved statistical treatment. Although statistics furnishes us with our most valuable tools for the handling of data, it never becomes an altogether effective substitute for more precise methods of collecting data.

BIBLIOGRAPHY

This bibliography represents a selection from approximately fifteen hundred titles which were considered. In general the selection was based upon the following principles: (1) articles written in English were taken in preference to those in foreign languages, (2) preference was given to studies of younger children, (3) recent articles were given preference over the earlier studies, (4) emphasis was placed on studies in the social sciences.

Very brief articles or notes were not included unless of special importance. A small number of articles and books were included because of their direct relationship to particular portions of this book. On the whole, an attempt was made to have the selection cover a fairly wide range of topics and methods.

For this reason, articles of somewhat less merit have occasionally been listed in preference to those of greater technical worth when the former deal with topics for which little information is available.

1. ALPERT, AUGUSTA, The solving of problem situations by preschool children. *Teachers' College, Columbia University, Contrib. to Educ.* No. 323, 1928, Pp. 69.
2. ANDERSON, J. E., The attendance of nursery school children. *School and Soc.* 1926, 24, 182-184.
3. ANDERSON, J. E., The dream as a reconditioning process. *J. Abn. and Soc. Psychol.* 1927, 22, 21-25.
4. ANDERSON, J. E., The clientele of a parental education program. *School and Soc.* 1927, 26, 178-184.
5. ANDERSON, J. E., FOSTER, J. C., and GOODENOUGH, F. L., The sleep of young children. *University of Minnesota, Institute of Child Welfare Monograph Series.* Minneapolis, University of Minnesota Press. To appear shortly.

6. ANDRUS, R., *An inventory of the habits of children from two to five years.* New York, Teachers' College, Columbia University Bureau of Pub. 1928, Pp. 51.

7. ATKINS, RUTH, The measurement of the intelligence of young children by an object-fitting test. *University of Minnesota, Institute of Child Welfare Monograph Series No. V.* Minneapolis, University of Minnesota Press, 1931.

8. BALDWIN, B. T., The physical growth of children from birth to maturity. *University of Iowa Stud., Stud. in Child Welfare.* 1, No. 1, 1921, Pp. 411.

9. BALDWIN, B. T., FILLMORE, E. A., and HADLEY, L., *Farm children; an investigation of rural child life in selected areas of Iowa.* New York, D. Appleton and Co., 1930, Pp. xxii + 337.

10. BALDWIN, B. T., and STECHER, L. I., *The psychology of the preschool child.* New York, D. Appleton and Co., 1924, Pp. 305.

11. BARR, F. E., A scale for measuring mental ability in vocations and some of its applications. M.A. thesis, Stanford Univ., 1918. Described in *Genetic Studies of Genius*, Vol. 1, *Mental and physical traits of a thousand gifted children* by L. M. Terman *et al.* See Chap. IV.

12. BARRETT, HELEN E., and KOCH, HELEN L., The effect of nursery-school training upon the mental-test performance of a group of orphanage children. *J. Genet. Psychol.*, 1930, 37, 102-122.

13. BAYLEY, N., Performance tests for three, four, and five-year-old children. *Ped. Sem.* 1926, 33, 435-454.

14. BAYNE, T. L., WINSOR, A. L., and WINTERS, E. S., Conditioned motor responses in children. *Proc. Soc. Exper. Biol. and Med.* 1929, 26, 342-343.

15. BECKMANN, HERMANN, Die Entwicklung der Zahlleistung bei 2-6 jährigen Kindern. *Zsch. f. angew. Psychol.* 1923, 22, 1-160.

16. BERNE, E. V. C., An investigation of the wants of seven children. *University of Iowa Stud., Stud. in Child Welfare.* 1929, 4, No. 2, Pp. 61.

17. BETZNER, JEAN, Content and form of original compositions dictated by children from five to eight years of age. *Teachers' College, Columbia University, Contrib. to Educ.* No. 442, 1930, Pp. v + 53.

18. BINET, ALFRED, *L'étude expérimentale de l'intelligence.* Paris, Alfred Costes, 1902, Pp. 308.

19. BLACKING, E., Standardization of a bead-stringing test. *Ped. Sem.* 1927, 34, 620-633.

20. BLANCHARD, P., A study of subject matter and motivation of children's dreams. *J. Abn. and Soc. Psychol.* 1926, 21, 24-37.

21. BLANCHARD, P., and PAYNTER, R. H. Jr., The problem child. *Ment. Hygiene* 1924, 8, 26-54.

22. BLANTON, MARGARET, The behavior of the human infant during the first thirty days of life. *Psychol. Rev.* 1917, 24, 456-483.

23. BLATZ, W. E., and BOTT, E. A., Studies in mental hygiene of children. I. Behavior of public school children —A description of method. *Ped. Sem.* 1927, 34, 552-582.

24. BOLTON, T. L., The relation of motor power to intelligence. *Amer. J. of Psychol.* 1892, 5, 123-204.

25. BOTT, E. A., BLATZ, W. E., CHANT, NELLIE, and BOTT, HELEN, Observation and training of the fundamental habits in young children. *Genet. Psychol. Monog.* 1928, 4, No. 1, 1-161.

26. BOYD, W., The development of sentence structure in childhood. *Brit. J. Psychol.* (Gen. Sect.), 1927, 17, 181-191.

27. BRAINARD, P. P., Some observations of infant learning and instincts. *Ped. Sem.,* 1927, 34, 231-254.

28. BRAINARD, P. P., The mentality of a child compared with that of apes. *J. Genet. Psychol.* 1930, 37, 268-293.

29. BRANDENBURG, G. C., and BRANDENBURG, JULIA, Language development during the fourth year. *Ped. Sem.* 1919, 26, 27-40.

30. BRIAN, C. R., and GOODENOUGH, F. L., The relative potency of color and form perception at different ages. *J. Exper. Psychol.* 1929, 12, 197-213.

31. BRIDGES, K. M. B., Occupational interests of three-year-old children. *Ped. Sem.* 1927, 34, 415-423.

472 Bibliography

32. BRIDGES, K. M. B., The occupational interests and attention of four-year-old children. *J. Genet. Psychol.* 1929, 36, 551-570.

33. BRYAN, EDITH S., Variations in the responses of infants during the first ten days of post-natal life. *Child Dev.* 1930, 1, 56-77.

34. BÜHLER, CHARLOTTE, *The first year of life*. Translated by Pearl Greenburg and Rowena Ripin, New York, The John Day Co., 1930.

35. BÜHLER, CHARLOTTE, HETZER, HILDEGARDE, and TUDOR HART, BEATRIX, *Soziologische und psychologische Studien über das erste Lebensjahr*. Jena, G. Fischer, 1927, Pp. vi + 250.

36. BURKS, BARBARA S., The relative influence of nature and nurture upon mental development. A comparative study of foster parent-foster child resemblance and true parent-true child resemblance. *Twenty-seventh Yearbook of the National Society for the Study of Education*. Part I, Bloomington, Ill., Public School Pub. Co., 1928, 219-316.

37. BURKS, BARBARA S., JENSEN, DORTHA W., and TERMAN, L. M., *Genetic studies of genius. Vol. III. The promise of youth. Follow-up studies of a thousand gifted children*. Stanford University, Cal., Stanford University Press, 1930, Pp. xiv + 508.

38. BURNSIDE, L. H., Coördination in the locomotion of infants. *Genet. Psychol. Monog.* 1927, 2, No. 5, 279-372.

39. BURT, CYRIL L., *Mental and scholastic tests*. London, King and Son, 1921, Pp. xv + 432.

40. BURT, CYRIL, *The young delinquent*. New York, D. Appleton and Co., 1925, Pp. xvi + 619.

41. BUZBY, D. E., The interpretation of facial expression. *Amer. J. Psychol.*, 1924, 35, 602-604.

42. CARMICHAEL, MAX, To what objective stimuli do six-year-old children respond with intentional misrepresentation of facts? *Ped. Sem.*, 1928, 35, 73-83.

43. CHAPIN, F. S., A quantitative scale for rating the homes and social environment of middle class families in an urban community; a first approximation to the meas-

urement of socio-economic status. *J. Educ. Psychol.*, 1928, 19, 99-111.

44. CHAPIN, F. S., *Scale for rating living room equipment*, Minneapolis, Institute of Child Welfare, Univ. of Minnesota, 1930.

45. CHAPMAN, J. C., and SIMS, V. M., The quantitative measurement of socio-economic status. *J. Educ. Psychol.* 1925, 16, 380-390.

46. CHAUNCEY, M. R., The relation of the home factor to achievement and intelligence-test scores. *J. Educ. Res.*, 1929, 20, 88-90.

47. CHEVALEVA-JANOOSKAJA, E., Les groupements spontanés d'enfants à l'age préscolaires, *Arch. de Psychol.*, 1924-1927, 19-20, 219-233.

48. CHEVALEVA-IANOVSKAIA, E., and SYLLA, D., Essai d'une étude sur les enfants meneurs. *J. de Psychol.* 1929, 26, 604-612.

49. Child Study Committee of the International Kindergarten Union. (M. D. Horn, chairman.) *A study of the vocabulary of children before entering the first grade.* Baltimore, Williams and Wilkins, 1928, Pp. 36.

50. COBB, M. V., and HOLLINGWORTH, L. S., The regression of siblings of children who test at or above 135 IQ. (Stanford-Binet). *J. Educ. Psychol.*, 1925, 16, 1-7.

51. COGHILL, G. E., *Anatomy and the problems of behavior.* Cambridge University Press, 1929, Pp. xii + 113.

52. COHEN, JOSEPH T., The dates of eruption of the permanent teeth in a group of Minneapolis children. *J. Amer. Dental Assn.* 1928, 15, 2337-41.

53. COX, CATHERINE M., *Genetic studies of Genius.* Vol. III. *The early mental traits of three hundred geniuses.* Stanford University, Calif., Stanford University Press, 1926, Pp. xviii + 842.

54. CUNNINGHAM, BESS V., An experiment in measuring the gross motor development of infants and young children. *J. Educ. Psychol.* 1927, 18, 458-464.

55. CUNNINGHAM, K. S., The measurement of early levels of intelligence. *Teachers' College, Columbia University Contrib. to Educ.* No. 259, 1927, Pp. v + 74.

56. Cushing, H. M., A perseverative tendency in preschool children. *Arch. of Psychol.* 1929, 17, No. 108, Pp. 55.

57. Darwin, Charles, A biographical sketch of an infant. *Mind.* 1877, 2, 285-294.

58. Davis, Clara M., Self-selection of diet by newly weaned infants. *Amer. J. Dis. Children.* 1928, 36, 651-679.

59. Davis, K. B., *Factors in the sex life of twenty-two hundred women.* New York, Harper Brothers, 1929, Pp. xx + 430.

60. Dearborn, G. V. N., *Moto-sensory development. Observations on the first three years of childhood.* Baltimore, Warwick and York. 1910, Pp. 215.

61. Descoudres, A., *Le développement de l'enfant de deux à sept ans.* Paris, Delachaux and Niestle. 1922, Pp. 327.

62 Dolch, E. W., Grade vocabularies. *J. Educ. Res.* 1927, 16, 16-26.

63. Doran, E., A study of vocabularies. *Ped. Sem.* 1907, 14, 401-438.

64. Dougherty, M. L., A comparative study of nine group tests of intelligence for primary grades. *Johns Hopkins University Studies Educ.* No. 10, 1928, Pp. vii + 112.

65. Douglass, H. R., The development of number concepts in children of preschool and kindergarten ages. *J. Exper. Psychol.* 1925, 8, 443-470.

66. Downey, J. E., Types of dextrality and their implications. *Amer. J. Psychol.*, 1927, 38, 317-367.

67. Downey, J. E., Dextrality types and the preschool child. *Twenty-seventh Yearbook of the National Society for the Study of Education.* Part II. Bloomington, Ill., Public School Publishing Co., 1928, 153-158.

68. Duffy, Elizabeth, Tensions and emotional factors in reaction. *Genet. Psychol. Monog.*, 1930, 7, No. 1, 1-79.

69. Eisler, E. R., The significance of physical disease in relation to behavior problems. *Ment. Hygiene*, 1926, 10, 85-89.

70. Enders, A. C., A study of the laughter of the preschool child in the Merrill-Palmer school. *Papers of the Mich. Acad. of Sci. Art and Letters*, 8, 341-356.

71. Fenton, J. C., *A practical psychology of babyhood.* Boston. Houghton, Mifflin Co., 1925, Pp. xvi + 348.

72. FERNALD, M. R., and ARLITT, A. H., A psychological study of a group of crippled children of various types.— A Preliminary Report. *School and Soc.*, 1925, 21, 449-452.

73. FLEMMING, B. M., A study of the sleep of young children. *J. Amer. Assn. Univ. Women.* 1925, 19, 25-27.

74. FOSTER, J. C., Verbal memory in the preschool child. *Ped. Sem.* 1928, 35, 26-44.

75. FOSTER, J. C., Distribution of the teacher's time among children in the nursery school and kindergarten. *J. Educ. Res.* 1930, 22, 172-183.

76. FOSTER, J. C., and ANDERSON, J. E., The young child and his parents. A study of one hundred cases. *University of Minnesota, Institute of Child Welfare Monograph Series No. 1.* Second Edition, Minneapolis. University of Minnesota Press, 1930, Pp. 241.

77. FOSTER, J. C., GOODENOUGH, F. L., and ANDERSON, J. E., The sleep of young children. *Ped. Sem.* 1928, 35, 201-218.

78. FOULKE, K., and STINCHFIELD, S. M., The speech development of four infants under two years of age. *J. Genet. Psychol.* 1929, 36, 140-171.

79. FREEMAN, F. N., HOLZINGER, K. J., and MITCHELL, B. C., The influence of environment on the intelligence, school achievement, and conduct of foster children. *Twenty-seventh Yearbook of the National Society for the Study of Education*, Part I, Bloomington, Ill., Public School Publishing Co. 1928, 102-217.

80. FROIS-WITTMAN, J., The judgment of facial expression. *J. Exper. Psychol.* 1930, 13, 113-151.

81. FURFEY, P. H., An improved rating scale technique. *J. Educ. Psychol.*, 1926, 17, 45-48.

82. FURFEY, P. H., The measurement of developmental age. *Cath. Univ. Amer. Educ. Res. Bull.* 1928, 3, No. 10, Pp. 40.

83. GALE, M. C. and GALE, H., The vocabularies of two children of one family to two-and-a-half years of age. *Psychological Studies by Harlow Gale, No. 1.* Minneapolis, privately printed, 1900, Pp. 70-117.

84. GASKILL, P. C., FENTON, N., and PORTER, J. P., Judging the intelligence of boys from their photographs. *J. Appl. Psychol.* 1927, 11, 394-403.

85. GATES, A. I., Variations in efficiency during the day, together with practice effects, sex differences and correlations. *University of California Publ. Psychol.*, 1916, 2, 1-156.

86. GATES, A. I., Recitation as a factor in memorizing. *Arch. of Psychol.* 1917, No. 40, Pp. 104.

87. GATES, A. I., and TAYLOR, G. A., The acquisition of motor control in writing by preschool children. *Teach. Coll. Rec.*, 1923, 24, 459-468.

88. GATES, A. I., and TAYLOR, G. A., An experimental study of the nature of improvement resulting from practice in a mental function. *J. Educ. Psychol.* 1925, 16, 583-592.

89. GATES, A. I., and TAYLOR, G. A., An experimental study of the nature of improvement resulting from practice in a motor function. *J. Educ. Psychol.*, 1926, 17, 226-236.

90. GATES, A. I., and BOCKER, E., A study of initial stages in reading of preschool children. *Teach. Coll. Rec.* 1923, 24, 469-488.

91. GATES, G. S., An experimental study of the growth of social perception. *J. Educ. Psychol.*, 1923, 14, 449-461.

92. GAUGER, M. E., The modifiability of response to taste stimuli in the preschool child. *Teachers' College, Columbia University, Contrib. to Educ.* 1929, No. 348, Pp. 53.

93. GESELL, A. L., *The mental growth of the preschool child.* New York, The Macmillan Co., 1925, Pp. x + 447.

94. GESELL, A. L., The influence of puberty praecox upon mental growth. *Genet. Psychol. Monog.* 1926, No. 1, 507-539.

95. GESELL, A. L., *Infancy and human growth.* New York, The Macmillan Co., 1928, Pp. xvii + 418.

96. GESELL, A. L., and LORD, E. E., A psychological comparison of nursery school children from homes of low and high economic status. *Ped. Sem.* 1927, 34, 339-356.

97. GESELL, A. L., and THOMPSON, HELEN, Learning and growth in identical infant twins: an experimental study by the method of co-twin control. *Genet. Psychol. Monog.* 1929, 6, No. 1, 1-124.

98. GILBERT, J. A., Researches on the mental and physical development of school children. *Studies from the Yale Psychological Laboratory*, 1894, 2, 40-100.

99. GOODENOUGH, F. L., A new approach to the measurement of the intelligence of young children. *Ped. Sem.* 1926, 33, 185-211.

100. GOODENOUGH, F. L., The relation of the intelligence of preschool children to the education of their parents. *School and Soc.* 1927, 26, 54-56.

101. GOODENOUGH, F. L., The consistency of sex differences in mental traits at various ages. *Psychol. Rev.*, 1927, 34, 440-462.

102. GOODENOUGH, F. L., The reliability and validity of the Wallin Peg Boards. *Psychol. Clin.* 1925-1928, 16, 199-215.

103. GOODENOUGH, F. L., The Kuhlmann-Binet tests for children of preschool age; a critical study and evaluation. *University of Minnesota Institute of Child Welfare Monograph Series No. 2*. Minneapolis, University of Minnesota Press, 1928, Pp. 146.

104. GOODENOUGH, F. L., Measuring behavior traits by means of repeated short samples. *J. Juv. Res.* 1928, 12, 230-235.

105. GOODENOUGH, F. L., A preliminary report on the effect of nursery school training upon the intelligence test scores of young children. *Twenty-seventh Yearbook of the National Society for the Study of Education*. Part I. Bloomington, Ill. Public School Publishing Co., 1928, 361-369.

106. GOODENOUGH, F. L., The relation of the intelligence of preschool children to the occupation of their fathers. *Amer. J. Psychol.* 1928, 40, 284-302.

107. GOODENOUGH, F. L., The emotional behavior of young children during mental tests. *J. Juv. Res.*, 1929, 13, 204-219.

108. GOODENOUGH, F. L., Inter-relationships in the behavior of young children. *Child Dev.* 1930, 1, 29-47.

109. GOODENOUGH, F. L., Anger in young children. *University of Minnesota Institute of Child Welfare Monograph Series*. Minneapolis, University of Minnesota Press. To appear shortly.

110. GOODENOUGH, F. L., and BRIAN, C. R., Certain factors underlying the acquisition of motor skill by preschool children. *J. Exper. Psychol.* 1929, 12, 127-155.

111. GOODENOUGH, F. L., and LEAHY, A. M., The effect of certain family relationships upon the development of personality. *Ped. Sem.* 1927, 34, 45-71.

112. GOODENOUGH, F. L., and TINKER, M. A., A comparative study of several methods of measuring speed of tapping in children and adults. *J. Genet. Psychol.* 1930, 38, Pp. 146-160.

113. GREENE, K. B., The influence of specialized training on tests of general intelligence. *Twenty-seventh Yearbook of the National Society for the Study of Education*. Part I. Bloomington, Ill., Public School Publishing Co., 1928, 421-428.

114. HAGGERTY, M. E., The incidence of undesirable behavior in public-school children. *J. Educ. Res.*, 1925, 12, 102-122.

115. HALL, G. S., The contents of children's minds on entering school. *Ped Sem.* 1891, 1, 139-173.

116. HALL, G. S., A study of fears. *Amer. J. Psychol.* 1896, 8, 147-249.

117. HALL, G. S., A study of anger. *Amer. J. Psychol.* 1899, 10, 516-591.

118. HALL, W. S., First 500 days of a child's life. *Child Study Monthly*, 1896-97, 2, 330-342; 394-407; 458-473; 522-537; 586-608.

119. HALLOWELL, D. K., Mental tests for pre-school children. *Psychol. Clin.*, 1925-1928, 16, 235-276.

120. HARTSHORNE, HUGH, and MAY, MARK A., *Studies in the nature of character, Vol. 1, Studies in deceit*. New York, The Macmillan Co., 1928, Pp. xxi + 414 and viii + 306.

121. HARTSHORNE, HUGH, and MAY, MARK A., *Studies in the nature of character, Vol. II. Studies in service and self-control.* New York, The Macmillan Co., 1929, Pp. xvii + 559.

122. HEIDBREDER, EDNA, Reasons used in solving problems. *J. Exper. Psychol.* 1927, 10, 397-414.

123. HEIDBREDER, EDNA, Problem solving in children and adults. *J. Genet. Psychol.* 1928, 35, 522-545.

124. HEINLEIN, C. P., A new method of studying the rhythmic responses of children together with an evaluation of the method of simple observation. *J. Genet. Psychol.* 1929, 36, 205-228.

125. HEINLEIN, J. H., A study of dextrality in children. *J. Genet. Psychol.* 1929, 36, 91-119.

126. HERTZBERG, O. E., The relationship of motor ability to the intelligence of kindergarten children. *J. Educ. Psychol.* 1929, 20, 507-519.

127. HERTZBERG, O. E., A comparative study of different methods used in teaching beginners to write. *Teachers' College, Columbia Univ. Contrib. to Educ.* No. 214, 1926, Pp. 61.

128. HICKS, J. ALLAN, The acquisition of motor skill in young children. *Child Dev.* 1930, 1, 90-105.

129. HILDRETH, G., The effect of school environment upon Stanford-Binet Tests of young children. *Twenty-seventh Yearbook of the National Society for the Study of Education.* Part I. Bloomington, Ill., Public School Publishing Co., 1928, 355-359.

130. HILL, A. B., and VAN ALSTYNE, D., *Learning levels of the children in the nursery school with reference to the eating situation.* New York, Teachers' College Bureau of Pub. 1930, Pp. v + 41.

131. HILL, DAVID SPENCE, The personification of ideals by urban children. *J. Social Psychol.*, 1930, 1, 379-393.

132. HIRSCH, N. D. M., An experimental study upon three hundred school children over a six-year period. *Genet. Psychol. Monog.* 1930, 7, No. 6, 487-549.

133. HOLLINGWORTH, L. S., Musical sensitivity of children who test above 135 IQ (Stanford-Binet). *J. Educ. Psychol.* 1926, 17, 95-109.

134. HOLLINGWORTH, L. S., and TAYLOR, G. A., Studies of physical condition and growth: Size and strength of children who test above 135 IQ. *Twenty-third Yearbook of the National Society for the Study of Education.* Part I. Bloomington, Ill., Public School Publishing Co., 1924, 221-237.

135. HOLLINGWORTH, L. S., and MONAHAN, J. E., Tapping-rate of children who test above 135 IQ. (Stanford-Binet). *J. Educ. Psychol.* 1926, 17, 505-518.

136. HORN, M. D., The thousand and three words most frequently used by kindergarten children. *Childhood Educ.* 1926-1927, 3, 118-122.

137. HULL, C. L., and HULL, B. I., Parallel learning curves of an infant in vocabulary and in voluntary control of the bladder. *Ped. Sem.* 1919, 26, 272-283.

138. HULSON, E. L., An analysis of the free play of ten four-year-old children through consecutive observations. *J. Juv. Res.* 1930, 14, 188-208.

139. HULSON, E. L., Block constructions of four-year-old children. *J. Juv. Res.* 1930, 14, 209-222.

140. HUNTER, W. S., The delayed reaction in animals and children. *Behavior Monog.* 2, No. 1, 1913, Pp. 86.

141. HUNTER, W. S., The delayed reaction in a child. *Psychol. Rev.* 1917, 24, 74-87.

142. HURLOCK, E. B., The value of praise and reproof as incentives for children. *Arch. of Psychol.* 1924, 11, No. 71, Pp. 78.

143. IRWIN, O. C., The amount and nature of activities of new born infants under constant external stimulating conditions during the first ten days of life. *Genet. Psychol. Monog.* 1930, 8, No. 1, 1-92.

144. JOHNSON, B. J., *Mental growth of children in relation to rate of growth in bodily development.* New York, E. P. Dutton, 1925, Pp. xix + 160.

145. JOINT COMMITTEE on methods of preventing delinquency. *Three problem children. Narratives from the case records of a child guidance clinic.* New York, The Committee, Pub. No. 2, 1925, Pp. 146.

146. JONES, D. C., and CARR-SAUNDERS, A. M., The relation between intelligence and social status among orphan

children. *Brit. J. Psychol. (Gen. Sect.)* 1926-1927, 17, 343-364.

147. JONES, H. E., A first study of parent-child resemblance in intelligence. *Twenty-seventh Yearbook of the National Society for the Study of Education.* Part I. Bloomington, Ill. Public School Publishing Co., 1928, 61-72.

148. JONES, H. E., The galvanic skin reflex in infancy. *Child Dev.* 1930, 1, 106-110.

149. JONES, H. E., and JONES, M. C., A study of fear, *Childhood Educ.* 1928, 5, 136-143.

150. JONES, M. C., The elimination of children's fears. *J. Exper. Psychol.* 1924, 7, 382-390.

151. JONES, M. C., A laboratory study of fear: the case of Peter. *Ped. Sem.* 1924, 31, 308-315.

152. JONES, M. C., A study of the emotions of preschool children. *School and Soc.* 1925, 21, 755-758.

153. JONES, M. C., The development of early behavior patterns in young children. *Ped. Sem.* 1926, 33, 537-585.

154. KELLEY, T. L., *The influence of nurture upon native differences.* New York, The Macmillan Co., 1926, Pp. vii + 49.

155. KIRKWOOD, J. A., The learning process in young children: An experimental study in association. *Univ. of Iowa Stud., Stud. in Child Welfare,* 1926, 3, No. 6, Pp. 107.

156. KNIGHT, F. B., and BEHRENS, M. S., *The learning of the 100 addition combinations and the 100 subtraction combinations.* New York, Longmans Green, 1928, Pp. xiii + 82.

157. KÖHLER, WOLFGANG, *The mentality of apes.* (Translated by E. Winter.) New York, Harcourt Brace, 1925, Pp. viii + 342.

158. LANDIS, C., Studies of emotional reactions. I. A preliminary study of facial expression. *J. Exper. Psychol.* 1924, 7, 325-341.

159. LANDIS, C., Studies of emotional reactions. II. General behavior and facial expression. *J. Comp. Psychol.* 1924, 4, 447-509.

482 Bibliography

160. LANDIS, C., National differences in conversations. *J. Abn. and Soc. Psychol.* 1927, 21, 354-357.

161. LANGFELD, H. S., The judgment of emotion by facial expression. *J. Abn. Psychol.*, 1918, 13, 172-184.

162. LEHMAN, H. C., and WITTY, PAUL A. *The psychology of play activities.* New York, A. S. Barnes and Co., 1927, Pp. xviii + 242.

163. LEVY, D. M., and TULCHIN, S. H., The resistance of infants and children during mental tests. *J. Exper. Psychol.* 1923, 6, 304-322.

164. LEVY, D. M., and TULCHIN, S. H., The resistant behavior of infants and children. *J. Exper. Psychol.*, 1925, 8, 209-224.

165. LINCOLN, E. A., The later performance of under-aged children admitted to school on the basis of mental age. *J. Educ. Res.* 1929, 19, 22-30.

166. LIPPMAN, H. S., Certain behavior responses in early infancy. *Ped. Sem.* 1927, 34, 424-440.

167. LORD, ELIZABETH E., A study of the mental development of children with lesions in the central nervous system. *Genet. Psychol. Monog.* 1930, 7, No. 5, 365-486.

168. LÖWENFELD, BERTHOLD, Systematisches Studium der Reactionen der Säuglinge auf Klänge und Geräusche. *Zsch. f. Psychol.* 1927, 104, 62-98.

169. McCARTHY, D., A comparison of children's language in different situations and its relation to personality traits. *J. Genet. Psychol.* 1929, 36, 583-591.

170. McCARTHY, D., The language development of the pre-school child. *University of Minnesota Institute of Child Welfare Monograph Series No. 4,* Minneapolis, University of Minnesota Press, 1930, Pp. xiii + 174.

171. McCARTY, S. A. (Ed.). *Children's drawings: A study of interests and abilities.* Baltimore, Williams & Wilkins, 1924, Pp. 164.

172. McGINNIS, ESTHER, Seashore's measures of musical ability applied to children of preschool age. *Amer. J. Psychol.* 1928, 40, 620-623.

173. McGINNIS, ESTHER, The acquisition and interference of motor habits in young children. *Genet. Psychol. Monog.* 1929, 6, No. 3, 209-311.

174. MAJOR, D. R., *First steps in mental growth.* New York, The Macmillan Co., 1906, Pp. xiv + 360.

175. MARGAIRAZ, EMILE, et PIAGET, JEAN. Le structure des récits et l'interprétation des images de Dawid chez l'enfant. *Arch. de Psychol.*, 1925, 19, 193-210.

176. MARSTON, L. R., The emotions of young children: An experimental study in introversion and extroversion. *Univ. of Iowa Stud., Stud. in Child Welfare,* 1925, 3, No. 3, Pp. 99.

177. MATEER, FLORENCE, *Child behavior; a critical and experimental study of young children by the method of conditioned reflexes.* Boston, R. G. Badger, 1918, Pp. v + 239.

178. MATHEWS, ELLEN, A study of emotional stability in children by means of a questionnaire. *J. Delinq.* 1923, 8, 1-40.

179. MEEK, L. H., A study of learning and retention in young children. *Teachers' College Columbia University Contrib. to Educ.* 1925, No. 164, Pp. ix + 96.

180. MERRILL, M. A., On the relation of intelligence to achievement in the case of mentally retarded children. *Comp. Psychol. Monog.* 1923-1925, 2, No. 10, Pp. 100.

181. MERRIMAN, C., The intellectual resemblance of twins. *Psychol. Monog.* 1924, 33, No. 5, Pp. 58.

182. MILES, W. R., The high-relief finger maze for human learning. *J. Gen. Psychol.* 1928, 1, 3-14.

183. MILES, W. R., The peep-hole method for observing eye-movements in reading. *J. Gen. Psychol.*, 1928, 1, 373-374.

184. MILLER, E. O., A study of the preschool child's picture and story books by the battery of tests method. *J. Appl. Psychol.* 1929, 13, 592-599.

185. MINKOWSKI, M., Sur les mouvements, les réflexes les réactions musculaires du foetus humain de 2 à 5 mois et leurs relations avec le système nerveux foetal. *Revue Neurol.* 1921, 28, 1105-1118; 1235-1250. (Brief abstract in English in Ref. No. 337, p. 487.)

186. MONAHAN, J. E., and HOLLINGWORTH, L. S., Neuromuscular capacity of children who test above 135 IQ. (Stanford-Binet). *J. Educ. Psychol.* 1927, 18, 88-96.

187. Moore, H. T., Further data concerning sex differences. *J. Abn. Psychol.* 1922-23, 17, 210-214.

188. Moore, K. C., The mental development of a child. *Psychol. Monog.* 1896, 1, No. 3. 1-145.

189. Moore, T. V., The reasoning ability of children in the first years of school life. *Cath. Univ. Amer.: Stud. Psychol. and Psychiat.* 1929, 2, No. 2, Pp. viii + 34.

190. Mosher, R. M., and Newhall, S. M., Phonic versus look-and-say training in beginning reading. *J. Educ. Psychol.* 1930, 21, 500-506.

191. Moss, F. A., Note on building likes and dislikes in children. *J. Exper. Psychol.* 1924, 7, 475-478.

192. Murchison, C., and Langer, S., Tiedemann's observations on the development of the mental faculties of children. *Ped. Sem.* 1927, 34, 205-230.

193. Myers, G. C., Infants' inhibition: A genetic study. *Ped. Sem.* 1922, 29, 288-295.

194. Myers, G. C., Evolution of an infant's walking. *Ped. Sem.* 1922, 29, 295-301.

195. Nice, Margaret, The speech development of a child from eighteen months to six years. *Ped. Sem.* 1917, 24, 204-243.

196. Nice, Margaret, Concerning all-day conversations. *Ped. Sem.* 1920, 27, 166-177.

197. Nice, Margaret, A child who would not talk. *Ped Sem.* 1925, 32, 105-142.

198. Nice, Margaret, Length of sentences as a criterion of a child's progress in speech. *J. Educ. Psychol.* 1925, 16, 370-379.

199. Olson, W. C., The measurement of nervous habits in normal children. *University of Minnesota, Institute of Child Welfare Monograph Series No. 3.* Minneapolis, University of Minnesota Press, 1929, Pp. xii + 97.

200. Olson, W. C., *Problem tendencies in children; a method for their measurement and description.* Minneapolis, University of Minnesota Press, 1930, Pp. v + 92.

201. Parten, Mildred, An analysis of social participation, leadership, and other factors in preschool play groups. *University of Minnesota Institute of Child Welfare*

Monograph Series. Minneapolis, University of Minnesota Press, 1931.

202. PETERSON, J., The comparative abilities of white and negro children. *Comp. Psychol. Monog.* 1922-1923, 1, No. 5, Pp. 141.

203. PIAGET, J., *The language and thought of the child.* (Trans. by M. Warden.) New York, Harcourt Brace, 1925, Pp. xxiii + 246.

204. PIAGET, J., *et al, Judgment and reasoning in the child.* (Trans. by M. Warden.) New York, Harcourt Brace, 1928, Pp. viii + 260.

205. PIAGET, J., *The child's conception of the world.* New York, Harcourt Brace, 1929, Pp. ix + 397.

206. PINTNER, R., Intelligence as estimated from photographs. *Psychol. Rev.* 1918, 25, 286-296.

207. PINTNER, R., The Pintner-Cunningham Primary Test. *J. Educ. Psychol.* 1927, 18, 52-58.

208. PRATT, K. C., NELSON, A. K., and SUN, KUO HUA, *The behavior of the newborn infant.* Columbus, Ohio State University Press, 1930, Pp. xiii + 237.

209. REAM, J. M., The tapping test. *Psychol. Monog.*, 1922, 31, 293-319.

210. REYNOLDS, M. M., Negativism of preschool children. *Teachers' College, Columbia University Contrib. to Educ.* No. 288, 1928. Pp. viii + 126.

211. ROGERS, MARGARET C., Adenoids and diseased tonsils; their effect on general intelligence. *Arch. of Psychol.* 1922, 7, No. 50, Pp. 70.

212. ROSE, M. S., GRAY, C. E., and FOSTER, K. L., The *relation of diet to health and growth of children in institutions.* New York, Teachers' College, Columbia Univ. Bureau of Publ. 1930, vii + 128.

213. RUGG, H., KRUEGER, L., and SONDERGAARD, A., Studies in child personality. I. A study of the language of kindergarten children. *J. Educ. Psychol.* 1929, 20, 1-18.

214. SALUSKY, A. S., Collective behavior of children at a preschool age. *J. Social Psychol.*, 1930, 1, 367-378.

215. SANGREN, P. V., Comparative validity of primary intelligence tests. *J. Appl. Psychol.*, 1929, 13, 394-412.

216. SAYLES, M. B., *The problem child in school. Narratives from case records of visiting teachers*. New York, Joint Committee on Methods of Preventing Delinquency, 1925, Pp. 287.

217. SCUPIN, E., and SCUPIN, G., *Bubi's erste Kindheit*. Leipzig, Grieben, 1907.

218. SCUPIN, E., and SCUPIN, G., *Bubi im vierten bis sechsten Lebensjahre*. Leipzig, Grieben, 1910.

219. SHALES, J. M., A study of mind-set in rural and city school children. *J. Educ. Psychol.*, 1930, 21, 246-258.

220. SHEN, EUGENE, The reliability coefficient of personal ratings. *J. Educ. Psychol.* 1925, 16, 232-236.

221. SHERMAN, M., The differentiation of emotional responses in infants. I. Judgments of emotional responses from motion picture views and from actual observations. *J. Comp. Psychol.*, 1927, 7, 265-284.

222. SHERMAN, M., The differentiation of emotional responses in infants. II. The ability of observers to judge the emotional characteristics of the crying of infants, and the voice of an adult. *J. Comp. Psychol.* 1927, 7, 335-351.

223. SHERMAN, M., The differentiation of emotional responses in infants. III. A proposed theory of the development of emotional responses in infants. *J. Comp. Psychol.* 1928, 8, 385-394.

224. SHERMAN, M., and SHERMAN, I. C., Sensori-motor responses in infants. *J. Comp. Psychol.*, 1925, 5, 53-68.

225. SHINN, M. W., Notes on the development of a child. Parts I and II. *University of California Studies*, Berkeley, University of California Press, 1893. Parts III and IV. *University of California Studies*, Berkeley, University of California Press, 1899.

226. SHINN, M. W., The development of the senses in the first three years of life. *University of California, Pub. in Education No. 4*. Berkeley, Univ. of California Press 1907.

227. SHINN, M. W., *The biography of a baby*, Boston, Houghton, Mifflin Co. 1908.

228. SHIRLEY, MARY, The first two years: a study of twenty-five babies. *University of Minnesota, Institute of Child*

Welfare Monograph Series. Minneapolis, University of Minnesota Press.

Vol. I. *Postural and locomotor development,* 1931.
Vol. II. *Intellectual development.* To appear shortly.
Vol. III. *Personality manifestations.* To appear shortly.

229. Sims, V. M., *The measurement of socio-economic status.* Bloomington, Ill. Public School Pub. Co., 1928.

230. Skalet, Magda, The home play of young children. A survey of play equipment and its use. *University of Minnesota, Institute of Child Welfare Monograph Series,* Minneapolis, University of Minnesota Press. To appear shortly.

231. Slaght, W. E., Untruthfulness in children: Its conditioning factors and its setting in child nature. *Univ. of Iowa Stud.: Stud. in Character,* 1928, 1, No. 4, Pp. 79.

232. Smith, Lois G., An experimental investigation of young children's interest and expressive behavior responses to single statement, verbal repetition and ideational repetition of content in animal stories. *Child Dev.* 1930, 1, 232-247.

233. Smith, M. E., An investigation of the development of the sentence and the extent of vocabulary in young children. *Univ. of Iowa Stud., Studies in Child Welfare.* 1926, 3, No. 5, Pp. 92.

234. Stern, W., and Stern, C., Erinnerung und Aussage in der ersten Kindheit. Ein Kapitel aus der Psychogenesis eines Kindes. *Beitr. z. Psychol. d. Aussage,* 1905, 2, 32-67.

235. Stern, W., and Stern, C., *Monographien über die seelische Entwicklung des Kindes. I. Die Kindersprache. Eine psychologische und sprachtheoretische Untersuchung.* Leipzig, Barth, 1907. *II. Erinnerung. Aussage, und Lüge in der ersten Kindheit.* Leipzig, Barth, 1909.

236. Stern, W., and Stern, C., Die zeichnerische Entwicklung eines Kindes vom 4 bis zum 7 Jahre. *Zsch. f. angew. Psychol.* 1909, 3, 1-31.

237. Strachan, L., Distribution of intelligence quotients of twenty-two thousand primary school children. *J. Educ. Res.* 1926, 14, 169-177.

238. Strayer, Lois C., Language and growth: The relative efficacy of early and deferred vocabulary training studied by the method of co-twin control. *Genet. Psychol. Monog.*, 1930, 8, 209-319.

239. Studencki, S. M., Children's relations to themselves. *Ped. Sem.* 1926, 33, 61-70.

240. Stutsman, R., Irene—A study of the personality defects of an attractive superior child of preschool age. *Ped. Sem.* 1926, 33, 61-70.

241. Terman, L. M., The vocabulary test as a measure of intelligence. *J. Educ. Psychol.* 1918, 9, 452-466.

242. Terman, L. M., and Hocking, A., The sleep of school children: its distribution according to age and its relation to mental and physical efficiency. *J. Educ. Psychol.* 1913, 4, 138-147; 199-208; 269-282.

243. Terman, L. M., *The intelligence of school children.* Boston, Houghton, Mifflin Co. 1919, Pp. xxii + 317.

244. Terman, L. M., *et al. Genetic studies of genius, Vol. 1. Mental and physical traits of a thousand gifted children.* Stanford University, Calif., Stanford University Press, 1925, Pp. xiii + 648.

245. Thomas, D. S., and others. Some new techniques for studying social behavior. *Child Dev. Monog.* 1929, No. 1. New York, Columbia University Press, 1929, Pp. 213.

246. Thorndike, E. L., The curve of work and the curve of satisfyingness. *J. Appl. Psychol.* 1917, 1, 265-267.

247. Thorndike, E. L., *The teacher's word book.* New York, Teachers' College, Columbia Univ. Bureau of Publications. 1921, Pp. vi + 134.

248. Thorndike, E. L., *The measurement of intelligence.* New York, Teachers' College, Columbia Univ. Bureau of Publications, 1926.

249. Thurston, F. M., A preliminary study of the factors affecting the time taken by nursery school children to eat their food. *J. Genet. Psychol.* 1929, 36, 303-318.

250. Thurstone, L. L., The absolute zero in intelligence measurements. *Psychol. Rev.* 1928, 35, 175-197.

251. Thurstone, L. L., and Ackerson, L., The mental growth curve for the Binet tests. *J. Educ. Psychol.* 1929, 20, 569-583.

Bibliography 489

252. Tilson, M. A., Problems of preschool children, a basis for parental education. New York, *Teachers' College, Columbia Univ. Contrib. to Educ.* No. 356, Pp. ix + 90, 1929.

253. Tinker, M. A., and Goodenough, F. L., A comparative study of finger tapping in children and adults. *Child Dev.* 1930, 1, 152-159.

254. Valentine, C. W., The color perceptions and color preferences of an infant during its fourth and eighth months. *Brit. J. Psychol.* 1914, 6, 363-386.

255. Valentine, C. W., Reflexes in early childhood: their development, variability, evanescence, inhibition, and relation to instincts. *Brit. J. Med. Psychol.* 1927, 7, 1-35.

256. Valentine, C. W., The foundations of child psychology and their bearing on some problems of general psychology. *School and Soc.* 1930, 32, 507-513.

257. Valentine, C. W., The innate bases of fear. *J. Genet. Psychol.* 1930, 37, 394-420.

258. Van Alstyne, D., The environment of three-year-old children; factors related to intelligence and vocabulary tests. *Teachers' College, Columbia University Contrib. to Educ.* No. 336, 1929, Pp. vii + 108.

259. Waddle, C. W., Case histories of gifted children. *Twenty-third Yearbook of the National Society for the Study of Education.* Part I. *The education of gifted children.* Bloomington, Ill. Public School Publishing Co., 1924, 185-207.

260. Wagoner, L. C., The constructive ability of young children. *Univ. of Iowa Stud., Stud. in Child Welfare,* 1925, 3, No. 2, Pp. 55.

261. Wagoner, L. C., and Armstrong, E. M., The motor control of children as involved in the dressing process. *J. Genet. Psychol.* 1928, 35, 84-97.

262. Ward, A., The only child: a study of one hundred only children referred to a child guidance clinic. *Smith College Studies in Social Work,* 1930, 1, 41-65.

263. Waring, E. B., The relation between early language habits and early habits of conduct control. *Teachers' College, Columbia University, Contrib. to Educ.* No. 260, 1927, Pp. 125.

264. WASHBURNE, J. N., An experiment in character measurement. *J. Juv. Res.* 1929, 13, 1-18.

265. WASHBURN, RUTH W., A study of the smiling and laughing of infants in the first year of life. *Genet. Psychol. Monog.* 1929, 6, Nos. 5 and 6, 403-537.

266. WATSON, J. B., and WATSON, R. R., Studies in infant psychology. *Scient. Mo.* 1921, 13, 493-515.

267. WEILL, B. C., The behavior of young children of the same family. *Harvard Studies in Educ.* 1928, 10, Pp. x + 220.

268. WELLMAN, B., The school child's choice of companions. *J. Educ. Res.* 1926, 14, 126-132.

269. WELLMAN, B., The development of motor coördination in young children: An experimental study in the control of hand and arm movements. *Univ. of Iowa Stud., Stud. in Child Welfare,* 1926, 3, No. 4, Pp. 93.

270. WICKMAN, E. K., *Children's behavior and teachers' attitudes.* New York, The Commonwealth Fund, Division of Publications, 1928, Pp. 247.

271. WILLSON, G. M., Standard deviations of age scores and quotients in typical groups. *J. Educ. Psychol.* 1925, 16, 193-207.

272. WILSON, C. A., SWEENEY, M. E., STUTSMAN, R., CHESIRE, L. E., and HATT, E., *The Merrill-Palmer standards of physical and mental growth.* Detroit, The Merrill-Palmer School, 1930, Pp. ix + 121.

273. WOODROW, H., A picture-preference character test. *J. Educ. Psychol.* 1926, 17, 519-531.

274. WOODROW, H., and BEMMELS, V., Overstatement as a test of general character in preschool children. *J. Educ. Psychol.* 1927, 18, 239-246.

275. WOODROW, H., and LOWELL, F. E., Children's association frequency tables. *Psychol. Monog.* 1916, 22, No. 5, Pp. 110.

276. WOOLLEY, H. T., Some experiments on the color perceptions of an infant and their interpretation. *Psychol. Rev.,* 1909, 16, 363-376.

277. WOOLLEY, H. T., Agnes: A dominant personality in the making. *Ped. Sem.* 1925, 32, 569-598.

278. WOOLLEY, H. T., The validity of standards of mental measurement in young childhood. *School and Soc.* 1925, 21, 476-482.

279. WOOLLEY, H. T., Peter: The beginnings of the Juvenile Court problem. *Ped. Sem.* 1926, 33, 9-29.

280. YOUNG, H. H., Slot maze A. *Psychol. Clinic,* 1922, 14, 73-82.

II. TEXTBOOKS AND REVIEWS

281. ADAMS, S., and POWERS, F. F., The psychology of language. *Psychol. Bull.* 1929, 26, 241-260.

282. ALLEN, C. N., Recent studies in sex differences. *Psychol. Bull.* 1930, 27, 394-407.

283. ANDERSON, J. E., and GOODENOUGH, F. L., *The modern baby book and child development record.* New York, Norton, 1929, Pp. 409.

284. BALDWIN, B. T., STECHER, L. I., and SMITH, M. General review: Mental development of children. *Psychol. Bull.* 1923, 20, 665-683.

285. BALDWIN, B. T., Child psychology. A review of the literature Jan. 1, 1923 to March 31, 1928. *Psychol. Bull.* 1928, 25, 629-697.

286. BÜHLER, KARL, *The mental development of the child.* New York, Harcourt Brace, 1930.

287. DALLENBACH, K. M., Attention. *Psychol. Bull.* 1926, 23, 1-18.

288. DALLENBACH, K. M., Attention. *Psychol. Bull.* 1928, 25, 493-512.

289. DALLENBACH, K. M., Attention. *Psychol. Bull.* 1930, 27, 497-513.

290. DISERENS, C. M., and Bonfield, M., Humor and the ludicrous. *Psychol. Bull.* 1930, 27, 108-118.

291. DOE-KULMANN, L., and STONE, C. P., Notes on the mental development of children exhibiting the somatic signs of puberty praecox. *J. Abn. and Soc. Psychol.* 1927, 22, 291-324.

292. FREEMAN, F. N., *How children learn.* Boston, Houghton, Mifflin Co., 1917, Pp. xiv + 322.

293. FREEMAN, F. N., *Mental tests, their history, principles and applications*. Boston, Houghton, Mifflin Co., 1926, Pp. xi + 503.

294. GARTH, T. R., A review of racial psychology. *Psychol. Bull.* 1925, 22, 243-367.

295. GARTH, T. R., A review of race psychology. *Psychol. Bull.* 1930, 27, 329-356.

296. GUILFORD, J. P., and BRALY, K. W., Extroversion and introversion. *Psychol. Bull.* 1930, 27, 96-107.

297. HALL, G. S., *Aspects of child life and education*. Boston, Ginn & Co., 1907, Pp. ix + 326.

298. HARRIS, J. A., JACKSON, C. M., PATERSON, D. G., and SCAMMON, R. E., *The measurement of man*. Minneapolis, University of Minnesota Press, 1930, Pp. vii + 215.

299. HOLLINGWORTH, H. L., *Judging human character*. New York, D. Appleton & Co., 1926. See Chap. 3 "Human character in photographs."

300. HOLLINGWORTH, L. S., *Gifted children. Their nature and nurture*. New York, The Macmillan Co., 1926, Pp. xxii + 374.

301. HORN, M. D., Selected bibliography on children's vocabularies. *Childhood Educ.* 1927, 3, 316-319.

302. JONES, H. E., and JONES, M. C., Genetic studies of emotions. *Psychol. Bull.* 1930, 27, 40-64.

303. KELLEY, T. L., *Interpretation of educational measurements*. Yonkers-on-Hudson, World Book Co., 1927, Pp. xiii + 363.

304. KELLEY, T. L., *Scientific method*. Columbus, Ohio State University Press, 1929, Pp. viii + 195. See Chapter 3.

305. Koos, L. V., *The questionnaire in education*. New York, The Macmillan Co., 1928, Pp. vii + 178.

306. LINCOLN, E. A., *Sex differences in the growth of American school children*. Baltimore, Warwick and York, 1927, Pp. xii + 189.

307. McCARTHY, D., The vocalizations of infants. *Psychol. Bull.* 1929, 26, 625-651.

308. McGEOCH, J. A., The acquisition of skill. *Psychol. Bull.* 1927, 24, 437-466.

309. McGEOCH, J. A., Memory. *Psychol. Bull.* 1928, 25, 513-549.
310. McGEOCH, J. A., The acquisition of skill. *Psychol. Bull.* 1929, 26, 457-498.
311. McGEOCH, J. A., Memory. *Psychol. Bull.* 1930, 27, 514-563.
312. MANSON, G. A., *Bibliography of the analysis and measurement of human personality up to 1926.* Washington, D. C., National Research Council. Repr. and Circ. Ser. No. 72, 1926, Pp. 59.
313. MARKEY, J. F., *The symbolic process and its integration in children.* New York, Harcourt, Brace, 1928, Pp. xii + 192.
314. MAY, M. A., and HARTSHORNE, H., Personality and character tests. *Psychol. Bull.* 1926, 23, 395-411.
315. MAY, M. A., HARTSHORNE, H., and WELTY, R., Personality and character tests. *Psychol. Bull.,* 1927, 24, 418-435.
316. MAY, M. A., HARTSHORNE, H., and WELTY, R. E., Personality and character tests. *Psychol Bull.* 1928, 25, 422-443.
317. MAY, M. A., HARTSHORNE, H., and WELTY, R. E., Personality and character tests. *Psychol. Bull.* 1929, 26, 418-444.
318. MAY, M. A., HARTSHORNE, H., and WELTY, R. E., Personality and character tests. *Psychol. Bull.* 1930, 27, 485-494.
319. MURCHISON, CARL (Editor). *Handbook of child psychology.* Worcester, Mass., Clark University Press. London, Humphrey Milford, Oxford University Press, 1931.
320. NATIONAL EDUCATION ASSOCIATION. The questionnaire. *Research Bulletin, N. E. A.* 1930, 8, No. 1, 1-51.
321. PATERSON, D. G., *Physique and intellect.:* New York, The Century Co., 1930, Pp. xxvii + 304.
322. PETERSON, JOSEPH, *Early conceptions and tests of intelligence.* Yonkers-on-Hudson, World Book Co., 1925, Pp. xiv + 320.
323. PINTNER, R., *Intelligence testing.* New York, Henry Holt and Co., 1923, Pp. vii + 406.
A revised edition of this book will appear shortly.

324. PINTNER, R., Intelligence tests. *Psychol. Bull.* 1926, 23, Pp. 366-381.

325. PINTNER, R., Intelligence tests. *Psychol. Bull.* 1927, 24, 391-408.

326. PINTNER, R., Intelligence tests. *Psychol. Bull.* 1928, 25, 389-406.

327. PINTNER, R., Intelligence tests. *Psychol. Bull.* 1929, 26, 381-396.

328. PINTNER, R., Intelligence tests. *Psychol. Bull.* 1930, 27, 431-457.

329. POWERS, F. F., Psychology of language learning. *Psychol. Bull.* 1929, 26, 261-274.

330. Proceedings of the third conference on research in child development. Papers and discussions. Issued by the committee on child development of the National Research Council, Washington, D. C. 1929, Two volumes.

Volume I includes critical reviews and bibliographies on the following topics: (a) *The measurement and analysis of human growth* by R. E. SCAMMON, (2) *Types and indices of growth in childhood* by T. WINGATE TODD, (3) *Review of recent literature on certain phases of nutrition research and its significance in child development* by LYDIA J. ROBERTS, (4) *A review of recent research pertinent to the clinical aspects of child nutrition* by C. A. WILSON, (5) *Measurement and prediction of mental growth* by F. L. GOODENOUGH, (6) *Clinical studies of child development* by ARNOLD GESELL, (7) *The development of motor, linguistic, and intellectual skills in young children* by J. E. ANDERSON, (8) *Implications for training contained in the recent literature of mental growth* by A. H. ARLITT, (9) *Studies of personality and social adjustment in early childhood* by H. E. JONES, (10) *Individual adjustments and community relationships* by W. E. BLATZ, (11) *Observations on several phases of present European research in child development* by FLORENCE POWDERMAKER and (12) *Notes on some Russian experiments* by L. K. FRANK. Volume II includes the addresses and discussions.

331. ROBERTS, LYDIA J., *Nutrition work with children.* Chicago, University of Chicago Press, 1927, Pp. xiv + 394.

332. RUCKMICK, C. A., The uses and abuses of the questionnaire procedure. *J. Appl. Psychol.*, 1930, 14, 32-41.

333. SHUTTLEWORTH, K. A., The social relations of children. *Psychol. Bull.* 1927, 24, 708-716.

334. SPEARMAN, C. E., *The abilities of man.* London, The Macmillan Co., 1927.

335. STERN, W., *Psychology of early childhood up to the sixth year of age.* (Trans. from 3d ed., rev. and enl. by A. Barwell.) New York, Henry Holt & Co., 1924, Pp. 557.
    See also 5th German Edition, revised and enlarged, Leipzig, Quelle & Meyer, 1928.

336. TAUSSIG, F. W., *Principles of economics.* Second revised edition. New York, The Macmillan Co., 1920, 2 vols. See Vol. II. Pp. 134-137.

337. THOMAS, W. I., and THOMAS, DOROTHY S., *The child in America.* New York, Alfred A Knopf, 1928, Pp. xiv + 583.

338. THORNDIKE, E. L., *Notes on child study.* New York, The Macmillan Co., 1903, Pp. 157.

339. THORNDIKE, E. L., *Educational psychology.* (3 vols.) New York, Teachers' College, Columbia Univ. Bureau Publ. 1913.

340. THORNDIKE, E. L., *et al.* Intelligence and its measurements; a symposium. *J. Educ. Psychol.* 1921, 12, 123-212.

341. TRAVIS, L. E., Recent research in speech pathology. *Psychol. Bull.* 1929, 26, 275-304.

342. *Twenty-eighth Yearbook of the National Society for the Study of Education. Preschool and parental education. Part I. Organization and development. Part II. Research and method.* Bloomington, Ill., Public School Pub. Co., 1929, Pp. 875. Part II contains brief abstracts of experimental studies on child development and training.

343. U. S. CHILDREN'S BUREAU, *References on the physical growth and development of the normal child.* Bureau

Pub. No. 179. Washington, U. S. Gov't Printing Office, 1927.

344. WATSON, J. B., *Psychology from the standpoint of a behaviorist*. Philadelphia, J. B. Lippincott Co., 1919, Pp. xi + 429.

345. WEISS, A. P., The measurement of infant behavior. *Psychol. Rev.* 1929, 36, 453-471.

III. MENTAL TEST MANUALS

346. ARTHUR, GRACE, *A point scale of performance tests. Vol. I. Clinical Manual*. New York, The Commonwealth Fund Division of Publications, 1930, Pp. ix + 82.

347. BAKER, H. J., *Detroit kindergarten test*. Yonkers-on-Hudson, World Book Co., 1920.

348. BAKER, H. J., *Detroit advanced first-grade intelligence test*. Yonkers-on-Hudson, World Book Co.

349. BIRD, G. E., The Rhode Island intelligence test. *J. Educ. Res.* 1923, 8, 397-403.

350. BIRD, G. E., and CRAIG, C. E., *Rhode Island intelligence test for children from three to six years of age*. Bloomington, Ill., Public School Pub. Co.

351. BRONNER, A. F., HEALY, W., LOWE, G. M., and SHIMBERG, M. E., *A manual of individual mental tests and testing*. Boston: Little, Brown & Co., 1927, Pp. x + 287.

352. DEARBORN, W. F., *The Dearborn group tests of intelligence. Rev. Ed. Series I. General examination A and B*. Philadelphia, J. B. Lippincott Co., 1922.

353. ENGEL, ANNA M., *Detroit first-grade intelligence test*. Yonkers-on-Hudson, World Book Co., 1920.

354. GOODENOUGH, F. L., *Measurement of intelligence by drawings*. Yonkers-on-Hudson, World Book Co., 1926, Pp. xi + 177.

355. GOODENOUGH, F. L., and FOSTER, J. C., *The Minnesota preschool tests*. Minneapolis, University of Minnesota Press.

Ready in 1931.

356. HAGGERTY, M. E., *Intelligence examinations, Delta I, for grades 1-3.* Yonkers-on-Hudson, World Book Co., 1920, Pp. 12.

357. HAGGERTY, M. E., and NOONAN, M. E., *Haggerty reading examination—Sigma I for grades 1-3.* Yonkers-on-Hudson, World Book Co.

358. HAGGERTY, M. E., TERMAN, L. M., THORNDIKE, E. L., WHIPPLE, G. M., and YERKES, R. M., *National intelligence tests.* Yonkers-on-Hudson, World Book Co.

359. HAYES, S. P., The new revision of the Binet intelligence tests for the blind. *Teachers' Forum for Instructors of Blind Children,* 1929, No. 2, 2-4.

360. HERRING, J. P., *Herring revision of the Binet-Simon tests. Examination manual.* Yonkers-on-Hudson, World Book Co., Pp. 56.

361. KELLEY, T. L., A constructive ability test. *J. Educ. Psychol.* 1916, 7, 1-16.

362. KELLEY, T. L., RUCH, G. M., and TERMAN, L. M., *New Stanford achievement test. Forms V, X, Y, Z.* Yonkers-on-Hudson, World Book Co., 1929, *Primary examination,* Pp. 8. *Advanced examination,* Pp. 24.

363. KINGSBURY, F. A., A group intelligence scale for primary grades. *Psychol. Monog.* 1924, 33, No. 6, Pp. 60.

364. KUHLMANN, F., *A handbook of mental tests.* Baltimore, Warwick & York, 1922, Pp. 208.

365. KUHLMANN, F., and ANDERSON, R. G., *Kuhlmann-Anderson intelligence tests.* Minneapolis, Minn.: Educational Test Bureau, 1927.

366. LINFERT, H. E., and HIERHOLZER, H. M., A scale for measuring the mental development of infants during the first year of life. *Cath. Univ. Amer. Stud. Psychol. and Psychiat.,* 1928, 1, No. 4, Pp. 33.

367. MYERS, G. C., and MYERS, C. E., *Myers mental measure,* New York, Newson, 1921.

368. OTIS, A. S., *Otis group intelligence scale: Primary examination: Forms A and B.* Yonkers-on-Hudson, World Book Co.

369. PINTNER, R., *Manual of directions for the non-language mental and educational survey tests.* Columbus, Ohio, College Book, 1920, Pp. 16.

370. PINTNER, R., and CUNNINGHAM, B. V., *The Pintner-Cunningham primary mental test.* Yonkers-on-Hudson, World Book Co., 1923.

371. PINTNER, R., and PATERSON, D. G., *A scale of performance tests.* New York, D. Appleton & Co., 1917, Pp. x + 218.

372. PRESSEY, L. C., *Pressey attainment scales.* Bloomington, Ill., Public School Pub. Co.
      Separate scales are available for each of the first three grades.

373. PRESSEY, S. L., and PRESSEY, L. C., *Pressey primary classification test, Form A. Grades 1 and 2.* Bloomington, Ill., Public School Pub. Co.

374. PRESSEY, S. L., and PRESSEY, L. C., *Pressey intermediate classification test.* Bloomington, Ill., Public School Pub. Co.

375. SANGREN, P. V., *Sangren information tests for young children.* Yonkers-on-Hudson, World Book Co., 1930.

376. STUTSMAN, R., *Mental measurement of preschool children.* Yonkers-on-Hudson. World Book Co., 1931. Pp. x + 368.

377. TERMAN, L. M., *The measurement of intelligence.* Boston, Houghton, Mifflin Co., 1916, Pp. xviii + 362.
      A revision of these tests is now being made.

378. WHIPPLE, G. M., *Manual of mental and physical tests. Part I. Simpler processes. Part II. Complex processes.* Baltimore, Warwick and York. Third edition, 1924.

379. YERKES, R. M., and FOSTER, J. C., *1923 revision. A point scale for measuring mental ability.* Baltimore, Warwick and York, 1923, Pp. vii + 219.

IV. STATISTICAL METHODS, FORMS AND TABLES

380. ANDERSON, JOHN E., *Correlation chart.* Minneapolis, Educational Test Bureau, 1928.

381. ANDERSON, R. G., A critical examination of test-scoring methods. *Arch. Psychol.* 1925, No. 80, Pp. 50.

382. *Barlow's tables of squares, cubes, square roots, cube roots, and reciprocals of all integer numbers up to*

10,000. London, E. and F. N. Spon, 1924, (First published in 1814), Pp. vii + 200.

383. CRELLE, A. L., *Calculating tables*. Berlin, O. Seelinger, 1908, Pp. 500.

384. GARRETT, H. E., *Statistics in psychology and education*. New York, Longmans, Green & Co., 1926, Pp. xiii + 317.

385. GOODENOUGH, F. L., A short method for computing the correlation between interchangeable variables. *J. Educ. Psychol.*, 1929, 20, 386.

386. HOLZINGER, K. J., *Statistical tables for students in education and psychology*. Chicago, University of Chicago, University of Chicago Press, 1926, Pp. v + 74.

387. HOLZINGER, K. J., *Statistical résumé of the Spearman two-factor theory*. Chicago, University of Chicago Press, 1930, Pp. 43.

388. INGLIS, A., *Inglis tables of intelligence quotient values*. Yonkers-on-Hudson, World Book Co., Pp. 16.

389. KELLEY, T. L., *Kelley correlation chart*. Yonkers-on-Hudson, World Book Co.

390. KELLEY, T. L., *Statistical method*. New York, The Macmillan Co., 1923, Pp. xi + 390.

391. KELLEY, T. L., and SHEN, E., General statistical principles. In *Foundations of experimental psychology*. Worcester, Mass., Clark University Press, 1929, Pp. 832-854.

392. KELLEY, T. L., and SHEN, E., The statistical treatment of certain typical problems. In *Foundations of experimental psychology*. Worcester, Mass., Clark University Press, 1929, Pp. 855-883.

393. OTIS, A. S., *Otis correlation chart*. Yonkers-on-Hudson, World Book Co.

394. OTIS, A. S., *Universal percentile graph*. Yonkers-on-Hudson, World Book Co., Pp. 4.

395. PEARSON, KARL, *Tables for biometricians and statisticians. Part I*. Second Edition, Cambridge University Press, 1924, Pp. lxxxiii + 143.

396. THORNDIKE, E. L., *An introduction to the theory of mental and social measurements. Second revised edi-*

tion. New York, Teachers' College, Columbia Univ. Bureau Publ., 1919, Pp. xi + 277.

397. THURSTONE, L. L., *The fundamentals of statistics*. New York, The Macmillan Co., 1925.

398. THURSTONE, L. L., A method of scaling psychological and educational tests. *J. Educ. Psychol.* 1925, 16, 433-451.

399. THURSTONE, L. L., The unit of measurement in educational scales. *J. Educ. Psychol.* 1927, 18, 505-524.

400. THURSTONE, L. L., Scale construction with weighted observations. *J. Educ. Psychol.* 1928, 19, 441-453.

401. WARREN, RICHARD, and MENDENHALL, R. M., The Mendenhall-Warren-Hollerith correlation method. *Columbia University Statistical Bureau Document No. 1.* 1929, Pp. ii + 37, 6 plates.

402. WOODWORTH, R. S., Combining the results of several tests: a study in statistical method. *Psychol. Rev.* 1912, 19, 97-123.

403. YULE, G. UDNY. *An introduction to the theory of statistics*. London, Charles Griffin & Co., 1919, Pp. xv + 398.

APPENDIX A

CLASSIFICATION OF OCCUPATIONS OF EMPLOYED MALES IN UNITED STATES, 1920

The data in these tables are taken from the Report of the Fourteenth Census of the United States, Vol. 4, 1920. By following this outline, corresponding percentages can be worked out from the census data for any state and for the larger cities.

GROUP I

Census
Classification

Prof. S.   Architects;
"   Artists, sculptors, teachers of art;
"   Authors editors, reporters;
"   Chemists, assayers, and metallurgists;
"   Civil engineers, surveyors;
"   Clergymen;
"   College presidents and professors;
"   Dentists;
"   Electrical engineers;
"   Keepers of charitable and penal institutions;
"   Lawyers, judges, and justices;
"   Librarians;
"   * Mechanical engineers;
"   Mining engineers;
"   Physicians and surgeons;
"   Professional service; (other occup.)
"   Teachers; (School)

TOTAL in United States 839,188

Per cent of total occupied 2.54

* Includes all technical engineers not elsewhere classified.

GROUP II

Census
Classification

Cler.	Accountants and auditors;
Prof. S.	Aeronauts;
Trade	Bankers and bank officials;
"	Books; (retail dealers)
"	Brokers, N.O.S.,* and promoters;
Mfg.	Builders and building contractors;
Trade	Buyers and shippers of grain; (retail dealers)
"	Buyers and shippers of livestock; (retail dealers)
"	Buyers and shippers of other farm produce; (retail dealers)
Trans.	Captains, masters, mates, and pilots;
Trade	Commercial brokers and commission men;
"	Department store dealers; (retail dealers)
Prof. S.	Designers;
"	Draftsmen;
Trade	Drugs and medicine, pharmacists, druggists; (retail dealers)
"	Furs; (retail dealers)
Trans.	Inspectors; (steam railway)
Prof. S.	Inventors
"	Interior decorators
Trade	Jewelry; (retail dealers)
Dom. S.	Laundry owners, officials, and managers;
Trade	Loan brokers and loan company officials;
Trans.	Locomotive engineers
Trade	Lumber; (retail dealers)
Mfg.	Managers and superintendents; (mfg.)
"	Manufacturers and officials;
Prof. S.	Musicians and teachers of music;
Trade	Officials of insurance companies;
Pub. S.	Officials, inspectors; (state)
Trans.	Officials and supt.; (steam and street R.R.)
Pub. S.	Officials, U. S.; (except postmasters)
Mining	Operators, officials and managers of mines;

* Not otherwise stated.

Census
Classification

Ag.	Owners and mgrs. of log and timber camps;
Pub. S.	Probation and truant officers;
Trade	Proprietors, officials, mgrs.—elevators and ware-
Trans.	houses;
	Proprietors, officials, mgrs.—for telegraph, tele-
	phone, and other transportation N.O.S.
Trade	Other proprietors, officials, and mgrs.;
Prof. S.	Religious, charity, and welfare workers;
Trade	Stockbrokers;
"	Wholesale dealers, importers, and exporters;

TOTAL in United States 1,553,626

Per cent of total occupied 4.70

Retail dealers includes managers and superintendents of retail stores.

GROUP III

Classification
Census

Prof. S.	Abstracters, notaries, justices of peace;
"	Actors;
Trans.	Agents of express companies;
Trade	Agr. implements and wagons; (retail dealers)
Mfg.	Annealers and temperers; (metal)
Ag.	Apiarists;
Mfg.	Apprentices to architects, designers, and drafts-men;
Trade	Art stores and artist materials; (retail dealers)
"	Automobiles and accessories; (retail dealers)
Cler.	Bookkeepers and cashiers;
Trade	Boots and shoes; (retail dealers)
Mfg.	Cabinet makers;
"	Carpenters;
Trade	Carpets and rugs; (retail dealers)
"	Clothing and men's furnishings; (retail dealers)
"	Coal and wood; (retail dealers)
"	Commercial travelers, traveling salesmen;

Census
Classification

Mfg.	Compositors, linotypers, and typesetters;
Trade	Crockery, glass, and queensware; (retail dealers)
"	Curios, antiques, novelties; (retail dealers)
"	Decorators, drapers, window dressers;
Prof. S.	Dentists' assistants and apprentices;
Mfg.	Dressmakers and seamstresses not in factory;
"	Electricians;
"	Electrotypers, stereotypers, lithographers;
Trade	Employment office keepers;
Mfg.	Engravers;
Trade	Florist; (retail dealers)
Trans.	Foremen of livery and transfer company;
Mfg.	Foremen, overseers, mfg.;
Trade	Foremen, floorwalkers in stores;
Ag.	Foresters, forest rangers, timber cruisers, etc.
Trade	Furniture; (retail dealers)
Trans.	Garage keepers, managers;
Trade	Gas fixtures and electrical supplies; (retail dealers)
"	General stores; (retail dealers)
Mfg.	Glass blowers;
Trade	Hardware stores and cutlery; (retail dealers)
Dom. S.	Hotel managers and keepers;
Trans.	Inspectors of street railway;
"	Inspectors of telephone and telegraph;
"	Inspectors, other transportation;
Trade	Insurance agents;
Mfg.	Jewelers, watchmakers, goldsmiths, silversmiths;
Ag.	Landscape gardeners and nurserymen;
Pub. S.	Lighthouse keepers;
Mfg.	Machinists;
"	Mechanics, other;
"	Millers (grain, flour, feed, etc.);
"	Milliners and millinery dealers;
"	Millwrights;
Trade	Music and musical instruments (retail dealers);
Pub. S.	Officials, inspectors, city and county;
"	Officials of lodge, society, etc.;

Census
Classification

Trade	Optician (retail dealers);
Prof. S.	Osteopaths;
Trade	Pawnbrokers;
Prof. S.	Photographers;
Mfg.	Piano tuners and organ tuners;
"	Plumbers, gas and steam fitters;
Pub. S.	Postmasters;
Trade	Produce and provisions (retail dealers);
Trans.	Proprietors and managers of transfer company;
"	Railway mail clerks;
Trade	Real estate agents and officials;
Mfg.	Skilled occupations (N.O.S.);
Trade	Stationery (retail dealers);
Trans.	Steam railroad conductors;
Cler.	Stenographers and typists;
Prof. S.	Teachers of athletics and dancing;
Trans.	Telegraph operators;
Prof. S.	Theatrical owners, mgrs. officials;
Trans.	Ticket and station agents;
Prof. S.	Trained nurses;
"	Turfmen and sportsmen;
Trade	Undertakers;
Prof. S.	Veterinary surgeons;
Cler.	Weighers;
Trans.	Yardmen, steam railroad;
Trade	Retail dealers (other specified);
"	Retail dealers (N.O.S.);
Mfg.	Wood carvers;

TOTAL in United States 4,767,285

Per cent of total occupied 14.42

GROUP IV

Ag.	Agriculture and animal husbandry, other and not specified pursuits;
"	Dairy farmers;
"	Dairy farm, farm, garden, orchard, etc., foremen;

*Census
Classification*

Ag.	Farmers, general farms;
"	Farmers, turpentine farms;
"	Florists, fruit growers, gardeners, and nursery men;
"	Inspectors, scalers, and surveyors (lumber);
"	Poultry raisers;
"	Stock raisers;

TOTAL in United States 6,197,191

Per cent of total occupied 18.74

GROUP V

Cler.	Agents, canvassers and collectors;
Mfg.	Apprentices to cabinet makers, carpenters, electricians, machinists;
"	Apprentices to jewelers, watchmakers, goldsmiths;
Prof. S.	Attendants and helpers (other-prof. service);
Trans.	Baggagemen , freight agents (railroad);
Mfg.	Bakers;
Dom. S.	Barbers, hairdressers, manicurists;
Trade	Bicycle (retail dealers);
Dom. S.	Billiard and pool room keepers;
"	Boarding and lodging house keepers;
Mfg.	Blacksmiths, foremen, hammersmiths, welders;
"	Boilermakers;
Trans.	Brakemen, railroad;
Mfg.	Brick and stone masons;
Trade	Butchers and meat dealers (retail dealers);
Dom. S.	Butlers;
Trade	Candy, confectionery (retail dealers);
Trans.	Chauffeurs;
Trade	Cigars and tobacco (retail dealers);
"	Clerks in stores;
Cler.	Clerks, other, not in stores (except shipping clerks and weighers);
Trade	Coffee and tea (retail dealers);

Census
Classification

Trans.	Conductors, street railroads;
Dom. S.	Cooks;
Mfg.	Coopers;
Dom. S.	Dance hall and skating rink, etc., keepers;
Trade	Delicatessen stores (retail dealers);
Prof. S.	Detectives;
Trade	Dry goods, fancy goods, notions (retail dealers);
Mfg.	Dyers (not retail dealers);
Trans.	Express messengers;
Prof. S.	Firemen (fire department);
Trade	Five and ten cent variety stores (retail dealers);
"	Flour and feed (retail dealers);
Trans.	Foremen and overseers, transportation N.O.S.;
Dom. S.	Foremen, and overseers of laundry operatives;
Trans.	Foremen and overseers, steam and street railroads;
Trade	Foremen (warehouses, stockyards, etc.);
"	Fruit (retail dealers);
"	Groceries (retail dealers);
Mfg.	Gunsmiths, locksmiths, and bell hangers;
Trade	Harness, saddlery (retail dealers);
Dom. S.	Housekeepers and stewards;
Trade	Ice (retail dealers);
Mining	Inspectors (extraction of minerals);
Trade	Inspectors, samplers, and gaugers, (trade);
Prof. S.	Keepers of pleasure resorts, race tracks, etc.;
Trade	Leather and hides (retail dealers);
Prof. S.	Librarians' assistants and attendants;
Pub. S.	Lifesavers;
Trans.	Livery stable keepers and managers;
"	Locomotive firemen;
Mfg.	Loom fixers;
Trans.	Mail carriers;
Pub. S.	Marshals and constables;
Trade	Milk (retail dealers);
Trans.	Motormen, steam and street railroad;
Mfg.	Molders, founders and casters (metal);
Trade	News dealers (retail dealers);

Census
Classification

Dom. S.	Nurses, not trained;
Trade	Oil, paint, wallpaper (retail dealers);
Mfg.	Painters, enamelers, glaziers, varnishers, etc.;
"	Paper hangers;
"	Pattern and model makers;
Prof. S.	Physicians' and surgeons' attendants;
Mfg.	Plasterers and cement finishers;
Pub. S.	Policemen;
Mfg.	Pressmen and plate printers (printing);
Pub. S.	Public service (other occupations);
Dom. S.	Restaurant, café and lunchroom keepers;
Mfg.	Roofers and slaters;
Trade	Salesmen, sales agents, auctioneers, demonstrators;
Mfg.	Sawyers;
Prof. S.	Semi-professional, other occupations;
Mfg.	Semi-skilled operatives, N.O.S. (mfg. and mech.);
Trade	Semi-skilled pursuits, fruit graders, meat cutters, packers, wholesale and retail trade, other occup.;
Trans.	Semi-skilled transportation, other occup.;
Pub. S.	Sheriff;
Cler.	Shipping clerks, not in stores;
Mfg.	Shoemakers, cobblers, not in factory;
Prof. S.	Showmen;
Pub. S.	Soldiers, sailors, marines;
Mfg.	Stationary engineers, cranemen and hoistmen, etc.;
"	Stone cutters;
"	Structural iron workers (building);
"	Tailors;
Trans.	Telegraph and telephone linemen;
"	Telephone operators;
Prof. S.	Theater ushers;
Mfg.	Tinsmiths and coppersmiths;
"	Toolmakers, dyesetters, and sinkers;
"	Upholsterers;

Census
Classification

Dom. S.   Waiters;
Mfg.   Wheelwrights;
            TOTAL in United States 9,059,457
            Per cent of total occupied 27.40

GROUP VI

Mfg.   Apprentices to blacksmiths, boilermakers, coopers, masons, painters, glaziers, varnishers, paper hangers, plasterers, roofers and slaters, tinsmiths and coppersmiths;
  "   Apprentices to printers and book binders;
  "   Apprentices (other);
Dom. S.   Attendants, cleaners and renovators of clothing, hunters, trappers, vendors, saloon keepers, umbrella menders, scissors grinders, and other occup. (domestic service), bartenders, bathhouse keepers and attendants, cemetery keepers;
  "   Bell boys, chore boys, etc.;
Trans.   Boatmen, canal men, and lock keepers;
  "   Boiler washers and engine hostlers;
Dom. S.   Bootblacks;
Cler.   Bundle, cash, messenger, errand, and office boys (except messengers);
Trans.   Carriage and hack drivers;
Dom. S.   Coachmen and footmen;
Mining   Coal mine operatives;
  "   Copper mine operatives;
Dom. S.   Chambermaids;
Trade   Deliverymen (bakers, laundries, stores);
Trans.   Draymen, teamsters and expressmen (not including teamsters in agriculture, forestry, and extraction of minerals);
Dom. S.   Elevator tenders;
Ag.   Farm laborers (home farms only);
Mfg.   Firemen (except locomotive and fire dept.);

Census
Classification

Ag.	Fishermen and oystermen;
Mining	Foremen and overseers (extraction of minerals);
Ag.	Foremen and overseers (forestry);
Prof. S.	Fortune tellers, hypnotists, spiritualists, etc.;
Mfg.	Furnacemen and smeltermen, heaters, ladlers, and pourers;
"	Filers, grinders, buffers, and metal polishers;
Mining	Gold and silver mine operatives;
Pub. S.	Guards, watchmen, and doorkeepers (public service);
Prof. S.	Healers (except osteopaths, physicians, and surgeons);
Mining	Iron mine operatives;
Trade	Hucksters and peddlers (retail dealers);
Dom. S.	Janitors and sextons;
Trade	Junk dealers (retail dealers);
"	Laundry operatives (other);
Trade	Newsboys;
Mining	Oil, gas, and salt well operatives;
Mfg.	Oilers of machinery;
Mining	Operatives in mines N.O.S.;
Dom. S.	Porters (domestic and prof. service);
"	Porters (steam railroads);
"	Porters (other except in stores);
Mining	Quarry operatives;
Trade	Rags (retail dealers);
Mfg.	Roller and roll hands (metal);
Trans.	Sailors and deck hands;
Dom. S.	Servants (other);
Prof. S.	Stage hands and circus helpers;
Trans.	Switchmen and flagmen (steam railroad);
"	Switchmen and flagmen (street railroad);
Ag.	Teamsters and haulers (lumber);
Trans.	Telegraph messengers;
Dom. S.	Valets;

TOTAL in United States 4,336,658

Per cent of total occupied 13.25

GROUP VII (Urban)

Census
Classification

Dom. S.	Cleaners;
Trans.	Hostlers and stable hands;
Mfg.	Laborers all industries, N.O.S., mfg. and mechanical;
Trade	Laborers, coal yards, stock yards, lumber yards;
"	Laborers, express company, pipe lines, telegraph and telephone, water trans. and other trans.;
Trans.	Laborers, garage, road and street;
Trade	Laborers, porters, helpers in stores;
Dom. S.	Laborers, (laundry operatives);
Trans.	Laborers, steam and street railroads;
Dom. S.	Laborers (domestic and prof. service);
"	Launderers not in laundry;
Trans.	Longshoremen, stevedores;
Pub. S.	Scavengers, garagemen, other laborers, (public service);

TOTAL in United States 3,963,398

Per cent of total occupied 11.99

GROUP VII (Rural)

Ag.	Cornshellers, hay-balers, etc.;
"	Dairy farm laborers;
"	Ditchers (farm);
"	Farm laborers (working out);
"	Farm laborers (turpentine farms);
"	Gardeners, greenhouse, orchard, and nursery laborers;
"	Irrigators and ditch tenders;
"	Poultry yard laborers;

*Census
Classification*

Ag. Lumbermen, raftsmen, and wood choppers;
" Stock herders, drovers, and feeders;

 TOTAL in United States 2,303,525

 Per cent of total occupied 6.97

 TOTAL GROUP VII in United
  States (Urban and Rural).. 6,266,923

 Per cent of total occupied 18.96

 GRAND TOTAL all classes for
  the United States 33,064,737

APPENDIX B

THE CHAPIN SCALE *

FOR RATING LIVING ROOM EQUIPMENT

DIRECTIONS TO VISITOR

1. The following list of items is for the guidance of the recorder. Not all of the features listed will be found in any one home. Entries on the schedules should, however, follow the order and numbering indicated. Weights appear after the names of the respective items. Disregard these weights in recording. Only when the list is finally checked should the individual items be multiplied by these weights and the sum of the weighted scores be computed, and then only after leaving the home. All information is confidential.
2. Check or underline the articles or items present. If more than one, write 2, 3, or 4, as the case may be.
3. Do not enter the *score* of any article or feature present. Complete recording before attempting to enter scores.
4. In cases where the family has no real living room, but uses the room at nights as a bedroom, or during the day as a kitchen or as a dining room, or as both, *in addition to use of room as the chief gathering place of the family, please note this fact clearly* and describe for what purposes the room is used.
5. When possible it is desirable to have a living room checked twice. This may be done in either of two ways.
    a. After an interval of two or three weeks the same visitor may recheck the room. The first schedule should be marked I, the second II.

* (43, 44, 258)

513

b. After an interval or simultaneously the room may be checked by two different visitors. One schedule should be marked A, the other B.

Scores of the same homes on two trials should be similar. If a group of homes are scored twice there should be a high correlation between the scores. Please report findings to F. Stuart Chapin, University of Minnesota.

SCHEDULE OF LIVING ROOM EQUIPMENT

I. FIXED FEATURES

  1. Floor ....—
    Softwood 1, hardwood 2, composition 3, stone 4.
  2. Floor covering ....—
    Composition 1, carpet 2, small rugs 3, large rug 4, oriental rug 6.
  3. Wall covering ....—
    Paper 1, kalsomine 2, plain paint 3, decorative paint 4, wooden panels 5.
  4. Woodwork ....—
    Painted 1, varnished 2, stained 3, oiled 4.
  5. Door protection ....—
    Screen 1, storm door 1.
  6. Windows ....—
    1 each window.
  7. Window protection[1]....—
    Screen, blind, netting, storm sash, awning, shutter 1 each.
  8. Window covering[1] .....—
    Shades 1, curtains 2, drapes 3.
  9. Fireplace ....—
    Imitation 1, gas 2, wood 4, coal 4.
  10. Fire utensils ....—
    Andirons, screen, poker, tongs, shovel, brush, hod, basket, rack, 1 each.
  11. Heat ....—
    Stove 1, hot air 2, steam 3, hot water 4.

  12. Artificial light ....—
    Kerosene 1, gas 2, electric 3.
  13. Artificial ventilators 1..—
  14. Clothes closets 1.......—

    Total Section I......—

II. BUILT-IN FEATURES

  15. Book containers ......—
    Shelves 1, cases 2.
  16. Beds ....—
    In a sideboard 1, in a ceiling 2, in a door 3.
  17. Desk 1...............—
  18. Window seats 1.......—
  19. Window boxes 1.......—

    Total Section II.....—

III. STANDARD FURNITURE

  20. Table ....—
    Sewing 1, writing 1, card 1, library, end, tea, 2 each.
  21. Chair ....—
    Straight, rocker, arm chair, high chair, 1 each.
  22. Stool or bench........—
    High stool, footstool, piano stool, piano bench, 1 each.
  23. Couch ....—
    Cot 1, sanitary couch 2, chaise longue 3, daybed 4, davenport 5, bed-davenport 6.

[1] If checked out of season, ascertain if used in season and so record.

24. Desk .... ——
    Business 1, personal-
    social 2.
25. Book cases 1 .... ——
26. Wardrobe or movable
    cabinet 1 .... ——
27. Sewing cabinet 1 ...... ——
28. Sewing machine ...... ——
    Hand power 1, foot pow-
    er 2, electric 3.
29. Rack or stand 1 .... ——
30. Screen 1 .... ——
31. Chests 1 .... ——
32. Music cabinet 1 .... ——

    Total Section III..... ——

IV. FURNISHINGS AND CULTURAL
    RESOURCES

33. Covers .... ——
    Furniture, table, chair,
    couch, piano, 1 each.
34. Pillows .... ——
    Couch, floor, 1 each.
35. Lamps .... ——
    Floor, bridge, table, 1
    each.
36. Candle holders, 1 each.. ——
37. Clock .... ——
    Mantel, grandfather, wall,
    alarm, 1 each.
38. Mirror, 1 each........ ——
39. Pottery, brass or metal.. ——
    Factory made 1, hand
    made 2 each.
40. Baskets .... ——
    Factory or hand made,
    waste, sewing, sandwich,
    decorative, 1 each.
41. Statues, 1 each........ ——
42. Vases 1, flowers or
    plants, 2 each........ ——
43. Photographs 1 each
    (portraits of personal
    interest) .... ——
44. Pictures .... ——
    Note if original or repro-

duction. If original, oil,
water color, etching,
wood block, lithograph,
crayon drawing, pencil
drawing, pen and ink,
brush drawing, photo-
graph (when treated as
a work of art), 2 each;
if reproduction, photo-
graph, half tone, color
print, chromo, 1 each.

45. Books [2] .... ——
    Poetry, fiction, history,
    drama, biography, phi-
    losophy, essays, litera-
    ture, religion, art, science
    (physical, psychological,
    social), atlas, dictionary,
    encyclopedia, .20 for
    each volume.
46. Newspapers [3] .... ——
    General, labor, local com-
    munity, sectarian, 1 for
    each type of paper.
47. Periodicals [3] .... ——
    News (current events),
    professional, religious, lit-
    erary, science, art, chil-
    dren's, 1 each; fraternal,
    fashion, or popular story,
    .50 each.
48. Telephone [3] .... ——
    Switchboard connection
    1, two-party line 2, one-
    party line 3 (Note social
    or business mainly).
49. Radio [3] .... ——
    Crystal 1, one-tube 2,
    two-tube 3, three-tube 4,
    five-tube and up, 5.
50. Musical instruments [3] .. ——
    Piano 5, organ 1, violin
    1, other hand instru-
    ments 1 each.
51. Mechanical musical in-
    struments [2] .... ——

[2] To be recorded if in another room (except professional library of
doctor, lawyer, clergyman).

[3] To be recorded if in another room.

Music box 1, phono-
graph 2, player-organ 3,
player-piano 4.

52. Sheet music [4] ....
Opera, folk, military,
ballads, classic, dance
(other than jazz), chil-
dren's exercises, .05 for
each sheet; jazz, .01 for
each sheet.

53. Phonograph records [4]...——
Type of music (as
above); type of instru-
ment reproduced; voice
—solo, duet, quartet,
chorus; instrumental—

solo, instrument (piano,
violin, etc.), trio, quartet, band, orchestra, .10
for each record; jazz .01
for each.

Total Section IV.....——

Sums of Weighted Scores

Total Section I...........——

Section II...........——

Section III...........——

Section IV...........——

Grand Total ....——

[4] To be recorded if in another room.

APPENDIX C

1. Key list of intelligence quotients for photographs shown in Figure 22, Chap. 26.

Picture	IQ	Picture	IQ	Picture	IQ
A	95	E	80	I	137
B	111	F	118	J	116
C	127	G	121	K	133
D	92	H	105	L	100

2. Key for matching Buchner pictures (Figure 29) to the numbered descriptions of situations given in Chapter 34.

Picture	Situation	Picture	Situation
A	8	E	11
B	4	F	3
C	9	G	10
D	1	H	7

APPENDIX D

LIST OF STATISTICAL FORMULAS

The following list includes only the formulas suggested for use in the experiments described in Chapters 15-55 inclusive. For further statistical methods the student is referred to the textbooks listed in the bibliography.

Symbols

a	= number of judges (Formula 22).
$A.D.$	= average deviation.
c	= correction to be applied when computations are made from an arbitrary origin instead of the true mean.
d	= difference between ranks.
D	= difference between groups.
$dis.$	= distribution.
f	= number of cases or *frequencies* in a class interval.
i	= size of class interval.
k	= coefficient of alienation.
M	= arithmetic mean.
Mdn	= median.
$M.V.$	= mean variation.
n	= number of times the original length of a test or series of observations is duplicated in applying the Spearman-Brown prophecy formula.
N	= number of cases.
p	= a proportion or percentage.
$P.E.$	= probable error.
q	= the proportion remaining after p has been subtracted $(1 - p)$.
r	= the product moment coefficient of correlation.
r_{11}	= a reliability coefficient.

$\bar{r}_{11}$ = mean intercorrelation between ranks.

S = sum of all ranks given to a single case (Formula 22).

$S.D.$ = standard deviation of a distribution.

x = a distance measured in terms of class intervals away from the mean or from an arbitrary origin. In a correlation chart the x distances are plotted on the horizontal axis.

$\bar{x}$ = the regression of x on y. The most probable x score corresponding to a given value of y.

$\bar{y}$ = the regression of y on x. The most probable y score corresponding to a given value of x.

y = a distance corresponding to x (above) plotted on the vertical axis of a correlation chart.

ρ = coefficient of correlation obtained by the rank-order method.

σ = standard error of a statistical measure (mean, coefficient of correlation, etc.) This symbol is also used to indicate the standard deviation of a distribution ($S.D.$).

Σ = the sum of.

Formulas

I. *Measures of central tendency.*

    1. The arithmetic mean (M)

       a. Long method:

$$M = \frac{\Sigma \, (\text{measures})}{N}$$

       b. Short method:

$$M = \text{Arbitrary origin} + \frac{i \, (\Sigma f x)}{N}$$

    2. The median (Mdn)

       a. Counting method:

$$Mdn = \text{the } \frac{N-1}{2} \text{ measure.}$$

II. *Measures of dispersion.*

   1. The mean variation (*M.V.*) or average deviation (*A.D.*)

$$M.V. \text{ or } A.D. = \frac{\Sigma x}{N} \text{ (disregarding signs.)}$$

   2. The standard deviation (*S.D.*)

     a. Long method:

$$S.D. = \sqrt{\frac{\Sigma x^2}{N}}$$

     b. Short method:

$$S.D. = \sqrt{\frac{\Sigma f x^2}{N} - c^2}$$

   3. The coefficient of variability

$$\text{Coef. var.} = \frac{S.D.}{M}$$

III. *Measures of probable variability. Standard errors* (σ)
(To reduce standard errors to probable errors, multiply by .6745.)

   1. Standard error of the mean:

$$\sigma_M = \frac{S.D.}{\sqrt{N}}$$

   2. Standard error of a percentage:

$$\sigma_p = \sqrt{\frac{pq}{N}}$$

   3. Standard error of a coefficient of correlation:

     a. $\sigma_r = \dfrac{1 - r^2}{\sqrt{N}}$

     b. $\sigma_p = \dfrac{1.05 \, (1 - \rho^2)}{\sqrt{N}}$ (approximately).

4. Standard error of a difference between correlated measures:

$$\sigma_D = \sqrt{\sigma_1{}^2 + \sigma_2{}^2 - 2r\sigma_1\sigma_2}$$

5. Standard error of a difference between independent measures:

$$\sigma_D = \sqrt{\sigma_1{}^2 + \sigma_2{}^2}$$

IV. *Measures of relationship.*

1. The Spearman rank-order coefficient of correlation:

$$\rho = 1 - \frac{6 \Sigma d^2}{N(N^2 - 1)}$$

2. The Pearson product-moment coefficient of correlation

   a. Long method:

$$r = \frac{\Sigma xy}{N \sigma_x \sigma_y}$$

   b. Short method:

$$r = \frac{\dfrac{\Sigma xy}{N} - c_x c_y}{\sigma_x \sigma_y}$$

3. The product-moment formula for use when variables are interchangeable:

$$r = \frac{\dfrac{\Sigma xy}{N} - c^2}{\sigma^2}$$

4. Short method for finding the mean intercorrelation between ranks:

$$\bar{r}_{11} = 1 - \frac{a(4N + 2)}{(a - 1)(N - 1)} + \frac{12 \Sigma S^2}{a(a - 1)N(N^2 - 1)}$$

5. The Spearman-Brown prophecy formula:

$$r_{nn} = \frac{nr_{11}}{1 + (n-1)r_{11}}$$

6. The coefficient of alienation:

$$k = \sqrt{1 - r^2}$$

7. The regression equations
   a. Regression of x on y:

   $$\bar{x} = r\frac{S.D._x}{S.D._y}y.$$

   b. Regression of y on x:

   $$\bar{y} = r\frac{S.D._y}{S.D._x}x.$$

GLOSSARY

(The terms marked by asterisks are defined elsewhere in the glossary)

abscissa—a distance measured along the horizontal axis (or base-line) of a graph or chart. This is also known as the x axis; hence in plotting correlations* the variable* which is entered along the abscissa is known as the x variable. *See ordinate.**

absolute measure—A measure expressed in equal units whose derivation is independent of the thing measured, and is determined only by the fundamental notions of space, mass, and time; *e.g.*, inches, seconds, pounds.

action pattern—See behavior pattern.*

alienation, coefficient of (k)—See coefficient of alienation.*

analysis, graphic—See graphic analysis.*

arbitrary origin—A point which is arbitrarily chosen for purposes of convenience as a zero point from which measurements are to be taken. In finding the arithmetic mean it is customary to make the initial calculation from an arbitrary origin or "guessed average" and apply a correction afterward.

arithmetic mean (M)—The sum of the separate measures divided by the number of measures.

array—A single row or column in a correlation table or "scattergram." *

average deviation ($A.D.$)—The sum of the values of the deviations of the separate measures from the mean * divided by the number of measures. Also known as the mean variation ($M.V.$)* or the mean deviation ($M.D.$)

axis—See abscissa * and ordinate.*

bar diagram—A graphic method of comparing two or more quantities or proportions by the use of bars with lengths proportionate to the values of each.

523

behaviorism—The view that only behavior which is or can be made open to observation by everyone is useful for scientific investigation.

behavior pattern—A complex act or sequence of acts which is regarded as making up a functional whole. Also known as *action pattern* * or reaction pattern.

case history—An organized summary of the available data regarding the past and present characteristics of an individual and his environment, assembled with reference to a particular problem.

category—A general class under which objects or actions are grouped. The term is commonly reserved for groupings made upon the basis of qualitative rather than quantitative characteristics. Analogous to class interval * in a quantitative series.

cell—That portion of a correlation table or scattergram,* which is formed by the intersection of an *x* array * with a *y* array.* (See ordinate * and abscissa.*)

central tendency, measure of.—The measure which is taken to be the most significant or meaningful expression of the general trend of the individual values in a group. In psychological and educational statistics the most commonly used measures of central tendency are the arithmetic mean,* the median,* and the mode.*

chartometer—An instrument for measuring the length of irregular lines.

class interval—A given range of scores within a continuous quantitative series.* Analogous to category * in a qualitative series.

code slip—A sheet on which the results obtained on a single individual on all phases of an investigation are brought together in a systematic and concise fashion, for purposes of sorting and classifying.

coefficient of alienation (*k*)—A quantitative expression of the lack of relationship between two variables * corresponding to the coefficient of correlation * which is a quantitative expression of the presence of relationship.

coefficient of correlation—See correlation, coefficient of.*

coefficient of variability—The quotient obtained by dividing the standard deviation * by the mean * of the group.

comparative method—Comparison of two or more groups known to differ with respect to some essential characteristic, such as race, biological classification, etc.

composite rating scale—The term is used here to denote a compound rating scale in which the general trait * to be rated has been broken up into a number of sub-traits which are rated separately and the results combined for the general rating. Any method of rating the items may be used.

conditioned response.—A response which a given stimulus was originally unable to evoke; but which has become attached to it through repeated presentation of that stimulus just before or along with the stimulus which normally evokes the response.

conditioning—The process of setting up a conditioned response.*

consistency, internal—See internal consistency.*

constant error—An error of measurement which is more likely to take one direction than another; that is, tends to yield results which are too high rather than too low or *vice versa.*

continuous variable or continuous series—A measurement which is theoretically capable of infinitely fine subdivision, *e.g.,* time or space.

control by pairing—See pairing.*

control group—A group of subjects used for comparison with the group who are acting as subjects of an investigation (the experimental group *). Control groups are employed chiefly in connection with experimental studies of learning when the performance of the subjects is likely to be influenced by incidental stimulation, practice or maturation. The extent to which the two groups differ from each other at the end of the experimental period is taken as a measure of the effect of the training given. See pairing.*

control, methods of—Methods of limiting possibilities of variation which are sources of error in experimental work. In the field of human behavior this is rarely, if ever, possible, hence methods of control are commonly partial rather than complete.

correlation—Concomitant variation. See Chapters 14 and 31.

correlation, coefficient of—A quantitative expression of the consistency with which two variables * tend to vary concomitantly.

correlation, partial—See partial correlation.*

co-twin control—A method of control in which one member of a pair or pairs of identical twins is subjected to an experimental condition while the other is used as a control.

criterion—A standard by which the validity * of a test or other measuring device may be determined.

curve—Representation by a line which may be either straight or curved of a series of values of a continuous variable.* *Growth curve*—A curve drawn to show the extent of the changes which take place with advancing age in a particular physical or mental trait.* *Learning curve*—A curve drawn to show the changes which take place with practice. *Seriatim curve*—Any curve designed to show serial changes in a trait.*

curve, normal probability—See normal probability curve.*

deviation, average (A.D.)—See average deviation.*

deviation, mean (M.D.)—See average deviation.*

deviation, standard (S.D. or σ)—See standard deviation.*

differences, individual—See individual differences.*

differentiation—The process through which new structures or functions appear.

discrete units—Units which are distinct or separate from each other, as persons, chairs, apples. Discontinuous quantities as opposed to continuous * quantities or variables.*

dispersion (of scores within a group)—Refers to the extent to which the scores or measures of a particular group scatter about their central tendency.*

distribution—See frequency distribution.

empirical—Based upon the results of observation.

error, constant—See constant error.*

error, experimental—See experimental error.*

error, instrumental—See instrumental error.*

error, intrinsic—See intrinsic error.*

error, observational—See observational error.*

error, sampling—See sampling error.*

error, variable—See variable error.*

experiment—A controlled investigation set up for the purpose of answering a scientific question or testing an hypothesis.*

experimental error—Error due to inaccuracy in the measuring instrument, to lack of precision on the part of the observer, or to errors in recording. *Per cent of experimental error*—The per cent which the average experimental error is of the mean of the group measured.

experimental group—A group of subjects who are exposed to the experimental conditions of an investigation as contrasted with a control group * of subjects who are inactive.

fluctuations of sampling.—Chance differences among different samples drawn from the same population.

fore-exercise—A practice exercise given at the beginning of an experiment or test in order to acquaint the subject with the procedure to be followed.

frequency—A term used in statistics to denote the number of cases in a given class-interval.*

frequency distribution or table—A tabular arrangement of a series of measures within successive class-intervals.*

frequency polygon—A graphic presentation of the data of a frequency table by means of a continuous line joining the points which represent the mid-values of the successive class-intervals.*

graphic analysis—The plotting or charting of data for the purpose of bringing out trends or relationships.

graphic rating scale.—A method of expressing estimates of individuals by indicating their relative position on a line supposed to represent the entire range of the trait * in question.

growth curve—See curve, growth.*

heterogeneity—As used in statistics, the term has reference to the amount of dispersion * of the individual measures and particularly to the increase in dispersion resulting from unlikeness of the cases in some correlated trait.* Thus, the dispersion of the height measures of a group of children will be increased if the children are not all of the same age.

histogram—A graphic representation of a frequency table *
by means of a group of adjacent rectangles of height
corresponding to the number of cases within each of the
successive class-intervals.*

hypothesis—A supposition made as a starting point for investigation.

individual differences—Differences of specified kind between
the individuals making up a group. The term is also
loosely used to include differences between categori-
cally * defined groups, as differences between sexes,
races, etc.

instrumental error—Error due to inaccuracy of the instrument used in measuring, in presenting the stimulus, or
in recording the response when this is done by means
of a mechanical device rather than by hand.

integration—The process of bringing together and uniting
into a whole of which the parts, although they may be
artificially distinguished, lose their separate identity.

intelligence quotient (IQ)—The quotient obtained by dividing the mental age * by the chronological age. The IQ
gives a rough measure of the average rate at which
mental growth has taken place in the individual. It has
approximately the same meaning regardless of age
(within the developmental period).

internal consistency—The extent to which the separate items
in a composite test or scale correlate * with each other
and with the total series.

interpolation—The process of calculating values for points
intermediate between those actually measured. Thus,
if standards are derived for ages five and six years respectively, it is possible by interpolation to compute
standards for each month of age between the birthdays.

intrinsic error—Error resulting from true but uncontrollable
variation in the subject measured when it is desired
to secure a measure of its most characteristic state.
Briefly, the error resulting from securing an inadequate
number of measures of a varying phenomenon.

introspective method—A method of obtaining psychological
data through the subject's verbal report of his own experiences, feelings, *etc.*, of the moment, usually as these

are aroused by some artificially presented stimulus. The introspective method differs from the behavioristic method * which takes account only of those aspects of the subject's response which can be observed by the experimenter.

learning curve—See curve, learning.*

maintenance level—A stage of development at which growth has ceased, and the organism is maintained in a relatively constant state. The term is approximate rather than precise, since small changes in structure and function continue to occur even after the adult level has been reached.

master sheet—A general form on which the results obtained by all the subjects on corresponding items are brought together for general purposes of summarizing.

mean, arithmetic (M)—See arithmetic mean.*

mean deviation—See average deviation.*

mean variation (M.V.)—See average deviation.*

measure, absolute—See absolute measure.*

measurement, direct—The measurement in absolute units* of structures and functions which are open to general observation and which can be described in terms of generally accepted meaning, as height, weight, time required to perform a given task, *etc.*

median (Mdn)—The point in a frequency distribution * on either side of which fifty per cent of the measures lie.

mental age (MA)—The level of mental development of a child expressed in terms of the typical performance of children of the age in question. Thus a child is said to have a mental age of seven if his performance on the test used is equal to that of the average seven year old child. Since different mental tests yield somewhat different results, the test used should always be specified when mental ages or intelligence quotients * are reported.

norm—A standard found by determining the average measurement or most typical kind of performance for a given group.

normal probability curve—The bell shaped curve obtained by plotting the nth expansion of the binomial theorem. It represents the relative frequency of occurrence of the different combinations of an infinite number of independent factors when the chances of the occurrence or non-occurrence of each factor is the same.

objective data—Data obtained from facts which are open to general observation. The opposite of subjective data.*

observational error—Error resulting from faulty observation; failure to see the right thing or to see it in its proper relationships.

observations, incidental—Observations made casually without formally conceived plan.

observations, systematic—Observations made according to a preconceived plan and recorded in a systematic way.

ordinate—A distance measured along the vertical axis of a graph or chart. The ordinate is also known as the y axis; hence in plotting correlations * the variable * which is entered along the ordinate is known as the y variable. See abscissa.*

origin—A point from which measurements are made to define position.

origin, arbitrary—See arbitrary origin.*

overlapping, per cent of—See per cent of overlapping.*

pairing—A method of selecting a control group * to match an experimental group with reference to all characteristics believed to have a bearing upon the performance to be studied.

partial correlation—A statistical technique used where three or more variables are involved for the purpose of cancelling out the effect of one or more variables * in order to determine the independent relationships of the remainder.

per cent of overlapping—The per cent of the cases in one group which equals or exceeds the median * score or measurement of another group with which it is compared.

percentile—The score on a particular test or measurement at or below which a given percentage of the cases in the group under consideration will fall. Thus, the 75th percentile for three-year-old children on a certain test is the score which separates the lowest 75 per cent from the highest 25 per cent.

percentile rank—The position or rank occupied by a given individual in a group of 100 who are ranked * in order of measurement from low to high. Percentile ranks are usually determined from percentile tables used as norms.

physiological limit—The limit of performance on a given task which is set by the physical or physiological capacities of the organism. For example, no matter how thoroughly a maze-pattern has been learned, it can never be traced in a shorter time than that required to make the needed muscular movements.

practice limit—The limit beyond which further practice without change in procedure brings no improvement. A true physiological limit can never be exceeded, but the limit of practice according to a particular method is sometimes greatly surpassed by the use of an improved technique.

probable error—The range between which 50 per cent of the cases in a normal distribution * will be found. Since distributions of finite numbers of cases are rarely exactly normal in form, the use of the probable error should be confined to the statistical computation of probable fluctuations of sampling.*

prophecy formula—(Spearman-Brown) A formula to determine the improvement in reliability * to be expected by increasing the length of a test or the number of observations in a series of time samples.

psycho-physics—The quantitative study of the relation between the physical attributes of the stimulus and the attributes of sensation.

quartiles—The 25th, 50th, and 75th percentiles.* Since the 50th percentile is the median, the term is commonly used with reference only to the 25th and 75th percentiles, often designated as Q1 and Q3.

questionnaire—A formal series of questions on a given subject designed for use with fairly large numbers of subjects.

range—In statistics the range of scores on a given test or measurement is defined as the difference between the two extremes of the group measured.

ranking—Arranging in order of merit.

rating scale—A formally organized series of descriptive categories * in terms of which individuals are to be classified by means of personal estimates of their various characteristics.

rating scale, composite—See composite rating scale.*

rating scale, graphic—See graphic rating scale.*

reaction pattern—See behavior pattern.*

reaction time—The interval elapsing between the presentation of a stimulus and the making of a specified motor response.

regression—When two variables * are imperfectly correlated * the mean of any array * will be found to have moved toward or "regressed" to a point nearer the mean of the other variable than the distance of the array itself from its own mean. Distance here must be expressed in standard deviation * units, and the number of cases in the array must be great enough to cancel out chance variations.

regression equation—The equation which shows the extent of regression * corresponding to a given magnitude of correlation,* and from which the most probable score in one variable can be predicted from a knowledge of the score in the correlated variable.

regression lines—Lines drawn through the means of the arrays * in each of two variables * showing the extent of the regression.*

reliability—A term used in statistics to indicate the amount of dependence which can be placed either in an individual score or measurement or in a group measure, such as the mean,* standard deviation,* *etc*. Reliability refers solely to the accuracy of the measurement *per se* and tells nothing about its meaning; *i.e.*, whether or not it measures what it purports to measure. The reliability of individual scores is usually expressed in terms of correlation; * the reliability of group-values in terms of the standard error * of the measure in question.

sampling—Refers to the methods by which a group of subjects for investigation are selected, *i.e.*, the general characteristics of the group of subjects as expressed in objective terms.

sampling error—Error resulting from extending the use of norms or other experimental findings to a group of significantly different character from the one actually studied. Errors of sampling are always likely to occur when general conclusions are drawn from experimental groups whose composition is inadequately described.

scale values—Values assigned to test-scores or other irregularly spaced measures on the basis of statistical treatment designed to establish their distance from each other on a scale of equal units.

scatter-diagram or *scattergram*—A correlation chart.

semi-interquartile range—One half the distance from the 25th to the 75th percentile,* *i.e.*, from Q1 to Q3.

seriatim curve—See curve, seriatim.*

situation—A general term used to denote all the conditions surrounding the subject of an experiment or an observation. Both the material factors such as the room-temperature, the number of people present, *etc.*, and the psychological factors such as the familiarity or unfamiliarity of the surroundings may be included. Also loosely used in a more specific sense to refer to a group of stimuli which elicit a particular reaction.

situational analysis—An analysis of the differences in behavior characteristically associated with different situations.*

skewness, measure of—A measure of the symmetry of a distribution. In a normal curve,* the cases cluster around the mid-point and decrease in frequency symmetrically toward the extremes. In a skewed curve, the cases tend to be concentrated at a point nearer one extreme than the other. The curve is said to be skewed toward the extreme at which the cases tail out, *i.e.*, positively skewed if the tailing out is toward the upper end of the curve, and negatively skewed if toward the lower end.

smoothing—The mathematical treatment of data for the purpose of ironing out irregularities in order to bring out a general trend.

standard deviation (*S.D.* or σ)—The square root of the mean of the squares of the deviations of the separate measures from the central tendency. Unless otherwise stipulated, the standard deviation is computed from the mean.* Under ordinary circumstances it is the most reliable measure of dispersion.*

standard error (σ) The theoretical standard deviation * of an infinite number of similar statistical measures (means, medians, standard deviations, *etc.*) obtained from successive samplings * drawn from the same population.

standard error of estimate—The standard error * of an array; * *i.e.*, the standard error of estimating a score on a second variable * from knowledge of a score in the first.

standardized test—A test which has been tried out on a sufficient number of subjects to yield fairly reliable norms.* Adequate standardization also implies examination of the test's reliability,* and validity,* and an objective description of the sampling * of subjects on which the norms were derived.

subjective data—Data derived from facts which can be observed only by the subject himself: such as his own thoughts, feelings, sensations, *etc*. The term is also used to include observations and estimates in which there is much disagreement among observers, leading to the assumption that the reports have been influenced in unknown ways by the personal characteristics and experiences of the individuals.

systematic error—See constant error.*

time sample or *method of short samples*—A method of taking systematic observations in which a constant unit of time is employed.

trait—A general characteristic or usual mode of reaction; a distinguishing factor in terms of which individuals may be classified.

validity—Theoretically the term indicates the accuracy with which a test or other device measures the thing it purports to measure. Actually, since it is often impossible to secure a really valid criterion * in terms of which the test can be tested, the term validity is used to denote the correlation * of a measuring device with some other measure or rating which is accepted as the best criterion available, though it may be recognized as imperfect.

variability, coefficient of—See coefficient of variability.*

variable—A trait * in respect to which the individuals composing a group differ from each other.

variable, continuous—See continuous variable.*

variable error—An error which is as likely to take one direction as another; hence an error which tends to be cancelled out in measurements of large groups.

weighting—The assigning of differential values to the separate items or sections making up a composite measure. Weights may be either arbitrary or determined by statistical procedure.

INDEXES OF SUBJECTS AND NAMES

Index of Subjects

Abbreviations, used in record keeping, 57

Abscissa, 85, 111, 523

Accuracy, checking for, 60 ff.

Adaptation, 13

Adapted information, 215

Adjustment of child to situation, 63 ff.

Alienation, coefficient of, 288, 524

Anger, 341, 433

Anterior-posterior development, 81

Arbitrary origin, 96, 268, 523, 530

Arithmetic mean, 79 ff., 96 ff., 100 ff., 111, 523

Arm span, 88

Attention, 175 ff.

Average deviation, 108, 129, 523

Average intercorrelation, 307 ff.

Bar diagrams, 120, 523

Barr Scale for occupational intelligence, 238, 451

Behavior problems, 117, 305 ff., 355, 356 ff., 358

Behaviorism, 16 ff., 524

Bibliography, method of preparing, 48 ff.

Biography, child, 4 ff., 365 ff.

Brain weight, 23

Case history, 32, 357 ff., 369 ff., 524

Causality, 37, 235, 358

Central tendency, 111, 519, 524

Chapin scale for living room equipment, 239, 513 ff.

Chapman-Sims scale for socio-economic status, 243 ff.

Chartometer, 145, 524

Checking for accuracy, 60 ff.

Child study movement, 7

Children, methods of handling, 62 ff., 387

Class interval, 85, 89, 99 ff., 524

Code slip, 58, 105 ff., 524

Coefficient of alienation, 288, 524

Coefficient of correlation, *see* Correlation

Coefficient of variability, 130, 524

Collection of data, 55 ff.

Color and form perception, 169 ff.

Color discrimination, 151 ff.

Comparative method, 12, 465, 525

Concepts, children's, 6, 345

Conditioning, 17, 365 ff., 525

Construction analysis of sentences, 216

Constructive ability, 352 ff.

Contacts between child and teacher, 330 ff.

Continuity of development, 19 ff.

Continuous quantity or variable, 99, 525

Control group, 326 ff., 525

Control of conditions, 7, 457 ff., 525

Controlled investigations, 6, 35, 457 ff.

Coördination, bodily, 141 ff., 337 ff.

Correction to arbitrary origin, 99 ff., 127 ff., 242, 269 ff.

Correlation, coefficient of, 133 ff., 526; effect of heterogeneity upon, 137, 281 ff., 527; effect upon reliability of a difference, 165; formulas for, 521 ff.; interchangeable variables, 240 ff.; meaning of, 136 ff., 280 ff.; partial, 466, 530; product moment, 240 ff., 263 ff.; ratio, 279; Spearman rank-order, 133 ff.

Co-twin control, 464, 526

Index of Subjects

541

Heterogeneity, effect upon correlation coefficient, 281 ff., 527
Histogram, 85, 91 ff., 528
Hypotheses, development of, 34, 456 ff., 528

Incentives, 70 ff.
Incidental observations, 4, 32, 35, 363 ff., 426 ff., 530; comparison with systematic, 428 ff.
Individual differences, 10, 12, 13, 308 ff., 528
Inflection, tonal, 67 ff.
Instructions, supplementary, 68 ff.; verbal, 67 ff.
Integration, 26 ff., 528; of problems in scientific field, 54
Intelligence, criteria of, 13, 222, 441 ff.; quotient, 228 ff., 445 ff., 528; estimating from photographs, 231 ff.; key for, 517; effect of environment upon, 351; tests, 11 ff., 14, 25, 33, 225 ff., 351, 441, 445, 450
Interests, children's in school subjects, 312 ff.
Interpretation of results, 53 ff.; from case history data, 376 ff.
Interviews with parents, 118 ff.
Introspective method, 6, 16, 528
Introversion, 145, 291 ff.
Investigations, controlled, 6, 455 ff.

Labelling, 57
Laboratories, psychological, 6, 7
Language development, 5, 210 ff., 344; in twins, 455 ff.
Laughter, 296 ff., 341
Learning, ability, 339 ff., 360; curves, 181, 192 ff., 337, 348, 526
Literature, need of studying, 47 ff., 364 ff.
Living room equipment, scale for, 239 ff., 513 ff.

Maintenance level, 21
Master sheet, 58 ff., 529
Maze-learning in children, 198 ff., 339
Mean, arithmetic, 79 ff., 111, 523; short method for finding, 96 ff.
Mean variation, 108, 523

Measurements, 33, 403 ff.; of bodily dimensions, 77 ff.; reliability of, 406 ff.; units of, 405 ff., 443 ff., 447
Median, 111, 529
Memory, 179 ff., 349 ff., 457 ff.
Memory transferences, 15 ff.
Mental age, 226, 227, 445, 529
Mental defects, 13 ff., 386
Mental growth, 23 ff., 352
Mental hygiene, 18, 305 ff.
Mental set, 13, 300
Mid point of class interval, 99 ff.
Monologue, 215
Motivation, 62, 70 ff.
Moving average, 195 ff.
Musical ability, 319 ff.; tests of, 320 ff.; relation to auditory acuity, 352

Normal probability curve, 88, 292, 529
Norms, 337, 345, 411, 450 ff., 529; control by, 465
Note-taking, methods of, 49 ff.

Obliviscence, 350
Observational period, length of, 331 ff.
Observations, incidental, 4, 32, 35, 363 ff., 426 ff., 530; comparison with systematic, 428 ff.
Observations systematic, 34, 144 ff., 246 ff., 296 ff., 334, 337, 341, 344, 353, 426 ff., 530; rules for, 427 ff.; comparison with incidental observations, 428 ff.
Occupation as related to socio-economic status, 237 ff.; classification of, 501 ff.
Oral habits, 431
Ordinate, 85, 111, 530
Organization of course in child study, 44 ff.
Orientation of problem in scientific field, 50 ff.
Origin, arbitrary, 96, 268, 523, 530
Overlapping, per cent of, 111 ff., 530

Pairing, control by, 326 ff., 462 ff., 530

4 / 1 53